The EXPERIENCE OF LIFE

WITNESS LEE

Living Stream Ministry
Anaheim, California • www.lsm.org

First Edition, 1973.

ISBN 978-0-87083-417-2

Published by

Living Stream Ministry
2431 W. La Palma Ave., Anaheim, CA 92801 U.S.A.
P. O. Box 2121, Anaheim, CA 92814 U.S.A.

Printed in the United States of America

14   15   16   17   /   15   14   13   12

CONTENTS

FOREWORD

The content of *The Experience of Life* is compiled from messages given during the Life Training given by Brother Witness Lee in Taipei, Taiwan, in 1953 and 1954.

PREFACE

We know that it is the desire and purpose of God's heart to secure a corporate man, having His image, manifesting His glory, and exercising His authority to deal with His enemy— all in order that He Himself may obtain eternal rest. Very few people, however, know that this great heart's desire and purpose can only be attained by God's own life. Even fewer understand how one can experience this life and thus fulfill the desire of God's heart. The saints are very weak and childish. Although many pursue, few find the path of life. There are yet many who confuse enthusiasm, knowledge, ability, and gifts with life.

Thank God that in these last days, days of such spiritual need, He has revealed through our brother His marvelous and mysterious way of life in such a way that every believer may comprehend and make it his own. We may say that these chapters contain the essence of the saints' understanding and experience of life during two thousand years, plus the thirty years of personal testing and experience, which enabled our brother to compile these precious writings. It is indeed magnificent. The contents discuss the experience of life in nineteen items, explaining the experience of the various stages of spiritual life and the way of pursuing the Lord. If the experience of each subject is sought after and exercised, one can go on in a straight course and rise to the stage of the maturity of life very quickly.

These chapters make real that science of life which is not easily seen or grasped. Any saint who loves the Lord and seeks to grow in life must not fail to read them.

Dr. Y. L. Chang

Taipei, Taiwan
November, 1956

INTRODUCTION

From the experiences of the saints throughout the ages, and in the light that we have seen in these recent years before the Lord, we may say that the experience of life can be divided into four stages with a total of nineteen points.

According to our experience, the first four stages may be designated as follows: the first stage may be called the salvation stage; the second, the revival stage; the third, the stage of the cross; and the fourth, the stage of spiritual warfare. But according to our relationship with Christ, these four stages should be designated in this way: the first stage, in Christ; the second, abiding in Christ; the third, Christ abiding in us; and the fourth, Christ fully grown in us. The experiences of these four stages are based on our relationship with Christ.

Life is God Himself, yet in order that God may be our life, this life must necessarily be in Christ. Therefore, the Scripture says, "Christ is our life" (Col. 3:4). Since life is Christ, when we experience life, we experience Christ. The experience of life may be expressed, therefore, as our relationship with Christ.

THE FIRST STAGE—IN CHRIST

The first stage of the experience of life is being in Christ. This is due to the fact that our relationship with Christ results in our being in Christ. Before we were saved, we were outside of Christ; we were in Adam. But when we are regenerated, God transfers us into Christ (2 Cor. 5:17). The experience of this stage, from our point of view, may be said to be the stage of salvation or the stage of regeneration, but from the standpoint of our relationship with Christ, it is simply being in Christ.

Chapter One

REGENERATION

The first experience of the first stage is regeneration.

From the point of view of knowing life, regeneration means that in addition to his original life man obtains the life of God. But from the standpoint of experience, what, actually, is regeneration, and what are the conditions of regeneration?

I. REGENERATION BEING:

1. The Part in the Experience of Salvation That Is a Matter of Life

The story of how we were saved is the story of how we experienced God's salvation. God's salvation is exceedingly full and complete. It includes forgiveness of sins, cleansing, sanctification, justification, freedom from bondage, regeneration, and so forth—all parts of God's salvation. Of all these parts, only regeneration is the part of life. The forgiveness of our sins is not a matter of life; neither are the cleansing away of our sins, our being sanctified, and our being justified matters of life. Even our being set free from bondage cannot absolutely be a matter of life, since part of this experience has to do with release from the law and another part with freedom from the bondage of sin, and these parts are not entirely of life. All these are only what God has done upon us. Only regeneration is the part of life in God's salvation. Therefore, when we experience God's salvation, only regeneration is the experience of the part that is of life.

2. The Center of the Experience of Salvation

Since regeneration is the part that is of life in the experience of salvation, it is then the center of the experience of

salvation, because the central purpose of God in saving us is
that we may have His life. It is for this that He has forgiven
our sins; it is for this that He has cleansed us; it is for this
that He has sanctified us; it is for this that He has justified
us; and it is for this that He has set us free. He has done all
these for one purpose—regeneration. Regeneration, therefore, is the central part of God's salvation, and it is also the
central part of our experience of God's salvation.

3. The Beginning of the Experience of Life

The first experience of life is regeneration. Without regeneration we have not yet begun our experience of life. When we
are regenerated, we then begin to experience life. Therefore,
from the standpoint of experience, regeneration is the beginning of the experience of life.

4. The Entering into Us of God's Life

Since regeneration is the obtaining of God's life in addition
to our original life, the moment we are regenerated is the very
moment that God's life enters into us. Regeneration, therefore, is the entering into us of God's life.

5. The Birth of Christ within Us

Regeneration is not only the entering into us of God's
life, it is also the birth of Christ within us. As God's life
enters into us in Christ and regenerates us, it is on one hand
God's life entering into us, and on the other hand, it can be
said that Christ is born in us. The birth of Christ in us means
that Christ is born once more. Every time a man is regenerated, Christ is born once more into humanity. Hence, regeneration is the birth of Christ within us.

6. The Beginning of the New Man

Regeneration is also the beginning of the new man within
us. All our experiences of spiritual life are matters of the new
man within us, and this new man begins at the time of our
regeneration. Before we are regenerated, we are in Adam, a
fallen sinner, the old man. Once we are regenerated, God's life
in Christ enters into us. This life is a new element, and when

it mingles with our spirit, it becomes the new man within us. Therefore, every one of us who has been regenerated is a double man: we are on one hand the old man in Adam, fallen; and we are on the other hand the new man in Christ, saved. This new man begins at the time of our regeneration. Hence, regeneration is the beginning of the new man.

II. THE CONDITIONS OF REGENERATION

The experience of regeneration is especially related to four things: our nature, our heart, our spirit, and God's life. From the aspects of these four things, therefore, we will look at our condition before regeneration, during regeneration, and after regeneration.

1. The Condition before Regeneration

First, our nature is corrupted. Jeremiah 17:9 says, "The heart is deceitful above all things, / And it is incurable; / Who can know it?" Although this verse speaks of man's heart, it actually refers to man's nature. Thus, we see that before regeneration our original nature is deceitful and crooked, incurable, and unable to match God's nature.

Second, the heart is hardened toward God. Ezekiel 36:26 speaks of our original heart as a "heart of stone." This means that before regeneration our heart toward God is always rebellious, stubborn, and as hard as stone.

Third, our spirit is dead toward God. Before regeneration, because of sins (Eph. 2:1), our spirit is dead toward God and has lost its function to contact God. We cannot, therefore, have fellowship with God, nor can we understand the spiritual things of God.

Fourth, man is separated from God's life. Since the nature of a man who is not regenerated is corrupted, his heart toward God is hardened, and his spirit toward God is dead, his entire person, therefore, is separated from God's life (4:18).

This is our condition before regeneration.

2. The Condition during Our Experience of Regeneration

First, we see that our nature is corrupt. Although before

regeneration our nature was corrupt, we did not know it. It is at the time of experiencing regeneration, because of the Holy Spirit's enlightenment, that we see ourselves to be corrupt. At this time we see not only that our external deeds are corrupt but also that our inner nature is corrupt.

Second, our heart is contrite and repentant toward God. When we experience regeneration and the Holy Spirit enlightens us, we see ourselves as corrupt, sinning against God and man. Our heart then reproaches us and is contrite and repentant before God.

Third, our spirit is contrite toward God. Because of the repentance of our heart, the spirit deep within us also feels extremely contrite. Our spirit at this time is like that of Psalm 51:17, "a broken spirit." When we are being regenerated of the Holy Spirit, our spirit deep within feels contrite—indeed, as if it were broken.

Fourth, man contacts God's life. Since man sinned and fell and was driven out of the garden of Eden, the cherubim with the flaming sword guarded the way of the tree of life (Gen. 3:24) so that man could no longer contact it and thereby obtain God's life. Not until the Lord Jesus shed His blood and died on the cross, thus satisfying the demand of God's glory, holiness, and righteousness, was the way that leads to God's life opened. Therefore, at the time of our regeneration, because of our contrition, repentance, and faith in receiving the Lord Jesus Christ as our Savior, we can then contact in our spirit the life of God, which is in Him, for the life of God is in His Son, the Lord Jesus Christ (1 John 5:11).

3. The Condition after Regeneration

First, we feel that our nature is corrupt. At the time of regeneration we *see* that our nature is corrupt. After regeneration, because of that initial seeing, we always feel that our own nature is corrupt.

Second, our heart is softened toward God. Our heart, which is as hard as stone toward God before regeneration, having experienced repentance at the time of regeneration, is softened toward God and becomes "a heart of flesh" (Ezek. 36:26). Our heart, having been softened, desires to love God and draws near to God; it longs to contact spiritual things and gladly receives and obeys God's commands; it is not stubborn or rebellious; and although at times it is unable to obey, yet it is still willing to obey.

Third, our spirit is alive toward God. Because of its contact with God's life at regeneration, the spirit that was dead before regeneration has been made alive by the resurrection power of God. The spirit, having been made alive, is able to contact God, to fellowship with God, and to apprehend the spiritual things of God, and it has the strength to do God's will.

Fourth, we have God's life. Because we have contacted and received God's life during regeneration, we have the life of God within us. At the same time we also have God's nature, since God's nature is in God's life.

When we speak of the experience of regeneration, therefore, in regard to the aspects of these four things—our nature, our heart, our spirit, and God's life—the changes that have taken place before and after regeneration are all very clear. Our nature before regeneration is corrupt; at the time of regeneration we see that it is corrupt; and after regeneration we always feel that it is corrupt. Our heart is hard toward God before regeneration; at the time of regeneration it becomes deeply repentant; and after regeneration it is softened toward God. Our spirit is dead before regeneration; it is contrite at the time of regeneration; and it is alive unto God after regeneration. Before regeneration we are separated from God's life; at the time of regeneration we contact God's life; and after regeneration we have God's life. If we are clear regarding these few points, we then have a thorough understanding of the experience of regeneration.

CHAPTER TWO

CLEARANCE OF THE PAST

Now we will look straightway at the second experience of life, namely, the clearance of the past.

Strictly speaking, the clearance of the past cannot be regarded as an experience of life in itself. It can only be considered as an appendix to the experience of regeneration, since a man who has been truly regenerated and saved will naturally bring all his past to an end. The normal experience, therefore, of regeneration certainly includes the element of the ending of the past. But because there are some who do not seem to be well regenerated and saved in a thoroughgoing way, although they have indeed been regenerated and saved, their past has not been immediately cleared. Not until they are once more revived by the Lord do they make up this lesson of clearing the past. It is proper, therefore, that we separate regeneration and the clearance of the past and consider them as two distinct experiences of life.

I. THE SCRIPTURAL BASIS

There is no clear teaching in the Scripture concerning the clearance of the past, but there are two very good examples: one is found in Luke 19:1-10—the story of Zaccheus's dealing with the past after his salvation; the other is in Acts 19:18-19—the account of the Ephesians' clearance of the past after being saved.

In Luke 19 we are told that as soon as Zaccheus was saved, he immediately felt that he had extorted others in the past and was thus unrighteous; he also felt that he was a money lover with a stingy manner of living. He said therefore to the Lord that if he had taken anything from anyone by false accusation, he would willingly restore him fourfold. Furthermore, he was willing to give half of his possessions to the poor. This was his clearance of the past. In Acts 19 we are told that many of the Ephesian saints, having been saved through Paul's leading, came to confess their practices, many of them willingly bringing their books of magic and burning them before the people. This was their clearance of the past.

II. THE OBJECT OF THE CLEARANCE OF THE PAST

What are the things of the past that need to be cleared away after we are saved? What are the objects that must be ended and cleared up? Altogether there are four categories: (1) unrighteous matters, (2) improper matters, (3) evil and unclean matters, and (4) old ways of living. After we have been saved, there needs to be a clearing up and conclusion of these matters.

(1) Unrighteous matters. *Unrighteous* means "unjust, illegal." All we have obtained in the past by unjust, illegal means, such as stealing, swindling, taking by force, encroaching upon others' properties, keeping things that have been lost by others, not returning things that were borrowed long ago, and all illegitimate relations with others and unjust dealings toward others—all these unrighteous matters—are things that we should clear up.

(2) Improper matters. *Improper* and *unrighteous* are close in meaning, and yet they are different. *Unrighteous* means that the method by which a certain thing is obtained, or the relationship of a certain matter, is unjust or illegal. *Improper* means that the very nature of a certain thing or matter is improper or indecent. For instance, things used in gambling and drinking can be bought and obtained by legal means, but these things are used for gambling and drinking. Since both gambling and drinking are improper and indecent, the very nature of these things is also improper and indecent. Furthermore, neither smoking nor reading obscene novels can be said to be unrighteous, but surely they are immoral and improper. All these improper matters are also things that we should put to an end.

(3) Evil and unclean matters. Evil and unclean matters

are things related to idols, such as graven or portrait idols, candlesticks, and censers used in idol worship; ornaments, furniture, and clothing with the image of a dragon; writings of worldly religions; unclean things related to curious arts, such as books on horoscope, physiognomy, magic, and so forth; also evil and unclean things, such as worshipping idols, worshipping ancestors, divining, fortune-telling, and so forth. These are hated by God even more than the things in the first two categories, and they are certainly intolerable to the life within us, which is holy and clean. Therefore, even more so must these things be thoroughly put to an end.

(4) Old ways of living. *Old ways of living* refer to our entire old manner of living before we were saved. After we are saved, we should not only put an end to all unrighteous, improper, and evil and unclean matters, but we must also put an end to our whole former manner of living and have a new beginning.

Usually, when we speak of the clearance of the past, we emphasize the ending of unrighteous, improper, and evil and unclean matters, but we are not likely to pay any attention to the ending of the old way of living. This is insufficient. As a matter of fact, when a man is regenerated, his old way of living ceases at once. Since regeneration enables man to obtain a new life, it naturally brings to man a new way of living. The old way of living ends with the old life, and the new way of living begins with the new life. Thus, man has changed to a new human living. It can be said, therefore, that what really wrecks the old manner of living is the salvation of the Lord. Whoever receives the Lord's salvation has his old human living wrecked and terminated and his new human living begun and being built up.

How then should we regard the ending of the old human living and the beginning of the new? We are not saying that after a person is regenerated he should change his present occupation—stop going to school, close his business, ignore caring for his family—and go out preaching. The ending of the old human living means that after a person is regenerated, he may continue in his original profession, provided that it is proper, but the taste within him is changed, his mood is changed, and his feeling is changed. No matter what a person does before he is regenerated, his taste, his mood, and his feeling are all toward the world, all desiring to accomplish something in the world. The more he works, the more he relishes his work, and the deeper he enters into it. But after regeneration, when God's life enters into him, that taste within him becomes tasteless, that mood is changed, and his feeling is also changed. He even has a different taste for eating, clothing, and other daily necessities. In this sense, his old way of living is ended, and his old life comes to a conclusion.

We have referred to Zaccheus's clearance of his past. His clearance included the ending of his old way of living. Formerly, he had extorted money from others and was thus unrighteous, so he put an end to his unrighteous deeds by restoring fourfold. Moreover, he also gave half of his possessions to the poor; that was to end his old way of living. Had he not given to the poor, would that be unrighteous? Would that be improper? Would that be evil and unclean? Indeed not! His unwillingness to give was his old way of living. In his former life he put an extreme value upon money; covetousness was his philosophy of life, and loving money was his old way of living. When he was saved and God's life entered into him, his concept concerning money was immediately changed; he esteemed it of little value; he was willing to give—this shows that his life was changed, and his old way of covetous living was ended. This does not mean, of course, that after he ended his old way of living, he did not possess or spend any more money. It is possible that afterward he still had much money and spent it. But his taste in possessing money was different; his taste in spending money was different. His old life was changed; his old way of living came to an end.

I recall my own experience of ending the old way of living. It was also a very evident change. When I was nearly twenty years old, I was pursuing the knowledge of this world, full of ambition and with great purpose. At this time a sister came to preach the gospel in my locality, and I was saved at the first listening. She spoke at that time from Exodus, telling how Pharaoh usurped the Israelites and would not allow them to leave Egypt. She said that this typifies Satan's usurping of man, not allowing him to worship God. Her words were indeed Spirit-inspired and moved me greatly. At that time I had a feeling within that said, "Never again do I want this world. I must serve God." Since then, this feeling within me has never died. On one hand, I felt that I could no longer walk in the way of this world and that it was henceforth no longer possible to possess my ambition and great purpose toward the world. On the other hand, I felt that a new path, a new life, was before me, causing me to follow the Lord and go on. In this way the taste within me was changed, my mood was changed, and my feeling was also changed. My old way of living then came to an end.

It seems difficult to find words to express these changes in taste, mood, and feeling, but they are definitely the result of being regenerated. Furthermore, the more thoroughly a person is regenerated, the more drastic these changes will be. For those who have more future in their enterprises or more accomplishment in society, the change will be more evident. Even those who are barely saved can still sense that these changes have taken place in their lives, although their experience of regeneration is not so clear. Once there are such changes within, the old way of living comes to an end.

Although this ending of the old way of living is a preliminary experience of a Christian, it has a deep effect upon his future walk with the Lord. When our old way of living comes to an end, our ambition and interest in the world are changed, our estimation and point of view toward men and all matters are also changed, and our purpose in life is different than before. Thus, we can escape from all anxieties, leave all our burdens behind, and run the race in the way of the Lord.

Since ending the old way of living is so important, we must give heed to this matter of the clearance of the past, whether in self-examination or in leading others, to see that the old way of living is ended and that there is such a change in taste, mood, and feeling. If these changes are not great enough, we must look for a deeper work of the Holy Spirit to make them stronger and more weighty. The more drastic these changes are, the more thorough will be the ending of the old way of living.

Strictly speaking, it is not necessary to wait till after a person is saved before he can be led to consider this change in the old way of living. When we are preaching the gospel, it is also necessary to add this point to enable others to see that regeneration means a change in their human living. A certain kind of life must have a certain kind of living. If a man is regenerated, he obtains a new life, and his old life then naturally comes to an end. Thus, once a man is saved, he will have this change of affection, and it follows that he will have a good ending of the past.

III. THE BASIS OF THE CLEARANCE OF THE PAST

The clearance of the past is not based on the demand of outward regulations but on the sense of life within. We have previously pointed out four matters that must necessarily be ended, yet these only enable us to recognize principles. They are not rules that demand we put an end to such matters. When we are practicing the clearing of the past, what needs to be ended really depends on the sense of life within. Therefore, the sense of life within is the basis for our clearance of the past.

We know that all the religions of the world are built on their various religious codes. Their followers live and behave according to these rules. But the Lord's salvation is not like that. The salvation of the Lord, through the regeneration of the Holy Spirit, gives us a new life. Since we have such a new life, we can now live and behave in the presence of God through the sense of this new life. This is the principle of all our living as Christians. Our clearance of the past is also based on this principle. When a person is regenerated and obtains God's life, this life moves within him, causing him to sense that in his past there have been many unrighteous, improper, and perverted matters, and that all these matters and even his entire old way of living are altogether incompatible with his present Christian state. Thus, he proceeds with his clearance of the past in accordance with these inner feelings.

The examples of Zaccheus and the Ephesian Christians

clearing their past also show us that neither the Lord Jesus nor the apostle Paul clearly taught anything in regard to the clearance of the past; they did not give any rules demanding what one must do to end his past. The "ending" of Zaccheus and the Ephesian Christians was such that, when the salvation of the Lord came upon them and the life of the Lord entered into them, they had a feeling toward the unrighteous and unclean things of the past and toward their old way of living; therefore, they put it all to an end. Their "ending" proves that this matter is not based on external regulations and teachings but on the sense of life within.

However, when we are first saved, we do not necessarily sense all the things that need to be terminated. Although there are many matters that need to be cleared up, we are only conscious of a portion of them. Even so, we still need to put an end to that portion of which we are conscious. At any rate, whatever we are conscious of, that much we must put to an end. The area of our consciousness should be the extent of our clearance. As for those things of which we are not yet conscious, we need only continue to move on and grow in the life of the Lord; in the future the Lord will naturally cause us to sense them. At that time there will be further dealing and further clearance.

Once there was an elderly sister in whose home were two things: a silk lampshade embroidered with dragons and a tea set also printed with a dragon design. Long after her salvation she did not sense anything. Then she was enlightened by the Lord and became possessed of a deep inner feeling toward these things. She had no peace whenever she saw these items with dragon designs. She then proceeded to destroy them according to her inner feeling.

In like manner, there was a brother who had an embroidering factory that specialized in making pajamas with dragon designs. In the beginning he lacked any feeling regarding this matter. Then one day he suddenly said to me, "Brother Lee, I feel that I cannot continue to run my factory. I am a Christian. How can I continue to sell clothing with dragon designs?" He proceeded to change his line of business in accordance with this feeling.

These two examples show how these people originally lived in the midst of unclean things without any feeling about them. Then one day, because of their love for the Lord, their following the Lord, and their allowing the life of the Lord to move actively within them, they felt the need of clearing up these matters. Accordingly, they obeyed their inner feeling and put an end to the past. This proves that the basis of clearing the past is the inner feeling of life.

Since the ending of the past is based on the sense of life within, we must continue to lay hold of this principle when we are leading others to end the past. Never establish for them any outward rules, teaching them that they ought to end this or that, but seek to stir the sense of life within and point them to that. We need first to cause others to know that the life of God is within them and lead them to know the sense of this life. Then, second, with the help of the ministry of the Word, spiritual literature, and the testimonies of other saints regarding their clearance of the past, cause them also to have some feeling or deeper feeling regarding what needs to be terminated in their own past. Once this feeling has begun and has been deepened within them, we can lead them to clear up their past according to their own feeling. This manner of clearance is in accord with the principle of the Lord's salvation and can help others to truly grow in life.

IV. THE DEGREE OF ENDING THE PAST

How far should we go in putting an end to the things of the past? To what degree should we proceed? The degree is expressed in Romans 8:6 as "life and peace."

We have already seen that the ending of the past is based on the sense of life within. This sense of life within is a feeling given to us through the inner anointing of the Holy Spirit. Since the ending of our past is based on the sense of life within us, the procedure is the same as that mentioned in Romans 8:5-6, namely, following the Spirit, or minding the Spirit. The result, therefore, will naturally be the same—"life and peace." Thus, life and peace are the degree to which we are required to clear up the past. If we follow the demand of our inner feeling to make restitution, to confess our sins, to eliminate improper and unclean things, and to end our old way of living, we will surely feel strengthened, enlightened, satisfied, and enlivened; we will also feel peaceful, secure, and full of the presence of the Lord. If we have made a clearance of the things of the past and we still sense the lack of fullness and manifestation of life and peace, we may be sure that we have not followed the Spirit to the uttermost; we have not sufficiently satisfied the demand of the inner feeling. We must look to the Lord for grace that we may clear up things more thoroughly, until we are full of life and peace.

The witness of life and peace within is not sufficient, of course, to prove that all our past that needs to be cleared up has already been dealt with. It only indicates that we have attended to everything according to the demand of our inner feeling. It is possible that later, when our life has grown and our feeling increased, we will feel there is more that needs to be put to an end. At this time we must again follow the leading of this feeling and deal with these matters until we again sense life and peace. After several thorough clearances and dealings, we will have cleared up to a much better degree things, deeds, relations, and concepts of the past that are not pleasing to the Lord. We can then follow the Lord and go on without dragging.

THE SECOND STAGE—ABIDING IN CHRIST

What we have seen in the preceding chapters is the first state of spiritual life, that is, the experience "in Christ." Now we will continue by looking at the second stage of the spiritual life, the experience of "abiding in Christ."

Abiding in Christ and *in Christ* are different. Although both speak of our relationship with Christ's life, yet the matters referred to are different. *In Christ* refers to the fact of our sharing what Christ is and our oneness with Christ. *Abiding in Christ* refers to the experience of our fellowship with Christ and of enjoying Christ.

Originally, we were in Adam and shared what was of Adam. When we received the Lord as our Savior, however, God transferred us from Adam into Christ. This is the first stage of our experience of life, so we call this stage "in Christ." After we are saved and have been attracted by the love of the Lord, we pursue the Lord more, consecrate ourselves, and have various kinds of dealings. Thus, we enter into the second stage of the experience of life. We begin to abide in Christ in a practical way, fellowship with Christ, enjoy Christ, and experience Christ. We call this second stage, therefore, the stage of "abiding in Christ."

Someone has designated the first stage as "the salvation stage" and the second as "the revival stage." The implication is that in the first stage man has only the Lord's salvation, being regenerated of the Holy Spirit. As to the other experiences of life, they are still very weak and vague to him, so this stage can only be called "the salvation stage." At the second stage he is constrained by the love of the Lord and is revived. He then loves the Lord, pursues the Lord, and gradually obtains the various experiences of life that come after regeneration. This stage is therefore called "the revival stage."

We cannot avoid dividing a Christian's early life experiences into these two stages. Yet, according to the truth, these

two stages should not and cannot be divided. Let us first consider the division of "in Christ" and "abiding in Christ." When a
man is saved, he is transferred into Christ and should then be
abiding in Christ. Once we share what Christ is, unite with
Christ, and possess the fact of being in Christ, we should have
fellowship with Christ, enjoy Christ, and have the experience of
abiding in Christ. No one ever moves into a house without
living in that house and enjoying it. Likewise, once a man is in
Christ, he should abide in Christ—these two events are closely
connected and take place almost simultaneously. Because of
this, "in Christ" and "abiding in Christ" can only be regarded as
one stage. "Abiding in Christ" should be the first stage, with "in
Christ" being simply the beginning of this first stage.

As to the division of the "salvation stage" and the "revival
stage," the situation is also the same. Regeneration in the
salvation stage is actually "revival." Originally, man lived in
the presence of God, but because of his transgression, he
became dead and fell into sins. Now because of the Lord's
deliverance, he is made alive together with the Lord and
raised up together with the Lord. This is regeneration, and
this is revival. Therefore, a regenerated and saved man
should also be a revived man. It is abnormal for a man to
be saved but not revived, since the central point of salvation
is regeneration, that is, revival. Only in the salvation that
does not reach the mark is there no condition of revival; salvation that reaches the mark is not only regeneration but
also revival. For this reason the salvation stage is the revival
stage, and the two should not be divided.

Strictly speaking, therefore, the four stages of the spiritual life are in reality only three stages, with the first two
stages regarded only as one. There are many, however, who
though they are saved, do not appear to have the condition of
revival; they are actually in Christ, yet they do not have the
practical experience of abiding in Christ. They still need the
mercy of the Lord to be attracted by Him, to love Him, to
pursue Him, and to follow Him so that they will manifest the
condition of revival and begin to enjoy Christ and experience
Christ. For this reason then, we divide the Christian's early
experience of life into two stages.

CHAPTER THREE

CONSECRATION

The second stage of the experience of life usually begins with consecration. Many Christians wait until they are consecrated before they abide in Christ, have fellowship with Christ, and thus enjoy and experience Christ. We can say, therefore, that the first experience of the second stage of spiritual life is consecration.

In a normal condition these two experiences, salvation and consecration, are closely related. A saved person should be a consecrated person. Once a person is saved, he should consecrate himself to the Lord. To be saved without being consecrated is a very abnormal condition. Our gospel work must be done strongly to such an extent that people will immediately consecrate themselves as soon as they are saved.

Concerning the experience of consecration there are five main points: the basis of consecration, the motive of consecration, the meaning of consecration, the purpose of consecration, and the result of consecration. These five points include all the content of consecration. We come now to look into this experience of consecration according to these points.

I. THE BASIS OF CONSECRATION—GOD'S PURCHASE

The first main point is the basis of consecration. On what basis must we consecrate ourselves to God? On what basis does God require us to consecrate ourselves to Him? We need to have a basis for whatever we do. For example, when we move into a house and live in it, it is because we have paid a price and rented or bought it. This renting or purchasing is the basis upon which we live there. When a creditor takes action to obtain payment of debt from someone, it is because the other party is indebted to him. The debt is the creditor's basis for seeking payment. Our God is One who is most legal and One who acts most reasonably. All His doings are legal and have a basis. He cannot obtain something in the universe without paying a price, and He also cannot demand something from us without a basis. When God, therefore, demands that we consecrate ourselves to Him, it cannot be without a basis. In this matter He has a very solid basis, that is, His purchase. He has already bought us. He can, therefore, demand that we consecrate ourselves to Him.

First Corinthians 6:20 says, "You have been bought with a price." Our consecration is based on this purchase of God. For instance, you may go to the Gospel Book Room and see a great number of books on display, but you cannot help yourself to any of them, because you have no basis for doing so. But if you pay three dollars for one of the volumes, then you can demand that the book be turned over to you and claim that it belongs to you. This demanding is based upon your purchase. The basis of consecration is exactly the same. How can God demand that we consecrate ourselves to Him? The reason is that He has bought us. Some think that the reason for consecrating ourselves to God is because God has created us. This is not right. Consecration is not based on God's creation; it is based on God's purchase. In Exodus 13:2 we see that after the passover, God commanded the Israelites, saying, "Sanctify to Me all the firstborn." The reason for this command is that all these firstborn were redeemed by God through the death of the lamb. They were bought by God with the blood of the lamb. To purchase is to acquire the right of ownership. When God has bought us, He then has the right of ownership; that is, He has a basis to demand that we turn ourselves over to Him to belong to Him. The basis of consecration, therefore, is God's purchase.

God has bought us with none other than the precious blood shed by His beloved Son on the cross (1 Pet. 1:19). How great "a price" (1 Cor. 6:20) is this precious blood! God used this precious blood as the price to buy us, that we may belong to Him.

We may further ask, From what did God buy us? Some think that God has bought us from the rule of Satan, or that

God has bought us from the bondage of sin, or that God has bought us from the world. But these concepts are not in accordance with the truth. To purchase a thing implies the recognition that the original right of ownership is legal; therefore, one must use the legal means—purchasing—to obtain that right of ownership. The rule of Satan, the bondage of sin, and the usurpation of the world are all illegal. God never admits that these are legal. It is not necessary, therefore, for God to purchase us with a price from Satan, sin, and the world. Satan, sin, and the world seized us by illegal means, captured us, and dominated us. God saved us from these by the saving work of the Lord at the cross. In this aspect, therefore, it is salvation and not a purchase.

From what then has God bought us? Galatians 4:5 says, "That He might redeem those under law." This verse reveals that God has redeemed us from under the law; God has bought us from under the law. Why is it that God has redeemed us from the law? The reason is that when we sinned and fell, we not only came under Satan, sin, and the world and became their captives, but we also offended God's righteousness, transgressed God's law, and became sinners. Because we became sinners, we fell under God's law and were kept and retained by this law. The fact that we were thus retained by the law of God is altogether righteous and legal. If God, therefore, wanted to release us from under His righteous law, He must pay the full price to satisfy the demand of His law. This price is the precious blood shed by His Son. Since this blood satisfied the requirements of the law, we are redeemed from under His righteous law; that is, we are bought from under the law. Since the day we obtained redemption, we have been released from the rule of the law; we are no longer under its authority. Formerly we belonged to the law, but now we belong to God. The right of ownership over us has been transferred from the law to the hand of God. It is on the basis of this transfer of right that God demands that we consecrate ourselves to Him. God's right of ownership over us through purchase, therefore, is the basis upon which we should consecrate ourselves to God.

When we lead others to consecrate themselves, or when

we examine our own consecration, we must attend to this basis of consecration. We must realize that we were bought by God and that the right of ownership over us has been transferred to God. We are no longer, therefore, in our own hands. We are no longer our own. When we thus realize the basis of consecration, our consecration is stable and secure.

If we were to investigate the consecration experiences of Christians, we would discover that most were constrained by the love of the Lord. This motive is truly good and reasonable. But if we were to consecrate ourselves to the Lord only because of the constraint of the Lord's love, would this consecration be sufficiently stable? Experience tells us that it is not. The reason is that love is the story of our heart's mood and desire. When we are happy, we love; when we are not happy, we do not love. Today we are in the mood to love, so we consecrate ourselves; tomorrow we are not in the mood to love, so we do not consecrate ourselves. Therefore, if consecration is purely a matter of love, it will not be sufficiently stable. It will be subject to as much change as our unstable mood. When we understand the basis of consecration and realize that consecration is based on the matter of purchase, our consecration will then be stable and secure. A purchase is not a matter of mood but a matter of ownership. God has already bought us and has the right to own us. Therefore, whether we are happy or not, we must consecrate ourselves.

I feel deeply that not many of those brothers and sisters among us who have already consecrated themselves truly realize God's right of ownership. We must return, therefore, and make up this lesson. Our consecration must not only be because of the love of the Lord; we must realize that God verily has the right to possess us. Following the Lord is not always exciting, and serving Him is not always pleasant. Even those of us who have served the Lord for many years sometimes feel that it is really not easy to serve the Lord, but the urge within forbids us to do otherwise. We often feel like giving up, but we cannot. The reason is that we have realized God has a right to us. We were bought by God, and we belong to Him; therefore, whether we like it or not, we cannot but consecrate ourselves and serve Him. In the world today, people get married when they feel like it and divorced when they feel like it. They act according to their mood without recognizing any right of ownership. Our consecration must not be like that. True consecration must sooner or later rest on the realization of God's right to us, based on His purchase. Whether we are in a happy mood or not, this fact remains the same. When we stand before the judgment seat to be judged by the Lord regarding our consecration, judgment will not be on the basis of whether we love Him or not, or whether we liked to be consecrated or not; it will be based on the fact of whether we were bought by Him or not. If we were bought by Him, we can do nothing but consecrate ourselves; we have nothing to say. From now on, therefore, whenever we speak about consecration, we must not neglect this basis.

When we read these words regarding the basis of consecration, we may understand with our mind and receive with our heart, but this is still not adequate. We cannot say that we thus have the basis of consecration. We need to experience this basis practically in our daily life. Each time something occurs that causes us to argue with God, we must bow before Him and say, "Lord, I am the slave You bought. My right of ownership has been purchased by You. I here and now declare Your right. Even in this matter I will let You be the Lord and decide for me." Every time we depart from the position of consecration, we should feel that we are in a state of rebellion similar to that of Onesimus, the slave who fled from his master, Philemon. Whenever we are confronted with the opportunity to make a choice, we should consider this basis of consecration, this purchase, as the foundation rock under our feet. We must stand securely thereon, never daring to depart from it. If we experience consecration in such a sincere way, we have truly laid hold of the basis of consecration.

At the time John Bunyan, the author of *Pilgrim's Progress,* was being martyred, he expressed that regardless of how God treated him, he would still only worship Him. He realized that he was but a purchased slave, one over whom God had the complete right of ownership. However God treated him, he had nothing to say; he only worshipped. He knew that to make his own choice meant to escape and that to accept

God's will meant consecration. For this cause he let God do all the choosing for him and was willing to accept His arrangement, whatever it might be. Until death he stood on the foundation rock of the basis of consecration. He really was one who knew God's right and the basis of consecration. Our realization of the basis of consecration must also go to the same extent.

II. THE MOTIVE OF CONSECRATION—GOD'S LOVE

The motive of consecration refers to one's heart in consecration. In order to have a good consecration, we not only need to realize its basis; we also need to have a motive. Although one knows the basis of consecration as having been bought and redeemed by God, yet this realization may not be sufficient to touch his feeling, move his heart, and cause him to consecrate himself willingly to God. If the things that God purchased were inanimate objects, such as a chair or a garment, He could proceed directly to use them as He pleases. But what God has redeemed today are living persons, each with a mind, an affection, and a will. Although God wants to have us, we may not be happy to let Him have us. Although God has the legal right and basis to possess us, we may not have the heart to let Him do so. Therefore, when God desires us to consecrate ourselves to Him, He must move our heart. He must give us the motive of love so that we might be willing to consecrate ourselves to Him.

The motive of consecration is the love of God. Whenever the Holy Spirit pours out the love of God in our hearts, we will naturally be willing to become the prisoners of love and consecrate ourselves to God. This kind of consecration, motivated by the love of God, is mentioned very clearly in two places in the Scriptures: 2 Corinthians 5:14-15 and Romans 12:1.

Second Corinthians 5:14-15 says, "The love of Christ constrains us...and He died for all that those who live may no longer live to themselves but to Him who died for them and has been raised." *Constrains* in the original has the meaning of the rushing of waters. In other words, these verses tell us that the dying love of Christ is like the rushing of great waters toward us, impelling us to consecrate ourselves to God and to live for Him beyond our own control.

Romans 12:1 says, "I exhort you therefore, brothers, through the compassions of God to present your bodies a living sacrifice." The compassions referred to here are the love of God. Therefore, in this place also, Paul is seeking to move our hearts with the love of God. He would cause us to have the motive of love so that we might consecrate ourselves willingly to God as a living sacrifice. We see from these two passages that the love of God is the motive of consecration.

In a normal consecration this motive of love is very necessary. If our consecration rests solely on the basis of consecration, the realization of God's right to us, this consecration will only be based on reason; it will lack sweetness and intensity. But if our consecration has love as its motive, if our feelings have been touched by the love of God, the constraint of this love will cause us to consecrate ourselves willingly to God. This consecration will then be sweet and intense.

The marriage relationship of a husband and wife is a case in point. If it rests solely on the basis of right, it will be difficult for their life to be harmonious and sweet. A true marriage relationship not only rests on the basis of right, but the more on love. Because the wife loves her husband, she becomes one with him and lives with him. So it is in a true consecration to God. When we touch the love of God and see that He truly is lovely, we will then consecrate ourselves to Him. Thus, although consecration based on love changes according to our mood, intense consecration is the result of constraining love. Those who have not had the experience of being constrained by the love of the Lord will not have a consecration that is good and intense. This is quite evident.

Hymns, #101 ("When I Survey the Wondrous Cross") tells a story of consecration because of the love of the Lord. It says that whenever I think of that love which saved me, I count everything but loss, because this love is so great. It goes on to say that I see His condition on the cross—His head, His hands, and His feet flowing with sorrow, love, and blood. All this because He loves me! Having seen such a love as this, if I offered to Him the entire universe, I would still feel ashamed, because His love is so noble, so excelling. If I should seek to repay His love, then I do not recognize His love; I even defile it. His love is like a priceless pearl, while my consecration is like filthy rags—we are simply unworthy of Him. One day, when the Spirit pours out this love in our hearts, we too will have such intense consecration.

Even after we have consecrated ourselves and have followed the Lord in the way of consecration, we need unceasingly the constraint of His love in order that we may touch its sweetness. In the way of consecration one often suffers pain and loss, and only those who frequently touch the love of the Lord can find sweetness in their pain. Though the early apostles were much despised and imprisoned, they considered their suffering a glorious and joyful thing, since they were counted worthy to be dishonored on behalf of the Lord's name (Acts 5:40-41). The martyrs throughout the generations could joyfully accept the suffering of death and were not willing to forsake the Lord's name, because they had touched the sweetness of the Lord and had been constrained by His love. The love between us and the Lord, therefore, must always be renewed. The motive of love must be maintained in us in order that our consecration and service may always be fresh and sweet.

In conclusion, a stable and intense consecration requires these two aspects: one aspect is to have a basis, that is, to realize that I myself have been bought by God, that I belong to Him, and that I ought to consecrate myself to Him; the other aspect is to have a motive, that is, to see that the love of God toward me is indeed very great, and that this love constrains me so that I willingly consecrate myself to Him.

III. THE MEANING OF CONSECRATION—
TO BE A SACRIFICE

When one sees the basis of consecration and also has the motive of consecration, he is willing to consecrate himself to God. What then is consecration? What is the meaning of consecration? Romans 12:1 says, "I exhort you therefore, brothers, through the compassions of God to present your bodies a living sacrifice." This verse shows us that the meaning of consecration is to be a "sacrifice."

What does the phrase *to be a sacrifice* mean? What is a sacrifice? The Scripture shows us that whenever a thing is set apart from its original position and usage and is laid on God's altar, specifically for Him, this thing is then a sacrifice. In the Old Testament men offered bullocks and rams as sacrifices. The principle is this: The bullock originally lived in a corral and was used for plowing the field and drawing carts. Now it is taken out from the corral and brought beside the altar. There is a change in its position. Then it is killed, placed on the altar, and consumed by fire to be a sweet-smelling savor unto God. This is a change in its usage. Thus, this bullock becomes a sacrifice. A sacrifice, therefore, is none other than a thing that is set apart for God and laid on the altar, with a change in position and a change in usage. Whether it is a bullock or a ram, whether it is fine flour or oil, once it is offered as a sacrifice, it leaves the hands of the offerer and can no longer be used for his own advantage and enjoyment. All the sacrifices on the altar belong to God and are for His use and enjoyment. To put it simply, to be a sacrifice means to be offered to God for His use.

When we present ourselves to God as a living sacrifice, there are also these two aspects: one is a change in our position, and the other is a change in our usage. When we understand this meaning of consecration, we can then discern the genuineness of the consecration of others. When a person says he is consecrated, we may ask whether he has changed his position and changed his usage. If not, he is not a sacrifice, and there is no true consecration. Nothing is offered as a sacrifice without a change in position and in usage. Those who truly offer themselves, therefore, must pass completely out of their own hands and into God's hands for His use.

Such a consecration is similar to the giving of gifts. When we give a gift to others, it changes position from our hands to theirs. It is no longer ours to use; it is for their use. In like manner, the day we truly consecrate ourselves, our position is changed. Formerly we were in our own hands; now we are in the hands of God. Formerly we walked in our own way; now we lie on God's altar. At the same time, our usage is also changed. Formerly we lived for ourselves and were toward the world; now we are set apart solely for God. Only this kind of consecration is true consecration.

When we thus present ourselves to God as a sacrifice, we become food for God; we are for His satisfaction. Among the offerings of the Israelites, some were for God's use, such as gold, silver, precious stones, threads of all colors, wool, and sheepskin (Exo. 25:2-7); and some were offered to God for food, such as the bullock, ram, pigeon, and turtledove used in the burnt offerings. When these were offered as a burnt offering, they were burnt on the altar and became a sweet savor, food for God (Lev. 3:11). When God accepted the sweet savor of these sacrifices, He was satisfied.

The offering of these sacrifices is a type of our consecration. The meaning, therefore, of offering ourselves as a sacrifice is offering ourselves to God as food that He will be pleased to accept and thus find satisfaction. We are people who were originally like a pile of uncooked rice, which might be used for this or for that. One day, because of God's need, we were separated from the original pile of rice and were worked on in such a way that we were cooked and placed on God's table— the altar—and became God's food for His satisfaction. This is the meaning of being a sacrifice, and this is the meaning of consecration.

Since the meaning of consecration is to offer ourselves to God as a living sacrifice for God's satisfaction, we should ask ourselves this question: Since our consecration, how much of our actual living and actual experiences have proved that we have indeed laid ourselves on the altar to be a sacrifice for God? Are we indeed willing to be God's food so that He might be satisfied? True consecration is never compelled by God; it is of our voluntary will. God takes nothing by force; everything is offered up by men willingly. Likewise, our consecration today must be made out of our voluntary will; it is we who willingly lie on the altar and dare not move off. Others may move about freely, but we dare not act in a casual way. Others may calculate and choose between the sweet and the bitter, but when we encounter a difficulty, we dare not consider escape. Others can reason and argue with God; we dare not say even one sentence. Others can evade God's will and avoid being bound and limited; we would rather be restricted by His will and willing to be imprisoned in His hand. All this, because we have already offered ourselves to God and have been laid on the altar. We are already a consecrated people. We should be able to say continually to God, "O God, I have no choice; I have already consecrated myself to You; I am in Your hand." Whenever anything happens to us, we must express ourselves in this way to God. We must remain thus in God's hand and actually be a sacrifice unto God. Only this is the true meaning of consecration.

IV. THE PURPOSE OF CONSECRATION— TO WORK FOR GOD

Since the meaning of consecration is to become a sacrifice, the thing offered is something that is entirely for God. The purpose of consecration, therefore, is to be used by God, to work for God. But in order that we may work *for* God, we must first *let* God work. Only those who have first let God work can work for God. We can only work for God to the extent that we allow God to work. If we do not let God work first, our labor can neither please Him nor be accepted by Him, no matter how diligent and enduring we are. Those things we do for God that are pleasing and acceptable to Him can never go beyond that which we allow God to work. "Let" is the basis, and "for" is the result. When we have the basis of "let," then we can have the result of "for." This is an unchanging principle. Therefore, when we consecrate ourselves to God, although it is to work for God, from our standpoint the emphasis is to let God work. The purpose of consecration then is to let God work in order that we might reach the stage of working for God.

The offering of the sacrifices in the Old Testament also sheds light on this matter. When the bullocks and rams were killed and offered to God as burnt offerings, it was first necessary for God to do His thorough work upon them, that is, to consume them by fire, if they were to be pleasing and acceptable to Him. If the sacrifices were not consumed by fire, they would be raw and foul smelling and could never be acceptable or pleasing to God. Our consecration today is just like that. We have already offered ourselves, yet if we do not allow God to work first but go out to work for Him and serve Him directly, that work and that service will be raw, untempered, and foul smelling. It can never be accepted by God, let alone satisfy Him.

When Nadab and Abihu offered strange fire before God, they were consequently consumed by God (Lev. 10). The offering of strange fire is the principle of working directly for God. Anyone who has not been dealt with by God and worked on by God and yet tries to work for God directly is offering strange fire. It is not only raw, untempered, foul smelling, and thus unacceptable to God; it is also dangerous and apt to involve one in much difficulty in God's work. This is why we earnestly hope many times, on one hand, that brothers and sisters would love God and offer themselves to God, but on the other hand, we are truly afraid that, when people love God and offer themselves to Him, they will want to work for God directly and serve Him directly. All such work and service is dangerous. I believe that if there are one hundred brothers and sisters in our midst who by the constraining love of the Lord consecrate themselves to Him, desiring to work for Him and yet not allowing Him to work first, these one hundred persons will quarrel every day. One will want to serve God this way, and another will want to serve God another way. The church will inevitably be divided.

One of the main reasons for the confusion in the church today is just this. Whenever someone offers himself to God, his purpose is to work for God, but he is either ignorant or neglects to allow God to work first. When people do not love the Lord or consecrate themselves to the Lord, it seems that everything is peaceful; but when there are those who love the Lord and consecrate themselves to Him, wanting to work for God directly, many problems are raised, and there is much confusion.

The same principle applies even to the reading of the Bible. If our head has not been worked on by God, if it is still in its natural state, it is dangerous to read the Bible. If we do, in each reading and in each expounding we will allow our fancy to run wild. If a person is not zealous to read the Bible, it is not so bad; but once he acquires this zeal, his reading becomes wild, and he gathers from it many strange and erroneous ideas. His zeal is good, but his untamed reading is indeed fearsome.

It is extremely dangerous whenever a man comes into direct touch with spiritual things without experiencing the working of God. If we want to touch spiritual things, whether it be to work for God, to study the Bible, to preach the gospel, or to oversee the church, we must first allow God to work on us so that we might be broken, subdued, and disciplined by Him. Then we may touch spiritual things and work for God; then we are safe and no longer dangerous.

We must, therefore, be severe with ourselves and ask whether our consecration to God is for working for God directly or for allowing God to work in us first. If we are not willing to allow God to work in us first, we cannot attain the object of working for God. Consequently, after our consecration we must not first be anxious to accomplish something for the Lord. We need to remain on the altar and allow God to work on us and consume us. The result of this consuming work will enable us to work for the Lord. This consecration, this service, is ripe and resurrected; it is acceptable to God and satisfies Him. In conclusion, the object of consecration is to let God work in us so that we may work for Him.

V. THE RESULT OF CONSECRATION— TO ABANDON OUR FUTURE

The result of consecration is that we are caused to cut off all our relationships with people, matters, and things, and especially to abandon our future and wholly belong to God. We need to consider this matter also in the light of the offerings of the Old Testament. When a bullock was taken for sacrifice and offered upon the altar, he was immediately cut off from all his previous relationships. He was severed from his master, his companions, and his corral. After he was consumed by fire, he even lost his original form and stature. All his choicest parts were changed to a sweet-smelling savor to God, and all that was left was a heap of ashes. Everything was cut off, and everything was finished. This was the result of the bullock being offered to God. Since our consecration is also an offering to God, the result must also be the same. There must be the giving up of everything to be burned to ashes by God to the point where all is finished. If evidence of this relinquishing of all things and burning to ashes is not seen in a man, there is something wrong with his consecration. Some brothers and sisters still have hopes after their consecration of becoming such-and-such a person. This proves that their future has not been given up.

The future we are speaking about includes not only our future in this world but also our future in the so-called Christian world. We all know how the world naturally attracts us and offers the hope of a future in it, but even the so-called Christian world holds an attraction to us and offers a hope of a future in it. There are some, for example, who hope to be famous preachers, some to be world-wide evangelists, and some to obtain the degree of doctor of divinity. All these are hopes for the future. Brothers and sisters, if we have been enlightened, we will discover that even in our hope for more fruit in our work, our hope for more people to be saved through our gospel preaching, our hope to lead more brothers and sisters to love the Lord, and our hope for more local churches to be built by our hand—even in these hopes—there are hidden many elements that are for the building up of our future. When we see the prosperity of others, we become envious. When we see the achievement of others, our heart is moved. All this proves that we still have hopes in our own future. All these hopes, however, never exist in a consecrated person. A truly consecrated man is a man who has given up his future. He abandons not only his future in the world but also his so-called spiritual future. He no longer has hopes for himself in anything; all his hope is in God. He lives purely and simply in the hand of God; he is what God wants him to be and does what God wants him to do. Whatever the outcome may be, he does not know and does not care. He only knows that he is a sacrifice, wholly belonging to God. The altar is forever the place where he stands, and a heap of ashes is forever the result. His future has been utterly abandoned.

This giving up of the future is not a reluctant act after

something has already occurred to wreck your future hopes; it is a willing surrender before such an event. It is not waiting till you have lost or failed in your business and then giving up. It is not waiting till you lose your job, till you cannot enter college, or till you fail to obtain a Ph.D. degree, and then give up. It is not this. When we speak of giving up the future, we mean that when a profitable business opportunity awaits you, when an excellent job awaits you, or when a Ph.D. degree awaits you, you willingly give it all up for the Lord's sake. This is truly called the giving up of the future. Even if the entire glory of Egypt is placed before you, you can say to it, "Goodbye, I must go to Canaan." Perhaps Satan will continue to call you from behind, saying, "Do come back. We have a Ph.D. degree here and an Egyptian palace for you. This is a rare opportunity." If at this time you can face him and tell him straightly, "Be gone; these are not my portion," this then is a true giving up of the future.

There is a very grievous situation today—many who serve the Lord have a future in the Christian world. We must understand that this is a very serious degradation. If this does not prove that there was something wrong with the original consecration of the people concerned, it does prove that they have fallen off the altar. A truly consecrated person knows from the outset that his future is through. If he still wants to have a future, he need not come to the church. He realizes that he should never have any future, because he is already on the altar. Sometimes he comes to a place of difficulty and finds that he has more courage because this difficulty proves to him that he is still on the altar and still under God's guidance. Sometimes he enters a period of ease, and he becomes on the contrary a little fearful, wondering if perhaps he has fallen off the altar and is no more under God's guidance. Brothers and sisters, we need frequently to ask ourselves: What is the result of our consecration? Has our all become ashes on the altar? Has all our future been abandoned? Or have we reserved something that is hopeful?

Every one of us must go before God and deal thoroughly with this problem of consecration. If our consecration is not sound, sooner or later problems will arise in our service and in our spiritual condition. The temptations of future prospects are very many and very great, and these temptations are particularly severe to those who are especially gifted and can be used outwardly to some extent by God. There are many matters, many environments, and many attractions that can cause us to lose our consecration unconsciously. There is only one way for us to overcome these temptations, and that is to relinquish thoroughly all our future on the very first day of our consecration. This means that since we have consecrated ourselves, everything is through.

From the life of J. N. Darby, we may see what a truly consecrated person he was. He was greatly used of the Lord in the last century, many thousands being helped spiritually through him. Even in his old age he was still walking a straight path with the Lord. He could very well have had fame and position, but he did not take them. At a certain time in his old age he went to work in Italy and spent a night in a very plain and lowly inn. He was exhausted, and he bowed his head between his hands and sang softly: "Jesus, I my cross have taken, all to leave and follow Thee..." Even in this condition he had no murmuring, no regrets; he could joyfully sing this hymn to the Lord. I was really touched when I came to this point in reading his life story. The fact that he could preserve the result of relinquishing his future right to the end moved me. Although he was old, his consecration was not old; it was still as fresh as it was in the beginning.

Brothers and sisters, this result of abandoning all our future prospects always needs to be kept fresh within us. We must never let our consecration become old. If it grows old, it is the same as if we had never consecrated ourselves. We should always be as ashes on the altar, always entirely for God to enjoy, always without any future.

A CONCLUDING WORD

After we have gone through the five main points of consecration, we should be quite clear concerning the lesson of consecration. From the standpoint of the truth, we can say that everything pertaining to the doctrine of consecration is included in these five points. From the standpoint of experience, as long as a person is truly consecrated, he will also have these five points; the only difference we can point out is that some may have experienced these matters in a stronger way, others in a weaker way; some more evidently, others more hiddenly. These five points of consecration, therefore, were not conceived in our imagination to indoctrinate people; rather, the *actual condition* of a consecrated person is our basis for unveiling these points and making them explicit. I do hope that through these explanations and investigations there will be, on one hand, a development of the consecration that is already in one's inner being and, on the other hand, that the defects or lack of intensity of one's consecration may be revealed, that by this, one will be enabled to pursue and progress continuously in this experience.

We must realize that it is not possible to hit the climax of any experience of life by experiencing it just once. We need to pursue continuously so that our experience will increase gradually and become fuller, until it reaches the stage of maturity. Although some brothers and sisters have consecrated themselves, they have only had a beginning; they have not had much experience in consecration. They need to pursue continuously and deepen their experience in this matter.

If we want to enter into a house, we usually need to walk a certain distance, after which we step into the door of the house. But in spiritual experience it is just the opposite. You must step inside the door first, and then you begin to walk. All experience of spiritual life requires that we first step inside the door and pass through a crisis to have a beginning; we should then walk another distance and continue to go forward, to pursue, and to experience further. The crisis experience of some people is quite weak and without weight, so they must still continue to pursue. On the other hand, some people have a crisis experience that is strong and weighty, yet they likewise need to go on continually and pursue a deeper consecration.

Although all five points of consecration are included in the normal consecration experience of a person at the beginning, as though they were already attained, this does not mean that his experience of consecration is complete. It has just begun; it is simply an entrance through the door. There is still a long way ahead in the path of consecration that he is required to walk. Consequently, we must be steadfast in our consecration in every environment and practice our consecration in every affair, and at every opportunity we must reconsecrate ourselves afresh. By so doing we can go straight forward in the path of consecration.

In Old Testament times the burnt offering had to be offered every day, not only in the morning but also in the evening. On every Sabbath, at every new moon, and during every festival, special burnt offerings were required (Num. 28). Special burnt offerings were also needed at times of great events (Lev. 8:18, 28; 1 Kings 3:4, 15; 8:62-64). One offering was not sufficient; offerings were required daily, at every festival, and at every event. The burnt offering, therefore, is one of the most important offerings in the Old Testament. Due to this, the bronze altar was even specifically called "the altar of burnt offering." The frequency of these offerings typifies to us the need for making a new consecration every day. When we come to special convocations and special events, we need to make special offerings. If we would consecrate ourselves repeatedly in this way, the experience of consecration would be increased and formed in us.

Many of us have read the biography of Madame Guyon. Through the account of her life we see that she was one who was steadfast in her consecration and one who advanced continually. Consequently, we can clearly distinguish the five points of consecration expressed in her when she was advanced in years. The basis of her consecration was as firm as a rock. Whenever there was a controversy between her and the Lord, there was a rock under her feet on which she stood continually. She said to the Lord, "Lord, You have bought me!" The motive of her consecration was just like the mighty force of rushing waters; therefore, her consecration remained sweet and absolute. In her autobiography she often mentions that she renewed her marriage vows to the Lord. This shows that in her inner being she was constantly touched and constrained by the love of the Lord, for a marriage vow is an expression of love at its highest. From the human standpoint, the path she trod was one of much suffering, but to her it was exceedingly sweet; because of the love of the Lord, her suffering was transformed to sweetness. The meaning of her consecration was even clearer. Although she was sometimes at home serving her husband and caring for her child, she was one who really remained in the hands of the Lord. She was willing to take her hands off and put herself entirely into the hands of God. She said to Him, "O God, if You want to use me, to beat me, to press me, or to mold me, I want to be at Your disposal; even if You want to cut me into pieces and kill me, I am at Your disposal. I am not in my own hands; I have handed myself over to You." This particular point is especially clear in Madame Guyon. The purpose of her consecration was not muddled at all. She was really one who through consecration let God work within her, carve her, break her, and press her. Her function, therefore, was expressed in a very full way—it shone as the midday sun. We consider that in the last three centuries she has provided more life to the saints than anyone else. Because she let God work in her the most, she had the most to minister to others. Although she is dead, to this very day we obtain help through her. Finally, the result of her consecration causes us to worship God even more. She had no success in the world, nor in her spiritual work were there any future prospects. She could say that she was just a heap of ashes; everything was gone. On the other hand, in the universe, before God she is ever producing a sweet-smelling savor to His satisfaction and to the joy of His people. The experience of consecration with her truly reached its full maturity.

Having gone through all these matters related to consecration, we are enabled to understand that consecration is not just a knowing of the right of ownership in the mind or a feeling of love in our affections, nor is it only an attitude and expression of ours toward God. Actually speaking, consecration itself is a part of life, a major part of life. The experience of consecration, therefore, is really the experience of life. The fullness of one's experience of life depends on the fullness of one's experience of consecration. Hence, if one pursues the experience of consecration, it will enable him to grow in life.

Furthermore, since consecration is a part of life, then by following this life and living in this life, the law of life will cause the five points of consecration to be clearly and spontaneously worked out in us. When we first consecrate ourselves, our experience is similar to an embryo in the mother's womb—one cannot distinguish the ears, the eyes, the mouth, and the nose. As we grow in life, however, these five points related to the experience of consecration gradually become formed in us. Then we have a definite feeling that we have been bought by God and that all our rights are in His hand. We become a prisoner of His love because His love has pierced our hearts. We become a sacrifice indeed, laid on the altar for God's enjoyment and satisfaction. We will be those who have been thoroughly worked over by God and are then able to work for Him. Our future will truly be as a handful of ashes. All our ways of escape outside of God's will shall have been cut off; God only will be our future and our way. At that time the experience of our consecration will indeed have become matured. May we all, by the grace of the Lord, pursue and go on together.

Chapter Four

DEALING WITH SINS

Now that we have considered consecration, we must look into various dealings. *Dealing* implies that we follow the leading of the Holy Spirit to purge away all the difficulties that hinder the growth of life. The more we are being dealt with, the more God's life grows in us. The more God's life grows in us, the more we are being dealt with. These two cannot be separated; they are two aspects of the same matter. Therefore, the dealings constitute an extremely important position in our experience of life. We can say that this is a major portion of the experience in life.

Why do we approach the subject of dealing directly after consecration? Because it is the natural result of consecration. Once we have consecrated ourselves to God so that He may use us, God must cleanse us, deal with us, and purge away all our problems so that we may be fit for His use. If we wish to use a glass, we would first want it to be washed. When it is completely clean, it is a glass that we can use. Before we consecrate ourselves, or when we depart from a consecrated position, we do not realize that we need to be dealt with. When we consecrate ourselves, or when we return to the position of consecration, we immediately discover that there are many difficulties in us that prevent God from using us. Therefore, if we desire to fulfill the purpose of our consecration, we need to have all our difficulties dealt with one by one. When we have purged ourselves in such a way, we will become a vessel unto honor, useful to the Master (2 Tim. 2:21). We should therefore deal with ourselves directly after consecration.

Of course, in the clearance of the past when we were newly saved, there were many dealings involved, but these dealings were primitive and shallow. The thorough and deep kind of dealings take place after consecration. We have said that under normal circumstances, once a person is saved, he will have a proper clearance. This proper clearance will bring forth a sound consecration. However, after we have consecrated ourselves, we discover that there are more things to be dealt with, and we deal with them more thoroughly. Thus, sound consecration brings forth proper dealings. The stronger the consecration, the more severe are the dealings; the truer the consecration, the more thorough are the dealings. When we have been completely dealt with so that there are no further difficulties in us, we shall be wholly used by God, and the purpose of consecration will be fully attained.

Among all the difficulties that need to be dealt with, sins are the crudest, the most defiling, and the most evident. After having consecrated ourselves, the first thing we need to deal with is sins. Dealing with sins is the first lesson in our experience of dealings.

I. THE SCRIPTURAL BASIS

The following references give the scriptural basis for dealing with sins:

Matthew 5:23-26: "Therefore if you are offering your gift at the altar and there you remember that your brother has something against you, leave your gift there before the altar, and first go and be reconciled to your brother, and then come and offer your gift. Be well disposed quickly toward your opponent at law, while you are with him on the way, lest the opponent deliver you to the judge, and the judge to the officer, and you be thrown into prison. Truly I say to you, you shall by no means come out from there until you pay the last quadrans." Here, *reconciled* and *be well disposed* refer to dealings concerning our relationships with others.

Second Corinthians 7:1: "Therefore since we have these promises, beloved, let us cleanse ourselves from all defilement of flesh and of spirit, perfecting holiness in the fear of God." Here, *cleanse* also refers to a kind of dealing.

First John 1:9: "If we confess our sins, He is faithful and

righteous to forgive us our sins and cleanse us from all unrighteousness." Here *confess* is again a kind of dealing.

Proverbs 28:13: "He who covers his transgressions will not
prosper, / But whoever confesses and forsakes them will obtain
mercy." Here *confesses* and *forsakes* speak also of a dealing.

We see from the above Scriptures how we are to deal with
sins: toward men, we must be reconciled with them and well
disposed; toward God, we must confess our sins; and concerning sin, we must forsake it. These kinds of settlement of sin
are what we mean by dealing with sins.

II. THE OBJECT OF OUR DEALING WITH SINS

The object of our dealing with sins is the sins themselves.
There are two aspects with regard to sin: the nature of sin
within and the action of sin without. The nature of sin within
us is in the singular form; the action of sin without is in the
plural form. The singular form of sin is the life of Satan
within us, with which we have no way of dealing—the more
we deal with it, the more alive it becomes. The dealing with
sins of which we are speaking is our dealing with the sins
that we commit outwardly, the sins in our actions.

What are the sins in our actions? First John 5:17 says,
"All unrighteousness is sin." First John 3:4 says, "Sin is lawlessness." Both references show that in our actions all acts of
unrighteousness and lawlessness are sins. It is difficult to
distinguish between unrighteousness and lawlessness. All
lawlessness is unrighteousness, and all unrighteousness is lawlessness. Therefore, all deeds of unrighteousness and lawlessness are the sins of our actions and the object of our dealing.

Romans 2:14-15 says that the Gentiles, who have no law,
are a law to themselves; they show the work of the law written in their hearts. Their conscience is the law within them
that bears witness, and their thoughts either accuse or else
excuse them. All deeds that are right and lawful are justified
by our conscience; all deeds that are not right and lawful are
condemned by our conscience. All actions therefore that are
contrary to our conscience are actions of sins and the object of
our dealing.

We have said that the object of our dealing with sins is the external action of sins. This external action of sins has two aspects: the record of sin and the fact of sinning. The record of sin denotes the unrighteous and lawless deeds that offend the righteous law of God and result in our having a record of sin before the law of God. In the future God will judge us according to this record. The fact of sinning is the very act that establishes the record of sin. These sinful acts always fall short of the glory of God and, in either a perceptible or an imperceptible manner, hurt others. For example, stealing is an act of sin. By so doing, not only do we put the name of God to shame, but we also cause damage to others. This constitutes the fact of sinning. At the same time, we have offended the law of God. Henceforth, before His law we have a record of sin. Therefore, whenever we commit a sin, we have immediately the fact of sinning not only against God but many times also against man. At the same time we have a record of sin before God.

Since the action of sins has these two aspects, the object in dealing with sins likewise has two aspects. One is the record of our sin before God; the other is the fact of sinning. On one hand, we need to deal with our record of sin before God, and on the other hand, we need to deal with the fact of our sinning.

III. THE BASIS OF DEALING WITH SINS

Our object in dealing with sins includes all the sins we have committed. In carrying it out, however, God does not require us to deal with all the sins at once, but to deal with all those that we are conscious of while in fellowship with Him. We do not mean to say that we must deal with all the sins that we have actually committed, but only with those we are conscious of while in fellowship with God. The basis, therefore, of dealing with our sins is the consciousness we have while in fellowship with God.

Matthew 5:23 says, "If you are offering your gift at the altar and there you remember that your brother has something against you..." then go and deal with it quickly. Offering the gift is for fellowship with God. Therefore, this means that when we are having fellowship with God and are conscious of any discord between ourselves and others, or vice versa, we should immediately endeavor to rectify this situation lest our fellowship with God be affected or hindered. First John 1:7 indicates that if we have fellowship with God, we can see our sins in His light; then, according to what we have seen in His light, we are to confess this to God and deal with it before God in order to obtain God's forgiveness and cleansing. Matthew 5 speaks of our problems with others; 1 John 1 about our problem with God. One is the remembering by the altar; the other is the seeing in the light. Both indicate our consciousness while in fellowship with God. It is based on this consciousness that we have dealings toward man and God. Therefore, the basis for our dealing with sins is our consciousness while in fellowship with God.

Our dealing with sins is based only on the consciousness while in fellowship with God, not on all the facts of all the sins we have committed. Therefore, the realm of the basis is much smaller than the realm of the object. For example, we may have actually committed one hundred sins; however, when we approach God, we remember only ten sins while in fellowship with Him. We should deal with those ten sins of which we are conscious. If we are aware of only ten percent, we deal with ten percent; if we are aware of twenty percent, we deal with twenty percent. In other words, we deal only with the number of sins that we remember. The number of sins we recognize are the ones with which we are obliged to deal. This is the principle of remembering as stated in Matthew 5, and this is our principle in dealing with sins. We can leave undealt with for the time being the sins of which we are not aware, until such time as we do become aware of them in fellowship with God. Practically speaking, dealing with sins is not an ordinance of the law but a requirement of fellowship.

How is it that we can leave those unconscious sins undealt with for the time being? We can do so because unconscious sins do not affect our fellowship with God. If a person is guilty of an unrighteous act, others may become conscious of his wrongdoing, but he himself may not be aware of it. His conscience is still blameless. For this reason he can still pray and have fellowship with the Lord, and he can serve God and testify for God as usual; his spiritual life and service remain unaffected. But whenever he is aware of this sin and still does not deal with it, he has a guilty conscience; his fellowship with the Lord is hindered, and his spiritual life and service are not normal. According to Matthew 5, if one remembers something that needs to be dealt with and neglects to deal with it, his fellowship with God is immediately interrupted. He must deal with it quickly until it is completely cleared up; then he can have fellowship once more with God. First John 1:7 states the same fact. If one recognizes his sin while in the light of fellowship and does not deal with it, his fellowship is immediately hindered. Therefore, if we are not conscious of the sins that we have committed, we do not need to deal with them. If, however, we are aware of them, we should deal with them quickly; otherwise, our conscience will accuse us, our faith will become shipwrecked, and all spiritual things will thereby leak out (1 Tim. 1:19).

Hence, when we help others to deal with sins, we do not ask them to deal with their unconscious sins but with their conscious sins. When one becomes aware of his sin and either neglects or refuses to deal with it, then we can help him and lead him to deal with it.

The same is true when we examine our experience in dealing with sins. We do not ask how many sins we have committed that we have not dealt with but how many conscious sins we have not dealt with. We can leave our unconscious sins undealt with for the time being, but the conscious ones should be dealt with speedily. Up to the present time there are many brothers and sisters who have not come to absolute obedience with regard to the feelings they have while in fellowship with God. For example, someone may have committed one hundred unrighteous deeds and has become aware of twenty of them while in fellowship with God, but in practice he deals with only five. A problem, therefore, exists in his fellowship with the Lord. His spirit is not strong, and his prayer cannot be released. His condition before the Lord is greatly damaged.

We see, therefore, that the consciousness of fellowship upon which we base our dealing with sins is not absolute but differs according to the degree of depth of fellowship the individual

has with the Lord. The same unrighteous deed may be a sin
in the eyes of one person, whereas in the eyes of another it is
not a sin. This is because the degree of fellowship in the one is
deeper than in the other, so the consciousness of fellowship of
one is keener than that of the other. For instance, one may
tell a lie in a very evident manner, and everyone knows that
it is a sin; others may lie by telling the truth. To the average
individual the latter may not be sin, but those in deep fellowship with the Lord know that this also is a lie and must be
dealt with.

For example, Brother A is entering the room of Brother B.
Brother B sees him coming and hurriedly arranges his bed.
Brother B comes later to Brother A in order to deal with this
situation, saying, "Brother, when I saw that you were coming into my room, I arranged my bed; this is pretension." By
arranging his bed in such a way he felt that he was pretend-
ing; hence, he had sinned and wished to clear it up. Others
who are not quite so sensitive would consider this act as a
polite and necessary gesture. This is because the degree of
fellowship differs, and so also the consciousness differs.

Furthermore, the feeling in the same individual may also
vary according to the difference in his stage and depth of fellowship. Should someone have told him about a certain sin
two years ago, he would not have admitted it, but his fellowship during the past two years has deepened, and he has
become more sensitive. No longer does he wait for others to
condemn him; within himself he recognizes the sin and realizes that it must be dealt with.

Dealing with sins, therefore, is based on the consciousness we have while in fellowship with the Lord, and the
consciousness we have while in fellowship with the Lord is in
turn based on the depth of this fellowship. If the degree of
our fellowship is deep, our consciousness will be keen and
strong. If, on the other hand, the degree of our fellowship is
shallow, our consciousness will be dull and weak. It is similar
to the air in the room, which at first glance seems quite clean
and free from dust. The fact is that the light is not strong
enough, so our vision is not able to pierce the atmosphere and
detect the dust. When the sunlight enters the room, under

such strong illumination, we may observe many dust particles in the air. In like manner, we are guilty of many unrighteous and unlawful deeds, among which may be the coarser and more serious sins that are easily recognized; but there are many finer or less serious sins that are not so easily discerned. Not until our fellowship in life deepens will we be enabled to recognize these and deal with them. Hence, we should never measure others by the yardstick of our own consciousness, nor should we accept the consciousness of others as a yardstick by which to measure ourselves. Everyone should learn to deal with sins only according to his own consciousness at the time he is in fellowship with the Lord.

We should realize at the same time that although we deal with our conscious sins, this by no means indicates that all ours sins have been completely dealt with, for there are still many sins of which we are not conscious. If we wish, therefore, to deal with our sins thoroughly, we should strengthen our fellowship with God. As this fellowship is strengthened, our consciousness concerning sin will become correspondingly broadened, and our dealing with sins more thorough.

How should we strengthen our fellowship? First, we should enlarge the sphere of our fellowship. The extent of our consciousness is the extent of our fellowship. In fellowship we unfold everything before the Lord. When we do this, we have a consciousness concerning everything and can thereby deal with everything. At the same time, as we deal with our conscious sin, our fellowship will naturally increase. Then, as our fellowship increases, more sins will be revealed, and we will increase our dealings. The more we deal with sins and the more our fellowship increases, the broader the area of our consciousness becomes, and the more our dealings increase. Thus, our dealings cover every aspect.

Second, we should deepen the degree of our fellowship. As the area of our fellowship broadens, we deal with every sin, but these dealings are not thorough. It is for this reason that our fellowship with the Lord needs to be deepened. As our fellowship is deepened, our consciousness is correspondingly deepened. Realizing that our former dealings were not sufficiently thorough, we deal again. More dealing brings in deeper fellowship, and as the fellowship is deepened, we experience more dealings. Then not only are all the sins dealt with which need to be dealt with, but they are dealt with in a very thorough manner.

IV. THE LIMIT OF OUR DEALINGS WITH SINS

The limit of our dealing with sins is similar to that of our clearance of the past. It is life and peace. When we deal with sins, we should do it until we have life and peace within. If we follow our consciousness in dealing with sins, we will feel inwardly satisfied, strengthened, refreshed, and enlivened; we will also feel joyful, restful, comfortable, and secure. Our spirit will be strong and living, and our fellowship with the Lord will be free and without hindrance. Our prayers will be releasing and with authority, and our utterance will be bold and powerful. All these senses and experiences are the conditions of life and peace. This is the limit of our dealing with sins, and this also is the result of our dealing with sins. What we have said before about dealing with sins thoroughly implies that we deal with sins to such a state of life and peace.

V. THE PRACTICE OF DEALING WITH SINS

We have previously said that there are two aspects with regard to the object of dealing with sins: one is the record of sin before God, and the other is the actual deed of sin. When we practice dealing with sins, therefore, these two aspects must be dealt with. First, the record of sin must be abolished, and second, we must deal with the actual committing of sin.

The abolishing of our record of sin before God is based upon the redeeming work of our Lord on the cross. Our Lord bore for us the righteous judgment of God. His blood satisfied the requirement of God's law on our behalf; therefore, all our record of sin before God has been abolished. However, if this objective fact is to become our subjective experience, there is still the need of application. We will speak of this application by dividing it into two stages: before we are saved and after we are saved.

Acts 10:43 says, "Everyone who believes into Him will receive forgiveness of sins." These are the words of the apostle when preaching the gospel to the unsaved. He told them that all the sins they committed before being saved would be forgiven if they would only believe. The abolishing of our record of sin before we are saved depends upon our believing. The application, therefore, is through our believing.

First John 1:9 says that "if we confess our sins, He is faithful and righteous to forgive us our sins and cleanse us from all unrighteousness." These words were written by the apostle to those who are saved, and they refer to all the sins we commit after we are saved. If we become conscious of them in His light, we must confess them before God; then we will be forgiven and cleansed. The abolishing of our record of sin after we are saved, therefore, depends upon our confession. Here the application is through our confession. If we do not confess, God will not forgive or cleanse. The moment we confess, we obtain forgiveness and cleansing. If we confess while still in this world, we obtain forgiveness while still here. If we do not confess while here, we will still have to confess in the coming kingdom before we can obtain forgiveness. This forgiveness is called the forgiveness in the kingdom. In conclusion, through our confession we obtain forgiveness for all the sins committed after we have been saved. This confession is our dealing before God.

How should we deal with the actual committing of sin? If we have offended God, we must deal with it before God and ask His forgiveness. If we have sinned against man, we should deal with it before man by asking man's forgiveness. If our act of sinning against man involves only a moral matter, we have only to confess this and apologize before man. If it also involves a loss of money and profits, then we should pay accordingly the amount we owe. This act of apologizing and reimbursing does not apply only to sins committed after we are saved. We must also deal with all those sins committed before we were saved; we must deal with them one by one before man according to the inner consciousness. Dealing with sins before man is the major part of this matter of dealing with sins, and we should take heed to practice it.

When we deal with sins before man, there are four basic principles we should remember and by which we should abide.

The first principle is to dispel all discord between others and ourselves. Every sinful act of ours, when it becomes known to others, whether it causes damage to them or not, results in a discordant condition between them and us. For instance, if we abuse or curse another person, we not only have a record of sin before God; we also have made a bad impression upon the one we have cursed and also upon any others who were present. Thus, it is difficult for us all to live together in harmony as before. Therefore, if, after being enlightened, we become conscious of this, we have to confess it to God and ask His forgiveness, and we also have to go to the persons concerned— the one who was cursed and any others who were present—to apologize and also to deal with what we have said. By doing this, the bad impression we have given them will be eradicated, and we can live together as formerly. The first principle, therefore, in dealing with sins is to dispel all discord between others and ourselves.

Therefore, under this principle, even our forgiving of others and our seeking peace with others are included in this dealing. Whether we are forgiving others or seeking peace with others, the purpose is to dispel all bad impressions and discordant situations between others and ourselves so that in the universe we can live peaceably and harmoniously with God and with man.

The second principle in dealing with sins is to have a clean conscience, void of offense. The dispelling of a discordant situation is in relation to man, but the possession of a clean conscience, void of offense, is in relation to ourselves. Every sin we have committed not only causes disapproval in others but also brings condemnation to our conscience. Not only will it cause others to have a bad impression of us, but it will also cause our conscience to have guilty stains. Therefore, our dealing with sin is not only to dispel the bad impressions caused in others but also to remove the guilt in our own conscience so that our conscience will be clean and void of offense.

The third principle in dealing with sins is to testify to the salvation of God. Because of the enlightenment of God's life, every person who has really been saved by God has a strong feeling about sins and therefore deals with them constantly. If one is willing to disregard loss and shamefacedness and deal with sins willingly and humbly, it is a strong testimony that God's salvation has come upon him. If he deals with sins continuously, it is proved even more that the grace of God is still working in him. Each real dealing with sins, therefore, is the issue of the grace of God working in him and is a strong testimony of God's grace.

The fourth principle in dealing with sins is to benefit others. Every time we deal with sins, the object is not only to dispel the discordant condition between ourselves and others, to cause our conscience to be clean and void of offense, or to testify to the salvation of God but also to benefit others. When dealing with our own sins, we should never cause damage or trouble to others. The result of our dealing with sins is peace within ourselves and peace also within others. Thus, we cause others to be benefited both spiritually and materially, and they are thereby edified.

We have mentioned four principles in dealing with sins. We should give heed to these principles in carrying out these dealings. Irrespective of the sin with which we are dealing and regardless of how we deal with it, we should always take care of these four principles by asking: Will this dealing dispel the discordant condition between others and ourselves? Will it cause our conscience to be clean and void of offense? Will it enable us to testify to the salvation of God and thereby give Him glory? And can we benefit others by it? If the answers to these questions conform to the four principles, we may bravely proceed then to deal with the sin. If, however, one of the answers does not conform to one of these principles, we should be careful; otherwise, the enemy will take advantage of our dealing and use it to produce an opposite result. In order that our dealings be properly and soundly carried out to the end that God may be glorified, that we obtain grace, and that others be benefited, we shall now discuss a few technical points in accordance with the four principles we have mentioned.

First, the object of our dealing. We should go to whomever we have offended and deal with the matter. If we have sinned only against God, we deal with God alone. If we have sinned against God and man, we deal with both God and man. We deal with sins according to the number of persons we have sinned against. It is not necessary to deal with those against whom we have not sinned. Concerning the principle of dispelling a discordant condition, we are obliged to go to those against whom we have sinned, who already have a bad impression of us, and deal with the sin in order that the discordant condition existing between them and ourselves may be dispelled. As for those against whom we have not sinned, the relationship is harmonious. If we go to them and deal with our sin, we thereby give them a bad impression about ourselves, thus violating the first principle of our dealing with sins.

If we confess our sin to those against whom we have not sinned or to those who do not know our sin, we not only give them a bad impression regarding us, but we may also arouse gossip, which would only do more harm to those against whom we have sinned. In the past there have been those who have not dealt with sins in a careful way. They confessed their sins publicly, with the result that those against whom they had sinned were completely ruined, even to the extent that husband and wife were divorced, and brothers hated each other. Irreparable damage was thus done. When we deal with sins, therefore, we should take the sphere of our sin as the sphere of our dealing. Our dealing should not exceed the sphere of the sin that we have committed. This is the safe way to obtain peace within and not harm others.

Second, the circumstance of our dealing with sins. In whatever circumstance we have sinned, we should deal with the sin accordingly. If we have sinned openly, we deal with it openly; if we have sinned secretly, we deal with it secretly. The sin we have committed in private does not require our dealing with it in public. If we have sinned against a person behind his back, we do not have to deal with him face to face; it is enough that we deal with it by ourselves secretly. Otherwise, we will increase the discordant condition and thus violate the principle of dispelling discord.

For example, if some have been dishonest regarding money

matters in an organization, unknown to the one in charge, they are not obliged to announce it publicly; they need only repay in private according to the amount they owe. If we hate someone without his knowing it, we need only repent in heart, without going to him. Thus, by not dealing with him regarding this sin, he will have no knowledge of it and will not receive any bad impression of us. If we deal with him regarding this sin, we may leave an unhappy trace upon his heart. However, if we hate somebody and this has become known to him, we should go to him and deal with the sin so that the hindrance may be eradicated between him and us.

Third, the responsibility of our dealing with sins. When we deal with sins, we should only deal with that part for which we are responsible; never involve others. For instance: I and others have together committed the same sin. In dealing with this sin, I must use wisdom in handling that portion for which I am responsible. I should not expose what others have done and cause them difficulty. Otherwise, my dealing will not conform to the principle that we have mentioned of benefiting others.

Fourth, the reimbursing of others. If the sin we have committed involves material things or gain from others, we should make restitution. When we restore what we have taken, we should pay according to the original value and add a little more to compensate for the loss. Leviticus 5 says that one-fifth should be added. In the New Testament we have the example of Zaccheus (Luke 19) restoring fourfold to those whom he had cheated. These are not laws or regulations but principles and examples to show us that whenever we make restitution, we should add something to the original value. With regard to the amount to be added, we may be guided by our inner feeling and our financial situation at the time. However, if we can afford it, we should see that the reimbursement fully repays the loss of those whom we owe and that we also have peace within.

Sometimes the amount we owe others is beyond our means to repay. In this case we should ask their forgiveness and request them to allow us to repay either when we have sufficient means or in installments until they are fully paid.

The object of our restitution, of course, should be the owner himself. If the owner has passed away, if he has gone to an unknown place, or if there is no way to communicate with him and it seems impossible for us to see him again, we can repay the debt to his nearest relative. If we cannot locate his nearest relative, we should give it to God (Num. 5:7-8). Everything comes from God and belongs to God. God is the origin of everything and the ultimate end of everything. Therefore, we give God everything in the absence of the owner.

Practically speaking, when we give to God, we give to His representative on the earth. God's representative on the earth today is, first of all, the church. We can, therefore, put the debt into the offering box of the church. God's representative is, second, the poor. Proverbs 19:17 says, "He who has pity upon a poor man lends to Jehovah." All human needs on this earth are supplied by God; therefore, when we give money to the poor, it is the same as giving to God. If there is no church where we live and it is not convenient to send the amount to another church in a different locality, we can give what we owe to the poor. In conclusion, the owner is the first to be reimbursed. If the owner is not available, we may give the amount to his nearest relative. If there is not such a relative, we should give it to the church. If there is no church, we should give it to the poor.

Anything we find that has been lost comes under the same principle. If we know the owner, we should return it to him. If we do not know the owner, we should dispose of it in a suitable manner or give it to the poor.

In conclusion, the purpose of our dealing with sin is that we might have a clean conscience, void of offense, and also that our will might be subdued. Whenever God enlightens us, we should be willing to deal with our sin, whatever it may be, not caring for our face or counting the loss. When we have reached such a stage, we can say that the purpose of God in having us deal with sins is accomplished. If at the time the environment does not permit, if we cannot possibly afford the financial burden, or if there is no value in dealing with the matter, we need not be too harsh on ourselves or adhere too much to the letter of the law. There is no harm if we do not

deal with it. However, when we first begin to practice dealing
with sins, it is better to be as thorough and severe as possible.
Even if we overdo somewhat and afterward regain our balance, it is still well. This overdoing is also helpful in making
our conscience clean and sensitive and our will subdued and
tender.

VI. DEALING WITH SINS BY LIFE

If we have studied every point with regard to dealing with
sins, we know that it is not an ordinance in the law but a natural demand and urge of God's life within us. If we live in
fellowship and obey the feeling of this demand of life to deal
with sins, our spiritual life and service will be strong and
released, we shall constantly receive light to know spiritual
things, and God's life in us will be free and far-reaching in its
growth. Conversely, if the spiritual condition is abnormal,
light is absent, and the inner feeling is weak, miserable, and
suppressed, whether it be in an individual saint or a corporate church, the reason is found largely in the lack of dealing
with sins. This is a very accurate measurement.

Since dealing with sins has such a close relationship with
our spiritual life, we should endeavor to experience this lesson
continuously. Although this experience is not a deep one, no
one can be so spiritual as to say that they have no need to
deal with sins. It is difficult to graduate from this lesson.
Therefore, we should not only ask ourselves if we have ever
had these experiences, but we should also ask ourselves if we
are now living in such an experience. We not only have to
wash our face, but we need to wash it every day. If we washed
our face three years ago and have not washed it since, it must
be a dreadful looking face! In the same manner, unless we are
free from committing sins every day, we need to deal with
sins daily.

There was a young believer who came to inquire of a servant of God concerning how to grow in his spiritual life. The
servant of God asked him, "How many days have gone by in
which you have not dealt with sins?" How true it is that if we
desire our spiritual life to grow, we need to deal with sins. A
day that we do not deal with sins is a day that our spiritual

life does not grow. By dealing with sins daily, our spiritual life will grow daily. This is an ironclad principle. May God have mercy upon us so that we may continue to go forward.

CHAPTER FIVE

DEALING WITH THE WORLD

Dealing with the world is very important in the initial experience of our Christian life; therefore, we shall study it carefully. First, we shall consider, according to scriptural light, the difference between sin and the world, how the world was formed, its definition, and its process of development. Finally, we shall see how God delivers us from the world. Precise knowledge of these truths enables us to have precise experiences in dealing with the world.

I. KNOWING THE WORLD

A. The Difference between Sin and the World

Immediately after our consecration, sin should first be dealt with and then the world. Because both are defiling in our lives and are abominable to God, they need to be dealt with and purged. However, the defilement of these two aspects differs. The contamination of sin is savage, rough, and ugly, whereas the contamination of the world is cultured and refined, often appearing beautiful in the sight of man. The contamination of sin is like a splash of mud or black ink on a white shirt, but the contamination of the world is like a colorful pattern printed on the white shirt. From the human standpoint, a shirt with black spots is considered dirty and undesirable, whereas a shirt with colorful prints is not dirty but rather desirable. However, in the sight of God, both are undesirable. He desires neither a stained nor a colorful shirt but a pure white shirt. Just as a dirty spot is not pure white, even so a colorful pattern detracts from the pure whiteness. Likewise, the world appears better than sin, but when related to purity, both are contaminating and require dealing.

Furthermore, the damage caused by sin and the damage caused by the world upon man differ greatly: sin contaminates man, whereas the world both contaminates and possesses man. It is far more serious for man's life to be possessed by the world than to be contaminated by sin. If Satan only uses sin to defile man, he can only cause man to be corrupted, but if he uses the world to usurp man, he can gain man for himself. For example, a child under the guardianship of his parents may be innocent and pure. Someone may contaminate and corrupt his pure nature by teaching him to lie, steal, and do many evil things, yet he remains under the guardianship of his parents and still belongs to them. If, however, the evildoer goes one step further by giving the child beautiful clothes, he can deceive and gain the child, causing him to leave his parents and become lost. Similarly, Satan corrupts man by using sin, but he gains man by employing the world, thus causing him to depart from the presence of God and become lost.

A study of Genesis makes this difference apparent. Although Adam was corrupted by sin, he had not left the presence of God. It was not until Genesis 4, when man invented civilization and formed the worldly system, that he was not only corrupted but usurped and gained by Satan through the world. Hence, man no longer belonged to God.

Although Abraham repeatedly failed in the matter of claiming his wife as his sister, that was but a sin which merely contaminated him but did not usurp him. He could still be one who served the Lord and prayed for others in a heathen land (see chs. 12, 20). However, Demas, a co-worker of Paul, was deprived of his usefulness before God because he loved the present age and became usurped by it (2 Tim. 4:10). This proves that the damage of the world upon man is greater than that of sin.

Generally, people feel only the damage of sin but not that of the world, because sin is against morality, whereas the world does not oppose morality but God Himself. Man is destitute of the concept of God; he has only a moral concept within him. For this reason he has a little knowledge concerning sin, that which is against morality, and is conscious of its contamination. But as for the world, which is in opposition to God, he has no knowledge of it, neither is he conscious of its usurpation. For example, a drunkard—licentious, wanton, and lustful, fearing neither God nor man—is considered immoral and condemned by men. But if someone is daily occupied with poetry and recitation and steeped in literature, being completely indifferent to the things of God and unwilling to be gained by Him, men will praise him, having no feeling that he is usurped by literature. This is due to the fact that men neither know God nor have the concept of God and therefore are ignorant of Satan's usurpation of man by the world.

Finally, the scope of sin differs from the scope of the world. The field of the world is much larger than that of sin. Sin includes all matters that are immoral and in opposition to the moral law of God, whereas the world includes all men, activities, and things that are outside of God. We cannot say that everything outside of God is sin. However, we can say that everything outside of God may become the world. Within the many things of the world, sin is only a part. The world includes sin, but sin does not include the world. Sin may not necessarily be the world, but in the world there certainly is sin.

A person may commit sin and not necessarily be possessed by the world. However, all who are possessed by the world are certainly contaminated by sin. For example, Adam sinned and fell into sin, but he did not fall into the world. Therefore, he was one who was only corrupted by sin but not usurped by the world. The world began with Cain. Lamech, one of Cain's descendants, was both a polygamist and a murderer. He was one who was usurped by the world and sinned as well.

Similarly, when Abraham was living in a tent in Canaan, he had not fallen into the world. Therefore, it was not necessary for him to commit sin. But when he went down to Egypt, falling into the world, it became necessary for him to lie and commit sin. This also proves that sin is not necessarily the world, but the world certainly includes sin. Once we fall into the world, we cannot avoid committing sin.

When we see the differences between sin and the world, we will perceive that the world's damaging scope is greater, its harmful effect more serious, and its opposition to God more hostile than that of sin. Because the world is in direct opposition to God Himself, it has become God's enemy. Sin is contrary to God's law and His procedure, that is, His righteousness, whereas the world is contrary to God Himself and His divine nature, that is, His holiness. Sin opposes the law of God, and the world opposes God Himself. For this reason the Bible states that the friendship of the world is enmity with God (James 4:4). If anyone loves the world, the love of the Father is not in him (1 John 2:15). When calling people to follow Him, the Lord stressed the fact that man should forsake houses, lands, brothers, sisters, parents, wife, children, and so forth (Matt. 10:37; 19:29; Mark 10:29; Luke 18:29). These constitute our human life and are the various terms of the world. If a man desires to follow the Lord, he must forsake these worldly things because they will possess him.

Sin is the primitive, superficial, and initial step of the fall. The world is the final, serious, and last step of the fall. Many people stress only victory over sin, but the Bible stresses even more the overcoming of the world (1 John 5:4). We need to overcome the world. If we desire to grow in life and be gained by the Lord, we must make an effort to deal with the world that enslaves us.

B. The Formation of the World

Since the world opposes God and has such a harmful effect upon man, we must consider its origin and process of development. The world did not exist when man was created, but it developed gradually after the fall of man. At the creation of man, there were only the universe, the heaven and earth, and all things; the world did not exist. The world was formed after the fall, when man became independent of God and forfeited His care. Therefore, in studying the formation of the world, we must first consider the daily requirements of man's existence.

Four general requirements for man's existence are clothing, food, housing, and transportation. The Bible, however, divides man's needs into three main categories: provision, protection, and pleasure. In order to maintain his existence, he needs not only the various provisions, such as clothing and food, but also a means of defense to protect himself from

being hurt and a form of amusement for his happiness. Therefore, the entire need for human living is included in these
three all-embracing categories.

Prior to the fall, God was responsible for providing for
these three needs of man. First, before man was created, God
had made provision for all necessities of human life. When
Adam was in the garden of Eden, various kinds of fruit and
vegetables, water, air, sunshine, and a place for shelter were
provided.

Second, protection or defense was also God's responsibility
in the beginning. Today man needs self-protection and self-
defense, but in the beginning God Himself was his defense
and protection. When man is under God's care, he can escape
any attack or danger.

Third, pleasure was also God's responsibility. Some people
think that amusement is sinful, but this concept is wrong.
Happiness is essential to human life and is found in amusement. "Out of the ground Jehovah God caused to grow every
tree that is pleasant to the sight and good for food" (Gen. 2:9).
All the trees in the garden of Eden not only bore fruit for food
but were also pleasing and enjoyable to the eye, making one
happy. God not only prepared this happy environment; at the
same time He Himself was the joy of man. If man has God as
his enjoyment, then man's joy is fulfilled.

In the beginning these three great needs—supply, defense,
and amusement—were planned and prepared for by God,
even as the needs of children today are planned and prepared
for by their parents. A wife's substance, protection, and joy
are entirely dependent upon her husband. In other words, her
husband is her life and her all. Likewise, Adam in the garden
of Eden had no need to worry, plan, or prepare anything for
himself, for God was responsible for everything. Since God
supplied all man's needs, then in reality God was his life and
his all.

Alas, man fell by committing sin and was expelled from the
garden of Eden! His relationship with God became abnormal.
But God prepared a covering of skins for man's redemption,
enabling him to remain in His presence. As yet, man had not
lost God. However, during Cain's lifetime, man fell deeper into

sin. Cain said to God, "Now You have driven me out this day
from the face of the ground, and from Your face I will be hidden"
(4:14). "And Cain went forth from the presence of Jehovah"
(v. 16). Thus, man left God's presence completely and lost God.

When he lost God, man naturally lost God's provision, protection, and pleasure. When man lost God's care for his livelihood, he first experienced fear; he feared the lack of supply,
defense, and happiness. In other words, he feared poverty,
danger, and boredom with life. Therefore, in order to meet the
necessities of life and survive, man used his own strength and
devised means of supply, defense, and amusement. From this
time, man created a godless civilization.

Genesis 4 clearly reveals this to us. After the fall of Cain,
out of his descendants were produced the founders of man's
own supply for these three great needs of life. These were the
three sons of Lamech. Jabal was the father of those who dwell
in tents and raise cattle. Tents and cattle are for the supply of
man's living and therefore belong to the category of provision.
Another son, Jubal, was the father of all those who play the
lyre and pipe. Playing the lyre and pipe is for pleasure; thus,
it belongs to the category of amusement. The third son, Tubal-
cain, was the forger of every cutting instrument of bronze
and iron. These instruments were formed for the purpose of
defense, thus referring to the category of protection. Since
these three important inventions originated at that time,
humanity found no need of God. Man found within himself
the answer to the need of supply, defense, and amusement.
This was the civilization produced after the human race lost
God—a godless life created by men.

When mankind lived a godless life, Satan immediately
disguised himself and utilized these avenues as a means to
possess man. He caused man to employ his entire effort to
seek food and clothing for self-nurture, to invent instruments
for self-defense, and to design various forms of amusements for
self-enjoyment. When man obtains all these, he tends to enjoy
them to the utmost and become thoroughly immersed in them.
The entire human life is completely usurped by these requirements, and man totally disregards God and His will. This is
the first step in the formation of the world.

In the beginning, these various forms of occupations involving man's livelihood seemed rather trivial, scattered, and unsystematized. Later, Satan organized these into a more tangible and systematized world, thus entangling mankind in a tighter web. Take, for example, the matter of eating. A man requires food for his existence, but when he is engrossed in labor in order to earn enough to feed himself, he is already possessed. Moreover, Satan has systematized eating by methods of preparation, order of courses, and different relishes for taste. Table and seating arrangements also involve a certain order and etiquette. Whenever man partakes of food, he is bound by these dining regulations. Other matters, such as clothing, housing, marriage, funerals, occupations, and amusements, have been organized by Satan into various manners, orders, and systems. Gradually, man has become heavily bound and thoroughly possessed by these systems and can find no way of escape.

Therefore, the formation of the world has five steps. First, man lost God. Second, he developed fear and was desperate concerning his needs. Third, he created a godless life. Fourth, Satan disguised himself and utilized man's needs. Fifth, Satan organized man's own supply for his needs into a system. At the completion of these five steps the world was finally formed.

C. The Definition of the World

Now that we have learned how the world was formed, it is easy to define the world. Originally, man belonged to God, lived by God, and relied entirely upon Him. Now Satan has systematized the world to replace God in providing for man's need. Man, having forsaken God, relies upon the world and is overcome by the world. Therefore, the world consists of everything that replaces God and all that usurps man. When people, activities, or things—whether good or bad, beautiful or ugly—enslave man, they comprise the world. Anything that causes man to disregard God, be removed from Him, or be independent of Him is the world.

The Greek word for *world* is *kosmos,* which means "system, or organization." Satan not only employs the necessities of life, such as people, activities, and things, to preoccupy man;

he furthermore organizes them into numerous individual systems in order to intensify his grip upon man. The world today resembles a university, in which are many different departments, such as eating, drinking, clothing, marriage, funerals, literature, music, money, and fame—more than we can enumerate. The aggregate result is a world university, occupying man with many courses. One by one, these courses enslave and possess man, causing him to completely forsake and forget God and go along with the current of the world. Man believes that he is handling and enjoying all these, but actually, without realizing Satan's deception, man has fallen into the hands of the evil one and is controlled and tricked by him. Therefore, the world denotes the enemy's scheme, system, and organization to usurp the place of God in man and finally to gain full possession of man.

Concerning the definition of the world, the Bible gives some explanations:

First, the difference between *the world* and *the things in the world* (1 John 2:15-17): "If anyone loves the world, love for the Father is not in him" (v. 15). The world and God are in direct opposition to each other. Verse 17 says that "the world is passing away, and its lust, but he who does the will of God abides forever." Here the world contradicts the will of God. In verse 16 that which is included in the things of this world is divided into three categories: the lust of the flesh, the lust of the eyes, and the vainglory of life. In conclusion, all that does not come from the Father, all that originates outside of God, and all that comes from the world are things of the world and are contrary to the will of God.

Second, the difference between the world and the age: "Do not be fashioned according to this age, but be transformed by the renewing of the mind that you may prove what the will of God is, that which is good and well pleasing and perfect" (Rom. 12:2). Here *this age* in the Greek is *aion*.

What is the world, and what is the age? The combination of all people, activities, and things outside of God is called "the world." *This age* designates the part of the world that we contact at the present. The part of the world that Cain contacted was the age of Cain; the part of the world that

Abraham contacted was the age of Babel. The part of the world that we come in touch with today is called the age of the twentieth century. Whereas the world is the entire organization used by Satan to usurp man, an age is a fraction of this organization. There are many ages within this organized world. Therefore, the apostle in Ephesians 2:2 refers to "the age of this world." The world signifies the whole, and the age, the part. Man can only contact the age, a part, but not the world, the whole. Usually we say that the world possesses us. In reality, only part of the age possesses us, not the whole world, and even in the age, we contact but a fraction of it by having a wife, a few children, a home, a bank account, and so forth. These constitute the practical world that binds and possesses us. In other words, the age is equivalent to the aforementioned things that are in the world.

The Greek word for *age* is *aion,* which means "modern." So, *age* means "modern," "fashion," "the course," the world that is revealed before us today, or the things that are in the world. In Romans 12:2 the *age,* not the *world,* is in opposition to the will of God; this corresponds to 1 John 2:17.

From this we see the relationships between the world, the age, and the things that are in the world. We cannot contact the world in its entirety but only a portion of it, called the "age" or "the things in the world." This is also true of the relationship between God and His will. Since God is so great, we cannot contact Him as a whole but only a portion of Him. This portion that we contact is called the will of God. Whenever we contact God, we contact only the portion emanating from Him, which we call the will of God. Thus, we see that the world is in opposition to God, and the age or the things in the world are in opposition to the will of God.

Love of the world is comprehensive, but love of the things in the world is more practical. Also, obedience to God is comprehensive, but obedience to the will of God is more practical.

D. The Development of the World

We have seen that the world was formed after Cain's fall and separation from God. At that time he dwelt in the land of

Nod and built a city called Enoch. This was the first city built by man; it was also the beginning of a man-made, godless culture and life. In the Bible a man-made city was a center and symbol of a godless life invented by man. Hence, a city symbolizes the world. These godless cities throughout the Bible reveal the development of the world in all generations.

The world described in the Bible consists of two main stages, or we may say, two worlds. The first world began with the city of Enoch built by Cain; the second world began with the city of Babel after the flood. The first world, beginning with Cain, developed and prospered gradually, until it reached its peak during the time of Noah. The human race had then completely fallen into the world, and the corruption therein was beyond cure. Genesis 6:11-12 states, "The earth was corrupt before God, and the earth was filled with violence. And God looked on the earth, and behold, it was corrupt; for all flesh had corrupted its way upon the earth." In position, the human race was completely submerged in the world; its condition was vile, sinful, and utterly corrupted. This condition brought in God's judgment. The flood not only judged the sins committed by men but also put an end to the sinful world. Only the eight members of Noah's family were saved, while the remainder of the first world was wiped out by the flood.

After the flood the human race again became gradually engulfed by the world. In Genesis 11 men began to rebel against God in a collective way by forsaking Him and His name. They established a name for themselves and built the tower and city of Babel. This was the second city built by man. This city was even more man's declaration that he desired self and relied upon himself rather than God. It also represented a godless life invented by man. Therefore, the city of Babel was the beginning of the second world.

This second world, beginning with the city of Babel, gradually developed by branching out into three lines and becoming three different cities as recorded in the Bible: the cities of Babylon, Egypt, and Sodom. The first world was an all-inclusive mixture, but the second definitely branched into three lines, each representing one aspect of the world.

The first line is represented by the city of Babylon, which

derived its name from Babel. This city was filled with idols and false gods. (According to some records, the city and tower of Babel were filled with idolatrous names.) Therefore, this city represents the idolatrous aspect of the world.

Babylon was in the land of Chaldea, the original home of Abraham (vv. 27-28). Abraham and his ancestors were idol worshippers (Josh. 24:2). Although God delivered Abraham from the land and its idols, his descendants were later captured and compelled to return to the land and worship idols (see Dan. 3). Babylon always destroys man's worship of God. The Babylonians destroyed the temple of God, took its vessels into Babylon as spoils, and placed them in the temple of their idols (2 Kings 25:8-9, 13-15; 2 Chron. 36:7, 10, 18-19). This proves that Babylon in the Bible is a world of idols.

The second line is represented by the city of Egypt. Egypt, a rich land, was irrigated by the Nile and produced an abundance of food (Gen. 42:1-2) with a variety of tastes (Num. 11:5). Hence, Egypt represents the aspect of livelihood and enjoyment of the world. The Bible records several occasions in which the children of God went down into Egypt to solve their problems of livelihood (Gen. 12:10; 42:3; 45:9-11, 18). Furthermore, once the children of Israel went down to Egypt to solve the problem of livelihood, they invariably came under the power of the Egyptians, were forced into hard labor, and became enslaved (Exo. 1:11-14). Therefore, Egypt also represents the aspect of hard labor and slavery under the dominion of the world. In conclusion, Egypt represents a world of livelihood, power, hard labor, and slavery.

The third line is represented by Sodom. Whenever Sodom is mentioned in the Bible, it always refers to her sins (Gen. 13:13; 18:20; 19:13). Therefore, Sodom represents the sinful aspect of the world, or a world of sins.

These three cities represent the three different aspects of the second world. They compassed the land of Canaan, the rightful position of God's elect, and posed a snare to engulf the children of Israel. Whenever they became careless and succumbed to temptations, they were drawn into the sinful world of Sodom and became contaminated by its filth. An example of this was Lot's descent into Sodom. Sometimes, when they failed the tests because of weakness, they went down to Egypt and were required to exert themselves in order to maintain their livelihood. They became the slaves of livelihood and were controlled by the world. This is the story of Abraham and the Israelites when they sojourned to Egypt. It seemed impossible for them to return to Babylon to worship idols. When they were extremely weak, however, they were captured and taken back to the city of Babylon, the world of idolatry, to worship the devil. This occurred during the decline of Israel.

These three aspects of the world are the enemies of God, destroying those whom God has gained for Himself. The Israelites were a people separated from the human race to be possessed and used by Him. But they never freed themselves from the corruption of these three aspects of the world. Either they went down to the world of Egypt in order to seek sustenance (Isa. 30:1-4; 31:1), or they became like the people of Sodom (1:9; 3:9; Ezek. 16:46, 49; Rev. 11:8), or worse still, they were taken into the idolatrous world of Babylon and forsook their worship and service to God (2 Chron. 36:14-21). Today these three aspects of the world are in like manner destroying the church that the Lord chose and called out for Himself. Look at the church today! Is she not relying on the power of the world of Egypt? Does she not have the worldly sins of Sodom? Has she not even been captured and taken into the idolatrous world of Babylon and thus been filled with the idols of the world? This is especially true of today's Roman Catholic Church.

These three cities, representing the different aspects of this second world, will evolve on parallel lines continuously until they become that great city of Babylon mentioned in Revelation 17 and 18. That city—the center and representative of the world at that time—will exert all her effort to multiply her animosity toward God and persecute the children of God. She will be the climax of the development of the second world, and its conclusion as well. She will be judged and destroyed by fire through the Lord's second coming. This judgment of fire and the judgment of the flood have a distinct resemblance. The judgment of the flood consummated the first world, and the judgment of fire will consummate the second world. For this reason the Lord compared the day of Noah with that of His coming (Matt. 24:37-39). The destruction of the great Babylon will bring the world to an end.

The development, as depicted by the two worlds, is an example of Satan's method of employing the world to possess and win man for himself and to destroy and nullify the purpose of God in man. First, Satan corrupted Adam by sin and gradually employed the world in order to usurp his descendants. Up to the time of Noah, all the descendants of Adam were submerged in the world. Satan had then successfully accomplished his first step in possessing man. But God judged and destroyed that world by the flood. After the descendants of Noah greatly multiplied, Satan aroused a mass rebellion against God, causing that generation to build the tower of Babel. Consequently, man was submerged even deeper into the world and again possessed by Satan.

Since Satan obtained Noah's descendants, God could not fulfill His purpose in them. God had no other alternative but to forsake this created race by choosing Abraham. Abraham's descendants, who were multiplied as the stars of the heavens and the dust of the earth, became God's chosen race to fulfill His purpose, that purpose which had been suspended by the created race at Babel. Satan, however, continued to work unceasingly by using the world to defraud and possess God's chosen people, leaving no way for God to fulfill His purpose.

The Old Testament shows that their downfall resulted in God's people coming under the control of the world. For example, after Abraham had been led by God into Canaan, he was drawn away by Egypt. Later, Israel, in their weak endeavors to meet the needs of their livelihood, fell under the power of Egypt. Eventually, the kingdom of Israel completely succumbed to the world of idols by being led captive to Babylon. Finally, God's elect will become integrated with the great Babylon, which represents the whole world system (Rev. 17 and 18). That will be the final fall of God's chosen race, wherein they will be corrupted and possessed by Satan to the uttermost.

The Bible divides the history of the human race into two

parts: Genesis 1 through 11:26 and Genesis 11:27 to the end
of Revelation. The first part began with the creation of man
and ended with the destruction of the first world by the flood.
The subject of this part is the created race of Adam. The
second part began with the call of Abraham and will end with
the destruction of the second world by fire. The subject of this
part is the chosen race of Abraham. Although after the call of
Abraham there were histories of the created race, they were
not recorded as the main subject of the Bible. In both sections
Satan's work is characterized by his use of the world to possess man. In the first part, Satan employed the first world to
possess the created race; then Satan used the second world
to possess the chosen race. The second world was fully ripened in Egypt, because it was there that Satan possessed the
entire chosen race, the Israelites.

In conclusion, Satan employed two worlds in order to possess two races, which bring forth two judgments of God. The
first judgment was by water and terminated the first world.
The second judgment is by fire and will end the second world.
Therefore, the Bible is divided into two sections: the first
from the creation of man to the destruction of the first world,
and the second from the calling of the chosen people to the
destruction of the second world. This is the line of the development of the world as recorded in the Bible.

In the process of the world's development, a great majority
of those prepared by God for Himself have become possessed
by Satan. Nevertheless, a small number of overcomers have
stood on God's ground of separation from the world. With the
tent and the altar, they bear a direct testimony against the
city, which is the symbol and center of the world. The Bible
has not only the line of the city, depicting the development of
the world, but also the line of the tent, showing the testimony
of the overcomers against the world. This is another important line in the Bible, running parallel with the line of the
development of the world.

In the first world Noah was the first man who lived a tent
life in direct opposition to the city life of the world. When God
judged the first world, he delivered Noah. After he left the
ark, he built an altar unto God (Gen. 8:20) and lived in a tent

(9:21), not in a city. This tent may be considered as contrary to the city of Enoch built by Cain. The first overcomer was delivered out from the world and lived in a tent as an opposing testimony against the city, the world's symbol. Therefore, he could have an altar to worship and serve God.

In the second world there have been many who have lived in tents and have borne an opposing testimony against the world. Abraham was the most outstanding one among them. He was called out of the world, from the city of Babel to the land of Canaan (Gen. 12). There he set up a tent in opposition to the city of Babel. This tent was not only a proof of his overcoming but also an opposing testimony against the world at that time. Because he refused to live in the worldly city that usurped man and chose to live a life for God in a tent, he had an altar to worship and serve God. His tent stood in opposition to the city of Babel, and his altar stood in opposition to the tower of Babel.

Whenever an overcomer fails, the testimony of the tent and the altar disappears. Abraham became weak and went down to Egypt. Upon his arrival in Egypt, both his tent and his altar vanished; therefore, his testimony against the world and his service to God disappeared. When he departed from Egypt and returned to Canaan, the tent and the altar were recovered, and likewise the testimony and the service were recovered.

Lot, who journeyed to Canaan with Abraham, also lived with him in a tent. Then he left Abraham and eventually moved his tent to Sodom. Finally, he lived in Sodom and lost both his tent and his testimony.

Later, all Israel succumbed to the world of Egypt. Their daily occupation was to make bricks and build cities (Exo. 1:11-14). Consequently, they lost their testimony and service. After their deliverance from Egypt and their arrival in the wilderness, they observed the tent life and the service of the altar. Furthermore, God dwelt with them in the tent, the tabernacle, as a testimony against the city of Egypt.

When the Israelites entered Canaan, Jerusalem became the center of their dwelling. Jerusalem was a miniature of the eternal tent of God, the New Jerusalem. Jerusalem is always in opposition to Babylon, and Babylon is always contrary to

Jerusalem. When the Israelites experienced complete failure, Babylon destroyed Jerusalem (2 Chron. 36:6-7, 18-19). But later, when there were overcomers among the Israelites, they set their faces toward Jerusalem (Dan. 6:10) and recovered Jerusalem (Neh. 2).

At the end of the New Testament the great Babylon will be destroyed (Rev. 18:2), and on the other hand, the New Jerusalem will descend from heaven (21:2-3). This New Jerusalem is also called the "tabernacle of God," or the tent. Thus at the end we still see the tent, the symbol of the overcomers, as an opposing testimony against the city, which represents the world.

These biblical records convey the spiritual meaning of the tent in opposition to the city. The city is the symbol and center of all human, self-devised life, and thus represents the world. The tent, erected in the wilderness, that is, outside the world, represents the pilgrim life outside the world. Those who live in tents testify that they are not submerged in the world; rather, they lead a sojourner's life outside the world. When man failed and lost God, he succumbed to the world; when man was saved by God, he subsequently left the world and lived in a tent as a stranger and sojourner, serving only God.

The Bible discloses that the altar always accompanies the tent. If there is a tent, there is an altar. If there is no tent, there is no altar. After his departure from the ark, Noah erected a tent and built an altar. When Abraham went to Canaan, he also erected a tent and built an altar. But during his sojourn in Egypt, he lost the tent, and consequently the altar was gone. Likewise, the Israelites during their slavery in Egypt had no altar, but when they left Egypt and came into the wilderness, they lived in tents and reestablished the altar. When there is the altar, then consecration, service, and worship follow because the altar is the place for man to consecrate himself and the means to serve and worship God. These were the natural outcome of man's life in the tent. Whenever man succumbed to the world, he lost his consecration, service, and worship.

The tent life is the position not only where man serves

God but also where God meets him. This principle is evident in the lives of Abraham and Lot. God appeared to Abraham while he sat at the entrance of his tent. This bears witness to his victorious position over the world, which enabled him to obtain God's manifestation (Gen. 18). However, God Himself did not appear to Lot (ch. 19); instead, two angels were sent to Sodom. They found Lot sitting in the gate, which proves that he had already succumbed to the world. Although the angels came to his rescue, God Himself did not appear to him. He cannot appear to those whom the world has claimed. Once man falls into the world, he is gained by Satan and can no longer see light in the face of God.

Since the world possesses God's children and destroys God's purpose, God saves man in two aspects: from sin and from the world. Salvation from sin delivers us only from our fallen state, whereas salvation from the world delivers us from our fallen position. When we preach the gospel, we give much attention to deliverance from sin, but we seldom speak about deliverance from the world. This is not sufficient.

In the Old Testament the salvation of God is seen in two important types: the ark of Noah and the exodus from Egypt. Each type shows both aspects of deliverance from sin and from the world. The eight members of Noah's family were saved by the ark and by the water. The ark delivered them from God's judgment of the flood; the water delivered them from the corrupt world. Similarly, Israel was saved by the passover and by the Red Sea. The passover denotes their deliverance from God's judgment of death; the Red Sea denotes their deliverance from the ruling power of the world.

Likewise, the perfect salvation we enjoy today also has two aspects—faith and baptism. Through faith we are delivered from sin by the blood. Through baptism we are delivered from the world by water. Noah's family was saved through the flood, which destroyed the world, and thus they were delivered from the corrupted world. The Israelites were saved through the water of the Red Sea, which drowned the Egyptian army, and they were thus delivered from the Egyptian world, which ruled over them. Baptism is foreshadowed by these two incidents of passing through the waters of death (1 Pet. 3:20-21;

1 Cor. 10:1-2). Baptism by immersion delivers us from the
world. Therefore, when a believer is baptized, he has passed
through both the flood and the Red Sea. His ascent from the
water denotes his separation from the world and his new
position relative to the life of the tent and the altar. We who
have been chosen and saved should continually live a tent life
as a testimony that we have been delivered and separated
from the world. In this manner we shall be delivered from
being possessed by the world and shall be a people living completely unto God by the way of the altar.

II. DEALING WITH THE WORLD

A. Scriptural Basis

(1) James 4:4: "Adulteresses, do you not know that the
friendship of the world is enmity with God? Therefore whoever determines to be a friend of the world is constituted an
enemy of God."

(2) Romans 12:2: "Do not be fashioned according to this
age, but be transformed by the renewing of the mind that you
may prove what the will of God is, that which is good and well
pleasing and perfect."

(3) First John 2:15-17: "Do not love the world nor the things
in the world. If anyone loves the world, love for the Father is
not in him; because all that is in the world, the lust of the
flesh and the lust of the eyes and the vainglory of life, is not
of the Father but is of the world. And the world is passing
away, and its lust, but he who does the will of God abides forever."

B. The Objects of Dealing with the World

The world in our daily living consists of people, activities,
and things that usurp the place of God in us. Therefore, these
objects are the aim of our dealings.

How do we know what objects are usurping us, and what is
the standard of measurement? First, we need to see whether
these objects exceed the necessities of our life. We can say
that anything that goes beyond our daily necessities is taking
the place of God and possessing us; thus, it needs to be dealt

with. Our existence depends upon certain people, activities, and things, such as parents, husband, wife, family, clothes, food, housing, transportation, and occupation. These are the necessities for our existence. If these necessities contribute to our purpose of living for God, they are not our world. But should these people, activities, or things exceed our daily necessities, they then become our world. For example: clothing as a necessity is not worldly, but if one pays too much attention to apparel and ornaments or squanders money in order to comply with present-day fashions, he has already exceeded the scope of his daily necessities. Consequently, these excesses have become his world. Another example: glasses to correct defective eyesight are not worldly. But some wear glasses to be fashionable; this then is not their necessity but the world they love.

What is the standard that regulates our daily necessities in regard to people, activities, and things? In the Bible there is no uniform or specific standard governing these matters. God has ordained that we be born in different families, receive different educational training, have different professions, and contact different social environments. In this way God permits us to have diverse concepts and standards relative to our living. Therefore, all living necessities vary with each person.

For example, one person may live in a city and another in a village. Both may be saved and have Christ as their life, but because each was born in a different family, their occupations and environments differ. Therefore, their standard of living is different. The brother living in the city wears a suit, which is not beyond his living necessities; but to the one living in the village, this same suit would be beyond his necessities. In the eyes of the brothers who are merchants in the city, the suit may be very modest and simple, but the same suit would be extravagant to the Christian farmers in the village.

Likewise, a manager and a janitor of a company, or a professor and a gardener of a college, may all be saved and love the Lord, but their concepts regarding their living necessities are not the same. Due to the fact that their lives and environments differ, their opinions and feelings also differ. For this reason the Bible does not give a uniform or fixed standard for the necessities of the believers. Even though 1 Timothy 2:9 forbids the adornment of costly clothing, it is a matter of principle, not a detailed, rigid rule. What is really costly depends upon the environment of people.

These various standards of living are sovereignly permitted. In the church God does not require different classes of people to behave in the same way. Some time ago in China, a group of Christians went to extremes because they lacked this light. They started a meeting and formulated certain rules. They said that no one could attend the meeting wearing leather shoes, but all must wear Chinese shoes made of cloth. Moreover, the men were required to shave their heads, and the women were required to wear skirts; otherwise, they were not allowed to attend the meeting. We know that this is not what God desires of His children, for this is extreme.

Therefore, the standard of our living necessities must be determined by ourselves through prayer and seeking the mind of God. We cannot measure our standard according to that of others or demand that they agree with our views and feelings. Furthermore, our own dealings before God should also be according to the standard of our daily living before God. We should neither go beyond nor fall short. Some people deal with their living necessities, things that do not usurp them, as if they were worldly, and thus go to the extreme. Once, in northern China I met a brilliant preacher who loved the Lord and testified for Him. However, he dealt with the world in an extreme manner. For example, he perspired while preaching but refused to use a handkerchief, thinking it to be an item of the world. Instead, he used his sleeve to wipe the perspiration from his forehead. He slept on the floor because he had no peace sleeping on a bed. Upon arising in the morning, he went out to the seaside to wash, because he had no peace when washing indoors. This kind of dealing was really extreme. Because he neither ate nor slept properly, his body was weakened, and he died prematurely in his fifties! This was indeed regrettable.

We must realize that God still requires us to live as a normal human being on this earth. For this reason we have certain living necessities. When Adam was in the garden of Eden, God presented him with trees pleasant to the eye. From this we may conclude that even beauty and happiness are needed for human living. If our appearance is shabby or our home is untidy, this does not prove that we are spiritual. The question is whether this particular object usurps you. If it occupies a place in you and usurps you so that you are unable to relinquish it, that undoubtedly is your world, and you have to deal with it accordingly.

Although any excess beyond our necessities constitutes the world, this does not mean that all living necessities may not become the world. If a certain living necessity binds and hinders us from doing the will of God or from being completely gained by God, we are then usurped by it. This then becomes the world and requires dealings. For example, food and clothing are both needed for our living, but if they usurp us and replace God, they become the world.

Actually, when a believer pursues the Lord, he is seldom usurped and entangled by things beyond his living necessities. On the contrary, he is usually usurped and entangled by things that are needed for living. Therefore, when the Lord on earth called people to follow Him, He did not ask them to forsake that which exceeded their daily needs but stressed that they should forsake the involvements of their daily life, such as parents, wives, children, lands, and houses. If these necessities usurp man, they seize the Lord's place in man. Of course, the Lord Jesus did not ask us to forsake our responsibility, but He desired us to relinquish the entanglements of people, activities, and things. For this reason, in the Epistles the Lord teaches us again through the apostles that we should honor our parents, treat our wives fittingly, and care for our relations.

Without a doubt, the emphasis in dealing with the world is on dealing with the usurpation of people, activities, and things. As long as these usurp us, whether they are the necessary provisions for daily living or excessive provisions, they still constitute the world and must be the aim of our dealing. Our daily necessities may or may not usurp us, but anything exceeding our daily necessities definitely usurps us.

In conclusion, the objects in our dealing with the world are not certain fixed people, activities, and things. What we have to do is to ascertain whether these objects usurp us and take God's place in us. It is possible that the identical necessities regarding people, activities, and things may usurp one person and not the other, and may take God's place in one and not in the other. Therefore, from the human standpoint it is difficult to determine what is and what is not the world. There is no fixed limit and standard.

Now we come to see from God's viewpoint what are the objects of dealing with the world. From the divine viewpoint there is a certain measuring rule regarding the world. This rule is God Himself. As we measure sin by the law of God, so we measure the world by God Himself. The standard of dealing with the world is based upon God. If God is absent, we cannot sense what the world is. God and the world are forever in opposition to each other. Wherever there is the world, there God is not; where there is God, there the world is not.

Therefore, by taking God as the standard, we can define the world as those people, activities, and things incompatible with God, replacing God in us, hindering the will of God being done through us, or preventing God's full control over us. All these that usurp us are classified as "unholy." Therefore, to deal with the world is to deal with these "unholy" objects.

Unholy is the opposite of *holy*. Holiness means to be separated and different from all else. In the whole universe only God Himself is separated and different from all else; therefore, only He is holy. Likewise, if a person, activity, or thing is separated unto God and for God, the Bible also calls it holy, being separated unto holiness. For example, the Lord Jesus in Matthew 23:17 and 19 showed us that gold, if used for the temple, and a gift, when placed on the altar, become sanctified. All the gold in this world is for human use and is common; however, if a portion is separated and placed in the temple for God's use, it becomes sanctified. Again, if an ox or a sheep are among the herd, they are for human use and are common. When chosen and placed upon the altar, however, they become an offering unto God, being separated unto holiness. It is altogether a matter of whether they are separated and belong to God. Before they are separated, they are common; after they are separated, they become holy. Simply speaking, holiness means all that pertains to God and all that is of God, unto God, and for God. All else is unholy and common. These unholy objects are to be dealt with in our dealings with the world.

Actually, what pertains to God? What is of God, unto God, and for God? God Himself and all that is in Him pertain to Him. When God and all that is in Him enter into us, we are of Him directly, which, in turn, causes all things belonging to us to be of Him indirectly.

Although a believer's wife and children are not saved, they are sanctified, because they are directly of him and indirectly of God (1 Cor. 7:14). The husband is of God directly, but his unsaved wife and children are of God indirectly by virtue of their relationship to him. Otherwise, the Christian husband, when dealing with the unholy things of the world, must deal with his unsaved family—this would not harmonize with the truth of the Scriptures.

What does it mean to be unto God? The sphere of being unto God is smaller than the sphere of being of God. For example, my house is mine, but it may not necessarily be unto me in order to be under my control. Likewise, for us who are saved, all that we have is of God but is not necessarily unto God. Not until we consecrate all to God will all be unto God.

What does it mean to be for God? This sphere is again less than that of being unto God. "For God" means to be used by God. We who are unto God are not necessarily fully used by God. Perhaps, we are of God one hundred percent, but only forty percent unto God, and only five percent truly used by God. When we attain to the degree of being completely used by God, we are then altogether holy.

We see from the above that all that relates to God, all that is of God, all that is unto God, and all that is for God is holy. All else is not holy. All that is unholy is the object of dealing with the world. The standard of measuring what is worldly is God Himself. All that is unfitting and incompatible with God and all that does not measure up to God is worldly and unholy.

Therefore, each person, activity, and thing with reference to ourselves, our environment, our family, our work, and our career must be examined before God by the following standard: Is this related to God, is it of God, is it unto God, and is it for God? Whatever does not agree with God and measure up to God must be dealt with. For example, although the unsaved wife and children are indirectly sanctified to God through the believer, he must quickly bring them to salvation. After they are saved, he must help them to consecrate themselves to God so that they may be unto God and be used by God. This is also included in the dealings with unholiness.

In conclusion, the objects of our dealing with the world include all things not pertaining to God, not of God, not unto God, and not for God. They include anything that takes God's place in us, as well as all people, activities, and things that exceed our living necessities. These unholy, worldly objects need to be dealt with.

C. The Basis of Dealing with the World

The basis of our dealing with the world is the same as dealing with sin. It is based upon the sense of life obtained during fellowship. God has never asked an individual to separate himself in a moment's time from all unholiness and all things that usurp him. God wants man to deal with the things that he feels are unholy and usurping. Practically speaking, there may be one hundred unholy things in us, but during our fellowship we become conscious, perhaps, of only ten. Therefore, God holds us responsible for only these ten. Temporarily, we are not responsible for the remaining ninety. Not until we have attained to a greater degree of fellowship in life do we become conscious of the remaining objects and deal with them.

Therefore, the basis of dealing with the world is the same as that of dealing with sin. We should pay attention to the following three principles:

(1) We should deal with the world upon the basis of the inner feeling gained through fellowship. The dealing should not exceed our inner feeling.

(2) We should gradually broaden the area of our fellowship

so that our inner feeling touches all aspects of our life. Thus, we will have dealings with the world in all aspects.

(3) We should gradually deepen our fellowship so that our inner feeling concerning the world deepens; thus, we may deal more thoroughly.

Besides these three principles, there are two factors that greatly influence our inner feeling toward the world: our love for God and our spiritual growth in life. We have said that God is the standard for dealing with the world. If we are far from God, we are not conscious of our worldliness. But once we draw nigh to God, we discover many worldly matters in us. Only those who love God desire to draw nigh unto God. Therefore, if we desire to deal with the world, we should first love God. The more we love God, the more we become sensitive toward the world, and the more the world is exposed in us. Once it becomes exposed, it is being disposed of. This exposure is the enlightenment. When our love for God causes us to meet God, who is light, He enlightens and exposes the world. Whenever this light appears, it shines away the world in us. Therefore, in dealing with the world, there is no law but God, who is our standard and our measure. The degree to which we deal with the world depends upon the degree of our love for God.

Our inner feeling toward the world also depends upon our spiritual growth. The more we advance in the spiritual life and knowledge of God, the deeper we will be in knowing the world. This knowledge of the world is the inner feeling we have toward the world and forms the basis of dealing with the world. The degree of our spiritual growth is always in proportion to the degree of our dealing with the world. The life of a new believer is immature, and his knowledge toward God is limited. Consequently, his inner feeling toward the world and his dealings with the world are shallow. By comparison, the one whose life is matured and whose knowledge toward God is increased has deeper feelings toward the world. Thus, his dealings with the world are more severe. The sky above is so immense and high. However, how immense and how high it is to us depends on our vision. If our vision is as narrow as the opening of a well, then the sky we see will be no larger than the opening of the well. Similarly, in each of us the world is very much, but our measure of dealing with it depends upon our inner feeling toward it, upon our knowledge of God, and upon the degree of our spiritual growth. Dealing with the world will cause us to grow spiritually, yet if we wish to deal to the end that God may have a complete place within us, we should ask Him to draw us so that we may love Him more and pursue more for our spiritual growth so that we may become more mature in life.

D. The Extent of Dealing with the World

The extent to which we deal with the world is "life and peace" (Rom. 8:6). Whenever we deal with the world that we are conscious of, we should deal with it until we have peace and life within. Since these dealings are based upon the feelings of life that are derived from fellowship, they are experiences of life. Dealing with the world causes us to experience life and sense the freshness, brightness, satisfaction, strength, joy, and peace of life. In other words, we should deal with the world to the extent that we have life and peace.

E. The Practice of Dealing with the World

If we wish to practice dealing with the world, we should pay our attention to one point—that is, to close our mind to the world.

When we begin to learn the lessons of dealing, sin and the world often return to our thinking; that is, we often have a mind to sin or to love the world. At such a time our responsibility is to close our mind and refuse these thoughts.

Of course, it is very difficult to close our mind toward the thoughts of sin, because sin lives within us. Not until we are raptured will we be delivered from this inward difficulty. Therefore, even mature and learned Christians are still tempted by thoughts of sin.

The difficulty of the world is something of an outward nature. The Bible states that sin dwells in us, but it never mentions that the world lives in us. Since the nature of the world is outward, it is easy to shut off the thoughts of the world. When speaking of dealing with the world, 1 John 2 admonishes the

young saints. Thus, this matter does not require much experience; it can and ought to be practiced when we begin to follow
the Lord. On the contrary, if a saint is constantly being disturbed by the world and is unable to shut out worldly thoughts,
this proves that he is still young and immature.

In conclusion, when we endeavor to deal with the world,
we should be determined and violent to shut out any thoughts
of the world. Not only should we close the door, but we should
also bar it and even make this door into a wall. In this manner
we can thoroughly solve the problem of the world. For this, we
should not simply wait for the Lord to constrain us with His
love or for His grace to support us. We must also use our own
initiative to deal with this matter. If so, worldly thoughts will
never intrude again.

CHAPTER SIX

DEALING WITH THE CONSCIENCE

Now we come to the sixth experience of life, which is dealing with the conscience. After we consecrate ourselves, we need to deal not only with sins and the world but also with the conscience. Sins and the world are outward matters, but the conscience is something within us. Therefore, dealing with sins and the world is dealing outwardly with our circumference, whereas dealing with our conscience is dealing with the central part of our being. We have said that dealing with sin is like removing dirty spots from our apparel. Dealing with the world is like removing the colorful, printed pattern in the apparel, and dealing with the conscience can be likened to the thorough removal of all the bacteria from the apparel. Then the apparel is totally clean. Therefore, dealing with the conscience is also of great importance in the growth of our Christian life. We need to know and experience this thoroughly.

I. THE KNOWLEDGE OF DEALING WITH THE CONSCIENCE

A. The Origin of the Conscience

Let us look first at the origin of the human conscience. When did it first exist, and how did it come into being? Although we find no definite record of this in the Bible, according to the whole truth of the Bible and also according to our experience, the conscience was created in man when God created man. In other words, the organ of the conscience came into being at the same time man was created. However, it was not until after man partook of the fruit of the tree of the knowledge of good and evil that the function of the conscience was made manifest.

According to the biblical record, man before the fall was in

a primeval state, like a newborn babe. At that time he was not
ashamed of his nakedness. This proves that within man there
was no concept of good and evil, right and wrong, which means
that there was neither the feeling nor the function of the conscience. After man fell by eating the fruit of the tree of the
knowledge of good and evil, he felt ashamed of his nakedness.
This shameful feeling was due to the conscience being activated to function, thus producing a certain consciousness.
Therefore, the feeling of the conscience, that is, the function
of the conscience, was manifested after the fall.

Although the function of the conscience was not made
manifest before the fall, the conscience itself already existed.
Since the conscience is an organ within man, it must have been
created when man was created. We cannot say that before the
fall there was not such an organ as the conscience and that it
was not until after the fall that God created a conscience for
man. Such a concept is illogical. Logically speaking, the conscience itself must have been created by God in the beginning,
and its function must have been activated and revealed after
the fall. We may liken this to an infant who is born with the
organ of the brain but who later unfolds the brain's function
by education. The more education it receives, the more the
function of the brain is revealed. Likewise, the organ of the
conscience existed when man was created, but since he had
no problem with good and evil, there was no need for his conscience to function. Not until after the fall did the concept of
good and evil enter into man, and thereby the function of his
conscience was manifested. From that time the conscience
began to bear the responsibility of refusing evil and accepting
good. This is the origin of the conscience.

B. The Position and Function
of the Conscience

The position of the conscience is in the human spirit. The
human spirit has three parts: fellowship, intuition, and conscience. Although this is not clearly stated in the Bible, we can
ascertain this fact by our experience. In our spirit there is a
part called the fellowship, the function of which is to fellowship with God. Another part, the intuition, functions to sense

God and know His will directly. Finally, the last part, the conscience, enables us to discern between right and wrong, good and evil.

There were progressive changes in revealing the three functions of the human spirit. Before the fall the function of the conscience was not yet revealed. Therefore, at that time there were only two functions in the human spirit, fellowship and intuition. After the fall, when man hid from the presence of God (Gen. 3:8), his fellowship with God was frustrated and his intuition became dull, but his conscience began to function. His newly activated conscience enabled him to sense and differentiate between right and wrong, good and evil, in every phase of his life. Directly after the fall, although the fellowship and intuition of the spirit became withered and insensitive, the conscience became activated. Unfortunately, when man sank deeper into sin, even the feeling of the conscience was cast aside. At this point, man's conscience became branded as with a hot iron (1 Tim. 4:2) so that even when he indulged in licentiousness and lusts, he hardly had any feeling at all (Eph. 4:19). Thus, the functions of his spirit were completely lost.

When we are saved and regenerated, the Holy Spirit enters into us and enlivens our spirit, giving us a new spirit (Ezek. 36:26). At this time, the three functions of our spirit are recovered. We can freely fellowship with God, directly know His will, and keenly differentiate between right and wrong. Therefore, the functions of the spirit today are not the same as they were after the fall, neither are they similar to their condition before the fall. Today all three functions are present at the same time; moreover, all are strong and keen.

We may divide the function of the conscience into three aspects. First, the conscience is the organ that enables us to differentiate between right and wrong, good and evil. Second, the conscience enables us to know both what God justifies and what He condemns (Rom. 2:15), what He delights in and what He hates. Thus, from this viewpoint, the conscience enables us to know the will of God. Third, the conscience represents God in ruling over us. Just as a nation governs its people through the police force, so also God governs us through the conscience. This universe cannot exist unless it is controlled by numerous laws and principles established by God. Whoever defies these laws and principles will be condemned and judged accordingly. God has also established numerous principles and laws in His ruling over man; these principles and laws are being executed to a great extent by the conscience. God set up the conscience within fallen man so that man might govern himself according to these principles and laws. If anyone acts contrary to or is about to act contrary to these principles and laws of God, his conscience immediately condemns him and restrains him from going further astray and falling into corruption. The conscience rules not only to uphold the existence of the individual but also to hold together all the relationships of man in the universe. Therefore, the major function of the conscience is to govern man. Actually, the purpose of the conscience in enabling man to discern right and wrong and to know what God justifies and what He condemns is also to represent God in ruling over man.

C. The Relationship of the Conscience with the Inward Parts

1. Positionally

Since the conscience is a part of the spirit, it is closely related to the intuition and fellowship. Since the soul surrounds the spirit, the conscience is also closely related to the parts of the soul—the mind and emotion and will. Furthermore, since the conscience is a part of the heart, it is also closely linked with the heart. Thus, positionally speaking, the conscience is closely related to all our inward parts—namely, our spirit, soul, and heart.

2. Functionally

Since the conscience, in position, is so closely related to the inward parts, naturally, in functions also, the conscience and the inward parts have their influence on one another.

First, let us discuss how the intuition affects the function of the conscience. When anyone has a lively and keen intuition in his spirit, his conscience is sensitive and delicate.

Take, for example, a very dark room. If an adjacent room has a bright, shining light, it will somewhat illuminate the dark room. Likewise, since the intuition is adjacent to the conscience, its function affects to a large extent the function of the conscience.

The same is true of the fellowship. When a person's fellowship with God is free, without any hindrance, the function of his conscience is also keen and accurate. The deeper his fellowship is with God, the livelier and brighter he is within, and his conscience becomes more keen and accurate.

The three parts of the soul also affect the function of the conscience in a very evident manner. A clear, understanding mind, a rich, balanced emotion, and a strong, pliable will greatly affect the function of the conscience. For example, a man's knowledge toward things greatly affects the feeling of the conscience. Some people are born with a dull mind. Their thinking is inaccurate; therefore, their conscience is confused and slow. This indicates how the mind affects the conscience. In like manner, the emotion and the will also affect the conscience. Therefore, in order to acquire a conscience that functions normally, our mind, emotion, and will must be guided into their proper course.

The function of the conscience is also under the influence of the heart. If a person has a righteous mind, a kind heart, and a pliable will, his conscience will be bright and keen. Should he hurt another even slightly, he will feel uneasy. On the contrary, if one has a crooked mind, a cruel heart, and a hardened will, his conscience will be dark and dull. Even though he hurts others deeply, he will be insensitive.

These influences are rather fine and delicate. We have to realize and experience them in a very practical way.

D. The Relationship of Conscience with Government

Some students of Scripture have divided the Bible into seven dispensations: the dispensations of innocence, conscience, human government, promise, law, grace, and the kingdom. The first three dispensations are categorized according to the principle of government. In the dispensation of innocence we see the principle of God's rule; in the dispensation of conscience, the principle of self-rule; and in the dispensation of human government, the principle of man's rule. Of the three kinds of government, the one that is under the rule of self is the one related to the conscience.

Before the fall, no sin barrier existed between God and man. This was the so-called dispensation of innocence, when man was ruled directly by God. He lived before God and was responsible to God. Unfortunately, man failed under God's rule and became sinful within and without, so the holy and righteous God had to leave man.

Consequently, from the time of Adam's expulsion from the garden of Eden to the time of Noah's departure from the ark, God established the conscience within man to represent Him in ruling over man. This is the so-called dispensation of conscience. In this period man was ruled by his own conscience and was responsible to his own conscience. Unfortunately, under this self-rule, man again failed. He ignored the rebuke and control of the conscience, the issue of which was murder and fornication, which proceeded unto utter corruption and fullness of wickedness. God judged this dispensation by the flood.

After the flood God told Noah, "Whoever sheds man's blood, / By *man* shall his blood be shed" (Gen. 9:6, emphasis added). Because man was neither subject to God's rule nor obedient to self-rule, God authorized *man* to represent Him in ruling over man. Therefore, not long afterward, there was the beginning of nations; there came into being among the human races the rule of political authorities, the power of the society, and the control in the family. For example, in a nation there are the president and the officials; in a factory, the supervisors; and in a family, the parents and elder brothers, and so forth. These are the authorities set up by God to represent Him in ruling man. This is why Romans 13:1 says, "Let every person be subject to the authorities over him." This is the dispensation of human government, in which man is ruled by man and is responsible to man.

From the point of view of government, man's fall was a fall from God's rule to self-rule, and then from self-rule to man's rule. The more one is ruled by God, the nobler he becomes, but

the more one is ruled by man, the more base he becomes. Today
man's condition is a complete rejection of God's rule. There
may be a few people who are under self-rule, being controlled
by their conscience; however, the impact of their conscience is
very weak. The majority are living under human rule and never
conform unless they are being ruled by someone. Yet many
still fail in this dispensation of human government. They not
only disobey but also endeavor to escape and even overthrow
man's rule. Today what is set before our eyes is a rebellious
and disorderly condition. Thus, man is a total failure whether
under the ruling of God, self, or man.

Since man has been degraded from God's rule to human
rule, God, in saving man, must recover him from human rule
to divine rule, that man may once more live before God in
simplicity and under His direct authority. However, this kind
of recovery cannot be realized in a moment. As man became
degraded by falling from divine rule to human rule, passing
through the stage of self-rule in between, so in God's plan of
recovery he must retrace his steps from human rule to God's
rule, passing through self-rule in between. Since self-rule is
the step between human rule and God's rule, when a man is
saved, he must first be delivered from human rule and return
to self-rule.

All those who live under human rule are living before
man. They dare not do many things because of the fear of
man. Whenever they are not under man's jurisdiction and
observation, they do as they please. However, those who are
under self-rule are not so. They live by the feelings of their
own conscience. Being controlled by their conscience, they do
not need to be ruled by others. They are restrained in all their
utterances and behavior, not because of their fear of man
but because of the ruling of their conscience. They are free to
act only when their conscience approves. Outwardly, they
appear to be still subject to the rule of man, yet practically,
this rule is unnecessary, because their conscience is sufficient
to rule and control them.

Sadly, the condition of many Christians today is not so.
Their behavior still requires the rule of man. Students must
be controlled by their teachers, children by their parents,

and business personnel by their supervisors. Often they care only for those who are around them outwardly but care not for the conscience within. This proves to a great degree that they are still living in the fallen condition of being ruled by man. Therefore, only severe dealings with our conscience will deliver us from the fallen condition of human rule to that rule by the conscience. Then in all things we can live and act according to the feelings of our conscience.

However, the final goal of dealing with the conscience is not simply to restore us to self-rule. If we remain only in the feelings of conscience, we are still in a half-fallen situation and fall short of God's will. Therefore, dealing with the conscience is not just to cause man to return from human rule to self-rule, from the eye of man unto the conscience, but even more to cause man to pass through self-rule and attain to God's rule, to pass through the conscience and live in the presence of God. To deal with the conscience so that we are brought back to the conscience is still a negative objective; the positive objective is that we be recovered to God Himself. Therefore, the final goal of dealing with the conscience is to bring us back to God's rule.

Self-rule and God's rule differ greatly. Self-rule means that man lives by the feelings of his conscience, being responsible to his conscience; whereas God's rule means that man lives by the intuition of the spirit, being responsible to the intuition, that is, being responsible to God. We know that God through the Holy Spirit lives in our spirit. Therefore, we can say that the intuition in our spirit is the feeling of God. Hence, when we live by the intuition and are controlled by the intuition, we are living in the presence of God and ruled by Him. The conscience has only the feeling of right and wrong. It condemns all that is wrong and evil and justifies all that is right and good. But the intuition is above right and wrong, good and evil. It is above wrong and also above right; it is above evil and also above good. It condemns all that is wrong and all that is evil, but it does not necessarily approve all that is right and all that is good. It accepts only that which is of God, of the Spirit, and of life.

For example, lying is condemned by the conscience, whereas

truthfulness is approved. If we live by the conscience, all is well as long as we do not lie but tell the truth. However, if we live by the intuition, walking according to the feeling of God, then not only can we not tell lies, but also we cannot always tell the truth. We have to ask: Are these words of God or of myself? God does not want us to lie; neither does He want us to speak the truth. What God desires is that we speak His words, words that are of Him, of the Spirit, and of life. Therefore, when a brother ministers, whether he is speaking the truth or not will be attended to by the conscience. But as to what he should minister, what subject he should choose, what God has in mind for him to speak—these are not within the limit of right and wrong, good and evil. The feeling of the conscience is unable to do anything in this respect. Only through the intuition can one touch the mind of God and be led by God to speak His words. These differences between the conscience and the intuition are also the differences between self-rule and God's rule.

Today there are too few who are living completely under the ruling of God! Many brothers and sisters are living in a condition that is a combination of the three kinds of government. The greater part of their being is under human rule; they still need to be ruled by man. Another part of their being is under self-rule, the rule of the conscience. But only a small part of their being is under God's rule so that they are controlled by God directly. This is a very abnormal condition. Therefore, there is the need to deal with the conscience more thoroughly so that we can, on the negative side, be delivered from human rule and, on the positive side, enter into God's rule to be directly under His control.

E. The Feeling of the Conscience

1. The Origin of the Feeling

Throughout the generations all saints who have been seeking life agree that the conscience is the window of our spirit just as the eye is the window of our body. The window itself has no light; all light is transmitted from another source. So also is the conscience. Although we dare not say that the conscience itself has no feeling at all, we can say that the greater portion of its feelings comes from its neighboring parts. There are a total of seven of these neighboring parts: the mind, the emotion, the will, the intuition, the fellowship, the life of God, and the Spirit of God. All these seven neighboring parts have feelings. When their feelings penetrate into the conscience, they become the feeling of the conscience. This is the origin of the feeling of the conscience.

2. The Different Kinds of Feelings

The feelings of the conscience of the saints are of many aspects. One who has a keen conscience will have the feelings of the conscience in all matters. These feelings of the conscience can be divided into three categories: The first is the feeling toward sin. In the chapter concerning dealing with sin we have said that the basis of dealing with sin is the inner consciousness. This inner consciousness is the feeling of the conscience. If we sin before God or before man, the conscience will immediately have the feeling of condemnation. This is the first category of the feelings of the conscience.

The second category is the feeling toward the world. In the chapter concerning dealing with the world we have said that the basis for dealing with the world is also the inner consciousness. This inner consciousness is still the feeling of the conscience. If we love other matters or are occupied with anything outside of God, the conscience will also give us a feeling of condemnation. This is the second category of the feelings of the conscience.

Beside these two categories of the feelings of the conscience, there is a third category: these are the uneasy feelings concerning anything apart from sin and the world. There are certain matters that are neither sinful nor of the world, yet they cause our conscience to lose the feeling of peace. If we do not deal with these matters, we simply cannot get through. For example, looseness and inaccuracy in our daily living are not sin nor of the world, yet our conscience is disturbed by them. If someone scatters clothing and other articles around, leaving the room in a state of disorder, his conscience will rebuke him. If our character has certain

shortcomings or peculiarities, if our behavior toward others is
unbecoming as a Christian, or if before God we have certain
undesirable or unsuitable attitudes, though they are neither
sinful nor worldly, our conscience is bothered. All these uneasy
feelings belong to the third category of the feelings of the conscience.

Among the three categories of the feelings of the conscience,
the first two concerning sin and the world are superficial,
whereas the third is deeper. In the early stage of dealing with
the conscience, our inner feelings are more or less sensitive
toward sin and the world. When we have dealt with all these
feelings, the third category of feeling will be made manifest.
The more severely and thoroughly we deal with our conscience, the more this third category of feeling is increased.
Our emphasis in dealing with the conscience is upon the issue
of our coming to deal with this third category of feeling.

Since the conscience of a Christian includes these three
categories of feelings, his conscience is richer and keener than
that of an unbeliever. An unbeliever has no feeling concerning
the world and none of the uneasiness of the third category. He
only has a feeling concerning sin, a feeling of right and wrong,
good and evil; and even this feeling is quite dull. The feeling
in the unbeliever's conscience is about one-third of that in the
Christian's conscience. The feeling in the Christian's conscience
is so rich because the heart of the Christian is a new heart, a
heart which has been softened and renewed by God; his spirit
is a new spirit, a spirit which has been revived and renewed
by God; his mind, emotion, and will have also been considerably renewed; and he has as well the life of God and the Spirit
of God. These are all rich in feeling and can influence the conscience of the Christian. For this reason the feelings of a
Christian's conscience are indeed rich!

F. Offense and Condemnation in the Conscience

The three categories of the feelings of the conscience are
the result of our offenses—we have either offended God or
sinned against man in our intention, motive, word, or action.
Therefore, these feelings can be considered as feelings of
offense. The keener one's conscience is and the more one lives

in the presence of God, the easier it will be for him to have a
feeling of offense. Whenever he offends either God or man,
there is immediately a feeling of offense in the conscience.
Hence, by the intensity of this feeling of offense, we can tell
the degree of keenness of one's conscience and the extent to
which he has been enlightened by God.

However, as far as the feeling of offense itself is concerned,
it is a serious damage to our spiritual condition. When one's
conscience has this feeling of offense, his fellowship with God
is hindered, and thus his entire spiritual condition is lowered.
Therefore, whenever a Christian has the feeling of offense in
his conscience, he must immediately go before the Lord to
confess his sin according to this feeling and claim the cleansing of His precious blood. Sometimes there is also the need to
go before man and deal with the matter. Then the feeling of
offense will vanish, and the conscience will be void of offense.
Therefore, dealing with the conscience, on the one hand, is to
cause our conscience to become keen and rich in feeling and,
on the other hand, to cause our conscience to be secure, at
peace, and void of offense. Hence, the result of dealing with
our conscience, on the one hand, is to bring us into the light of
God so that we will become more enlightened and, on the
other hand, under such an enlightenment, to cause us to get
rid of all the things that are outside of God, not agreeable
with God, and not acceptable to God so that we may experience a deeper cleansing.

Now we come to the condemnation of the conscience. Condemnation issues from the feeling of offense in the conscience.
When our conscience senses that we have done wrong, it condemns. Therefore, these two are really one; they are difficult
to distinguish. Some define the condemnation of the conscience as the accusation of the conscience. These are also
two aspects of one thing. For example, the judge in a law
court condemns, whereas the prosecutor accuses. Likewise,
when our conscience feels that we have wronged, it will, on
one hand, represent man to accuse us and, on the other hand,
represent God to condemn us. The feeling of offense in the
conscience causes our spirit to become depressed and powerless in spiritual things because the feeling of offense brings

with it the accusation and condemnation of the conscience. Therefore, if we would be delivered from the accusation and condemnation of the conscience, there is no other way but to deal carefully with the feeling of offense. When the feeling of offense in our conscience disappears, the accusation and condemnation of the conscience will naturally vanish.

G. The Sensitiveness and Weakness of the Conscience, and Satan's Accusation and Attack

The sensitiveness of the conscience issues from a serious and thorough dealing. If there is no dealing with the conscience, the feeling of the conscience will certainly be slow and dull. When the conscience goes through severe dealings, its feeling becomes keen, even to the point of being sensitive. Hence, the sensitiveness of the conscience is a good phenomenon. It proves that the conscience has already been dealt with quite thoroughly. If our conscience has not been dealt with to the point of its becoming sensitive, then that dealing is not thorough enough.

Some deal so thoroughly with their conscience that they feel convicted should their speech or actions be just slightly off color. They are sensitive not only after they have wronged but even when they are about to do any wrong. Furthermore, the degree of keenness of the conscience in such persons can develop to such an extent of sensitivity that they feel wrong about their every action and word. If they do not act or speak, they also feel wrong. At this point, their whole being appears completely confused. However, when a man passes through such a stage of keenness and emerges from it unto sensitivity of the conscience, he has learned the lessons of dealing with the conscience quite well; the feeling in his conscience will then be constantly keen and normal. Therefore, the sensitiveness of the conscience is a necessary phenomenon.

However, when a man's conscience is dealt with until it becomes sensitive, it may develop into an oversensitive state and thereby become a weak conscience. This weakness due to oversensitivity is the result of over-dealing with the conscience. A Christian who is newly saved or who is not seeking will not acquire weakness of the conscience. Only those who are seriously seeking the Lord and dealing severely with their conscience, but who are still immature and tender in life, will have this weakness. Such persons, when gained by the Lord, deal thoroughly with their conscience, purging away all its darkness and wrongdoings. Their conscience is like glass, clear and bright. At this time their conscience has been sufficiently dealt with; there is no need to have any further dealings. But because they are young and inexperienced in spiritual things, they frequently deal too much, thus producing an oversensitive conscience, which causes weakness of the conscience. Like the skin of our body, some parts are calloused and dull in feeling, whereas other parts are tender and keen in feeling. New skin formed over a wound is tender and extremely sensitive, hurting at the slightest touch. We may say that this is the weak condition of the skin. Likewise, if the conscience is dealt with so much that it becomes oversensitive, it produces a feeling of offense in everything. In many matters such a one condemns himself even before God has condemned him; he loses his peace even before God has disallowed anything. This kind of condemnation and uneasiness may continue to exist even after he has dealt with the matter, causing much needless suffering and affliction. This condition of a weak conscience is the result of oversensitiveness of the conscience.

Several conditions of a weak conscience can be both described and illustrated. One condition is that after we have dealt with the conscience according to its feeling of offense, the conscience still feels condemned and accused. For example, if you have sinned against a brother, when you fellowship with God, you become enlightened and conscious of it; hence, you confess before God and to the brother. When you have done this, if your conscience is strong and normal, you should have peace and let the matter go. However, if the matter still remains in you and you continue to feel uneasy and condemned, it is a sign of a weak conscience.

Another condition is related to certain sins that need not be dealt with, yet your conscience requires you to deal with them also. For example, if you are inwardly disgusted with a brother and you feel that this is wrong, all you need to do is confess it before the Lord and let it go. This is just a personal matter in the heart before the Lord; it was not manifested in words and attitudes so as to involve the opposite party. However, after you have confessed this matter before God, if you still feel that you have to confess to the brother and seek his forgiveness, then this is too much. If after you have confessed to your brother, your inner being is still not at ease and feels the need to confess to him once again, because you feel that in some matter you have said too much and in another too little; yet you are afraid that by your going to him again he may be disgusted; therefore, you feel so perplexed within that you have lost all peace; this is an even weaker condition of the conscience.

Another condition is that of the conscience having the feeling of offense, and the person not finding the sure way to deal with it or always feeling that the dealing is not thorough enough. For example, a brother may have stolen a thousand dollars ten years ago. Now that he is saved, he tries to deal with this situation, but when he does so, he finds it difficult to decide what amount to pay back. According to the principle of the Old Testament (Lev. 6:5), he should add one-fifth to the original amount, yet he feels this is insufficient. Since no principle is given in the New Testament, he reasons that he should return the amount with interest. The question arises, however, concerning the amount of interest. Should he pay bank interest or loan-institution interest? Should it be yearly, monthly, or weekly interest? No matter how long he figures, his heart is still not at ease. This indicates another weak condition of the conscience.

A sensitive conscience is proper and normal, but a weak conscience, being oversensitive, is abnormal. First, this causes one to undergo much needless suffering and torture. Second, this causes one to have continual unrest, which results in ground being given for Satan to accuse and attack. Therefore, a weak conscience is not a good sign. Yet a weak conscience is a necessary product of our initial dealing with the conscience. A sensitive conscience, which comes from a thorough dealing with the conscience, usually becomes a weak conscience. If we have not dealt with the conscience until it becomes sensitive, the dealing is not thorough enough, and we have not yet learned the lesson. However, when the conscience has been dealt with so that it becomes sensitive, then certainly it will become oversensitive and weak. Therefore, when we follow the Lord and deal severely with our conscience, we must try by all means to avoid this weak condition. When our conscience becomes sensitive, we must exercise our will to hold it in place lest it go too far and thus become weak and restless. In this way we will not suffer loss.

We have already said that a weak conscience gives Satan ground to accuse and attack. What is the accusation of Satan? The accusation of Satan and the accusation or condemnation of the conscience are different. The accusation or condemnation of the conscience is always based upon definite fact—either sin, the world, or other matters. It arises from the fact that we have wronged either God or man. But the accusation of Satan is not so. It has no fact as its basis but is just a stirring without cause to deceive us, causing our conscience to have the feeling of failure and loss of peace. Sometimes Satan uses the facts of the past to accuse us. He reminds us again of certain things that have already been dealt with in the past, thus causing us to lose our peace. Therefore, all the accusations of Satan are false. He accuses us by taking advantage of a weak conscience in order that we may fall into needless sufferings, and that our spiritual condition may lose its balance, and that we may not peacefully pursue the growth of life, and thus we suffer great loss.

When a person is under the accusation of Satan, not recognizing the scheme of Satan but accepting again and again the needless accusation, thinking it to be the voice of conscience, his conscience will be made weaker, and the accusation of Satan will become more severe. Consequently, this accusation of Satan becomes his attack. Once man falls under this attack in the conscience, his spirit, soul, and body will be greatly afflicted. In more severe cases he may lose his reason, become insane, and even die.

We have previously considered the brother who did not use his handkerchief when he perspired while preaching.

This is because he dealt too severely with his conscience, thus causing a weak conscience and opening the way for Satan's accusation and attack. He was attacked to such an extent that he would not sleep on his bed but on the floor; otherwise, he would have no peace within. Thus, his body suffered great damage, and he died prematurely.

Another elderly sister, when dealing with the world, also suffered the attack of Satan. Even when she ate the coarsest of food, Satan told her that she was too concerned for her flesh. Neither would she sleep on her bed but on the floor; otherwise, she had no peace. Shortly thereafter, she died. These are a few serious illustrations exposing the dreadfulness of Satan's attack.

The blood of the Lord is our only weapon to overcome Satan's accusation and attack. Revelation 12:10-11 tells us that Satan accuses us day and night before God but that we can overcome him by the blood of the Lamb. First John 1:7 and 9 tell us that if we confess our sins, God will forgive our sins, and the blood of the Lord will cleanse us from all unrighteousness. If we have dealt accordingly with all the feeling of offense in our conscience before the Lord, we must hide under the blood through faith. Only then can we avoid all the accusations and attacks of Satan.

H. Leakage of the Conscience

Leakage of the conscience is also a kind of feeling of offense in the conscience. This condition is also extremely damaging to the spiritual state of a Christian.

In a normal situation the feeling of the conscience is based on the enlightenment of the Holy Spirit, which in turn is based on the measure of our life. The extent to which we have grown in life will be the extent of the enlightenment of the Holy Spirit. The degree of the Holy Spirit's enlightenment will be the degree of the feeling of our conscience. Thus, the feeling of our conscience can be adequately dealt with according to the measure of our life. Whatever the Holy Spirit demands of us through our conscience can also be adequately met by the supply of the power of our life. If we are willing to obey, we will have the strength to deal with the demand.

Thus, this kind of feeling of the conscience will not cause a leakage in the conscience.

However, sometimes the condition becomes abnormal: the conscience produces a kind of feeling that cannot be adequately met by the degree of life. This kind of feeling does not come from the enlightenment of the Holy Spirit. The enlightenment of the Holy Spirit is always based upon the growth of life. Since this kind of feeling cannot be adequately met by the growth of life, it must have come from premature knowledge. This situation is like a ten-year-old child who knows the things of a twenty-year-old man and accepts all the requirements for a twenty-year-old man, but since his life is not adequate, he has no strength to meet the requirements. This is equally true of one who has premature feelings in his conscience. On one hand, he feels that he should not do a certain thing because, if he does, his conscience will feel condemned and uneasy. On the other hand, he is not strong enough to overcome, so he goes ahead and does it. This causes a breach or violation of his conscience that cannot be reconciled. We call this condition the leakage of the conscience.

For example, a brother who has recently been saved has a bad habit. Since the light in him is not strong, his conscience does not condemn him. He is able to pray, attend the meetings, and have fellowship with the Lord—all with peace and joy. Later, a brother tells him that this bad habit is not pleasing to the Lord and that he must get rid of it immediately. He replies, "When I pray, I am not aware that the Lord is displeased." To prove his point, the brother then explains to him all the biblical truths concerning the matter. Finally, the new convert is convinced and compels himself to obey these truths that he may get rid of the bad habit. This results in failure because his growth of life is not adequate, and there is not a sufficient supply of the power of life. Therefore, he continues to live in this bad habit. At this point, his conscience condemns him severely, and a feeling of offense overwhelms him constantly. Originally, he could pray, consecrate himself, and attend the meetings, but now he says to himself, "Can someone like me pray, consecrate myself, and attend the meetings?" Thus, his conscience has a great leakage. The leakage is so serious that he can no longer pray, testify, and attend the meetings. Finally, his whole Christian life suffers bankruptcy.

Therefore, the leakage of the conscience is a very serious and dangerous matter. First Timothy 1:19 tells us that a leakage in our conscience is like a leaking boat doomed to sink in the water. The conscience of a Christian will suffer shipwreck once it has a leak. While faith and love are essential to the Christian himself, they are equally essential in our relationship toward God and in some degree toward others. The life that a Christian lives before God should be a life of faith and love. But once a conscience leaks, both faith and love escape, and the spiritual life of a Christian suffers bankruptcy. As a cracked light bulb has no light, so a leaking conscience causes the Christian's spirit to be deflated and all spiritual things to wither within him.

Since the leakage of the conscience is such a serious matter, we must strive to avoid it in the pathway of pursuing the growth of life. The way to avoid it is to not accept any feeling that comes from premature knowledge and to not respond to any demand that exceeds the supply of the life within. This applies both to ourselves and to others. We should not impart to others advanced knowledge that causes premature feelings, nor should we point out the problems in others without considering whether or not they have the strength to deal with them. Otherwise, their conscience will be damaged, causing a leakage. We should only help others positively in the aspect of life so that they may grow in life. As time goes by, the feelings of their conscience will spontaneously increase, and their dealings will also increase accordingly.

If we already have a feeling derived from premature knowledge, we need the Lord's blood to cover us. We may say to the Lord, "Lord, I know that I need to deal with this matter, but I am unable to cope with it; it is no match for my strength. Cover me with Your blood, and do not let Satan attack me." If we rely upon the blood in this way, though we are weak on the one hand, we can still on the other hand have fellowship with the Lord, and our spiritual life will not suffer loss.

While we are hiding under the blood, we should have

another attitude: we must look to the Lord for the supply of His grace. When the supply of His grace comes upon us and affords us the necessary strength, we must then deal immediately with the things that need to be dealt with. This supply of God's grace is related to the inner life supply and the outward environmental arrangement. For example, in dealing with our financial debts, we have to look to the Lord on one hand to work in us, causing us to have an adequate inward feeling. On the other hand, we must also look to the Lord to provide in the environment the adequate amount of money so that we can deal with the matter according to the inner feeling. This outward supply is also a kind of divine provision to enable us to deal with the matter concerned.

I. The Feeling of the Conscience and the Growth of Life

The feeling of our conscience is closely related to life. First, we shall study this relationship at the time before and after we were saved. Before we were saved, death and darkness were in us, and our conscience had very little light and feeling. After we were saved, God's Spirit brought God's life to dwell in us, and our spirit was quickened. At the same time, our inward parts were all renewed, the function of the conscience was restored, and the feeling of the conscience was revived. Therefore, the feeling in the Christian's conscience originates from the birth of his spiritual life.

This is the true condition when we are saved. After we are saved, the feeling of the conscience increases as the life grows. To the extent our life grows, to the same extent the feeling of our conscience increases. The more we advance in the growth of life, the richer and keener will be the feeling of our conscience. Therefore, if we desire a keener and richer feeling, we need to pursue further after life. If our life is abundant, the feeling of our conscience will be strengthened. Moreover, if we deal with all matters according to the feeling of the conscience, then the growth of life will increase. The growth of life affects the feeling of the conscience, and the feeling of the conscience aids the growth of life. These two are in a mutual cause-and-effect relationship that brings us onward in the path of life.

J. The Feeling of the Conscience and the Enlightening of the Holy Spirit

The feeling of the conscience is also connected with the enlightening of the Holy Spirit. This feeling, derived from the birth of life and increased according to the growth of life, passes through the Holy Spirit and the enlightening of the Holy Spirit. We can never separate life and the Holy Spirit, because the life of God is in the Spirit of God; therefore, we cannot sever the growth of life from the enlightening of the Holy Spirit. The more the Holy Spirit shines in us, the greater is our growth in life, and the greater growth of life we have, the stronger is the enlightening of the Holy Spirit. These two also act as a mutual cause and effect on one another and always exist in the same proportion.

Since the feeling of the conscience is based on the measure of life, and the measure of life is inseparable from the illumination of the Holy Spirit, the feeling of the conscience is naturally affected by the enlightenment of the Holy Spirit. When the life within us increases in growth, the enlightenment of the Holy Spirit will become greater, and the feeling of the conscience will become stronger. It is like a teacher who bases his instruction upon the grade level of the pupil. Normally, the grade level of a pupil conforms to his age, which in turn affects the teacher's lesson. The Holy Spirit within us is our best teacher. The measure of life we possess is our spiritual age. Whatever feeling we sense in our conscience is the lesson that the Holy Spirit enlightens within us. The feeling of conscience differs in each one because we all have a different measure of life. Thus, the enlightenment of the Holy Spirit in each one of us differs accordingly.

Conversely, the feeling of the conscience can also strengthen the enlightening of the Holy Spirit. If we deal with matters according to the feeling of our conscience, the Holy Spirit will naturally gain more ground and give us more enlightening; therefore, the enlightening of the Holy Spirit and the feeling of conscience mutually affect each other both as a cause as well as an effect.

K. The Feeling of the Conscience
and Spiritual Knowledge

Another strong basis for the feeling of the conscience is spiritual knowledge. Spiritual knowledge does not mean mental understanding and comprehension of Bible truths or spiritual things but denotes the understanding and realization of God and all the things of God through divine revelation and enlightenment. This kind of knowledge is both in life and in the Holy Spirit. If a certain kind of knowledge is not derived from life and the Holy Spirit, it is not spiritual knowledge. Real spiritual knowledge must come from life and the Holy Spirit.

Since it is derived from life, our spiritual knowledge is determined by the degree of life that we possess. If a certain kind of knowledge precedes our growth in life, it is premature and intellectual; it is not real spiritual knowledge. Hence, it cannot afford us the supply of life and is of no profit to us. If, however, our growth of life increases to a certain extent, a certain kind of knowledge will be produced. This is the proper and normal spiritual knowledge. It can supply us with life and is beneficial to us.

Spiritual knowledge is in proportion to the growth in life because real spiritual knowledge is derived from the enlightenment of the Holy Spirit, and this enlightenment is in proportion to the growth of life. If there is no enlightenment when we listen to messages, read the Bible, study books, and hear the testimonies of others, we merely accumulate much knowledge. This is not real spiritual knowledge. From this we can see the absolute relatedness of real spiritual knowledge, growth of life, and the enlightening of the Holy Spirit.

What then is the real spiritual knowledge that results from the enlightening of the Holy Spirit? First, it is a feeling in our spirit, the deepest part of our being, whereby we sense by inner revelation what needs to be dealt with. Second, this feeling brings with it the manifestation of God, causing us to feel that it is God who has spoken to us in His presence.

For example, a sister testifies that during prayer she was enlightened by the Lord not to wear many of her fashionable dresses. Another sister, upon hearing her testimony, says in her heart, "If she cannot wear her style of dress, how can I wear my dress, which is more fashionable?" The fact is that the concept of this second sister concerning modern dress is merely the result of mental knowledge mixed with emotion. This is not spiritual knowledge resulting from the enlightening of the Holy Spirit. But she could also possibly have another condition; that is, she not only comprehends the matter with her mind but is touched within by the testimony. She senses the finger of the Lord pointing to her stylish dress and giving her a feeling that she can never wear that dress again. This is the light of the Holy Spirit shining upon her. In the former situation she can merely nod her head and agree, but she cannot kneel down and pray. In the latter situation, even before she arrives home, she prays, "Lord, forgive me, and deliver me from this stylish dress." In this case, God through this testimony not only moves her but speaks and manifests Himself to her. Hence, she knows for certain that she can no longer wear her stylish dress. This is real spiritual knowledge, knowledge that originates from the enlightening of the Holy Spirit.

Each time God gives us spiritual knowledge, He desires that we meet the shining light of His face and sense the revealing of the Holy Spirit. This shining and revealing rebukes us in certain matters, makes us humble ourselves before God, and causes us to seek His forgiveness and deliverance as well as His supply and power of life to deal with whatever is being rebuked.

Take, for example, the messages that have been delivered in the church. Because of the different degrees of growth in life among the brothers and sisters, the enlightening of the Holy Spirit also differs. Therefore, the spiritual knowledge gained by each one varies greatly. A deeper growth in life gives the Holy Spirit more ground to enlighten some. Consequently, the spiritual knowledge they obtain is greater and deeper. With those whose spiritual growth is shallow, the revealing light of the Holy Spirit is limited, even though they sit in the same meeting and hear the same message. Hence, the spiritual knowledge within them is restricted and shallow. Therefore, these three—spiritual knowledge, the degree of growth in life, and the enlightening of the Holy Spirit—are related and mingled together.

Real spiritual knowledge is derived through our growth in life and the enlightenment of the Holy Spirit. This knowledge not only includes the comprehension of the mind but much more. It is a feeling in the spirit. After it touches our conscience, this feeling in the spirit becomes a feeling in the conscience. A lack of spiritual knowledge means no feeling in the conscience. Almost all normal feelings in the conscience come from real spiritual knowledge.

L. The Feeling of the Conscience and the Supply of Grace

Since a normal feeling of the conscience originates from life, the Holy Spirit, and spiritual knowledge, it certainly carries with it the supply of grace. This is a glorious characteristic of the New Testament. The Old Testament laws given to man contained only demands without supply. The New Testament law of life dispensed into man contains not only demand but, even more, supply. The demand in the law of life is met by itself as the supply. Therefore, whenever our conscience reveals the demand of the law of life, giving us a normal feeling to deal with a certain matter, we need but to bow down, worship, and acknowledge that this feeling of God's demand is a preliminary announcement of the supply of grace.

The demand of the feeling in the conscience carries with it the supply of grace, yet if we desire to realize this supply, we must fulfill one requirement: we must respond to this demand in faith. The supply of God's grace is always dependent upon our trust and obedience. If we trust and obey, the supply of God's grace follows. Otherwise, the supply will not be forthcoming. God always desires that we first obey by faith in response to all His demands. Then He will supply us with His grace. Therefore, our response to God's demands is our application for God's supply.

For example, when we ask someone to send a telegram, according to the business principle in the world, we first supply him with money, and then he proceeds to act. But the spiritual principle is that he must first obey and act accordingly;

then the money follows. If someone is afraid to act because of no means, then the money surely will not come forth. But while he is acting in faith to pay the expense, the money will be in hand. Many historical facts in the Bible illustrate this principle. When God brought Israel through the Jordan, the water did not separate before they stepped down; rather, they stepped down by faith, and then the waters were separated. The supply of grace is also obtained by faith and experienced in faith. Therefore, anyone learning to deal with the conscience needs to learn the lesson of receiving the supply of God's grace in faith. Every time the feeling in the conscience brings forth a demand, we ought to realize that this is God's supply for us. If we answer this demand in faith, God's supply will surely come. Our obligation is to respond; God's obligation is to supply.

We should be grateful to the Lord that even our believing and obeying are God given; they do not necessitate our striving or struggling. Normally, when a feeling of the conscience corresponds to the growth in life, we spontaneously have faith and submit in obedience. If ever a feeling of the conscience surpasses our trust in the supply of God's grace and our ability to obey, it is a premature feeling and proves that our growth of life has not reached this stage. In this case we should hide under the blood and wait until our life advances to this stage. Then spontaneously we will have sufficient faith to apply the grace of God and obey the feeling of conscience.

In conclusion, to fulfill the demand of the feeling in the conscience, we certainly need God's supply of grace. This supply is received through faith. When we fulfill in faith the demand that is in the feeling of our conscience, immediately God's grace comes to supply us. On one hand, it gives us strength to deal with the matter and obtain cleansing; on the other hand, this supply and grace become interwoven within us, bringing about the growth of life.

II. THE PRACTICE OF DEALING WITH THE CONSCIENCE

The above twelve points belong to our knowledge in dealing with the conscience; the following refers to the practical application in dealing with the conscience.

A. The Scriptural Basis

(1) First Timothy 1:19: "Holding...a good conscience, concerning which some, thrusting these away, have become shipwrecked regarding the faith." The good conscience mentioned by the apostle means a conscience that deals with all blemishes in order to maintain a blameless condition. If one permits some offense to linger in his conscience, his faith will become shipwrecked, and gradually his spiritual treasure will leak out; he himself will also fall away before the Lord.

(2) First Timothy 1:5: "Love out of a pure heart and out of a good conscience and out of unfeigned faith." In order to have the love that is necessary in a Christian's walk, we need to have a good conscience, for this love comes out of a good conscience.

(3) Acts 24:16: "I also exercise myself to always have a conscience without offense toward God and men."

(4) Acts 23:1: "I have conducted myself in all good conscience before God until this day."

The apostle testifies twice about his conscience being without offense. This reveals one reason why he had such strength and boldness in the Lord's work; that is, he continually dealt with his conscience, keeping it from being condemned.

B. The Object of Dealing with the Conscience

It is not the conscience itself but rather the feeling of the conscience that is the object of our dealings. Besides the premature feelings, oversensitive feelings, and the feelings of Satan's accusations and attacks, all normal feelings of the conscience are the object of our dealings.

Ephesians 4:19 tells us that sinners "cast off all feeling" (Darby). The feeling emphasized here is the feeling of the conscience. Before a man is saved, he is submerged in sin. In his living and behavior he endeavors to ignore and nullify the feeling of his conscience. Therefore, among the Gentiles a moral man may respect the feeling in his conscience, but the evil man is void of feeling in his conscience. The principle is the same with those who are saved. The more spiritual one is, the more sensitive the feeling of his conscience becomes. On the other hand, if he has little prayer and lacks fellowship with the Lord, the feeling in his conscience is insensitive.

In the context of Ephesians 4, the apostle admonishes us to put off the old man and put on the new man, and to walk according to the grace whereby we were called. Thus, the normal Christian life is seen to be absolutely related to the feeling of the conscience. In the past, when living in the old man, we cast away all the feeling of the conscience; now, having put off the old man and having put on the new man, we should live with due attention given to the feeling of the conscience and have dealings according to these feelings.

C. The Basis of Dealing with the Conscience

The basis of dealing with the conscience is also the feeling of the conscience. All normal feelings in our conscience, if in agreement with our growth of life and derived from the enlightening of the Holy Spirit, form the basis of dealing with the conscience.

We have mentioned previously that there are three categories of the feelings of the conscience—namely, the feeling toward sin, the feeling toward the world, and all other uneasy feelings. When dealing with sin, we must deal only with the feeling that exists in our conscience toward sin; when dealing with the world, we must deal only with the feeling in our conscience toward the world; when dealing with other matters apart from sin and the world, we must deal only with the uneasy feelings in our conscience. According to the objects of dealings, these three categories seem different, but their sole basis is the feeling of the conscience.

In the former chapters we did not base the dealing with sin and the world on the feeling of the conscience but rather on the feeling of life within. We did this because the feeling of the conscience is originally the feeling of life within. Although this feeling of life comes from the life of God and the Holy Spirit, it is through the conscience that we sense it. Therefore, although it is the feeling of life, it is also the feeling of the conscience.

D. The Extent of Dealing with the Conscience

The extent of our dealing with the conscience is the same as that of dealing with sin and the world—"life and peace." We must deal to such an extent that we sense not only peace within but also life. Not only do we need to feel restful, secure, and assured, but we must also feel strengthened, enlightened, and satisfied. Anything short of life and peace means that our dealings are not thorough enough.

However, in our experience, the feeling of life and peace cannot always be maintained without change. On the contrary, after a period of time, we may again feel empty and confused, uneasy and insecure, as if the feeling of life and peace were gone. Two factors are responsible for this condition. One is our carelessness and failure, which has caused us to become contaminated again and possessed of things not pleasing to God. Another is that the standard of God's inward demand of life is greatly uplifted when we continue to submit to our conscience, receive the supply of grace, grow in life, and increase with the enlightening of the Holy Spirit: These two reasons can cause us to feel neither life nor peace.

At first, this kind of feeling is a vague feeling within us that we lack life. In other words, we no longer feel "life." Whenever we sense a lack of life, we must realize that God has a deeper lesson within for us to learn and additional matters without for us to deal with. If at this time we enter more deeply into His presence, seeking more revealing light, God will go a step further and show us what matters need to be dealt with. When the light on the matter becomes clear, our vague feeling concerning the lack of life becomes a definite feeling of unrest. This feeling is a feeling in the conscience. We ought to deal accordingly with this feeling until we have recovered the inward condition of life and peace. Such cycles of repeated dealings will purge us again and again and take us forward in the way of life.

E. The Standard of Dealing with the Conscience

In dealing with the conscience we need to deal to such an extent that we have life and peace, but we also need a governing standard of dealing. Generally speaking, the inward lack of life and peace must be dealt with until we obtain life and peace, but this does not mean that all feelings lacking life and peace demand dealings. We only need to ask ourselves if this feeling meets the standard of dealings. If it corresponds with the standard, then we proceed to deal with it; otherwise, it is not necessary. Therefore, the standard of dealing is an important yardstick when we begin to practice the dealings.

When a Christian is touched by the love of the Lord and decides to follow Him, he is willing to yield to the Lord's thorough dealings, even to the point of losing his face and at any cost. At this time Satan often comes with many counterfeit feelings. In some cases people have been so deceived by him that they have felt obliged to deal unnecessarily, thereby suffering spiritual loss. Hence, we must recognize a standard to gauge all our dealings and measure carefully all the feelings that lack life and peace. In this way we can avoid many dangers and mistakes. Consequently, the standard for our dealings is a boundary and a protection as well.

We have said that the standard of dealing with sin is righteousness. Only the matters that are not righteous need to be dealt with. If there is no unrighteousness, there is nothing to consider. The standard of our dealing with the world is whether or not we are slavishly possessed by the world in our daily living. All that is not necessary for our existence or all that possesses us needs to be dealt with; other than that, there is no further need of dealing. However, the standard of our dealing with the conscience is whether or not a matter is meaningful or sensible. This applies when we intend to deal with the lack of peace in our conscience. We must ask, "Is this lack of peace meaningful? When I deal with it, am I edified? Can others be helped? Can God be glorified?" If it is meaningful, we accept it and deal accordingly. However, if it is meaningless, we should reject it and not deal with it.

For example, consider a brother who after reading a book throws it down carelessly. Immediately, a lack of peace is registered inwardly, and his carelessness is rebuked by his conscience. In such a case, he ought to go and carefully handle and replace the book. He must handle the book according to his inner feeling; then he will have the inward peace. In such a case, this lack of peace is evidently meaningful, teaching him not to be a careless person. However, if this brother has no peace while sitting in a chair, yet he has peace while sitting on the floor, he has dealt with his conscience to a meaningless degree. If he has no peace when carrying his Bible in his hand, but he has peace when it is on his shoulder, this lack of peace is nonsense. The more he deals with these meaningless feelings, the more such feelings will multiply. Consequently, the ground is given to Satan's attacks, causing much unnecessary suffering.

On one hand, we should deal with our conscience strictly according to the demands of our inner life and peace. On the other hand, we should also be governed by the standard of meaningfulness. According to the principle, we will then have balanced and profitable dealings that will cause us to grow in life and give no ground to the enemy to attack us.

CONCLUSION

In this second stage of our spiritual life, we have studied consecutively the three lessons of dealing: sin, the world, and the conscience. Everything that requires dealings in the initial stages of the Christian pursuing the Lord are included in these three lessons. After a Christian deals with sin, the justification that he receives from God is lived out through him and is also manifested before men. After he deals with the world, he experiences the sanctification in Christ, becomes wholly separated from the world, and belongs completely to God. Finally, after he deals with the conscience, the feelings within him are sensitive and rich, and the function of his spirit is strong and evident. At this point, everything outside of him that is not pleasing to God or agreeing with God is resolved, while the life inside is being made manifest. He then begins to turn from without to within and learns to follow the Lord inwardly in the path of life.

Practically speaking, after a Christian begins to seek the Lord and consecrates himself, there is a long period of time wherein the emphasis of the Lord's work upon him is in these three areas of dealings. The more he accepts these dealings, the more blessed is his spiritual condition before God, and the more rapid is his growth in life. Therefore, if we want to know our condition before the Lord, or the condition of our spiritual growth, we must check with our experiences to see how much we have been dealt with by the Lord in these aspects. Many brothers and sisters grow very slowly in life. They grieve daily over their poor condition, and they ask daily for the Lord's mercy. Yet, after a lapse of several years, their growth in the inner life still lingers in the initial stage. Other brothers and sisters are in a state of death and numbness before the Lord. The moving of the Holy Spirit is not discernible in them, nor can they be seen functioning in the Holy Spirit. The reason for this is largely that they have not learned these lessons of dealings.

We often speak of obedience, but many times our obedience before the Lord has nothing to do with dealings. Yet, besides the dealings, what else requires obedience? If our dealings are not thorough, how can our obedience be absolute? We dare not say that one hundred percent of all obedience lies in the matter of dealing, but we can say that out of one hundred demands for obedience, ninety of them fall in the category of dealings. Thus, obedience is largely a matter of dealings.

Our problem today is that we are disobedient in the matter of dealings. It is not that we have had no dealings at all, but we are neither thorough nor serious. Either we would not be definite and thorough in dealing, or we would procrastinate in dealing. This greatly discounts our obedience. Thus, we act contrary to the law of life, oppose the teaching of the anointing, and offend God. Therefore, our conscience is dull and insensitive; our spirit becomes deflated and low. Although we listen to messages and read spiritual books including the Bible, we receive little light. We are fruitless in our work, and our whole spiritual condition remains withered and weak.

Not only is this true individually but also in meetings. Many meetings are weak, poor, and low because everyone lacks dealings. If everyone deals strictly and severely in their daily lives, the condition of the meetings will change greatly and become very living.

We always beseech the Lord to work and even tell Him that if He does not work, we have no way to go on. But the problem is not that He refuses to work but that we refuse to allow Him to work. The work of the Lord is to arouse our inner sense. If we let the Lord work, spontaneously we will have dealings according to this inner feeling. Each step of the Lord's work is to expose our difficulties and demand that we deal with them. The minute the Lord works in us, immediately we must have dealings. To let the Lord work is to let Him deal with us. If we deal thoroughly with each feeling, the Lord will be able to work in us through and through. Our whole being will become living. We will become as dynamite in the Lord's work, exploding the Lord's work out from within us.

We must look to the Lord to lead us into the experience of these lessons. The more we neglect the dealings, the more our inner feeling will become indifferent to our being left in darkness. But the more we are willing to practice these dealings, the more our inner feeling will compel us to deal thoroughly, until we have dealt with all our feelings before the Lord. However, even at this point, we cannot say that we have graduated from dealings. There can be no graduation from these dealings, nor can they be terminated. Daily we must face the problem of the dealings. Whenever we discover new mistakes or things not yet dealt with in the past, we must immediately deal with them. Thus, we will be enabled to progress deeper and deeper in the Lord.

CHAPTER SEVEN

OBEYING THE TEACHING OF THE ANOINTING

The seventh lesson of the experience of life is that of obeying the teaching of the anointing. There are various ways of describing this lesson, such as walking according to the Spirit, abiding in the Lord, living in fellowship with God, walking with God, and living in His presence. However, the most precise is obeying the teaching of the anointing. If we understand this expression, the others will also be clear.

Although obeying the teaching of the anointing is an experience in the second stage of our spiritual life, it is the most crucial and central experience of all four stages. No matter what kind of dealing we experience on the negative side or how much building up there is on the positive side, we cannot depart from this lesson. This lesson causes the experience of life in the first and second stages to come forth spontaneously and to become deeper and more thorough. At the same time this lesson can bring us into the deeper experiences of the third and fourth stages. Therefore, our obedience to the anointing is the secret of our growth in life. If we desire to follow the Lord in the way of life, we should have a thorough knowledge and experience of this lesson.

I. SCRIPTURAL BASIS

First John 2:27 says, "As for you, the anointing which you have received from Him abides in you, and you have no need that anyone teach you; but as His anointing teaches you...and even as it has taught you, abide in Him."

II. THE ANOINTING

In the teaching of the anointing, there are two major parts: the anointing itself and knowing the anointing. We shall examine these two aspects carefully. Let us first look at the anointing.

A. The Meaning of the Anointing

What is the meaning of the anointing? We can understand this by the term itself and by its origin in the Bible.

First, let us look at the meaning of the term itself. *The anointing* in 1 John 2:27 in the original Greek is not a noun but a verb pertaining to a certain kind of motion. It is not an ointment in a quiescent state, inactive and motionless, but it is an ointment in a state of motion and activity, involving the movement of anointing.

Then what does *the anointing* refer to? Simply speaking, it is the movement of the Holy Spirit in us. Throughout the whole Bible, ointment symbolizes the Holy Spirit. When man receives the ointment from God, it signifies spiritually that man receives the Holy Spirit from God. When the Lord Jesus received the Holy Spirit at His baptism, He said, "The Spirit of the Lord is upon Me, because He has anointed Me" (Luke 4:18). Thus, the ointment that we receive from the Lord undoubtedly points to the Holy Spirit that we have received of Him. This Holy Spirit is not motionless in us but is always active and moving. This kind of movement gives us an inward feeling of being the recipient of a very delicate and soothing ointment.

Now let us look at the anointing according to its origin in the Bible. Although the term *anointing* is mentioned for the first time in 1 John, nevertheless, the matter of the anointing existed in the Old Testament when the Israelites erected the tabernacle. When they built the tabernacle in the wilderness, God commanded that they should apply the holy ointment to the tabernacle and all the articles within it. All the priests who served and the high priest also had to be anointed with ointment. Once the people and the articles were anointed, they became separated and sanctified unto God (Exo. 29:7, 21;

40:9-16; Lev. 8:10-12, 30). Later, kings and prophets were anointed by God for His service (1 Sam. 10:1; 16:12-13; 1 Kings 1:39; 19:16; 2 Kings 9:1-6; 11:12). Therefore, the anointing occurred very early in the Bible.

The purpose for which God anoints people and things is that the anointed ones may be sanctified. What does it mean to be sanctified? In the past we realized that to be sanctified means separation of the anointed one from what is common, thereby causing him to belong to God. However, this is a shallow understanding, for it refers merely to position. If we have a deeper comprehension, we will see that to be sanctified not only changes the position but also the nature of the anointed one. Since the ointment signifies the Holy Spirit, it signifies also the Triune God. Wherever this ointment is applied, there is God Himself. Whoever has the anointing of the ointment, in him shall the component of God be increased. When Moses anointed the tent, the altar, and the priests, the tent became the tent of God, the altar became the altar of God, and the priests became the priests of God. Due to the application of the ointment, God the Creator became mingled and united with men and things, the creatures. This is why, after the tent was erected and anointed with the ointment, God's glory filled the tent (Exo. 40:2, 9, 34-35). Although there were many tents among the Israelites, only this tent had the glory and the presence of God. This is because only this tent had the ointment applied to it and had the components of God; thus it was sanctified.

In conclusion, the anointing is the Triune God, through the moving of the Holy Spirit within us, anointing Himself into us. The more this ointment anoints us, the more God will be increased in us, bringing a greater and deeper mingling and uniting of Himself with us. Thus, the purpose of the anointing is that we may be mingled and united with God.

B. The Relationship between the Anointing and the Purpose of Salvation

The anointing and the purpose of God's salvation are closely related. The central purpose of God's salvation is to work Himself into human beings and be mingled with them as one.

Likewise, the function of the anointing is to anoint God into us so that we may be mingled with God as one. Therefore, practically speaking, the purpose of God's salvation is achieved through the anointing. If there is no anointing, the purpose of God's salvation can never be fulfilled. The anointing is thus a significant factor in the entire salvation of God.

In order that we may be clearer concerning the relationship of the anointing to the purpose of God's salvation, we will now study three steps of God's work in bringing about this purpose.

His first step was that of the Word becoming flesh. The Word was God (John 1:1), and *flesh* denotes man; therefore, the phrase *the Word became flesh* means that God became man and mingled Himself with man (v. 14). The incarnated Jesus of Nazareth is the first and master product in this universe of God being mingled with man, as well as the first accomplishment of God's purpose of salvation. When He was born on this earth, God obtained in this universe a specimen and model of His mingling with man. From this time forth, God intended to mingle Himself with humanity according to *and by Jesus Christ.*

The second step that achieved God's purpose of salvation was the death and resurrection of the Lord Jesus. The Lord's death released Him from the flesh, and His resurrection transferred Him into the Holy Spirit. Therefore, the death and resurrection of the Lord Jesus made it possible for Him to have another form, namely, the Holy Spirit. Before the incarnation, in eternity, He was the Father. When He was incarnated on this earth and lived among men, He was the Son. After He passed through death and resurrection, ascended to heaven, descended to earth again, and entered into man, He is the Spirit. As the Father expressed Himself in the Son through the incarnation, so the Son expressed Himself as the Spirit through death and resurrection. The Father came unto men as the Son, and the Son entered into man as the Spirit. This is the Triune God who mingles Himself with man through His salvation.

The third step that God used to achieve the purpose of His salvation was the entering of the Holy Spirit into man. When the Holy Spirit enters into man, the Son enters into him, and the Father also enters into him. Therefore, the Holy Spirit entering into man is the same as the Triune God entering into man. The Bible gives at least two references concerning this matter: Romans 8:9-11 says that the Spirit who dwells in us is the Spirit of God, the Spirit of Christ, and Christ Himself. When we put these various expressions together, we see that the Spirit of God being in us also means that both Christ and God are in us. Another reference is 1 John 4:13: "In this we know that...He [abides] in us, that He has given to us of His Spirit." This also proves that for the Holy Spirit to be in us means that God is in us.

When the Triune God came into us in the Holy Spirit, He became mingled with us. Thus, the purpose of His salvation— the mingling of God and man—is accomplished in us in a practical way.

However, the work of God to mingle Himself with man is not an instantaneous process. Since we were regenerated and the Holy Spirit entered into us, this mingling has been going on continuously. Throughout the entire lifetime of a Christian, all the work of the Holy Spirit upon him is to fulfill the work of mingling God with man.

Of course, there is another aspect of the work of the Holy Spirit, which is His outward discipline. This outward discipline is His work on the negative side, whereas the mingling within us is His work on the positive side. The outward discipline is to break us, whereas the inward mingling is to anoint God into us so that God may increase in us. The outward discipline is so that we may decrease, and the inward mingling is so that God may increase. Therefore, the outward discipline of the Holy Spirit is a secondary work; His inward mingling is the major work, directly achieving the purpose of salvation.

How does the Holy Spirit work this mingling into us? He does it by anointing us as the ointment. We have said that the moving of the Holy Spirit is the anointing. He is not motionless within us but is ever moving and active. This movement and action is a kind of anointing, which anoints more and more of God into us. Hence, the more the Holy Spirit anoints

us, the more God can mingle with us, and the more He can
fulfill His purpose of salvation upon us.

The way the Holy Spirit anoints God Himself into us is
comparable to the way we paint a room. For example, if we
wish to paint the walls and the furniture golden, we use gold
paint. By applying a portion of the paint to the walls and the
furniture, they assume the color of gold. If we paint the room
continuously, it will become mingled with the gold paint, and
the whole room will take on a golden hue.

So also the Holy Spirit anoints us to cause God to be mingled with us. God Himself is both the Painter and the paint.
We are like the furniture. God delights to mingle with us
so that we may be filled with His nature. Therefore, in the
Holy Spirit He acts as the ointment to anoint us continually.
This illustration falls short because when the paint is being
applied to the furniture, each retains its own identity—the
paint is still the paint, and the furniture is still the furniture.
However, when the Holy Spirit comes into us as the anointing, there is a compounding reaction that causes *both* to be
mingled as *one*. The result is that we cannot tell which part is
the Holy Spirit or which part is us. The more this mingling
continues, the more God increases in us.

Many brothers and sisters merely understand the teaching aspect of the teaching of the anointing. They think that
the purpose of the anointing is to teach us to know what God
desires us to do or not to do. If we obey such a teaching, we
have peace within; if we do not obey, we do not have peace
within. This kind of understanding, however, is not sufficient.
For example, when Moses applied the ointment to the tent and
its utensils, was he thereby instructing them what to do or
what not to do? Absolutely not. His intention was not for them
to know what to do or what not to do, and even less did he
intend for them to experience a peace regarding what was
done. His purpose in applying the ointment was that they
would wholly belong to God and be sanctified. Therefore, the
experience of the anointing in our spiritual life has more to do
with the anointing itself than with the teaching. The main
purpose of the anointing is that God Himself may be applied
to us. The teaching that comes with it is secondary.

Even in 1 John 2:27, where the teaching of the anointing is mentioned, no emphasis is placed on the matter of our having peace, but it states, "Even as it has taught you, abide in Him." Here, the abiding in Him is the mingling with the Lord and union with Him as one. Therefore, the emphasis of the Bible is on the matter of mingling. I trust that we will change our former concept.

C. The Relationship between the Anointing and the Fellowship of Life

There is a very close relationship between the anointing and the fellowship of life. The fellowship of life is the flowing of life, the flowing together of God and all those possessing His life. The anointing is the mingling of God with all those belonging to Him. The purpose of the flowing of life is to flow God into us, and the purpose of the anointing is to anoint God into us. These are two aspects of one thing; they are very closely related and difficult to separate.

Let us now see why the anointing and the fellowship of life are two aspects of the same thing. We know that God is life, and God is the Spirit. Concerning God as life, He flows in us unceasingly—this is the fellowship of life. Concerning God as the Spirit, He moves in us continually—this is the anointing. However, life and the Spirit are inseparable, for the Spirit includes life, and life is in the Spirit. Life is the content of the Spirit, and the Spirit is the reality of life. These two are the Spirit of life (Rom. 8:2), which is two-in-one and indivisible. Therefore, the fellowship of life and the anointing are also inseparable, being two aspects of one thing.

For this reason, we can see that in the entire Bible the anointing is mentioned in 1 John, a book that especially speaks about the fellowship of life. If we want to know the fellowship of life, we must first know the anointing. People often speak about the fellowship of life and also about the anointing mentioned in 1 John, but very few connect these two together. Even fewer have discovered the reason that the anointing is mentioned in John's book on the fellowship of life. The reason is that both the fellowship of life and the anointing are two inseparable aspects of one thing. As life is in the

Holy Spirit, so the fellowship of life is in the moving of the Holy
Spirit as the anointing. For a person to obtain the life of God,
he must first have the Spirit of God; likewise, for a person to
have the fellowship of life, he must first have the moving of
the Holy Spirit, that is, the anointing. Only when we have
touched the anointing can we experience the fellowship in life
in a practical way. Therefore, when 1 John mentions the fellowship of life, the anointing is inevitable, because the anointing
is for the fellowship of life.

We can also find proof in the types of the Old Testament that the anointing is for the fellowship of life. In Old
Testament times, three groups of people were required to
be anointed: the priests, the kings, and the prophets. Of
these three groups, the kings were sent from God to men to
rule for Him, and the prophets were sent from God to men
to speak for Him. As for the priests, they went from man into
God's presence to have fellowship with Him. It was absolutely necessary for them to be anointed. Every priest must
be anointed. The anointing is necessary in order to enter into
the presence of God, to have fellowship with God, and to
be mingled with God. In other words, a man must first be
anointed before entering into God's presence for fellowship.
This is why the matter of being anointed was especially significant in relation to the priests. This proves to us that the
purpose of the anointing is to anoint man into God, thus
enabling him to have fellowship with God and be united with
God as one. To have the fellowship of life, the anointing is
absolutely essential.

In order to have a clear understanding of the relationship
between the anointing and the fellowship of life, we shall speak
more concerning the significance of the anointing in 1 John,
according to the light of the Scriptures. We know that in the
New Testament the apostle John wrote one Gospel and three
Epistles, all of which speak of the mutual relationship between
God and man. However, there is a great difference between his
Gospel and his Epistles. His Gospel speaks of God coming to
man, while his Epistles speak of man going to God. His Gospel
says that in the beginning was the Word, and the Word was
God. One day the Word became flesh to live among men, and

this was the Lord Jesus. When men beheld Him, they saw the Father, because He and the Father are one (14:9; 10:30); He is God coming to man. His Epistles reveal that such a God, who was manifested, came into our midst, and entered into us, is eternal life. Once this life is preached to us and received by us, it brings us back into the fellowship of the Father and of His Son Jesus Christ (1 John 1:2-3). This is man going to God.

When God came to man, He brought with Him grace and reality: "The Word became flesh and tabernacled among us... full of grace and reality" (John 1:14), and "grace and reality came through Jesus Christ" (v. 17). When we received grace and saw the reality, we returned to God and met love and light. Therefore, 1 John says, "God is love" (4:8, 16) and "God is light" (1:5). Grace comes from love, and reality issues from light. That which is hidden in God is love, and when this love comes forth from God to us, it is grace. Likewise, that which is hidden in God is light, and when this light comes forth from God to us, it is reality. Therefore, when God comes to man, He brings grace and reality, and when we go to God, we touch love and light. When God came to man, He brought with Him His grace; when we received this grace and returned to Him, we met His love. Likewise, when God came to man, He brought His reality; when we saw His reality and returned to Him, we met His light.

This story of God's coming to us to impart grace and reality and our returning to Him to meet love and light is the story of the fellowship of life and the function of the anointing. The ointment anoints God into us and us into God. In other words, the ointment anoints God's grace into us and then anoints us into God's love; further, the ointment anoints God's reality into us and then anoints us into God's light. This coming as grace and going as love and this coming as reality and going as light causes us to be in God's grace as well as in His love, in God's reality as well as in His light. Thus, we are more deeply united and mingled with God.

Therefore, the anointing and the fellowship of life are inseparable. If the work of the anointing in us is shallow, then our fellowship with the Lord will be shallow; if the work of the anointing in us is deep, then our fellowship will also be deep. If the anointing in us is sporadic, then our fellowship with the Lord will also be sporadic. Thus, the anointing is very important for the fellowship in life.

D. The Relationship between the Anointing and the Applying of the Blood

A very close relationship also exists between the anointing and the applying of the blood. The purpose of the anointing is to anoint God into us, that we may have fellowship with God and be mingled and united with God. However, many areas of our being are incompatible with God, and many situations in our lives do not match God's righteousness, holiness, and glory; these make it impossible for God to mingle or unite with us. Hence, there is the need to first apply the blood. The purpose of the blood is to cleanse all the areas that are incompatible with God and to remove all the situations that do not match Him. First we have the applying and cleansing of the blood; then God's holy ointment anoints us with God Himself. Therefore, to experience the anointing we must first have the blood. The blood is the basis for the anointing.

The relationship between the anointing and the applying of the blood is also seen very clearly in the Old Testament. When a priest intends to apply the ointment to a leper at the time of his cleansing, the blood had to first be applied. Some of the ointment was placed "upon the blood," or "upon the place of the blood" (Lev. 14:14-18, 25-29). It would be a great sin against God to apply the ointment before the blood. Because the ointment prefigures the Holy Spirit who came to mingle God with man, it was never to be applied to one who had not been cleansed by the blood. It was necessary first to apply the blood, which would cleanse away all the filthiness and all the areas that were incompatible with God; then, the ointment, signifying God mingled with man, could be applied.

This principle remains unchanged in the New Testament. We have said that because 1 John speaks of the fellowship of life, it mentions the anointing. But not only so, it also mentions the blood. Furthermore, it mentions first the blood in chapter 1, then the anointing in chapter 2. This also indicates that in order to have the fellowship of life, we need not only the anointing of the ointment but also the cleansing of the blood. Furthermore, the blood comes before the anointing. The blood is required to wash away all iniquity in order that the anointing may subsequently bring in the fellowship with God in life. Therefore, if we wish to experience the anointing, we must first experience the blood. The more we apply the blood and allow it to wash us continually, the more we will experience the anointing and feel the living presence and moving of God; thus, we will have fellowship with God. Therefore, the anointing and the applying of the blood are also inseparable.

III. KNOWING THE TEACHING OF THE ANOINTING

First John 2:27 says, "His anointing teaches you concerning all things." In the teaching of the anointing, there is not only the teaching aspect but also the anointing aspect; there is not only the teaching of the Holy Spirit but also the moving of the Holy Spirit. The teaching does not come from the ointment or the Holy Spirit but from the *anointing* of the ointment, or the *moving* of the Holy Spirit.

A. The Relationship between the Teaching of the Anointing and the Anointing

The teaching of the anointing comes from the anointing and is the natural result of our being anointed. When the anointing is moving within us, on the one hand, it anoints God into us, and on the other hand, it reveals God's mind to us. Since the ointment is the Holy Spirit and God Himself, when this ointment anoints us, it anoints us with the components of God. However, since this anointing is the moving of the Holy Spirit, it definitely causes us to have inner feelings. Once we have the feeling of the anointing within us, our mind is able to comprehend some part of God's mind in this feeling of the anointing. We can know what pleases or displeases Him and what He desires and does not desire. This comprehension or knowing is the teaching that we obtain from the anointing. Therefore, the teaching of the anointing has two aspects: first, through the anointing we gain more of God Himself, more of

God's components; second, through the teaching we know His mind and live in Him.

Of these two aspects, to have God Himself is primary, and to know God's mind is secondary. Furthermore, to have God Himself always comes first, and then to know His mind. Each time we experience the anointing within us, we first gain more of God Himself, more of God's components; this, then, produces a result—it causes us to know what God wants us to do. It is impossible to know His will without having Himself.

This is similar to the illustration of painting. When we paint the furniture, both the paint and its color are applied. Our emphasis is on applying the paint, but once we apply the paint, its color naturally appears. Therefore, it is first the paint and then the color. Furthermore, to paint is the primary purpose; to obtain the color is secondary. Likewise, when the Holy Spirit anoints us, the main purpose is to paint God into us. Once God is painted into us, we spontaneously know His mind. Therefore, the teaching of the anointing is a subordinate function of the anointing.

The teaching of the anointing includes three items: the ointment, the anointing, and the teaching. The ointment is the Holy Spirit, the anointing is the moving of the Holy Spirit, and the teaching is the understanding of our mind concerning this moving. Our previous understanding of the teaching of the anointing was to ascertain only the teaching itself. In other words, we limited the teaching of the Holy Spirit to what we should or should not do: if we obey, we will have peace; if not, we will have no peace. In this teaching, we and the Holy Spirit remain two separate entities, having no relationship of mingling whatsoever. This kind of knowing is not sufficient and does not correspond with the principle of the New Testament. In the Old Testament, God revealed His will to man apart from Himself. In such a revelation God and His will were separated; man could only know God's will but could not gain God Himself. However, in the revelation in the New Testament, God and His will are inseparable. In the New Testament, God reveals His will to man in Himself; in order to know the will of God, man must first have God Himself. Therefore, here it is not just a matter of our knowing but also a matter of the mingling of the Holy Spirit with us. If the Holy Spirit gave only His teaching, we could either obey or disobey. If we obey it, we have His teaching; if not, we do not have it. But if the Holy Spirit as the ointment anoints us to teach us, our obedience is immaterial to Him. He has anointed us with something whether we obey His anointing or not. If we obey, He has anointed us; if we do not obey, He still has anointed us. We may disobey the *teaching* of the anointing, but we cannot eradicate the *anointing*.

For example, God may demand that a person leave his occupation and serve Him in faith. Apparently, this is an inspiration, a revelation, a guidance, or a teaching given to him by God; but, practically speaking, it is the result of the ointment that has anointed him either once or for some time. He may have disobeyed the teaching of the anointing and continued in the same occupation without any apparent change, but his inward taste regarding his occupation was different. The anointing, to which he was exposed, remained within him, and he could not disregard it and its effects.

The real spiritual walk and work of a Christian should be the result of such an anointing, an anointing that not only gives us some teaching but also adds some living element within us. We may disobey the teaching, but the element that remains in us continues to be very active so that before long we cannot go on without obeying it. For example, a brother may have originally liked the movies, but the anointing within him has been regulating him ever since he was saved. Eventually, he knows that he should no longer go. He may go again, but after he is seated, something within him will bother him so much that he can no longer stay there. Later, when he is on his way to the movies again, something within him will trouble him continuously and thus prevent him from going. After a longer period of time, when he even contemplates going again, something within him will bother him so much that he will forsake all such thoughts. Therefore, the teaching of the anointing does not merely show us what to do or what not to do, but it anoints the element of God into us while teaching us. This element within motivates us, thereby enabling us to obey the teaching.

In the past, concerning the teaching of the anointing, we paid very much attention to the matter of obedience. Indeed, obedience often brings a greater anointing, whereas disobedience often causes the anointing to cease and the fellowship of life to stop. Therefore, obedience is closely related to the teaching of the anointing. However, it would be too much to say that if one disobeys, he will never have the anointing and the fellowship of life, and that if one continually disobeys, the fellowship will never be recovered. No doubt, if we disobey, the anointing sometimes ceases, but many times when we disobey, it still anoints us. Even though we continue to disobey, it unceasingly anoints us until we do obey. The fact is, we are very disobedient. Should we obey the teaching of the anointing even twenty out of one hundred times, we would be the best Christians. But the anointing has not stopped because of our disobedience. The anointing in our experience often does not care whether we obey or disobey, whether we agree or disagree. If we agree, it anoints us; if we disagree, it also anoints us. Thus, after such an anointing, we are different from what we were before.

Brothers and sisters, this is grace, and this is characteristic of God's work in us in the New Testament era. If we really know this, we will neither be anxious for ourselves nor worry about others. When we help others merely by some outward encouragements, methods, and attractions, it is of little value. Today it seems that a brother is helped to be up, but tomorrow he may be down again. Only when God anoints man in a living way will he truly be possessed by God. If a man comes under such a living anointing several times, he can only follow and obey the Lord. Therefore, when we lead others to the Lord, we should help them to realize this living anointing.

In conclusion, when we mention this lesson of the teaching of the anointing, our purpose is to stress the matter of the anointing. Mere outward teaching is of no value. Only the teaching resulting from the anointing is of value. When we obey the Lord, we do not merely obey a teaching outwardly, but we obey the anointing inwardly. Only then will the result be of spiritual value.

B. The Teaching of the Anointing
and the Understanding of the Mind

The teaching of the anointing comes from the anointing; nevertheless, these two occupy different parts in our being. The anointing is in our spirit, whereas the teaching of the anointing is in our mind. The anointing is in our spirit because the Holy Spirit dwells in our spirit; therefore, the anointing that emanates from the moving of the Holy Spirit is definitely in our spirit. When our spirit is motivated by the Holy Spirit, we become conscious of it. Such a consciousness is the feeling of the anointing. At this time, provided that our mind has been taught, we are able to interpret this feeling from our spirit. We can understand its meaning and thus obtain the teaching that emanates from the anointing. Therefore, the teaching of the anointing is in our mind and is entirely a matter of the comprehension of our mind.

The work of the Holy Spirit within us, whether it be enlightening, watering, revealing, or guiding, is all derived from His anointing within our spirit. Hence, the scope of the anointing is extremely large and includes almost all the work of the Holy Spirit within us. However, the teaching of the anointing includes only the portion that our mind is capable of understanding; thus, the scope is much narrower. Frequently, the anointing can fulfill its purpose without passing through our mind and understanding. For example, during our fellowship with the Lord, we obtain the supply of life, and our spirit becomes watered, refreshed, brightened, and strengthened. Furthermore, when we touch the law of life, we can live and act according to God's nature. These experiences are purely of the anointing and have nothing to do with the teaching. However, there are also many times when the anointing must pass through our mind and be understood before it can manifest its function. For example, our spirit may be enlightened, have a revelation, know God's truth, understand His will in our work and move, and receive the guidance of the Holy Spirit; however, if these items merely remain as the anointing or a consciousness in the spirit, we will not be able to understand the meaning. They need to pass through the interpretation of the mind and become the teaching of the anointing; then we can understand the meaning.

The teaching of the anointing is the interpretation and understanding of the mind with regard to the anointing in the spirit. Therefore, if we desire to follow the teaching of the anointing, we should have not only a keen feeling in our spirit but also an experienced and spiritual mind. Such a mind includes the renewing of the mind, the exercising of our comprehension in spiritual matters, and the collecting of spiritual knowledge. These require that we love the Lord more, seek spiritual experiences, live in fellowship, study the Bible, read spiritual books, and listen to messages. Through these, our mind will receive spiritual unveiling and become enriched in knowledge; thus, it will be able to comprehend the meaning of the anointing in our spirit. Consequently, we will realize the teaching of the anointing.

The importance of our mind comprehending the feeling of the anointing can be illustrated by the case of one going to the movies. A newly saved person, who is ignorant of what movies involve, still feels inwardly pressed down, uncomfortable, and unnatural while watching a movie. He does not realize that the sanctifying Spirit within him is forbidding this, and that the anointing is teaching him not to go again. This is due to the fact that his mind and understanding have not been enlightened; hence, he does not understand the moving of the Holy Spirit regarding this matter. He has the anointing but not the teaching.

Later, his mind receives instruction about the movies, and he realizes that it is ungodly to watch movies. There are three reasons for this. First, the majority of movies are filthy, for they describe, represent, and advocate the evils of an adulterous generation. Everyone who frequently attends movies is constantly contaminated by their corruption. How can Christians partake of this? Second, some movies are not filthy and do afford a degree of knowledge, such as educational films, war films, and films of adventure; however, the environment of the theater is not a suitable place for the saint. Many of those who are in the theater are ungodly in their clothing, attitude, behavior, and conversation. If we attend a movie and come into contact with this kind of atmosphere, it hurts our spirit of godliness. Third, a film may not be filthy, and the environment may even be proper, but after you have watched the film, are you closer to the Lord or further from the Lord? We firmly believe that a spiritual man like Paul, after watching good films once a week for two or three months, would become a loose Christian.

From the above three points we learn that regardless of whether a film is good or bad, the atmosphere and environment of a theater are not fitting to the taste of a Christian. When a brother has this knowledge but again goes to a movie and experiences an anointing that causes him to feel unpleasant and uneasy, his mind immediately understands that this is the Holy Spirit forbidding him to see the movie. At this time, not only has his spirit experienced the anointing, but his mind has learned to understand the teaching of the anointing.

C. The Teaching of the Anointing and the Feeling of the Conscience

There is an absolute relatedness between the teaching of the anointing and the feeling of the conscience. We have said that the normal feeling of the conscience is derived from the Holy Spirit, who is in our spirit, and passes through our mind to enlighten us. This enlightenment is also a kind of anointing of the Holy Spirit as the ointment. Therefore, the feeling of the conscience and the teaching of the anointing are both derived from the feeling of the anointing. The anointing, after having passed through the intuition of the spirit and having been understood by the mind, becomes the teaching of the anointing. However, the anointing, having passed through the conscience and being understood by the mind, becomes the feeling of the conscience; this, then, is their relatedness.

There are, however, differences between the teaching of the anointing and the feeling of the conscience. First, the conscience is an organ to differentiate right from wrong. The feeling of the conscience, which is derived from the anointing, is also limited to right and wrong, good and evil. But the teaching of the anointing, which comes by way of the anointing and is sensed directly in our spirit, is related in scope to God Himself. It surpasses right and wrong and touches directly the will of God Himself. If we only care for the feeling of the conscience, we can only be a faultless Christian. We must go beyond this to live in the teaching of the anointing; then we can touch the mind of God and live in God.

Second, the main purpose of the teaching of the anointing is that we may touch God, possess God, and understand the mind of God. Its emphasis is upon positive guidance, which also indicates that which is forbidden. But the feeling of the conscience simply shows one's offense. It emphasizes the negative condemnation and dealing. God always gives us first the teaching of the anointing, not the feeling of the conscience. If we obey the teaching of the anointing, we will thereby eliminate the necessity for the feeling of the conscience.

However, if at any time we should not obey the teaching of the anointing, we immediately become aware of the condemnation of the conscience, which makes us aware of our offenses. This may be likened to the executive and judicial departments of a nation. When the executive department operates smoothly, there is no need for the judicial department to take any action. However, whenever the executive organ loses its effectiveness or steps beyond its power, the judicial then exercises its power of impeachment. So also is the relationship between the teaching of the anointing and the feeling of the conscience. The teaching of the anointing is always a positive move, while the feeling of the conscience is always a negative impeachment. In other words, the Holy Spirit as ointment first anoints the intuition of our spirit in order to guide or prohibit us. If we do not obey, it proceeds to anoint our conscience in order to produce a feeling in the conscience. Therefore, if we want to maintain a normal spiritual condition, we should always live in the teaching of the anointing, without having to wait for the feeling of the conscience to correct and impeach us.

D. The Nature of the Teaching of the Anointing

We now come to see the nature and characteristic of the teaching of the anointing:

First, the teaching of the anointing is a feeling rather than something clearly spoken. Although the teaching of the anointing must first pass through the understanding of our mind, yet what we comprehend is not a spoken sentence or a word. Its nature is still a feeling in the spirit. At the most, it may seem to be a spoken word as well as a feeling, but it can never be a clearly and definitely spoken sentence. It may be likened to a certain kind of color, which evidently is not a spoken word but a display that can be known when seen. Likewise, when we live in the presence of the Lord and have fellowship with Him, the Holy Spirit as the ointment gives an unveiling to our feeling. If our mind has been educated with the proper knowledge, we can understand the meaning of this unveiling and thereby obtain the teaching. However, this understanding signifies the meaning and not the literal teaching. Though sometimes the Holy Spirit reveals the words to us from the Bible, He does not give us the printed letters; rather He causes us to touch the principle of the Bible. If the complete Bible consisted of printed words, it would be inadequate for our use. For example, consider someone who seeks the Lord about purchasing a pair of glasses. If he seeks a sentence as an answer from the Lord, it is impossible, for glasses are not mentioned in the Bible. Therefore, the Lord can only give him a feeling and a certain knowledge based upon a principle. Practically speaking, the principle is more precious than the letters. The more matured a saint is and the deeper he experiences the anointing, the more free he is from the letters of the Bible, and the more attention he pays to the feeling in the spirit concerning the principle of the Bible.

Many who learn this lesson of the teaching of the anointing still like to seek reassuring words and obtain verbal confirmation. This kind of seeking very easily deceives us and is dangerous. For example, someone may seek the will of the Lord about marriage and pray for a definite answer—either a yes or a no. This kind of seeking is very dangerous and causes one to be easily mistaken; actually, it is a mistake in itself. The Lord makes known His will to us mostly by way of our inner feeling; He seldom uses words. When we pray and commit a matter to the Lord and sense inward peace and sweet fellowship, we know that the Lord agrees with the matter. However, when we pray about this matter and feel hindered, or whenever we think about it, we feel uneasy, this signifies that the Lord does not agree. Therefore, the teaching of the anointing is a feeling, not verbal words.

Second, the teaching of the anointing is inward rather than outward, subjective rather than objective. It is a feeling deep within and not a voice outside of us. Therefore, it is in us and not outside of us; it is subjective and not objective. Often our inward feeling is influenced by outward matters, but these outward influences still need the response from the inward anointing. Mere outward influences should be rejected.

Since the teaching of the anointing is so subjective, many times the feeling that comes from the teaching appears to be our own feeling. Under this condition we often doubt whether it is the feeling of the Holy Spirit or our own feeling. Often we question, "This is apparently my feeling; how can it be the Holy Spirit's?" It is because this feeling, which comes from the Holy Spirit within us, passes through us and is mingled with us, thus giving us this feeling. Therefore, it is difficult to separate it from our own feelings.

However, this feeling is indeed from the Holy Spirit; thus, we can still differentiate it from our own feelings. For example, when our fellowship with the Lord ceases, it is difficult for us to have this kind of feeling again. But when our fellowship with the Lord is recovered, this kind of feeling, which seemingly is our own feeling, reappears. This proves that this feeling does not originate from us but from the Holy Spirit passing through us.

Third, the teaching of the anointing is natural and not forced; neither is it something that is purposely sought after. It may be while you are in fellowship with the Lord, or it may be while you are working, resting, or walking on the street, that spontaneously there is a feeling or teaching within you, in your deepest part. This spontaneous feeling in your innermost being almost always comes from the anointing. If our spiritual life is normal, we should be able to feel the teaching of the anointing in such a very spontaneous way; otherwise, there is a problem with our living before the Lord. For example, while we are buying a dress, the anointing within will naturally show us whether or not we should buy it. If we need to pray for three days before we are clear about buying it, this proves that an abnormal condition exists in our spiritual life. This not only applies to trivial things in our daily life; the principle remains the same in important or special events. We may pray and wait specifically for an answer, but the Holy Spirit will still make the will of God known to us in a natural way. Therefore, concerning the teaching of the anointing, the more spontaneous it is, the more normal it becomes.

Fourth, the teaching of the anointing is constant, not coincidental or sudden. The teaching of the anointing, though very precious, can be frequently obtained. The Holy Spirit grants us this feeling in our daily life as well as for important events. From dawn until dusk, in all our activities, the anointing gives a continual feeling that enables us to understand the will of God and live according to His guidance. We can feel the teaching of the anointing when our spirit is watered; even when we feel that we have lost the presence of the Lord, we still can feel the teaching of the anointing, and the feeling at that time proves to be more accurate than when we were watered. Although we may not feel the presence of the Lord, we often feel the forbidding of the Lord in some things and the presence of the Lord in other things. This seems to be contradictory, but in spiritual experience this is so, because the characteristic of the anointing is constant. If someone obtains the teaching of the anointing only sporadically, his spiritual condition is abnormal.

Since the teaching of the anointing is constant, we should experience it frequently and live in it consistently. Since some people do not heed the feeling of the anointing during the routine of daily life, it becomes difficult for them to obtain it when serious matters occur. Even if they have some inward feeling, it is not reliable. It may be their own imagination or the disguise of Satan; therefore, it is dangerous. For example, consider a brother who does not follow the Lord and obey the teaching of the anointing in his ordinary daily living and who one day plans to be married. He seeks the feeling from the Holy Spirit and finds it very difficult to obtain. Since the feeling from the anointing is so regular, we can sense it in important matters such as marriage as well as in matters of daily living. To live in the feeling of the anointing is similar to a train running on two tracks. As long as we keep moving on the tracks, we are all right. Should we have a tendency to jump the tracks, the feeling of the anointing automatically forbids us and restricts us so that we are kept in the will of God.

This is exactly the same situation as that of the apostles' moving on in the Holy Spirit while doing their work. In Acts 16:6-7, when Paul and his party intended to remain in Asia, they were forbidden by the Holy Spirit; and when they tried to go into Bithynia, the Spirit of Jesus did not allow them. This forbidding and restricting is the story of the anointing. They are like two tracks that kept the apostles within the scope of God's guidance. Paul did not pray for several days in order to know the mind of the Holy Spirit. It was while he was working that the anointing of the Holy Spirit constantly taught him and planned his path.

When we live in the teaching of the anointing, this same condition should exist. If we are often checked in our actions by the forbidding and restricting of the Holy Spirit, this proves that we are constantly living in the feeling of the anointing. However, if we do not regularly have this feeling, and something special occurs that forces us to seek the Holy Spirit, this proves that we are not living continually in the teaching of the anointing. Therefore, a normal condition requires us to be constantly under the teaching of the anointing.

E. The Teaching of the Anointing and Its Results

The real teaching of the anointing comes from the Holy Spirit; therefore, if we obey it and live in it, it causes our heart to love the Lord, to be closer to Him, and to fellowship more with God in our spirit. These are the results of our obedience to the teaching of the anointing. If we obey a feeling within, and the results are not more love for the Lord or a deeper fellowship with God, we can judge that this feeling has been our own and not the teaching of the anointing. Thus, we can use these results to measure and judge whether any of our inner feelings are from the teaching of the anointing.

IV. OBEDIENCE TO THE TEACHING OF THE ANOINTING

Concerning the teaching of the anointing, the Holy Spirit attends to the anointing, and we take care of the obedience. If there is no obedience, it is difficult to have the experience of this lesson; therefore, we will also look into this matter of obedience.

A. Obeying the Teaching of the Anointing and Walking according to the Spirit

We often speak about the spiritual life as walking according to the spirit, living in fellowship, or living in the presence of God. These are various ways of expressing the obedience to the teaching of the anointing. Let us discuss each expression in its relationship to the teaching of the anointing.

We have already seen that the teaching of the anointing is the feeling generated by the moving of the Holy Spirit within us. Therefore, if we obey this feeling, we are walking according to the spirit. If we desire to walk according to the spirit, we need to obey and live in the teaching of the anointing. If we are able to obey the teaching of the anointing, then we are also able to walk according to the spirit. Thus, these are two different ways of expressing the same thing.

If we desire to have the experience of walking according to the spirit, we need to know what is the teaching of the anointing and what is the feeling derived from the inward moving of the Holy Spirit. We need to know and live in the apprehension of this feeling. It is only in this feeling that we are able to walk according to the spirit. Twenty years ago, I heard people speaking about following the Lord. But how do we follow the Lord, and what does it mean to follow the Lord? At that time I neither understood nor touched the reality of it, but praise the Lord, now I know. To follow the Lord means to follow the Spirit, which, specifically speaking, means to obey the teaching of the anointing. We are not following an objective, external Lord but One who is subjective and lives in us. The shining of His face and the manifestation of Himself is the anointing; whereas the will He reveals in the light of His face is the teaching of the anointing. If we obey this teaching, we are obeying the Lord. If we follow this teaching, we are following the Lord.

B. Obeying the Teaching of the Anointing and Living in Fellowship

When we mentioned the relationship between the anointing and the fellowship of life, we saw that these are two aspects of one matter and are inseparable. As life is in the Holy Spirit, so the fellowship of life is through the moving, or anointing, of the Holy Spirit. Each anointing of the ointment anoints the Lord into us and also anoints us into the Lord; thus, it creates a flow of life between the Lord and us. Therefore, when we experience the anointing, there also is the fellowship of life.

If our fellowship with the Lord is limited only to our time of private prayer or morning watch, it is still very shallow. We need to live in fellowship every moment and be in close contact with the Lord, even while we are the busiest; then our fellowship will be deep. In order to live in fellowship, we must live in the anointing and always sense the anointing. This living in the anointing is obeying the teaching of the anointing. If we obey the teaching of the anointing constantly, we can constantly experience the anointing and live in fellowship. Otherwise, we cannot experience the anointing and abide in fellowship.

It is not difficult to experience the anointing and obey its teaching, because its characteristic is constant and natural. By *natural* we mean that we automatically have the anointing without requesting it, and *constant* means that it is always available. If we obey the teaching of the anointing, the result is constant fellowship with the Lord in a very natural way; this is living in fellowship.

Here we would say a little word about the practical way of entering into fellowship:

First, we must know that the feeling of the anointing is the teaching of the anointing. If we desire to enter into the fellowship of life or, in other words, to enter into the anointing, we must first understand the teaching derived from the feeling of the anointing that is moving within us.

Second, we must cease all outward activities. Our whole

being should cease from all outward activity and movement in order to turn within and give full attention to the inner feeling. If we are busy with outward activities, it is impossible for us to take care of the inner feeling of the anointing. The previous point is to know the feeling, whereas this point is to take heed to the feeling. All Christian work and activities that are of any spiritual value should come from within us. First, we should have an inward incentive and guidance, then work and act according to it. But many Christians until this day are constantly living in outward activities. Being zealous for the Lord, they carry their Bibles and run to meet the outward need while neglecting the feeling within. They do not know the feeling within them, neither do they pay attention to this inner feeling. Consequently, these people have no way to enter into fellowship. Therefore, if we desire to enter into fellowship, we must cease from all outward activities.

Third, we must have a fixed time to practice this fellowship with the Lord. The beginner, learning how to fellowship with the Lord, should set aside several fixed times each day to practice this fellowship. At this time, do not try to bring in many items of prayer (we should even cease from praying outward prayers), but pray according to the inner feeling. During this kind of prayer, we sense mostly our sins and offenses and deal with them accordingly. Later, we feel mostly that we have to turn to the Lord and consecrate ourselves to Him. Then spontaneously we look to the grace of the Lord; through His supply of grace we enter into deeper fellowship. Finally, thanksgiving, praise, and worship follow. If we practice this fellowship daily at these set times, our spirit will be strong and living, making it easier to touch the Lord and enter into His fellowship.

Fourth, we must practice fellowship with the Lord at all times. After we spend quite a period of time in practicing fellowship at specific times, we should practice fellowship with the Lord at all times. Appointed times of fellowship are possible by laying aside all outward activities and by praying and seeking wholeheartedly after the Lord. It is comparatively easy for us to do this. However, continual fellowship should be maintained during the whole day, whether at work or at rest. We may be very busy outwardly or occupied with many business affairs, yet inwardly we are always with the Lord, experiencing constantly and naturally the anointing in His presence so that we can continuously live in fellowship. This point is higher and more difficult to attain but is possible through continuous practice.

C. Obeying the Teaching of the Anointing and Living in the Presence of God

To obey the teaching of the anointing means to walk according to the spirit, live in fellowship, and live in the presence of God. However, walking according to the spirit is related to the Holy Spirit, living in fellowship is related to the Lord, and living in the presence of God is related to God. Therefore, these three are a relationship between the teaching of the anointing and the Triune God.

As for the Holy Spirit, He anoints and moves within our spirit; hence, we need to walk according to the spirit. As for the Lord, He lives within us and becomes our life so that we may have the flow of life; hence, we need to live in fellowship with Him. As for God, He is in us to impart the light of His face so that we may enjoy His presence. Therefore, we need to live before Him. We may obtain all three of these aspects by obeying the teaching of the anointing.

According to the truth, God has ever been with us since the day we were saved. His presence has never departed from us, and we can never lose it. This presence is the Holy Spirit. The Holy Spirit within us is God's presence. Therefore, this presence is not a condition or a matter but a person. This person is the Holy Spirit, whose being in us is the presence of God. From the day we are saved, this presence is never lost.

However, according to our experience, we are not always conscious of His presence. Sometimes, it seems that His presence has disappeared, and we have lost the light of His face. It all depends upon the anointing. Without the anointing, the presence of God cannot be made real within us, and we cannot feel the light from His face. With the anointing, the reality of His presence and the sense of the light from His face follow.

Therefore, by the anointing we can experience the presence of God in a practical way.

We have already said that the function of the anointing in letting us know what to do and what not to do is secondary. The main purpose of experiencing the anointing is that we touch God Himself and have His presence. For example, if we deliver a message, it is not only a question of whether or not we should speak but whether or not we have the presence of God while speaking. If God is not present, no matter how much or how well we speak, our inward being becomes emptier and emptier until at the very end of the message our spirit is completely empty; we cannot even pray for some time. On the other hand, if there is the presence of God, we feel inwardly watered; the more we speak, the more we are satisfied. It is just like the Lord Jesus, who after He finished His talk with the Samaritan woman, was inwardly satisfied (John 4:31-34). Such watering and satisfaction were the result of the anointing. Therefore, when one ministers under the anointing, others receive the supply and are benefited, and he himself receives a greater portion of the element of God. Another example is that when planning to go somewhere, we should ask not only whether we should go but also whether God is with us. "Do I have the presence of God like the Israelites in the wilderness, with the pillar of cloud and the pillar of fire?" If God's presence is not within us, though we are doing the best thing, it is of no spiritual value. Therefore, the presence of God is of primary importance and depends upon His anointing. Once we have the anointing, we sense the light of God's face and obtain His presence. Without the anointing, we lose the light of His face and fail to touch His presence.

In the past, although some brothers and sisters learned the lesson concerning the anointing, they placed their attention upon the outward guidance, thereby neglecting the increase of God's element within them. Therefore, the element of God within them was of a limited measure, and after a few years His element within them remained the same. During those few years they did nothing wrong or licentious; they feared the Lord and lived as though they were in the presence of God, but God's element did not increase within them. Actually, their spiritual life had not increased, because in their experience of obeying the teaching of the anointing, they gave attention only to God's guidance and neglected the aspect of God's presence.

D. The Result of Obedience to the Teaching of the Anointing

Since the anointing is vital to God's presence, we need to obey the teaching so that we can experience more of the anointing. Then we can live at all times and in all places in the presence of God, living in the light of His face and touching His presence moment by moment. At this time we can enter into the reality of *Hymns,* #551, which says,

> I have passed the riven veil,
> Here the glories never fail,
> Hallelujah! Hallelujah!
> I am living in the presence of the King.

When man passes through the veil of the flesh and lives in the presence of God, he enters into the Holy of Holies and lives in the spirit, having fellowship face to face with God. It is at this time that his spiritual experience reaches its peak.

In conclusion, the key to all our spiritual life is the anointing. We should continually touch the anointing and obey its teaching. When we live in the teaching of the anointing, we are walking according to the spirit, living in the fellowship of the Lord and in God's presence. If once we lose the teaching of the anointing, the leading of the Holy Spirit is absent, our fellowship with the Lord ceases, and the light in God's face is lost; consequently, we have no way to live in His presence. Therefore, the teaching of the anointing is truly the center of all spiritual experience and is also a very wonderful part of God's salvation. May we pay more attention to it and experience it more!

Chapter Eight

KNOWING THE WILL OF GOD

We now come to the lesson of knowing the will of God or the leading of the Lord. This lesson is closely related in experience to the teaching of the anointing. The purpose of the anointing is to anoint the substance of God into us so that we may reach the goal of the mingling of God with man. Moreover, the teaching of the anointing is given so that we may know the leading of the Lord and His mind toward us. The leading and the mind of the Lord is the will of God. Therefore, if we want to know the will of God, we must have the experience of obeying the teaching of the anointing. Only those who experience the anointing are capable of knowing the will of God. For those who do not experience the anointing, it is almost impossible to know the will of God.

However, when we discuss this lesson on knowing the will of God, we cannot begin with the teaching of the anointing, because the anointing emphasizes the moving of the Holy Spirit in us and is not the will of God itself. At the same time, the will of God is too great a matter and can never be discussed merely as a part of the teaching of the anointing. Therefore, we must devote one lesson wholly to discuss it in detail.

I. THE SCRIPTURAL BASIS

Ephesians 5:17: "Do not be foolish, *but understand what the will of the Lord is*."

Colossians 1:9: "That you may be *filled with the full knowledge of His will* in all spiritual wisdom and understanding."

Romans 12:1-2: "I exhort you therefore, brothers, through the compassions of God to present your bodies a living sacrifice, holy, well pleasing to God, which is your reasonable service. And do not be fashioned according to this age, but be transformed by the renewing of the mind *that you may prove what the will of God is, that which is good and well pleasing and perfect.*"

Hebrews 10:5, 7: "Coming into the world, He says...Behold, I have come...*to do Your will, O God.*"

Matthew 6:10: *"Your will be done,* as in heaven, so also *on earth.*"

Hebrews 13:21: *"...for the doing of His will.*"

II. THE MEANING OF THE WILL OF GOD

What, actually, is the will of God? Christians often mention the will of God in relation to trivial affairs, such as their occupation and marriage. They use this phrase in a very casual manner, thus belittling and underestimating the will of God. When we carefully study the will of God throughout the New Testament, we discover that it points to matters great and lofty. For example, in Ephesians 5:17 to *understand what the will of the Lord is* seems to be a very common phrase, but the context of the book of Ephesians reveals that this phrase indicates depth. Ephesians is a very special book in the Bible; many of its words and principles speak of God and eternity. Therefore, the will of God mentioned there can never merely refer to common, insignificant matters. Furthermore, Ephesians 5 is based on the preceding chapters. Chapter 1 speaks of the mystery of God's will (v. 9), and chapter 3 speaks of the eternal purpose of God which He made in Christ Jesus our Lord (v. 11); both refer to extremely great things. Then chapter 5 exhorts us to understand the will of God, which naturally refers to the great matters previously mentioned, not to trivial matters in our life.

The same is true of Colossians. After Colossians 1:9 speaks of our being filled with the full knowledge of God's will, the following chapters mention the mystery of God in Christ, God's plan concerning Christ, and God's desire that Christ have the preeminence in all things and become all in all. Therefore, when the Holy Spirit speaks of the will of God in chapter 1, it again must refer to the extremely great matters.

After Romans 12:2 exhorts us to prove what the will of God is, verses 3 through 5 continue by speaking of our different functions and our coordination in the Body of Christ. Hence, the will of God mentioned here is also of great importance.

Hebrews 10:7 is a direct quote from the Lord Himself: "I have come to do Your will." The context of this verse is the incarnation of the Lord Jesus, a matter of great importance; therefore, when He declared His obedience to God's will, He did not refer merely to small matters, such as clothing, eating, lodging, and other trivial matters of life, but to His whole move on this earth in fulfilling God's eternal plan. This is a matter of great significance.

In Matthew 6:10 the Lord taught us to pray that the will of the Father be done, as in heaven, so also on earth. This means that the Lord wants the will of God done in heaven to be accomplished on earth. Again, this is of ultimate importance.

Hebrews 13:20-21 speaks of the God of peace, He who brought up from the dead our Lord Jesus, the great Shepherd of the sheep, in the blood of an eternal covenant perfecting us in every good work for the doing of His will. Since this God who perfects us to do His will is such a great God, His will must also refer to great matters.

These Scriptures speak of God's will as originating from God and coming to us both from eternity to the present time and from heaven to earth. Thus, God's will mentioned in the Bible is of great magnitude. How different this is from our past concept regarding the will of God! May the Lord open our eyes and change our concept.

What really, then, is the will of God? We will discuss this from three aspects:

A. The Will of God Being His Heart Desire

When we speak of God's will, we must trace it to the desire of His heart. Ephesians 1:5-12 is one of the most important portions in the Bible concerning the will of God. It says that God in eternity had a plan, which was according to His good pleasure. This portion mentions three related items: "purpose," "pleasure," and "will." Pleasure is of the heart, since the heart is an organ for delight. God has a heart as well as man. Therefore, God also has things of His pleasure, delight, and affection, which means that He also has His heart desire.

To attain His pleasure, He had a plan, which He purposed to fulfill in order to reach His goal. This purpose is His will. Therefore, God's will and His heart desire are the same. Anything not touching God's heart desire is not His will.

For example, the Bible reveals that God's heart desire from eternity is to have a group of people as the companions of His Son. To reach this goal, God planned the creation of heaven, earth, and man according to His pleasure. Then He created everything according to His plan. At that time creation became His will.

Plainly speaking, God's will is His heart desire, planned according to His pleasure. From His viewpoint, anything hidden in God is His heart desire. From our viewpoint, when His heart desire is executed upon us, it becomes His will. Therefore, the will of God that comes upon us is His heart desire, because His will is derived from His heart desire.

B. The Will of God Being the Mingling of God with Man

Since God's will is His heart desire, we must learn what that desire is. It is the mingling of God with man. To mingle with man is both God's desire and His will.

A thorough study of the Bible will help us discover the amazing fact that God in eternity planned according to His heart desire to attain the goal of mingling Himself with man. God in the universe has this one will: to work Himself into man and to mingle Himself with man. His creation, redemption, sanctification, and all other aspects of His work are for this one purpose. This is the one desire of His heart in the universe: it is the only goal, and it is the basic principle of all His work in the New Testament. Therefore, if we desire to know God's will in any situation, we must first ascertain whether the situation is conducive to the mingling of Himself with us. Without this mingling, no matter how good or praiseworthy the situation may be, it is not God's will. This is a strict measurement.

The earthly life of our Lord Jesus is the perfect expression of this principle. The Lord said, "Behold, I have come to do Your will" (Heb. 10:7, 9), and "I do not seek My own will but the will of Him who sent Me" (John 5:30). We see how the Lord's behavior on this earth was according to God's will. To Him, His entire life on this earth was God's will. However, He also said, "The words that I say to you I do not speak from Myself, but the Father who abides in Me does His works" (14:10). This means that while He was on this earth, His words, His deeds and all His living did not originate from Himself, but the Father, who was abiding in Him, mingled with Him and worked through Him. From these three scripture quotations we see that the Lord's life on this earth was in obedience to God's will and that it was a life of the mingling of God with man.

We cannot separate the will of God from the desire of God's heart; neither can we separate the will of God from God Himself. If we depart from His heart desire, we cannot know His will. Likewise, if we depart from God Himself, we cannot have His will. You may feel that you have understood and obeyed His will, yet if you have not touched God Himself, He remains God, and you remain you; there is no mingling whatever between you and Him, and you can be certain that what you have felt to be His will is not His will. A Christian should be like the Lord Jesus in obeying God's will. Not only must we be able to say in every matter that it is not my will but God's will; we must be able to say further that it is not I who work but God who works in me. It is not enough just to say that I know something to be God's will. We must also be able to say that when I do this thing, it is God who does it in me. We must ask two questions: "Whose undertaking is this, God's or my own?" and, "Who is doing it, God or myself?" If we can only ask the first question and not the second, the subject of His will remains doubtful. Anything that I do on my own is certainly not God's will; only what He does is His will.

For example, a brother may be planning to go to a certain place. If he can only say, "I am clear that it is God's will for me to go," this is not enough. He still must ascertain whether God goes with him and mingles more with him. As another example, when we offer money on the Lord's Day, we should not only ask, "Is this offering God's will?" but also, "Am I offering it myself, or is God offering it through me?" Therefore, in every matter, not only must we know what God's pleasure and desire is, but we must also definitely determine whether we have the presence of God and whether God mingles and works with us. It is not enough to say that we are doing the work of God. We should also be able to say that it is God who mingles with us to do His work. This is His will.

From God's viewpoint, the aspect of God's will as His heart desire is difficult for us to fathom. But from the human viewpoint, the aspect of God's will being His mingling with man is absolutely subjective and easy to comprehend, because God mingles with us through the anointing. Whenever there is the anointing, there is also the mingling of God and the presence of God. Without the anointing, it is impossible to have His mingling and His presence with man. Therefore, to understand His will, we must touch the anointing. Whenever we feel the inner anointing and the presence of God, we are in God's will; otherwise, we are not in God's will.

For years we have been speaking about God's will, but somehow we have felt that it was remote and vague. Now we believe that God has given us light, that He has caused us to have a clearer insight, and that He has enabled us to present it in a more concrete manner. God's will is now substantiated; it is no longer vague and abstract. The God we believe in is not only real and living, but He lives in us. In anything that is His will, He is in us anointing and mingling Himself, making His presence felt in us. If we can touch God inwardly in all matters, His substance is increased in us and mingled with us. Then we can be assured that this is the will of God and proceed accordingly.

Although God's will is an extremely great matter, speaking from the standpoint of God mingling Himself with man, it is not too difficult for us to touch, and it is not unfathomable. If we can comprehend this point thoroughly, then not only can we touch His will as something lofty and deep, but we can also easily know His will.

C. The Will of God Being
the Fulfillment of His Plan

God's will is not only His heart desire and His mingling with man but also the fulfillment of His plan. Generally, we are used to belittling and underestimating the will of God. Many people ask, "Is it God's will that I go to a certain place today? Is it His will that I seek a doctor for my sickness? Is it His will that I seek this occupation?" We miserable beings can never forget ourselves when we mention the will of God! Nor can we be separated from the trivial matters of life! We always view the will of God from an earthly standpoint, from our present situation, and from ourselves. Actually, none of these trivial matters of life can come up to the will of God. How great and how high is the will of God! God's will fulfills His eternal plan.

The book of Ephesians reveals to us God's heart desire and God's plan. God's plan in Christ originated from His heart desire. God in eternity had a plan, which He purposed to fulfill. This plan is the will of God. Therefore, the will of God is for the fulfillment of His plan. All the works of God in this universe are according to His will and for the fulfillment of His plan.

Hence, if we want to understand the will of God, the preliminary requirement is that we must know the eternal plan of God. We must be clear concerning what God is going to do on this earth, in this age, and in this locality. When we are clear about these matters, then we are qualified to touch the will of God and ascertain what His will is for us today.

Some brothers and sisters, who are indeed born again and realize that they are God's children, are ignorant and even unconcerned about what God is doing in this universe, what His economy is on this earth, and what His move is for this day. They themselves, their daily living, and their business as well are all for themselves, not for God. They are completely outside of God's economy. Yet they pray daily for God's will in their own living, behavior, and career. Consequently, the result of their inquiry is something of their own will, not God's will. They neither know nor are they in the plan of God. Any such person has no way of understanding the will of God.

To understand the will of God, the basic problem we must solve is to realize that God, to whom we belong and whom we serve, has a great plan in the universe. He desires to obtain a group of people for the building up of the Body of Christ and a corporate man to be the mystical bride of His Son. Furthermore, we need to know what God would do in our locality. If we touch the plan of God and place ourselves into the plan of God in this manner, we are taking God's economy as our career. Thus, when we engage in business, teach, or whatever we do, we are for God's economy; our entire living and all our actions are for His economy. Then we shall have the ground and qualification to touch God's will and be clear about His guidance regarding all the affairs of our daily life.

Therefore, each one of us should first ask ourselves, Do I clearly see the economy of God on this earth? Do I really see what God desires to do in this locality today? Even though we pursue the growth of life, the fellowship in life, and the presence of the Lord, these afford us but a little spiritual enjoyment for ourselves and fall short of the will of God if we do not know His economy.

Before we see the plan of God, though He is in charge of our affairs and our living, we are only under God's providential care, not under His will. When we have seen God's plan, we dare not use the term *God's will* in a light manner. We will not carelessly refer to trivial situations as being God's will. We can only speak of these matters in general as God's care for us.

III. THE MEANS OF KNOWING THE WILL OF GOD

How does God show us His will? By what means do we come to know God's will? Basically, there are five categories by which we may know His will.

A. Creation

First, we need to know God's will through His creation of all things, including matter, nature, and mankind. Revelation 4:11 says that all things were created according to His will.

Everything that exists in the universe speaks forth a measure of God's will. All things in heaven and on earth are certain components that enable us to know the will of God. Therefore, to know God's will, we must take note of all things that He created in the universe. They are like a book for us to study; hence, we must search out and discover why God needed to create all things in heaven and on earth. What was His purpose in creating man? Why is the human race distributed as it is on the earth? If we thoroughly study the matter of creation, the magnitude of God's will in this universe will be understood to a certain degree.

Examples of this aspect can be found in the Old Testament. There people learned a part of God's plan through all things that He created. Psalm 8 is a very good example. This psalm, which is a spiritual psalm, covers the creation, the present age, and the kingdom. The Lord Jesus quoted this psalm in Matthew 21:16, and it is quoted again in Hebrews 2. The writer was inspired to write this psalm while he was observing heaven and earth. When he saw the heavens, the work of God's fingers, and the moon and the stars, which He ordained, he praised the Lord: "O Jehovah our Lord, / How excellent is Your name / In all the earth, / You who have set Your glory over the heavens!" (v. 1). He saw the heavens speaking forth the glory of God and the earth telling the sweetness of His name. Through the means of creation he knew God and His will regarding the whole earth.

In another instance, the psalmist of Psalm 19 discovered that although this universe uttered "no speech and no words, yet their voice is heard" (v. 3, cf. Sept.). Their line is gone out through all the earth and their language to the end of the world. Therefore, the heavens declare the glory of God, and the expanse proclaims the work of His hands. This shows how the psalmist knew the will of God through His creation.

If we desire to understand God's will, we cannot neglect His creation. We must be enlarged to such an extent that we recognize God speaking to us through all things. Everyone who loves God and pursues after Him must at some time be brought to the place where he can comprehend God's will in the universe. First, such a comprehension of creation will enlarge his heart. The universe will enlarge him to become a universal man. Thus, he can read the will of God from a high and lofty ground and from eternity. Second, he will not be concerned about matters of minute importance. He will not argue with others for the sake of making a dollar in business, nor will he neglect God's work in the entire earth by being overly concerned about the situation and need in his own local church. He will indeed be able to say as the writer in Psalm 8, "O Jehovah our Lord, / How excellent is Your name / In *all* the earth." Every day he will labor faithfully on behalf of his local church, yet his heart will be enlarged to include the burden of all the churches on earth. Third, in his concern for the work and move of the Lord, he can easily be led anytime and anywhere—the whole earth is his field, and all souls are the object of his work. He can be led to show concern for the church far away as well as for the church nearby. The Lord's work in the whole earth has become the goal of his concern.

We regret to say that today many brothers and sisters have never read the creation of God in order to know God's will. Meanwhile, they give daily attention to the occurrences in their own little circles. They themselves are their own universe, their all. They are completely trapped in themselves. Therefore, whenever they seek to understand the will of God, their little self is their only starting point and base. What they ask is, Should I teach in a certain school? Should I consider marrying a certain sister? Should I take the train or the plane to travel somewhere? Should I see a certain doctor or go to a certain hospital regarding my ailment? All day long God's children inquire about God's will concerning such matters of daily living. Actually, these are not worth being listed under the category of the will of God. They are not God's will. Does God's will deal with our eating and clothing, our marriage and occupation, our healing and peaceful living? If our eyes have been opened by the Lord, we will see that our common talk about the will of God has nothing to do with God Himself. It is certainly not the will of God that is mentioned in the Bible.

The strange thing is that today's Christians are occupied

with many things that are not mentioned in the Bible. Conversely, many things that are mentioned in the Bible are unknown to them. Such is the case of many in knowing the will of God. The Bible never tells us to pay continuous attention to sickness, occupation, traveling, and other matters pertaining to our living and to study the will of God concerning them. However, most Christians are fully occupied with these matters. Every time the will of God is mentioned in the Bible, it touches God's heart desire, God's plan, God's work on this earth, the church of God, the Body of Christ, and so forth, all of which are matters of great importance and eternal value. Among God's children, we have seldom seen or heard these things mentioned.

For example, one brother may testify concerning some article of his possessions; it had been borrowed from him a long time ago and had not been returned. Therefore, he prayed to the Lord, and after a few days that article was returned. He was very glad and praised the Lord exceedingly. When we hear this kind of testimony, our heart groans. This type of person has seen neither heaven nor earth. He is completely enveloped in himself. All he sees is his little earthly benefits. When he seeks the will of God, he can never forget himself or be severed from his selfish interests of gain. This kind of person is not qualified to talk about the will of God.

If anyone wants to talk about the will of God, he must first come out of himself. Moreover, to come out of himself and understand the eternal and lofty will of God, he must study God's creation carefully. Man must thoroughly study creation in order to become enlarged, withdraw from himself, touch a little upon God's desire and plan in the universe, and understand the will of God. The more spiritual a person is, the more he will realize God in all things. The deeper he lives in the Lord, the more he will understand the will of God through creation.

God promised Abraham that he would become a great nation and that his descendants would be as the sand upon the seashore. But Abraham, still in himself, could not believe God's word. He still thought that his steward, Eliezer of Damascus, would be his heir. Therefore, God led him out and

said, "Look now toward the heavens, and count the stars"
(Gen. 15:1-6). God then promised him that his descendants
would be as great in multitude. When Abraham looked, he
believed. Because he beheld God's creation and realized the
deeds of God, he found faith. At that moment God accepted
him and accounted it to him as righteousness in the eyes of
God.

Take, as further illustration, the story of Job. Although
Job was repeatedly stricken by the hand of God, he failed to
realize God's intention because he was completely in himself.
His speeches were full of "I," full of himself. Thus, in order to
bring him out of himself, God brought him to His creation.
From Job 38 through 41, God questioned Job repeatedly
regarding the created things in the universe. From this he
finally came to see God's greatness and transcendency and
thus came out of himself, saying with repentance of heart,
"Who is this who hides counsel without knowledge?" (42:3).
Originally, because he lived in himself, God's will was obscured
from him. Now since he withdrew from himself, he saw God
with his own eyes and understood His will. Therefore, it was
through God's creation that Job was delivered from himself
and touched the will of God.

Since the understanding of God's will has much to do with
our knowing of God's creation, we need a scheduled plan to
study God's creation, as though we were attending school. We
must spend time to expose ourselves to nature in order to
comprehend God's will. The study of both astronomy and
geography would prove very helpful.

B. The Bible

The second means of knowing God's will is the Bible. God's
creation is only a piece of God's work; it is not sufficiently clear
in revealing His will. The Bible as God's Word tells us thoroughly and clearly what God desires to do in the universe and
what His purpose is. Therefore, the Bible is the clearest revelation regarding God's will. We should study the Bible and be
familiar with the Bible in order to understand His will.

However, many people, by studying the Bible, cannot ascertain God's will. At times, they may have some light regarding

His will, but only in trivial matters. For example, they extract from the book of Ephesians the minor points: the one who stole should not steal again, the wife should obey her husband, the husband should love his wife, the children should obey their parents, and the parents should not provoke their children. But important matters, such as God's plan and the mystery of Christ, are never discovered, because the person who reads the Bible in this way is so small and so much in himself. He studies the Word of God from his own pitiful view, and, as a result, he is like a man who views the sky from the bottom of a well—his view is limited to the scope of his narrow self.

Therefore, the study of both creation and the Bible are inseparable. If we wish to study the Bible, we should first study creation and allow the universe to enlarge us; then we may comprehend the magnificent things in the Bible. Actually, the Bible itself is closely linked with all things in the universe. In the beginning we read about God creating the heavens and the earth, and at the end, about the new heaven and new earth. All God's works and His will as revealed in the Bible are largely related to the universe. Therefore, the universe should first be studied so that our heart may be enlarged; then the Bible should be studied so that our view may be broadened. Thus, we will become one who has a clearer understanding of the will of God.

This category of study also includes spiritual literature, messages, spiritual fellowship, words of encouragement and testimonies of the saints. These all originate from the Bible and serve as a means by which God reveals His will.

C. The Environment

The third way that we know God's will is by our environment. When speaking of God's creation, we emphasize the sun, the moon, the stars, all things in heaven and on earth, and the vastness of His creation. But when we speak of environment, we are referring to our immediate surroundings, including people, things, and circumstances, which affect our lives. In order that we may understand and obey His will, God arranges and changes our environment. Therefore, we need to study both God's will and His guidance in our environment.

When we first came to Taiwan, it appeared to not offer much for the Lord's work. Later, the Lord opened our eyes: we saw that in times past it was difficult to preach the gospel to the many provinces on the mainland of China. However, the political situation has now changed, and people out of all the different provinces have been gathered in Taiwan before our very eyes. Was not this a golden opportunity for the gospel? If we helped these people to be saved, would they not spread the gospel to all China upon their return to their provinces? With this vision, we exerted ourselves wholeheartedly in the work of the gospel. As a result, the rapid increase of new believers included many from all the provinces. Originally, they had neither opportunity to hear the gospel nor a heart toward the gospel; now their environment forced them to come to Taiwan. Consequently, they were saved. This is a good example of how God accomplished His will through the change of environment. When we are alert to the environment about us, we can often touch God's will and know His move for today.

D. The Heart, Spirit, and Mind

The fourth means by which we understand God's will is our heart, spirit, and mind. God created these organs mainly for us to understand His will. If we were like a chair, without a heart, spirit, or mind, we would not understand His will, even though God had prepared all things in the universe, including the environment about us, and had given us the Bible. Therefore, the three organs—heart, spirit, and mind—are of great importance in our understanding of God's will. The creation, the Bible, and the environment are but instruments for God to reveal His will to us; whereas the heart, spirit, and mind are organs for us to comprehend His will.

When we speak of these three organs, we are referring to the parts of the new creation. Since the heart is a new heart, it inclines toward God, loves Him, seeks after Him, and chooses Him. Because the spirit is a new spirit, it can contact God and fellowship with Him. Since the mind is a renewed mind, having a renewed understanding, it can comprehend and interpret the feeling it obtains while in fellowship, and thus it can understand the will of God. If our heart is not new, our spirit is not keen, and our mind is not clear, we will be greatly hindered in the understanding of God's will. The men whom God has greatly used throughout the generations are those in whom these three organs have been renewed, made keen, and made clear.

E. The Holy Spirit

The fifth means by which we understand God's will is the Holy Spirit.

Creation and our environment are outside of us; they are indistinct and not easily understood. The Bible and spiritual books that pertain to God's Word are more practical, yet still objective. However, the Holy Spirit enters into us to reveal God's will in us; hence, this is both practical and subjective. Furthermore, all the previous four means by which we understand God's will are entirely dependent upon the working of the Holy Spirit. If the Holy Spirit does not inspire us from within, even though our heart, spirit, and mind are in perfect condition, we still cannot understand the will of God through creation and the environment. Neither will we understand the revelation that God has given in the Bible. Creation, environment, and the Bible are the material means by which God reveals Himself, but it is the Holy Spirit who makes them meaningful to us. Our heart, spirit, and mind are the organs through which we understand God's will, but it is only through the Holy Spirit that these organs can properly function. Therefore, without the Holy Spirit, the four means we have mentioned will be ineffective in revealing God's will.

There are no other means through which we understand the will of God than the five mentioned above. Dreams and visions mentioned in the Bible are included in the category of the Holy Spirit and will not be listed separately.

In order to understand the will of God, we need to be familiar with these five categories: (1) God's creation, (2) His Word, (3) our environment, (4) our heart, spirit, and mind, and (5) the Holy Spirit. A full knowledge of these will certainly cause us to know the lofty and eternal will of God. We will be able to ascertain that God's eternal plan is to use the universe as a sphere and all things as a means to gain a group of people to be the mystical Body of His Son, thereby manifesting His glory. He has placed us in the very center of His plan so that we may have a position in the Body of His Son and become His members. By knowing this, we will view the present through eternity and God's eyes; then we will immediately ask ourselves, "Am I a part of this plan? What kind of member am I in the Body?" Thus, we will be able to understand the will of God.

Regrettably, many brothers and sisters not only have failed to give attention to these five means, but they do not have any knowledge of them. They neither give attention to God's plan in this universe and to God's revelation in the Bible, nor do they care about His guidance in them through the Holy Spirit. Their only concern is to have a wonderful, peaceful life for themselves. All they ask is, "Should I go to a certain place?" or, "Is it God's will for me to do a certain thing?" How can such a person understand God's will? This is definitely not the understanding of God's will as mentioned in the Bible. What the Bible mentions is His lofty and eternal will, which can only be understood by those who know these five categories. May God grant us mercy that we may have a drastic change in our concept toward His will.

Furthermore, we need to practice these items. First, we need to study creation. We must often leave our immediate setting and expose ourselves to nature, studying and observing it carefully. If possible, we should make extended trips in order to enlarge our horizon as well as our vision.

Second, we need to study the Bible. We must study the truths and revelations that are of great importance, giving special attention to those passages that deal with God's eternal will and His mystical plan.

Third, we must study our environment. Always learn to comprehend the meaning of the environment with its circumstances. Realize why God put you in such a place to meet certain kinds of people under certain circumstances. We need to study all our surroundings and the world situation as well in order to understand the will of God in this present time.

Fourth, regarding the heart, spirit, and mind, we must first ask God to give us a heart to love Him, be drawn to Him, and long for Him. Then we should always worship Him in our spirit, draw nigh to Him, and fellowship with Him. Furthermore, we need a renewed mind. We should learn to forsake the viewpoint of the worldly people, as well as our own selfish viewpoint, in order to grasp the mind of God and His viewpoint. The minds of some brothers and sisters are occupied with financial matters, clothing, business, and children; they never concentrate on matters pertaining to God. Therefore, their understanding concerning the will of God appears to be very dull and slow. This is unfortunate. Our minds must always be fixed on the things of God so that we may be taught of God and so that the Spirit may permeate more of our mind, thus making it a spiritual mind. Finally, as a result, we will easily comprehend the feeling in our spirit and understand spiritual things. This, however, depends upon constant practice.

Last, we need to give careful attention to the Holy Spirit. We should always sense the moving and understand the revelation of the Holy Spirit within us. Our condition should always be right before the Lord so that the Holy Spirit can speak and reveal Himself to us. It is only by the Holy Spirit that God manifests the meaning of the universe and reveals the truths of the Bible to us. By seeking Him to do this, we will know His mind and our position in His plan.

In all these categories we need to be constantly exercised and continually learning in order to use them as the means of understanding God's will in our experience.

IV. THE PATHWAY OF KNOWING THE WILL OF GOD

We have seen the definition of God's will and the means by which God reveals His will. Now we will consider the pathway or the procedure leading to the knowing of God's will. In other words, how can we understand God's will? We will cover this pathway by the following eight steps.

A. Presenting Ourselves as a Sacrifice

The first step is to present ourselves as a sacrifice.

The first two verses of Romans 12 show the clearest way to know God's will: "I exhort you therefore, brothers, through the compassions of God to present your bodies a living sacrifice, holy, well pleasing to God...that you may prove what the will of God is, that which is good and well pleasing and perfect." Here, both the presenting of our bodies and the knowing of His will are joined together in one passage because the presenting of ourselves as a sacrifice is the primary condition for knowing God's will. When a man presents himself as a sacrifice, he becomes qualified and has the ground to know God's will.

Why must a man present himself as a sacrifice in order to know God's will? When a person has not yet presented himself as a sacrifice, he himself is the center of his life and the motivating factor of all his behavior and activities. He naturally thinks of himself and loves himself; even his slightest pursuing in the spiritual realm is for his own pleasure and enjoyment or for his future reward. However, he is oblivious to what God desires to do in this universe and never inquires into the purpose of God's salvation for him. Apparently, he is seeking God's will, but actually, he is wishing that God's will would fulfill his own satisfaction. When he is sick, he asks God whether he should go to a doctor, because he believes that if his going to a doctor is God's will, his sickness should soon be healed. Before going on a business trip, he asks God whether he should go, because he thinks that if the trip is God's will, he will be blessed, and everything will go well. These people can only understand their own will and not the will of God; much less can they understand His lofty and eternal will. Therefore, if one desires to know God's will, he must first put himself and his all on the altar as a consecrated sacrifice to God. He is not for himself but for God. He lays down his own career and enters into God's economy. In this way it is possible for him to know God's will. The altar is the only place and the only ground upon which man can understand God's will.

Our experience of following the Lord involves two different stages of consecration. In the first stage, consecration is usually the result of our being touched and constrained by the Lord's love. As far as emotion is concerned, this kind of consecration is correct and acceptable to the Lord, but as far as consecration itself is concerned, it is insufficient. Since the consecration in this primary stage is mostly a matter of the emotion, it changes according to our mood. Therefore, it is not dependable or stable.

Only after a certain period of time, when our life has grown, our spirit is enlightened, and our view is broadened, will we gradually see the plan of God in this universe and recognize the working of God in this age. Then, naturally, we will have a deeper consecration by placing ourselves in His plan and work in order to meet His need and answer His call for this age. This is the second stage of consecration; it is deeper and higher than the first. It goes beyond our emotion and brings us into the reality of consecration. If we wish to understand God's will, we need this deeper kind of consecration. Man must see God's need concerning His plan and work and consecrate himself to God; then he has the ground to understand God's will.

This is the kind of consecration that Romans 12 speaks about, that is, to present our bodies to God. This is the practical side of consecration. Because our being exists in our body, we must present our body so that our whole being may be given over to God in a practical way. Many people have a heart to consecrate themselves, but because their physical body has not been offered, their consecration is useless. Real consecration means that our body has been presented; it is neither a mere desire nor a verbal yieldedness but a giving of ourselves entirely and practically to God.

The purpose of presenting our body is to become a living sacrifice. Negatively, this means to be cut off from all our past activities. For example, before an ox in the Old Testament was brought as a sacrifice, he was in his own place and acted according to his own will. Once he was placed on the altar, he no longer moved by his own will, and his activities ceased. The principle is identical when we become a living sacrifice. Before we were consecrated to God, we were like a wild ox or sheep living in the mountain wilds; we acted completely by our own will. Only when we become a living sacrifice to God do we cease from our own activities in order to await God's command.

The positive meaning of a living sacrifice is to live for God and be used by God. Once the sacrificial animal in the Old

Testament became a sacrifice, it was killed and then burned completely. We may say that it was a dead sacrifice. However, in our case, after we consecrate ourselves, we are still alive; we are a living sacrifice. The difference is that in the past we lived for ourselves, but now we live for God. Before, we sought after our own benefit; now we seek His pleasure. Formerly, we were interested in our own affairs; now our concern is about God's work.

If a person consecrates himself as a living sacrifice and lives for God, it is then God's good pleasure to reveal His will in him so that he can understand His will.

B. Denying the Self

The second step in the pathway of knowing the will of God is to deny the self.

The two most important passages relative to knowing God's will are Romans 12 and Matthew 16. The former speaks of the relationship between being a sacrifice and understanding God's will; the latter speaks of the relationship between God's will and the denying of self. To be a sacrifice is to solve the problem of living *for* ourselves. To deny the self is to solve the problem of living *according to* ourselves. If we are merely a sacrifice and have not denied ourselves, even though we are living for God, we are still living according to our own opinion and ideas. As such, we cannot understand His will. Therefore, the denying of self is also a basic requirement for knowing the will of God.

Matthew 16:21-24 discloses three sections relating to the denial of self. The first consists of verses 21 and 22, where the Lord showed the disciples that He had to go to the cross and die. Peter rebuked the Lord, saying, "God be merciful to You, Lord! This shall by no means happen to You!" *God be merciful to You* in another translation is "Pity yourself." Peter meant that the Lord should pity Himself and not accept the cross. The Lord mentioned the cross, but Peter mentioned the self. These two are contrary to each other. The acceptance of the cross means the annihilation of the self. Whenever we pity ourselves, we lay aside the cross.

Therefore, in the second section the Lord rebuked Peter

and said, "Get behind me, Satan! You are a stumbling block to Me, for you are not setting your mind on the things of God, but on the things of men" (v. 23). *The things of God* means the will of God. This rebuke contains at least two explanations: First, if we pity ourselves, laying aside the cross, it is doubtless the work of Satan within us. Satan causes man to pity himself and to refuse the cross. Second, the Lord exposed two contradicting things—the will of God and the thought of man. Since the Lord's rebuke followed the preceding verses, the will of God means the cross, and the thought of man means the self. When man accepts the suggestion of Satan, pities himself, and rejects the cross, the result is that he sets his mind not on the things of God but on the things of men.

Hence, the Lord concludes in the third section: "If anyone wants to come after Me, let him deny himself and take up his cross and follow Me" (v. 24). Here again the Lord emphasizes the opposition between self and the cross. If we desire to follow the Lord and obey His will, we must, on one hand, deny ourselves and not set our mind on the things of men and, on the other hand, bear the cross and set our mind on the things of God.

In Matthew 16 *self* indicates the things of men. The things of men include all the varied kinds of ideas, viewpoints, perceptions, and opinions. When man touches our ideas, viewpoints, perceptions, and opinions, he touches our "self."

Our natural being is full of self with its ideas and opinions. Even though we zealously love the Lord and consecrate our all for the Lord in order to serve Him, yet we are full of our own ideas and opinions. We always want to do this and that for the Lord; we never pause to inquire what He desires us to do and how to do it. The human concept is that it is a good thing to be zealously serving the Lord, but according to Matthew 16 this kind of zeal can originate from Satan. When Peter laid hold of the Lord and said, "Lord, pity Yourself," he was not opposing but loving the Lord. However, the Lord's rebuke exposed this to be Satan's injection. When man serves God by his own zeal, it is horrible and abominable in God's sight. Because Satan is hiding within man, man's will is ever the enemy of God's will. When he lives in himself and does something for God according to his own idea and opinion, it is absolutely impossible for him to understand the will of God.

Again, the Word of the Lord shows us that God's will and man's will ever contradict each other. Man's will is his self, and God's will is the cross. Whenever God's will is revealed to man, it is like the cross, which puts man to death. The will of God kills primarily the self in man. It kills man's ideas, viewpoints, perceptions, and opinions. Therefore, the will of God and the self of man are ever contrary to each other. If we are in the self, we are out of God's will. It is impossible to have His will and keep the self. Each time we accept God's will, it kills the self. If we stand on the ground of death, accepting the cross, we will understand God's will. All who do not accept, or are not willing to accept, the killing of the cross cannot understand or receive God's will.

Miss M. E. Barber, who served the Lord in China, said that if one is willing to deny and reject his self, he has already ninety-nine percent passed through the path of knowing God's will, and the one percent left is just to know it. This has proven to be true in our experience. Beside denying self, there is no other way for us to understand the will of God.

C. Dealing with the Heart

The basic requirements for knowing the will of God are: (1) presenting ourselves as a sacrifice and (2) denying our self. The next step is to deal with the heart. Even though this step is not as basic as the first two requirements, it is still very important in the matter of knowing God's will.

As previously mentioned, the heart, spirit, and mind are organs for us to know God's will. The condition of the heart, whether aimed in the right direction or occupied by various involvements, vitally determines our knowing of God's will.

The following four quotations from the Scriptures clearly show the relationship between the heart and the knowing of God's will and especially the importance of dealing with our heart.

(1) Second Corinthians 3:16: "Whenever their heart turns to the Lord, the veil is taken away." If our heart fails to turn toward the Lord, it becomes a veil to cover us and keep us

from seeing the light; hence, we have no way to know God's will. When our heart is not turned toward God, we cannot see. But when we turn our heart toward God, we see. Thus, it is imperative that our heart be absolutely turned toward God.

(2) Second Corinthians 11:3: "I fear lest somehow...your thoughts would be corrupted from the simplicity and the purity toward Christ." A lack of simplicity and purity means that we are corrupted and have another goal besides God. God alone should be our goal. Once we pay more attention to other people, matters, and activities, immediately our heart becomes corrupted and thus loses its simplicity and purity. Consequently, we cannot understand God's will. Again, we are told that our heart must be absolutely turned toward God.

(3) Matthew 6:21-23: "Where your treasure is, there will your heart be also. The lamp of the body is the eye. If therefore your eye is single, your whole body will be full of light; but if your eye is evil, your whole body will be dark." These verses mention first the matter of our heart going after the treasure; then the light and darkness involving the eye follow. If our heart is set on God, our vision is clear; if our heart is set on other matters, our eye is evil and fails to see God's will. Here, again, is an exhortation to have our heart absolutely turned toward God.

(4) Matthew 5:8: "Blessed are the pure in heart, for they shall see God." The pure in heart are those who have no mixture in the heart. Their heart is single and pure, desiring nothing else but God. Many people are seeking and desiring something other than God Himself. Therefore, lacking a pure heart, they can neither see God nor understand His will. By this we see that our heart must be definitely turned toward God and desire nothing but God.

These four passages show that the relationship between the heart and knowing God's will is determined by the condition of the heart—whether it is absolutely turned toward God. Just as a compass, regardless of the changes in the surroundings, always points to the north, so also our heart should always turn toward God and take God as its goal. Thus, we can understand His will. We regret, however, that among God's children there are very few whose hearts are absolutely turned toward Him. The hearts of the majority are turned either to the left or to the right; they are never absolutely turned toward God in simplicity. These people not only fail to see God, but their consecration and denial of self are a problem. Since their heart is not right before God, their consecration is full of reservations, and their self stubbornly retains its own ideas and opinions. Therefore, it is impossible for them to understand God's will.

The dealing with the heart, although not as basic as consecration and the denial of self, is very fine and deep. We ought to bring all the details and hidden areas of our heart into the light of God, letting the Holy Spirit examine and correct us until our heart is completely toward God, and desires and chooses only God.

D. Exercising the Spirit

Once our heart has God as its goal, we can touch the will of God in a practical way. At this time we need to exercise our spirit. Since God and His will are inseparable, and since God dwells in our spirit as the Holy Spirit, our first practice in understanding God's will must be the exercise of our spirit to touch the feeling of the Holy Spirit in the depths of our spirit. Under normal conditions this feeling in our spirit is God's will.

However, our problem is not only that our heart is not absolute but also that our spirit is too weak. A heart that is not absolute causes us to be confused and unclear about God's will. A spirit that is weak causes us to be numb and dull in knowing God's will. This is why, when God's will is revealed unto us, we are frequently unconscious of it.

Therefore, to know God's will, our spirit must be strengthened by the constant practice of exercising it. The best way to do this is to have much fellowship and prayer with the Lord. If we can set aside an hour a day to enter into the inner chamber for prayer and fellowship with the Lord, after a certain period of time, our spirit will most assuredly be strengthened and become very keen.

Beside setting a certain time aside for prayer and fellowship with the Lord, we need to practice exercising our spirit in all matters of our daily living. On one hand, we need to deny the self in order to sense the feeling of the Holy Spirit; on the other hand, we need to walk in obedience to this feeling. For example, if someone should discuss business with us, our natural disposition would immediately express our own feeling and opinion. However, if we exercise our spirit to reject our feeling and opinion and seek the mind of God in our spirit, we will touch the feeling of God regarding this very matter. Once we have obtained this feeling and are clear about God's mind, we will speak and act according to this feeling. We will not employ craftiness or guile but merely conduct ourselves in a truthful manner according to the spirit. As a result, such exercise of the spirit will lead to a more strengthened and sensitive spirit. Then, knowing God's will is not difficult.

E. Training the Mind

After having contacted God and obtained the feeling in our spirit, we still need our mind to interpret and apprehend His will practically. Otherwise, the feeling in our spirit is but an unknown burden, and it is not meaningful to our understanding. Hence, we will not know God's will. For example, if we listen to a speech given in a foreign language, we hear the voice, but if our mind has little training in that language, we can neither interpret the meaning nor understand the mind of the speaker. Thus, the interpretation by the mind is an indispensable factor in the understanding of God's will. If our mind has not been trained in spiritual things, we have no access to this realm and no way to understand God's will.

It is regrettable that with many brothers and sisters there is a serious lack of training of the mind in the spiritual realm. Some brothers, when predicting the fluctuations in the stock market and calculating profits and loss, have very clever minds. In addition, some sisters, when chatting with their neighbors, display a very active mind. But when they sit in a meeting and listen to a message, they are incapable of understanding it. It is neither that they are unwilling to listen nor that the message is too profound but that their mind simply cannot grasp the spiritual content. Even though they strive to concentrate, before long they become very sleepy and doze off.

Their mind has not been trained in spiritual things; therefore, they are very ignorant and dull.

The training of the mind is the work of the Holy Spirit. The more the Holy Spirit renews the mind, the more it becomes spiritual and able to cooperate with our spirit. We also have our responsibility, which is to exercise our mind in spiritual matters, set our mind on them, and always turn to the spirit, paying attention to the movements therein. In this way, because our mind is always in contact with the spiritual realm, it becomes keen and living in understanding the feeling in our spirit, and thereby it understands God's will.

F. Fellowshipping with God and Studying the Inward Feeling

A practical understanding of God's will in our daily living demands fellowship with God. Those who lack fellowship with God are unable to understand creation and the Bible. Moreover, they cannot have a normal heart, spirit, or mind; neither can they touch the feeling of the Holy Spirit or be led by Him. Fellowship with God is one of the vital keys to understanding His will. A person who understands God's will must be one who has continual fellowship with God.

To set aside a certain time for prayer and fellowship with God is insufficient. We must have continual fellowship throughout our daily living. Furthermore, we need to grow and increasingly touch the Lord through this fellowship.

When we touch the Lord in fellowship, we thereby have an inward feeling. We should study this feeling in order to understand the will of God.

However, we generally have a common problem that causes us to be unable either to understand the feeling or to understand it accurately. The problem is that we do not believe what we feel. We usually overanalyze the feeling, fearing it is either not from God or a wrong feeling. Often our fear is not that we may be wrong and sin against God but that the outcome may not be to our advantage. Such a fear proves that we are considering our own gain or loss. If so, it makes it difficult for us to understand God's will.

Therefore, each time we touch a feeling from our fellowship

with God, as long as it is not in obvious conflict with the teaching of the Bible, we should believe and accept it as from God. Even though, due to our childish condition, we sometimes accept the feeling wrongly, we still have to believe that we are in the hand of God, and God will still keep us. Although we may be wrong in a certain affair, yet our being and our spirit are still right, and God is still pleased with us.

Furthermore, there is another factor within us that hinders us from understanding the feeling; that is, the self, which includes our opinions, ideas, prejudices, and concepts. These old things within us always keep us from studying the feeling we obtain while in fellowship or having a pure understanding of it, and thus they keep us from a clear perception of God's will. Therefore, we need to deal severely so that we may not be bound or influenced by self. This allows the Holy Spirit to freely give us the feeling and guidance of God's will in a manifested and unlimited way.

G. Studying the Bible

Another way of knowing God's will is to study the Bible, because God has revealed Himself and His will through His Word. We need to study carefully God's great revelations, such as His mysterious plan and the Body of Christ. We also need to study the minor principles in the Bible, such as those concerning clothing, eating, and spending money, as well as teachings, illustrations, examples, prophecy, and types. Not only should we study the Scriptures daily but also for special occasions. For example, when a brother who studies the Bible daily is contemplating marriage, he should also study the principles, detailed teachings, and examples of marriage given in the Bible. Then he needs to apply them so that he may realize the will of God about marriage.

Moreover, we should pay attention to messages given in meetings, read spiritual books, and take heed to the various kinds of fellowship and sharings. Since their origins are found in the Bible and are very applicable and practical in revealing God's will, they should be heeded.

It is not enough that we know God's will as revealed in His Word. We must also apply the principles and details in our daily life. Of course, when we apply the principles, we need the anointing. Then we will not be merely following the regulations of letters, but in the light of life we will be walking according to the spirit.

H. Studying the Environment

To know God's will more fully we need to study the environment. Remember, the environment is also a means by which God reveals His will. When God leads and guides us according to His will, He usually arranges the appropriate environments for this purpose. For example, after Jacob remained twenty years with his uncle, Laban, God wanted him to return to his father's house. Hence, He caused the sons of Laban to utter words against Jacob, which resulted in Laban changing his countenance toward him (Gen. 31:1-3). Through this, God proved His will to Jacob. The environment is always a means by which God reveals His will and is also a proof of His will. Therefore, if we are to know God's will, we need to observe the environment that He arranges for us.

Environment is practical and is comprised of many phases; therefore, we need to seek out the spiritual meaning and God's will from the many phases. The practical environment includes the people about us and the existence of situations with their manifold variations. A Christian seeking to know God's will should not only study (1) his feeling within and (2) the Bible without but also (3) the environment about him. If one learns to study these three aspects thoroughly, he is to a great extent in the will of God.

CONCLUSION

Beginning with obeying the teaching of the anointing, the spiritual experience of a Christian gradually progresses to a higher ground. When we come to the experience of knowing God's will, its requirement of spiritual growth and strict dealing with the self surpasses all the previous lessons. If one is still living in the self and does everything for self, it is impossible for him to know God's will. Since God's will is lofty and eternal, man must come out of his own little circle and get into the larger circle of God. It is as he is brought into the great circle of God that he will see God's eternal plan and his part in it. This will cause him to deny the self and lay his self aside in order to fulfill God's will.

This lofty realization, once it is established in one's life, will solve all the basic difficulties in knowing God's will. He can then be regulated by God's will in his practical daily living, that is, in what God wants him to do and how he should live and behave himself. Because he is consecrated to the Lord and has committed himself to His eternal plan, when he has fellowship with God, he will spontaneously experience the anointing and know what he should do. Then all the feelings he experiences in fellowship with God can be counted as His will. Not only does he study the great revelations and truths in the Bible, but he also studies the minor teachings and principles of the believer's life and conduct so that he may know God's will in all things. Furthermore, he always watches his environment and God's sovereign arrangement of it. After he puts all these factors together, he can clearly understand God's will.

THE THIRD STAGE—CHRIST LIVING IN ME

We come now to study the third of the four stages in our spiritual life, that is, "Christ living in me," or, the experience of "the stage of the cross."

If a Christian, after he consecrates himself to the Lord, deals thoroughly with all unrighteousness, unholiness, and the feelings of the conscience and has certain experiences in obeying the teaching of the anointing and understands God's will, then the Lord will lead him to accept the dealings of the cross. Thus, he will obtain experiences of the stage of the cross.

The experience of the stage of the cross is different in many respects from the previous spiritual experiences. The first two stages of the experience of life can only be counted as the experience of one stage, because all those dealings can be experienced once a person is saved. A person who is saved in a very thorough way begins immediately to clear the past and deals with sin, the world, and the conscience. Even in the deeper lessons, such as obeying the teaching of the anointing and understanding the will of God, he has already made headway. Therefore, these experiences actually belong to the stage of salvation. However, there is definitely a difference when we come to the third stage. It brings us to the starting point of another aspect in Christian experience, and this serves as a great turning point for a Christian before the Lord. Mrs. Penn-Lewis named this stage "the way of the cross." She used the term *way* to denote that it is at this stage that a Christian begins to walk formally in the way of the cross, having the experience of the cross and walking entirely under the cross. Therefore, from this time on, his spiritual walk enters into a new stage.

Moreover, all the dealings during the first two stages with regard to unrighteousness, unholiness, and even the unpeaceful feelings in the conscience are related to matters outside of us and have nothing to do with our own self. In the first two stages we conceive of all our problems as being things related to sin and the world, and that if we have dealt with them, we will have no further problems. However, not until we consecrate ourselves to the Lord and obey Him in an absolute way, making progress in the Lord and entering into the third stage, do we gradually discover that, in following the Lord, not only do we have problems related to matters outside of us but also problems of our very being, such as our flesh, our self, and our natural constitution. Furthermore, these inward matters hinder and offend the Lord most severely. At this time we will be led by the Lord to see how the cross can solve all these difficulties pertaining to our being. Then we will have deeper dealings with regard to these matters. This is why we say that if a Christian can enter into this third stage of the experience of the cross, then indeed a great turning point and a new beginning will be effected in his life.

The matter concerning the cleansing of leprosy (Lev. 14:2-9) is a type that very clearly shows these two different kinds of dealing related to the matters outside of us and the things of our selves. In the Bible a leper always typifies our fallen, sinful man. The problem of a leper is really not in his outward filthiness and ugliness but in the poison of the disease within. Likewise, the main problem with us fallen sinners is really not our outward sinful deeds but the sinful nature within us, which originates from the evil life of Satan. Therefore, the typology regarding leprosy is a very accurate and thorough description of our sinful condition before God. Hence, the way of cleansing related to the leper, as recorded in Leviticus, is also the way of our being cleansed and dealt with before God.

The first requirement for the cleansing of a leper was to bring him to the priest. The priest typifies the Lord Jesus. "The priest shall go forth outside the camp" (v. 3) to examine the leper, because the leper could not enter into the camp but had to remain outside. This tells us that we sinners cannot come into the midst of God's people, where God manifests His grace; but the Lord Jesus has come out to examine us. If we

have really repented from our heart, then the plague of leprosy is healed in the sight of God. After it is healed, "then the
priest shall command that two living clean birds and cedar
wood and scarlet strands and hyssop be taken for the one who
is to be cleansed. And the priest shall command that one of
the birds be slaughtered in an earthen vessel over running
water. As for the living bird, he shall take it and the cedar
wood and the scarlet strands and the hyssop, and shall dip
them and the living bird in the blood of the bird that was
slaughtered over the running water. And he shall sprinkle it
on the one who is to be cleansed from the leprosy seven times
and shall pronounce him clean. Then he shall let the living
bird go into the open field" (vv. 4-7). The filthiness of the
leper is a sin before God; therefore, it requires the cleansing
of the sprinkling of the blood. This is not for the cleansing of
the sinful nature but for the abolishing of all record of sin
before God. The procedure in the sprinkling of the blood is to
prepare two birds: one to be slaughtered in an earthen vessel
over running water, and the other, which is living, to be dipped
in the blood, and the blood to then be sprinkled over the leper.
The bird that is slaughtered typifies the Lord Jesus shedding
His blood and suffering death, the living bird typifies the
Lord Jesus resurrected from death, and the running water
typifies the eternal life of our Lord. Therefore, this indicates
that the Lord Jesus shed His blood and suffered death in His
eternal life. Furthermore, the blood, shed by His death, and
His eternal life are brought to us and become effective in us
through His resurrection. The sprinkling of the blood seven
times indicates the completeness of the cleansing of the Lord's
blood; it can abolish all our sinful record before God and
make us acceptable to God. After the living bird was dipped
in the blood, it was set loose into the open field. This means
that after a person receives the death of the Lord Jesus in his
stead, the blood of the Lord becomes effective upon him, and
the power of the resurrection of the Lord is manifested in him
and sets him free.

When a person is resurrected and liberated through the
death and resurrection of the Lord, he is saved. From this

time forth, he must cleanse away all his filthiness, dealing with both his inward and outward difficulties.

"The one who is to be cleansed shall wash his clothes" (v. 8). Clothing, which is something put upon the human body, typifies our living, deeds, and actions. Therefore, the washing of the clothes indicates dealing with all improper and wrong deeds in our lives. This includes all that we have mentioned before—the clearance of the past and the dealing with sin, the world, and the conscience, which belong to the first two stages of the experience of life.

It follows then that the leper has to "shave off all his hair... and bathe his flesh in water, and he shall be clean" (v. 9). The hair, which is something grown out from a man's body, signifies the difficulties within ourselves. Therefore, shaving the hair means dealing with the difficulties of our own self. This is the work of the cross in dealing with our being. After one passes through the dealing of the cross, his whole being is cleansed in a practical way. This kind of dealing is not once for all; it must be repeated again and again to become thorough. Therefore, "on the seventh day he shall shave off all his hair; he shall shave his head and his beard and his eyebrows, even all his hair. Then he shall wash his clothes and bathe his flesh in water, and he shall be clean" (v. 9). This continuous dealing is not only thorough but detailed; that is, it is not only the shaving of the hair in general, but it also differentiates between the hair of the head, the beard, and the eyebrows, and the hair of the whole body. These areas must be dealt with one by one, and eventually the whole body completely shaved.

In the Bible each of the different kinds of hair has its own significance. The hair of the head signifies the glory of man, the beard represents the honor of man, the eyebrows speak of the beauty of man, and the hair of the whole body denotes the natural strength of man. Everyone has his boasts in certain areas. Some boast of their ancestry, some of their education, some of their virtues, some of their zeal in their love for the Lord. Almost everyone can find an area in which to boast, to glorify himself, and to make a display before man. This is typified by the hair of the head. Moreover, people esteem themselves honorable with regard to their position, their family background, or even their spirituality; they always have a superior feeling that they are above others. This is their beard. At the same time, men also have some natural beauty, that is, some naturally good and strong points, which did not issue from the experience of God's salvation but from natural birth. This is the eyebrows of man. Finally, as human beings, we are full of natural strength, natural methods and opinions, thinking that we can do this or that for the Lord and that we are capable of doing all things. This means that we still have very long hair all over our body; we have not been shaved. All these are not outward contaminations but problems of our natural birth. The outward contaminations need only to be washed with water; however, our own natural problems must be shaved with a razor, which means that they must be dealt with by the cross. This kind of dealing is deep and severe, hurting us within and causing us much pain.

What we will discuss in the third stage are the experiences of "shaving the hair," that is, dealing with the problems of our own self. We will divide these dealings into the following items: dealing with the flesh, dealing with self, and dealing with the natural constitution. These are the major experiences of dealing in the third stage of the experience of life.

CHAPTER NINE

DEALING WITH THE FLESH

The first experience in the third stage of our spiritual life is dealing with the flesh by the cross. As we have mentioned before, dealing with sin can be likened to removing the dirt from a shirt; dealing with the world, to removing the colorful prints in the shirt; and dealing with the conscience, to removing the minute bacteria from the shirt. Then the shirt is completely cleansed. From the human viewpoint, it is sufficient to be dealt with to such an extent. However, it is not so with God. God has to further cut the shirt into pieces with a knife. This is dealing with the flesh. Although this seems unreasonable, it is real in our spiritual experience. After we have dealt with sin, the world, and the conscience, it seems that all the outward filthiness has been dealt with. But if the Lord enlightens us, we will discover that the greatest difficulty encountered by the life of God within us is our natural life, our own being. Although we have dealings with unrighteousness, unholiness, and all the feelings in the conscience, we still live by our natural life, not by God's life; we still live in ourselves, not in the Holy Spirit. Therefore, we are still soulish, not spiritual. If we want to be delivered from this kind of difficulty, the only way of salvation is the cross. Only when we accept the cross to break our natural life shall the life of God be manifested and overflow. Only when we put ourselves to death shall we let the Holy Spirit do an enlivening work within us. When the Israelites passed through the Jordan, the wandering in the wilderness came to an end; they entered into the realm of new life. Thus, they were able to enjoy the produce of the land of Canaan, fight for God, and bring in the kingdom. The Israelites' passing through the

Jordan signifies our experience of the death of Christ so that we may be delivered from the flesh and enter into the riches of God's life. If we receive the mercy of God and go on faithfully in the path of life, we will also fully experience the putting to death of our flesh by the cross and be conformed to His death. Only when we experience the deliverance of the putting to death of our flesh by the cross shall we be delivered out of the realm of desolation and failures and enter thereby into the riches and rest of Christ, living in the heavenly realm to fight for God and bring in God's kingdom. Therefore, the experience of the stage of dealing by the cross is a very important crisis. Blessed are they who can experience it in a full and thorough way, for they are close to maturity in their spiritual life, and Christ will grow and be formed in them.

I. SCRIPTURAL BASIS

(1) Romans 8:7-8: "Because the mind set on the flesh is enmity against God; for it is not subject to the law of God, for neither can it be. And those who are in the flesh cannot please God." This speaks of the condition of the enmity of the flesh toward God. A fleshly person can never please God or be accepted by Him.

(2) Romans 6:6: "Knowing this, that our old man has been crucified with Him in order that the body of sin might be annulled, that we should no longer serve sin as slaves." The *old man* refers to the flesh when it is not expressed. This passage reveals that our old man, or our flesh, has been crucified with Christ, and that it is a fact that has been accomplished long ago.

(3) Galatians 5:24: "They who are of Christ Jesus have crucified the flesh with its passions and its lusts." In the sight of God, dealing with the flesh is also a fact that has been accomplished long ago. Hence, we should no longer live by the flesh.

(4) Romans 8:13: "If you live according to the flesh, you must die, but if by the Spirit you put to death the practices of the body, you will live." This tells us that we need to put to

death the practices of the body by the Spirit and thus experience the dealing of the cross in a practical way.

II. THE DEFINITION OF THE FLESH

We can find at least three definitions in the Bible of the flesh:

A. The Corrupted Body

The first definition of the flesh in the Bible is our corrupted body. When God first created man, he had only the physical body, not the flesh. At that time, there was no sin or lust in the human body; it was simply a created body. However, when Satan induced man to eat of the fruit of the tree of the knowledge of good and evil, then Satan and his sinful life, which was signified by the fruit, entered into the human body, causing the human body to be transmuted and corrupted and thus become the flesh. Therefore, today, the human flesh, which has sin, lust, and many other impure substances of Satan within it, is much more complicated than the original human body.

We can easily find scriptural ground to show that the flesh is the corrupted body. For example, Romans 6:6 mentions "the body of sin," which is the sinful body. Romans 7:24 mentions "the body of this death," which means the dead body. This sinful and dead body refers to the corrupted body, or the flesh. Sin and death are the characteristics of the life of Satan. Our body, which has sin and death, has become the flesh. Therefore, Romans 7:18 says, "In my *flesh,* nothing good dwells"; again, verse 20 says, "Sin that dwells in *me*"; and again, verse 21 says, "Evil is present with *me.*" These verses tell us that "sin" or "evil," which is within us, is in our flesh. Then verse 23, which mentions "the law of sin which is in my members," shows in a more practical way that the law of sin is in the members of the body. This reveals that our body, having been mixed with satanic poison, is corrupted.

Galatians 5:19-21 lists the manifestations of the flesh, such as fornication, uncleanness, and lasciviousness, all emanating from our corrupted body; therefore, the first definition of the flesh is our corrupted body.

B. The Whole Fallen Man

The second definition of the flesh in the Bible is our whole fallen being. Romans 3:20 says, "Out of the works of the law no flesh shall be justified before Him." Galatians 2:16 states, "A man is not justified out of the works of law." In these two passages we see that "flesh" and "man" are identical. In the Lord's eyes, man not only *has* the flesh but *is* flesh as well.

How did man fall and become flesh? Immediately after man was created, his body was in subjection to the soul, which, in turn, was in subjection to the spirit. On one hand, man had fellowship with God by the spirit, thereby understanding the will of God; on the other hand, he exercised his spirit to bring his whole being into subjection to God's will. Hence, at that time, man lived by the spirit and was controlled by the spirit. When man was induced by Satan to eat from the tree of the knowledge of good and evil, man fell away from the spirit and no longer lived by the spirit. Meanwhile, the human body, having been poisoned by Satan, became transmuted into flesh. This was the first step of the human fall. Then Cain sinned and fell, in that he was rejected by God because he served God according to his own delight and opinion. Thus, man fell completely into the realm of the soul; he lived by the soul and became a soulish man. After Cain, man fell even deeper and sinned more violently. As a result, the spirit of man became withered, and his flesh grew stronger and stronger until it usurped the place of the spirit to control the whole being. In this way, man fell completely into the flesh and lived by it. Therefore, before the flood, God said that man "is flesh" (Gen. 6:3). Then, again, He said, "All flesh had corrupted its way upon the earth" (v. 12). At that time, in the sight of God, man was not only of the flesh but was the flesh. As those who are evil are the flesh, so also those who are good are the flesh. As those who hate are the flesh, so also those who love are the flesh. All people of this world are flesh. Therefore, in the Bible, flesh refers also to the whole fallen human being.

C. The Good Aspect of Man

Usually when we mention the flesh, we think that the flesh

is corrupt and wicked, just as mentioned in Galatians 5:19-21. But the Bible shows us that the flesh has not only an evil aspect but also a good aspect. The good flesh desires to do good and to worship and serve God. Paul in Philippians 3:3-6 indicates that there were some who worshipped God in the flesh and boasted in their flesh. The flesh there undoubtedly refers to flesh in its good aspect, for by it man worships God and through it man boasts.

Why is there a good aspect of man or of the flesh? Because although we are the people who fell deeply, we still have some good element that was originally created by God. Therefore, we often want to do good and serve God. But, after all, man or the flesh in its good aspect is weak and powerless, desiring to do good or serve God but not being able to do either. In the sight of God, we, the fallen men, controlled by the flesh, wholly became flesh. Anything that originates in us, whether good or bad, is of the flesh and does not please God. Therefore, not only our temper, hatred, or anything against God that originates in us is of the flesh, but the gentleness, love, and even the service to God that originate in us are also of the flesh. Whatever originates in us, whether good or bad, is of the flesh. We have to know the flesh to such an extent; then we have really touched the meaning of the flesh. Therefore, in the Bible, flesh also denotes the good aspect of man.

III. THE POSITION OF THE FLESH BEFORE GOD

What is the position of the flesh before God? What is God's attitude toward the flesh? This matter is clearly mentioned in many places in the Bible; however, we can only point out here the most important passages.

A. God Not Mingling with the Flesh

Exodus 30:32 says, "Upon the flesh of man it [the holy anointing oil] shall not be poured." The holy anointing oil typifies the Holy Spirit, which is God Himself. Therefore, the declaration that the holy anointing oil must not be poured upon man's flesh means that God cannot mingle or unite with the flesh.

B. God and the Flesh Not Existing Together

Exodus 17:14 and 16 say, "Jehovah said to Moses...I will utterly blot out the memory of Amalek from under heaven... Jehovah will have war with Amalek from generation to generation." Why did God determine to exterminate Amalek and to have war with him from generation to generation? It is because Amalek in the Bible typifies our flesh.

The Israelites as the descendants of Jacob typify the chosen, regenerated part within us, which is the new man in our spirit belonging to Christ. The Amalekites as the descendants of Esau typify the fallen natural part within us, which is the old man in the flesh belonging to Adam. Esau and Jacob were twins, but their descendants, the Amalekites and the Israelites, were mutual enemies; they could not stand together. Likewise, our fleshly old man is very close to our spiritual new man; the two are also mutual enemies and cannot stand together. The fact that God would have war with Amalek shows us how God hates the flesh and desires to exterminate it. If the flesh is not exterminated and there is no dealing with it, our spiritual life will have no way to grow. The two can never compromise or coexist.

When Saul became the king of Israel, God commanded him to smite the Amalekites, destroy all that they had, and not spare them (1 Sam. 15). However, Saul spared Agag, the king of the Amalekites, and the best of the sheep and of the oxen. All that was good he would not utterly destroy, but everything that was despised and worthless he utterly destroyed. Since Saul did not absolutely obey the command of God, he forfeited God's favor and lost his throne. This indicates that if man does not absolutely reject the flesh but retains what is good and honorable in the sight of man, he cannot please God, because between God and the flesh there is no compromise.

In the book of Esther, Mordecai chose to die rather than to bow down to Haman, an Agagite, the descendant of Agag, the Amalekite. Because Mordecai withstood firmly to the end, he pleased God and also brought deliverance to the Jews. This is further proof that only when we do not give in to the flesh, even unto death, can we please God and become fitting vessels for Him. God and the flesh cannot exist together!

C. God Being Determined to Remove the Flesh

In the Old Testament God did one specific thing to express His attitude toward the flesh—He established circumcision. The first man whom God commanded to perform the act of circumcision was Abraham (Gen. 17). God promised Abraham that his descendants would be as the stars in the heavens and as the sands of the sea. But as God delayed in the fulfillment of His promise, Abraham took Hagar as his wife and bore Ishmael. Thus, he used the strength of his flesh to fulfill God's promise. God was not pleased with him, and for thirteen years God hid Himself. Then, when Abraham was ninety-nine years old, God appeared again to him (16:15; 17:1). At this appearance God commanded Abraham and all that belonged to him to be circumcised. This means God desired that the flesh be removed so that henceforth they would not serve God in the flesh.

The second time that circumcision is mentioned in the Bible is in Exodus 4. As Moses answered the call of God to deliver the Israelites from Egypt, God met him on the way and sought to put him to death, because his two sons had not been circumcised. Hence, Zipporah, the wife of Moses, circumcised her son. From this we see that if man desires to serve God, he must first remove the flesh; otherwise, even if he gives up everything for God, he can never please Him.

The third instance of circumcision was at Gilgal, after the Israelites passed through the Jordan (Josh. 4—5). On the day of the passover, the Israelites buried their sins under the blood of the lamb. When they left Egypt, they buried their enemy, the hosts of Egypt, in the waters of the Red Sea. As they entered Canaan, they buried their self, or flesh, in the waters of the Jordan. In other words, they dealt with their sins at the passover and the world at the Red Sea, but before the Jordan they had never dealt with their flesh. Therefore, they wandered for forty years in the wilderness until they passed through the Jordan, where the Israelite of the old creation, that is, the flesh, was dealt with. When they passed through the Jordan, they gathered twelve stones from the bed of the river and carried them to the other side of the river; they also put another twelve stones in the midst of the Jordan. This means that their old man was buried under the river and that it was the new Israel that entered Canaan. Therefore, once they passed through Jordan, they were all formally circumcised and rolled away their flesh. Henceforth, they were able to fight for God and bring in His kingdom.

Furthermore, the New Testament mentions circumcision for Christians. Colossians 2:11 says, "In Him also you were circumcised with a circumcision not made with hands, in the putting off of the body of the flesh, in the circumcision of Christ." This further reveals, and that most clearly, that the spiritual meaning of circumcision is the putting away of the flesh. Circumcision, a sign of the covenant of God with His people, signifies that God desires His people to put away the flesh and live in His presence.

D. The Bible's Conclusion of the Flesh

Romans 8:8 says, "Those who are in the flesh cannot please God." The Bible has spoken much about the flesh, and at this point it concludes that the flesh cannot please God. If man belongs to the flesh, minds the flesh, and lives by the flesh, whatever he does, either good or bad, cannot please God.

E. The Rightful Position of the Flesh

Galatians 5:24 says, "They who are of Christ Jesus have crucified the flesh with its passions and its lusts." The rightful position of the flesh is on the cross. The final consequence of the flesh before God is death. God's verdict upon the flesh is that it must be put to death. Only when the flesh is put to death can God have His place and His way in man.

By studying the above five points, we realize how the whole Bible proves that the flesh is abominable before God and that God would forever destroy it. The greatest reason that God so deeply hates the flesh is that Satan lives in the flesh. The flesh is the camp of God's enemy and the largest base for his work. We can say that all the work of Satan in man is accomplished by means of the flesh. And all his work through the means of the flesh destroys the plan and the goal of God. Therefore, we can say that God hates the flesh in the same manner that He hates Satan, and He wants to destroy the flesh in the same manner that He wants to destroy Satan. God and the flesh can never exist together.

IV. THE RELATIONSHIP BETWEEN THE FLESH AND THE OLD MAN

The Bible mentions both the flesh and the old man. What is the relationship between the flesh and the old man? How do we differentiate between these two? To put it simply, the flesh is the living out of the old man; the two are one. In the old creation we are the old man. When the old man is lived out and expressed, it is the flesh. Therefore, both the old man and the flesh actually refer to our very being. As to the objective fact, we are the old man; as to the subjective experience, we are the flesh.

This matter is clearly stated in the book of Romans. Romans 5 speaks about the inheritance we have in Adam, chapter 6 speaks of what we have obtained in Christ, chapter 7 tells of our bondage in the flesh, and chapter 8 proclaims the release we have in the Holy Spirit. Chapters 5 and 6 are related to the objective facts concerning Christ and the old man, while chapters 7 and 8 are related to the subjective experiences concerning the Holy Spirit and the flesh. Just as Christ is related to the Holy Spirit, so the old man is related to the flesh. Just as Christ cannot be experienced without the Holy Spirit, so also the old man cannot be experienced without the flesh. Christ is lived out in the Holy Spirit; likewise, the old man is lived out in the flesh. For example, the Bible says that our old man has been crucified with Christ. This is a fact that was accomplished nineteen hundred years ago, though at that time we had not been born, and our old man had not been lived out. Today, more than nineteen hundred years later, we have been born, and we know how to lie and lose our temper. This is the living out of the old man, and we call it the flesh. Therefore, that which was crucified with Christ was our old man, which had not yet been lived out at that time; whereas that which is being dealt with today is the flesh, the living out of our being. Therefore, the flesh is the living out and the expression of the old man; that is, the flesh is our experience of the old man.

From this we can clearly see that when the Bible states that our old man has been crucified with Christ, it refers to the objective fact in the past, and when it says that our flesh must be crucified, it refers to the subjective experience today. Therefore, dealing with the flesh is entirely a matter of experience.

V. DEALING WITH THE FLESH

We have said before that there are three definitions of the flesh, which represent its three aspects. In dealing with the flesh we are dealing with these three aspects. First, we need to deal with passion, lust, pride, selfishness, dishonesty, covetousness, contentiousness, jealousy, and all other corrupt elements that are in the flesh. Second, we need to deal with the fleshly man. Our very being has fallen into the flesh and is bound and controlled by the flesh; hence, our whole being has become flesh. Therefore, our whole being must be thoroughly dealt with by the cross. Third, we need to deal with the good aspect of the flesh. All our natural goodness, our strong points by virtue of our birth, man esteems to be good, but they are abominable to God; thus, they also need to be dealt with.

Therefore, whatever belongs to our being, because it is flesh, needs to be dealt with. But how do we deal with the flesh? We will discuss this in two aspects: the objective fact and the subjective experience.

A. The Objective Fact

The objective fact in dealing with the flesh is completely related to Christ. Galatians 2:20 says, "I am crucified with Christ." Again, Romans 6:6 says, "Our old man has been crucified with Him." These two passages clearly show us that when Christ was nailed to the cross, we were crucified with Him. Our fleshly being has been dealt with on the cross of Christ. This is a fact, which has been accomplished long ago in the universe. The fact that we have been crucified with

Christ is the basis of our dealing with the flesh. If we had never been crucified with Christ, none of us could deal with the flesh. Therefore, our dealing with the flesh is to bring forth in experience the fact that we have died with Christ.

Therefore, the first step in our dealing with the flesh is to ask the Lord to enlighten us so that we may obtain revelation to see the fact of our having been crucified with Christ. Romans 6:11 says, "Reckon yourselves to be dead to sin." This reckoning is a matter of seeing. When we have seen the fact that we have died with Christ, we can automatically reckon ourselves as dead.

B. The Subjective Experience

The subjective experience in dealing with the flesh is completely related to the Holy Spirit. Being dead with Christ is merely a fact that Christ has accomplished for us before God; to us it is still objective. There is the need for the Holy Spirit to work in us and execute the fact that Christ has accomplished on the cross; then the dying with Christ will become our subjective experience. A very major and basic work of the Holy Spirit dwelling in us is to work into us the fact that Christ has crucified the flesh on the cross. In other words, the work of the Holy Spirit is to have the cross on Calvary wrought into us to become the cross within us. Therefore, the subjective experience in dealing with the flesh is being executed by the Holy Spirit in us.

Romans 6 and 8 show clearly both the death that Christ accomplished and the death being executed by the Holy Spirit. After Romans 6 tells us that we have been crucified with Christ, Romans 8:13 says, "By the Spirit you put to death the practices of the body." Since chapter 6 says that we have been crucified, why then does chapter 8 speak of the putting to death? It is because the deaths mentioned in these two chapters are different. The death in chapter 6 is that which was accomplished in Christ, whereas the death in chapter 8 is that which is being executed in the Holy Spirit. Chapter 6 speaks about the objective death, and chapter 8, the subjective death; chapter 6, the fact of dying together, chapter 8, the experience of dying together; chapter 6, the death of the old man, chapter 8, the death of the flesh. The death in chapter 6 needs our faith; the death in chapter 8 requires our fellowship, that is, our living in the fellowship of the Holy Spirit. Therefore, we need both aspects of this death. Some think that since the problem of our flesh has been solved long ago by the cross, if we just believe this fact and receive this truth, we are quite all right, and we have no need to spend time for dealing. Others think that dealing with the flesh is altogether our responsibility and that we need to spend our effort daily in dealing with it point by point. Both ways of thinking stress only one aspect; thus, both are unbalanced and partial. If we wish to have a real experience in dealing with the flesh, we need both aspects.

VI. THE PROCESS OF EXPERIENCING DEALING WITH THE FLESH

Now we come to see the practical process of experiencing dealing with the flesh.

A. Desiring a Sinless Life

When a man is willing to deal with his flesh, he always begins with the first step of desiring a sinless life. The part of the flesh that is easiest to recognize is its corrupted aspect. Therefore, in dealing with the flesh, we always start with the corrupted aspect. The corrupted flesh that we are considering here has a wider and deeper scope than that of dealing with sin. Everything hidden in man that displeases God, that has nothing to do with God's heart desire, and that cannot attain to God's will is the corrupted flesh. When a man is being drawn by the Lord to pursue on, he automatically sees the filthiness and abominable traits of the corrupted flesh. He naturally desires to be delivered from it and live a holy, sinless, and victorious life.

B. Discovering the Difficulties of the Flesh

When a man so desires a sinless life and wishes to be delivered from the bondage of sin, he naturally uses his own strength to deal with the sin that he is conscious of. Moreover, he asks the Lord for strength to help him deal with the

sins. But the result is disappointing, because although he
deals with some sinful deeds, he is not able to deal with the
nature within him, which inclines toward sin. He summons
all his efforts and deals with one sin, but another ten make
their appearance. It seems that the more he deals, the stronger
the power of sin is, so that he usually experiences complete failure. In all these failures he gradually discovers that within
him is the corrupted flesh. He also knows that this corrupted
flesh is the origin of all the sins. Sins are but the expressed
corruptions; the flesh is the true root of all these corruptions.
To deal only with the sins and not with the flesh is to neglect
the cause and to deal with the consequence, the result of which
is vain labor. It is not possible to live a sinless life unless there
has been a thorough dealing with the flesh. Thus, this person
discovers that the flesh is his greatest problem.

The Bible depicts the same experience regarding our dealing
with the flesh. First, Romans 6 tells us that being baptized in
Christ, we no longer should live in sins, nor should we present
our members as weapons of unrighteousness to sin. Therefore,
we need to deal with sin and present our members as weapons
of righteousness. Then chapter 7 follows by telling us that
this person who deals with sin discovers that sin and the flesh
are inseparable. The flesh, being the body of sin, has no goodness in it. The reason that man sins is because he is fleshly.
Therefore, chapter 8, on one hand, speaks of the fact of being
set free in Christ Jesus by the law of the Spirit of life, and, on
the other hand, of dealing with the flesh. Only when the flesh
has been dealt with can we be freed from the entanglement of
sin. After one has desired the sinless life, he will gradually
discover the difficulty of the flesh, knowing that we, the man
of the old creation, are the flesh, and all our problems are of
our very being. If we do not deal with our very being, the problem of the flesh cannot be solved, and we cannot live a holy,
sinless life.

C. Seeing That Our Flesh
Has Been Crucified with Christ

When we have really seen the difficulty of the flesh in the
light of God and realize that there is absolutely no way for us

to deal with the flesh by ourselves, we are totally in despair in ourselves. The Holy Spirit will then give us a revelation concerning the deliverance of the cross as mentioned in Romans 6:6: "Our old man has been crucified with Him in order that the body of sin might be annulled, that we should no longer serve sin as slaves." The Spirit will show us that this old man of the flesh has been crucified with Christ and that our body of sin has already been done away and has lost its function; then why should we still be under its bondage? In Romans 6 it is mentioned again and again that we have died to sin, that we have been released from sin, and that sin can no longer have dominion over us; hence, we have already been freed from sin. Once we come to the light of God's Word and receive this fact through faith, this word becomes the declaration of our emancipation and the song of our triumph. We can then reckon ourselves as dead to sin but living to God in Christ Jesus. What a glorious grace!

D. Allowing the Holy Spirit to Execute the Death of Christ

After we see and receive the fact that our old man has been crucified with Christ, we should allow the Holy Spirit to execute this fact within us. Christ has accomplished the objective fact for us, but we must be responsible for the subjective experience through the Holy Spirit. All the experiences of dealing with the flesh will not be real unless they are experienced subjectively. Whoever merely believes the fact that we have died with Christ on the cross does not have the real experience of dealing with the flesh. When the Lord died on the cross, the veil was rent in two. That veil was His flesh. He had put on our flesh and was nailed to the cross. This fact was to Him a subjective experience, but to us it is an objective fact. We must let the Holy Spirit execute this within us so that it will become our practical, subjective experience.

Galatians 5:24 says, "They who are of Christ Jesus have crucified the flesh with its passions and its lusts." This passage reveals that we, those who are saved and are of Christ Jesus, are the initiators of crucifying the flesh. It does not say here that the Lord crucified our flesh but that we ourselves have crucified the flesh. From this we see that we have the responsibility to take the initiative in crucifying the flesh. Crucifying the old man is the responsibility of God, but crucifying the flesh is our responsibility.

What Galatians 5:24 speaks about, therefore, is the subjective experience that we have crucified the flesh, not the objective fact that Christ has crucified our old man, as is the concept of many. The reasons are, first, that the crucifying of the flesh mentioned here is an act of our own initiative, not what Christ has done for us. Second, what is mentioned here is crucifying the flesh, not crucifying the old man. We have said that the old man refers to the objective aspect, whereas the flesh always refers to our subjective experience. Moreover, the same verse also mentions the passions and lusts, which are matters of our practical daily living. Third, all the verses preceding and following this verse speak about the work of the Holy Spirit; thus, the crucifying of the flesh mentioned in this verse must be something that we experience through the Holy Spirit. Hence, it refers to our subjective experience. With these three points in view, we can see that this verse speaks entirely of our subjective experience.

Why then does it say here that all who are of Christ Jesus *have* crucified the flesh? Why is the crucifying of the flesh an accomplished fact? How can this correspond to the experience of many? Do not the majority of Christians still live by the flesh? The answer is that the apostle was speaking according to the normal working of the Holy Spirit. Normally, all who belong to Christ Jesus should have already crucified the flesh through the Holy Spirit. If anyone belongs to the Lord and has not crucified the flesh by the Holy Spirit, he is abnormal. Many of the saints in Galatia were in such an abnormal stage. Even though they were saved and belonged to Christ, they lived by the flesh and did not crucify the flesh by the Holy Spirit. The apostle told the Galatians that according to the normal way, all who are of Christ Jesus have crucified the flesh: "Since you, the Galatians, are of Christ, how can you still live by the flesh? Since God has already crucified your old man with Christ, you also should have crucified the flesh by the Holy Spirit. Therefore, you should not live by the flesh any longer and fulfill the lust of your flesh." This is the meaning of the apostle in Galatians 5:24.

Some people think that the "crucified...with" in this verse means crucified *with* Christ. But if we read the words of the apostle carefully, we will realize that this means the crucifying of the flesh *with* "its passions and its lusts." Here the apostle is not dealing with the objective fact that we have been crucified with Christ but with the subjective experience of crucifying the flesh through the Holy Spirit.

The main purpose of discerning the correct meaning of this verse is that we may see that in this matter of dealing with the flesh we must bear our responsibility. It is not enough that we merely believe our old man has been crucified with Christ; we must take the initiative to crucify the flesh through the Holy Spirit. The Bible never says that we must crucify the old man, because this is an accomplished fact in Christ. Nor does the Bible say that Christ has already crucified our flesh, for this is our responsibility through the Holy Spirit.

Even our experience tells us this. It may be that half a year ago we definitely realized the fact that our old man was crucified in Christ. But if we do not put the flesh to death by the Holy Spirit, then to this very day we are still living by the flesh. When we see the fact that our old man was crucified on the cross, we still need to use the cross through the Holy Spirit as the knife to slay our flesh. We need to put our flesh to death daily through the power of the Holy Spirit. Thus, we shall have the real experience of dealing with the flesh.

We have to put the flesh on the cross; but, of course, this cross is not ours. In the whole universe there is only one cross that is considered effective by God. This the cross of Christ. Therefore, our subjective dealing is based on the objective crucifixion. When we realize that our being, the old creation, the old man, has already been dealt with by the cross of Christ, and that this old man is still being lived out again in the flesh, we should let the Holy Spirit apply the cross of Christ to us step by step in our daily life. Thus, step by step we put our flesh to death through the Holy Spirit. This is the practical experience of the Holy Spirit's crucifying work within us.

Once we have seen that Christ has solved all our problems on the cross, we must immediately allow the Holy Spirit to make this fact effective in us. This effectiveness is our subjective experience.

When God commanded Saul to kill the Amalekites, God Himself would not do the killing; Saul was the one to go to execute the Amalekites. Yet the power through which Saul killed the Amalekites was not of himself but of God. When the Spirit of God descended upon Saul, He gave him the power by which he was to kill all the Amalekites. Today, in dealing with the flesh, the principle is the same. On one hand, God Himself does not deal with our flesh; we ourselves must be responsible to deal with the flesh and put it to death. On the other hand, it is absolutely through the power of God that we are able to deal with the flesh. Our dealing with the flesh is not at all like the religion of the Gentiles, which uses human effort to bring the flesh under subjection. In other words, we must bear the responsibility to deal with the flesh through the power of the Holy Spirit.

In summary, the crucifying of the "I," our "being," is an accomplishment in Christ. But the crucifying of our flesh is an accomplishment in the Holy Spirit. To put the cross upon the "I," upon the "old man," was the objective fact accomplished by the Lord Jesus at Golgotha. It is when the Holy Spirit puts this cross upon our flesh that it becomes our subjective experience. This is what Galatians 5:24 says: "Have crucified the flesh with its passions and its lusts"; what Romans 8:13 says: "By the Spirit you put to death the practices of the body"; and what Colossians 3:5 says: "Put to death therefore your members which are on the earth."

VII. THE APPLICATION OF DEALING WITH THE FLESH

After we pass through the above process, we begin to experience dealing with the flesh. Yet this kind of experience and dealing is not once for all. We need to apply this experience and dealing to our practical living continuously, allowing the Holy Spirit to execute the putting to death in us, so that in every matter we may have the experience of dealing with the flesh. This continual experience is what we mean by the application of dealing with the flesh. We can divide this topic into three points:

A. In the Fellowship of the Holy Spirit

The application of dealing with the flesh is a matter that is completely in the fellowship of the Holy Spirit. None can experience the dealing of the cross outside the fellowship of the Holy Spirit. Therefore, in order to experience and apply continuously the dealing with the flesh, the most basic requirement is to live in the fellowship, or to live in the Holy Spirit. Whenever we are not in the fellowship of the Holy Spirit, we immediately lose the reality of dealing with the flesh.

Romans 6 speaks of the fact that the old man is crucified in Christ, whereas Romans 8 speaks of dealing with the flesh in the Holy Spirit. Romans 6 speaks of the death of Christ solving our problem of sin and the resurrection of Christ solving our problem of death. Yet these are the objective facts, which can only become experience in the law of the Spirit of life of Romans 8. Therefore, we have said emphatically that the fact in Romans 6 can never be our experience unless it is placed together with the Holy Spirit of chapter 8. It is very possible that someone may clearly realize the fact mentioned in chapter 6 and also accept it by faith; yet if he does not live in the fellowship of the Holy Spirit of chapter 8, this fact cannot become his experience. On the other hand, there have been many saints throughout the generations who have neither known the truth in chapter 6 adequately nor seen it clearly, yet they have remained living in the fellowship of chapter 8; as a result, they have spontaneously experienced release from the flesh. Therefore, the fellowship of Romans 8 is absolutely necessary in the application of dealing with the flesh.

When we have fellowship with the indwelling Holy Spirit and allow Him to move freely in our fellowship, then we touch the life of the Lord in the Holy Spirit. One of the elements of this life, the death of the cross, or the element of death, will then be applied to us in a practical way. The more the Holy Spirit moves in us, the more the element of the Lord's death will accomplish a killing work in us. This killing is the applying of the cross, or the application of dealing with the flesh. Therefore, if we wish to apply dealing with the flesh, we need to live continuously in the fellowship of the Holy Spirit.

B. Allowing the Holy Spirit to Execute the Death of Christ upon All Our Actions

When we are in the fellowship of the Holy Spirit, allowing Him to execute the death of Christ in us, His activity is limited in the beginning to a few actions of ours and occurs only occasionally. It is not until our experience gradually grows deeper that this death will be executed generally upon all our actions. In the early stage, we have dealings only when we discover our fleshly actions. Later, we allow the Holy Spirit to purify all our actions, whether good or bad, by executing the death of the cross in us. Consequently, all that we are in the natural constitution, the old creation, the self, will be solved by the cross. What remains should be of God and the substance of His life.

Take for example the matter of visiting the saints, offering a gift, and other such things that we think are good and spiritual. Even in these matters, we need first to allow the Holy Spirit to execute the death of Christ. Thus, we can be clear whether we should do any visiting or give an offering. The flesh of man fears the cross more than anything, for once it meets the cross, it is through. Yet God and His life in us become more living by contact with the cross. The cross of Christ is the dividing line between the old and the new creations. If we have never passed through the cross of Christ, we cannot discern the new creation from the old, the Holy Spirit from the flesh, or the resurrection life from the natural. The two are always confused one with the other and are difficult to differentiate, especially with regard to good and so-called spiritual things. Yet once we pass through the death of the cross, the new and the old are separated. All that falls and is finished is of the old creation, of the flesh, and of the natural constitution. All that can stand and remain is of the new creation, of the Holy Spirit, and of the resurrection life. Thus, the cross is the best filter. It retains the flesh and all that pertains to it, whereas it releases God and all that is of God.

If we continually apply the experience of the cross and allow the Holy Spirit to execute the death of the cross upon every aspect of our living and action, the flesh will be dealt with in a most effective manner and thus become atrophied. If we live continually under the shadow of the cross, the flesh will have no way to raise its head. Only thus can we be in the church without causing any trouble and be knit together with the brothers and sisters as one Body for the best service to the Lord.

Praise the Lord, in the past years we have served the Lord with many co-workers, yet among us there has been no quarrel or division. Apparently, it is because we all sought the Lord and loved the Lord with one heart and were all for the Lord. But the deeper reason is that we all have to some extent learned the lesson of dealing with the flesh by the cross. The cross within us kills all the strife and jealousy of the flesh, to the end that we cannot quarrel or be divisive.

C. Walking according to the Law of the Spirit of Life

If we apply dealing with the flesh to all our actions, we will eventually walk according to the law of the Spirit of life. Romans 8 shows us that the overcoming of the flesh is the result of obeying the Holy Spirit. The moving of the Holy Spirit within us is a law, the law of the Spirit of life. In other words, when we are in fellowship and apply, through the power of the Holy Spirit, the death of the cross to every part of our living, this application is the obeying of the law of the Holy Spirit in us and also the allowing of the Holy Spirit to move spontaneously in us. Therefore, our dealing with the flesh and putting it to death through the Holy Spirit have a positive relationship with the spontaneous law of the Holy Spirit within us. One who really experiences dealing with the flesh is one who allows the Holy Spirit to move within him and also one who allows the law of the Spirit of life to operate in him.

When we absolutely obey the law of the Spirit of life, we

do not set our mind on the flesh but on the Spirit. At all times we put to death the deeds of the body and leave no room for the flesh. Not only will we not sin or err according to the flesh, but we will not even touch spiritual things or serve God in the flesh. Only then will we have thoroughly dealt with our flesh in a practical way; only then will we be completely released from the flesh and live in the Holy Spirit.

VIII. SUMMARY

The first point in dealing with the flesh is that we must know what the flesh is and sense the flesh within us. In spiritual experience, all dealings are based on our knowledge and sense regarding that very matter. The degree to which we have attained in our knowledge will be the degree to which we have dealings. The thoroughness and depth of our dealing is according to our knowledge and sense in this matter. Therefore, if we wish to have a real experience in dealing with the flesh, we need to have a clear knowledge and sense of the flesh.

The meaning of the flesh has three aspects, namely: the corrupted flesh, the whole fallen man, and the aspect of man's good. It is easier for us to discern the flesh as the corrupted body, that is the corrupted aspect of the flesh; therefore, the first stage in our dealing with the flesh is more in this aspect. But as we go on with the Lord, we need to have a deeper knowledge and dealing concerning the other two aspects of the flesh. Not only should we know that sinning, losing our temper, and doing other evil things are of the flesh, but we should also realize that even the matter of worshipping and serving God, plus the matter of godliness, can also be full of the flesh. Plainly, whatever we do must be the outcome of our touching the Lord and the Spirit while in fellowship, and we must do it by trusting in God; otherwise, no matter how good it is, we must still condemn it as something of the flesh.

The second point in dealing with the flesh is that we must know the position of the flesh before God. We must receive light from the Bible to see how the flesh resists God and is in enmity toward God. We also need to see how the nature of the flesh is incompatible with God, how God rejects it and considers it abominable, and how He has determined to exterminate it and have no coexistence with it. This revelation will cause us to see as God sees, condemn what God condemns, and annihilate what God annihilates. Then we will seek release from the flesh, cooperate with God, and let the Holy Spirit put our flesh to death.

The third point in dealing with the flesh is that we must know the relationship and difference between the flesh and the old man. We should see that the old man, or our old I, is the real being of the flesh, and that the flesh is the expression of the old man or the old I. When the old man, or our old I, is being lived out in our experience, it is the flesh. Therefore, dealing with the flesh is entirely a matter of experience—that of dealing with the old man in a practical way.

The fourth point in dealing with the flesh is that we must know the dealing itself. The dealing consists of two aspects: the objective fact and the subjective experience. Both aspects are equally needed; neither one should be neglected. The aspect of the objective fact is what God has accomplished for us in Christ, whereas the subjective experience requires our cooperation with God in the Holy Spirit.

After we realize these four basic points in dealing with the flesh, we will have the experience of dealing with the flesh. The procedure of our experience in dealing with the flesh begins with a deeper longing and seeking for spiritual things. Once we love the Lord and pursue after Him, we naturally long that we may have a deeper life in the Lord and that the Lord would live in us in a deeper way. But in practice, our desire often is frustrated, and we fail. What we desire, we cannot do, but what we do not desire, we do. The result of our repeated failures is that we are brought to the place of total misery and despair. Although we often seek the Lord's deliverance, we cannot find the way of deliverance. At this time, the Holy Spirit gradually reveals that the reason for failure is that we live in the flesh. The thing that hinders us most from a deeper mingling with the Lord and hinders the Lord from living more deeply in us is our flesh. At the same time, the Holy Spirit shows us how filthy, corrupt, evil, and wicked our flesh is. Not to mention the evil aspect of our flesh, even what we ordinarily consider as good is also full of the element of man and the self. Our flesh, the good as well as the evil, is condemned by God and unacceptable to Him. When we have seen this, we will naturally, in the light of the Holy Spirit, hate our flesh. At this time the Holy Spirit will impress us with the fact of our being crucified with Christ. This impression, as vivid as picture taking, causes us to see that our flesh, our old I, or our old man, has already been nullified on the cross of our Lord Jesus. The entrance of this light immediately produces a killing effect that causes our old man, or our old I, to become gradually paralyzed and withered, eventually losing its position and power. Then all the fleshly elements in our practical living will automatically be exterminated. The more we allow the light of the Holy Spirit to shine within us, the more the old I, or old man, loses its position, and all the fleshly elements in our living gradually diminish and disappear. At this time we will have a little subjective experience in the matter of dealing with the flesh through the death of the cross.

However, our dealing with the flesh must not stop here. In our fellowship with the Lord and through the Holy Spirit who dwells within us and causes us to partake of the death of the Lord, we must apply the putting to death of our flesh and its expressions time after time and step after step. This is our application of the death of the cross through the Holy Spirit. This is also what Galatians 5:24-25 speaks about: the subjective experience of crucifying the flesh with its passions and its lusts through the Holy Spirit. Because we give Him the opportunity, the ground, and our cooperation, the Holy Spirit within us will enable us to put our flesh to death so that we may live the life God wants us to live and do what God wants us to do. At this time, we will not only live by the Spirit but also walk by the Spirit; then we will no longer be fleshly but spiritual.

We should always examine ourselves regarding the process of dealing with the flesh. Do we really see the objective fact? Do we ever let the Holy Spirit impress this fact into us? How much subjective experience do we have? How often do we apply the death of the cross in our practical living? After we strictly examine ourselves, we can be clear regarding the degree to

which we have attained in our experience and look to the Lord
for His further leading.

The process of dealing with the flesh that we have mentioned cannot be thoroughly experienced in a short period of
time. We need to go deeper, step by step. Many items of the
flesh are not recognized in the beginning; therefore, we have
no way to deal with them. It is not until our spiritual experience grows deeper that we gradually recognize our flesh and
have further dealings. Therefore, in our dealing with the
flesh, we deal first with the corrupted aspect and then with
the good aspect of the flesh. Finally, we put our whole being
under the death of Christ and deal completely with the flesh.

With regard to the experience of dealing with the flesh,
there is more dealing with the corrupted aspect of the flesh
among the brothers and sisters, but too little with the good
aspect of the flesh. We all have a natural concept concerning
the flesh; naturally, we only know the corrupted flesh. Therefore, our dealing with the flesh tends to be focused on this
aspect. For example, a brother may testify that sometimes
when giving a message he feels that he does fairly well and
also senses the presence of the Lord; therefore, he is quite
elated. Then he condemns the elated feeling as flesh, because
there is the element of pride. This condemnation is right and
necessary, but actually this kind of dealing is not of primary
importance. The important thing is this: when you deliver a
message, are you the one speaking, or is the Holy Spirit
speaking through you? This is what we should judge. It is not
a matter of whether the speaking is successful but rather of
who is speaking. Perhaps you have spoken quite well, and
many people were helped by you, but if you spoke in yourself,
according to what you knew and memorized, that is flesh and
must be condemned.

A certain brother may testify that he lost his temper while
he was with a brother. Later, he was sorry because he felt
that he was in the flesh; thus, he dealt with the matter and
condemned it. This is also a very shallow dealing. If we have
learned the deeper lesson of the experience of dealing with
the flesh, we will feel that even though we did not lose our
temper but, on the contrary, were good to others, helped them,

and even prayed with them, yet, if these things were not done in the Holy Spirit, it was but some good deeds of ourselves. Later, we will still feel that we are in the flesh. If we deal with our flesh to such an extent, then we really have a thorough dealing with the flesh.

Actually, if our dealing with the flesh is only limited to the corrupted aspect, then it differs little from dealing with sin, because there is not much of the real substance of dealing with the flesh in it. If we really want to deal with the flesh, we need to pay attention to dealing with the good aspect of the flesh and even the whole fleshly being. Not only in ordinary, small matters do we need to have dealings, but also in pious, spiritual things and matters pertaining to the worship of God, we need to ask: Am I doing this in myself, or am I doing it by abiding in the Lord? Am I doing this according to my own wishes, or am I being led by the Holy Spirit? Unless I abide in the Lord and have fellowship with Him, all that I have done, however good it may be, is still fleshly and should be condemned.

Not only should we deal with the "doing" of the flesh but also with the "not doing" of the flesh. Some brothers and sisters have some knowledge concerning the flesh, and the Holy Spirit shows them how much of their service, such as visiting and sharing, is done according to their own natural self, not through the fellowship of the Holy Spirit. Therefore, they decide that from now on they will never serve, visit, or share. But if this inactivity is not derived from fellowship with the Holy Spirit, but rather from their own decision, it is a worse kind of flesh. Some brothers and sisters have been enlightened to see that their former prayers were of the flesh; therefore, they do not pray anymore. Yet they do not know that their not praying expresses the flesh even more. Therefore, our "not doing" is never a way of release from the flesh. On the contrary, many who have been released from the flesh are those who are most capable in doing. The Bible reveals that God is a working God, a God who has been continually working until now. For several thousand years He has been speaking and working and has never ceased His work among humanity. Likewise, all those who live in the Holy Spirit can never stop

working, for the Holy Spirit is their motivating power, causing them to work even more. Therefore, we should not think
for a moment that inactivity is not of the flesh but of the
Spirit. All those who are inactive are even more of the flesh.
The flesh is nothing more than making your own decision
and having your own opinion; it is simply being what you
are and doing what you want. Therefore, dealing with the
flesh means that I recognize I have been crucified on the cross;
today it is not I who decide whether I should minister or pray,
but the Lord who decides for me. What He does, I do; what He
does not do, neither do I. When we have really dealt with the
flesh, we will not decide anything according to ourselves,
either to do or not to do. We should always live in fellowship
and abide in the Lord, always have a heart that puts no trust
in ourselves, but ever have a spirit that relies upon the Holy
Spirit. A relying spirit and a trusting attitude are marks of
our flesh being dealt with.

Again, let us use the illustration of the ministry of the
word. Many times when a brother speaks, he has full confi-
dence, knowing what he should say and how to say it.
Therefore, he has everything well prepared and has laid the
Lord aside. It seems that if there were not a Lord in the universe, he could still deliver the message successfully. This
situation proves that his message is being delivered in the
flesh. This is not so with one whose flesh has been dealt with.
Although he also prepares himself to deliver the message, he
has learned the lesson of rejecting the flesh and depending
upon the Spirit. It may be that originally he prepared to
speak about justification, but when he stands to speak, the
Holy Spirit suddenly moves him to speak about sanctification; thus, he will change his subject without hesitation. Or it
may be that before he speaks, the Lord has not shown him the
subject on which he should minister. On the Lord's Day, the
meeting starts at ten o'clock. At 9:50 he still does not know
what he will talk about. It may be that after the singing and
the prayer, he still does not know what to say; yet at this
point he still does not decide by himself. He looks to the leading of the Lord in his deepest being. It is not until he stands
and opens the Bible, saying, "May we read..." that he knows

which scripture to read and the subject upon which to minister. Sometimes in the beginning he still is uncertain of the point, but while speaking he tries to contact the Lord inwardly until he finally touches the source. It is similar to hitting a fountain when digging a well. Since he touches the stream of living water, words simply flow out of him. This kind of ministry is the condition of all those who have their flesh dealt with.

The life of the Lord on this earth shows that He is One who put His trust entirely in God. Our Lord has no sin nor fault, yet He said, "I can do nothing from Myself" (John 5:30). When He was on this earth, He neither acted nor spoke from Himself. He was in the Father, and the Father in Him. He did all things and spoke all things through fellowship with the Father. This is the example for our dealing with the flesh. We must abide in the Lord and act as the Lord works within us; we must also speak as the Lord speaks within us. It is only in this way that we will not be in the flesh.

Romans 8 speaks of dealing with the flesh as well as walking according to the Spirit or minding the Spirit. These two always go together. Whenever we do not walk according to the Spirit, mind the Spirit, or live in the Spirit, we are in the flesh. When we deal with the flesh, we do not stress dealing with jealousy, selfishness, or pride of the flesh, but with our works and activities, behavior, and manner of living that are outside the Holy Spirit. Inasmuch as what we do is outside the Holy Spirit and has nothing to do with the Holy Spirit, whatever we do is the flesh, and whatever we do not do is also the flesh. Therefore, there is no other way, no other method, of release from the flesh but the Holy Spirit. It is only by walking according to the Spirit, minding the Spirit, and living in the Spirit that we are released from the flesh. Therefore, the outcome of our dealing with the flesh is that we live in the law of the Spirit of life, depending on the Holy Spirit in all matters, never upon ourselves. It is not until this point is reached that we experience dealing with the flesh in its fullest measure. May the Lord be gracious to us.

CHAPTER TEN

DEALING WITH THE SELF

Now we come to see the matter of dealing with the self. This experience is very closely related to dealing with the flesh. This is an important experience in the stage of the cross.

If we desire to deal with the self, we need first to define what the self is. There are many spiritual terms that we use quite often, but when we press for the real meaning, it is difficult to explain them. So it is with the self. We often hear people speak about the self, but few can define it. What, really, is the self? Simply, the self is the soul-life with the emphasis on human thoughts and human opinions. We can discover this from the Bible, where the self is clearly mentioned.

Let us first read Matthew 16:21-25: "From that time Jesus began to show to His disciples that He must go to Jerusalem and suffer many things from the elders and chief priests and scribes and be killed and on the third day be raised. And Peter took Him aside and began to rebuke Him, saying, God be merciful to You, Lord! This shall by no means happen to You! But He turned and said to Peter, Get behind Me, Satan! You are a stumbling block to Me, for you are not setting your mind on the things of God, but on the things of men. Then Jesus said to His disciples, If anyone wants to come after Me, let him deny himself and take up his cross and follow Me. For whoever wants to save his soul-life shall lose it; but whoever loses his soul-life for My sake shall find it."

In this passage the Lord showed His disciples in verse 21 how He must suffer, be killed, and raised up again. All that the Lord said here is the will of God, because the cross of the Lord is the will of God ordained in eternity. But in verse 22 Peter had an opinion, and he voiced it to the Lord: "God be

merciful to You, Lord!" Therefore, the Lord in verse 23 rebuked
Peter, saying that he was not setting his mind on the things of
God but on the things of men. The things of God are the will
of God, or the cross. The things of men are to pity yourself and
to not receive the cross. What the Lord desired was the will of
God, but what Peter cared about was the human thought.
Therefore, in verse 24 the Lord asked the disciples to deny
themselves, take up the cross, and follow Him. When we compare this word with the preceding verse, we comprehend that
this self that the Lord asked us to deny is the human thought.
The Lord asked the disciples to deny and forsake the self,
which meant to lay aside their own thought. When the Lord
asked the disciples to receive the cross, this meant that they
should receive the mind of God or the will of God. Therefore,
the Lord was asking the disciples here to put aside their own
thought and receive the cross, which is the will of God.

From this we see that the self has much to do with human
thought. Yet the self is not human thought, and human thought
is not the self per se. Therefore, in verse 25 the Lord went on
to say that whoever wants to save his soul-life shall lose it,
and whoever loses his soul-life for the Lord's sake shall find
it. The denying of the self mentioned in the preceding verse
was followed immediately by the losing of the soul-life. This
indicates that the self that was mentioned is the soul-life
spoken of directly following. The soul-life is the self.

In this passage the word of the Lord follows step by step.
In verse 22 Peter admonished the Lord to pity Himself; in
verse 23 the Lord pointed out that this is human thought or
human opinion; in verse 24 the Lord traced this to the root by
saying that this opinion is the self. Therefore, we need to forsake and deny it. Then in verse 25 the Lord touched the root
of the self by showing that the very self is the soul-life. If the
soul-life is being put to death, which means that the self is
being denied, there will be no more human opinion. In this passage, verse 23 speaks about the opinion, verse 24 about the
self, and verse 25 about the soul-life. Each verse mentions one
matter, step by step, very clearly.

Therefore, we can find here a definition for the self: the
self in essence is the soul-life, whereas the expression of the

self is opinion. Self, soul-life, and opinion are three aspects of one thing. This may be likened to Christ Himself as the very God, and the expression of Christ as the Holy Spirit. The three are one. God incarnated and expressed is Christ, and the soul-life expressed is the self. When Christ is expressed before men and touched by men, He is the Holy Spirit. Likewise, the self is expressed before men and touched by men in the form of human opinion and human viewpoint. Just as when we touch the Holy Spirit, we touch Christ, so when we touch human opinion and viewpoint, we touch the self as well as the soul-life.

Let us read John 5:30: "I can do nothing from Myself; as I hear, I judge...I do not seek My own will but the will of Him who sent Me."

From this verse we learn that it is the same with the Lord Jesus as it is with us in the self being expressed in the form of opinion. First, the Lord said here that He can do nothing from Himself; then He said that He does not seek His own will. From this we see that "Myself" and "My own will" are identical. His doing nothing from Himself means that He does not seek His own will. Hence, it is clear that the self is focused in the idea and opinion. The self is expressed in opinion, and opinion is the expression of the self. For example, if in a certain fellowship meeting concerning service, a certain brother continually expresses his ideas and opinions, we cannot say that that is sin, the world, or the flesh. But we will surely say that that is the self, because the self expresses itself in opinions. A person who is full of ideas and opinions is full of the self and the expression of the self as well.

Now let us read Job 38:1-2: "Then Jehovah answered Job out of the whirlwind and said, Who is this who darkens counsel / By words without knowledge?"

Job 3 through 37 is a record of human words and opinions. In these thirty-five long chapters Job and his three friends, and later Elihu, were talking, arguing, and expressing their opinions continually. Therefore, soon after they had completely expressed themselves, God came forth and rebuked them, saying, "Who is this who darkens counsel / By words without knowledge?" After Job was enlightened by God, he said in

42:3-6, "Who is this who hides counsel without knowledge? /
...I had heard of You by the hearing of the ear, / But now my
eye has seen You; / Therefore I abhor myself, and I repent / In
dust and ashes." At first Job spoke words without knowledge
and expressed his own opinion, but at the end he abhorred
himself and repented in dust and ashes. From this we see that
Job's opinion was his self, which he abhorred. His opinion was
the expression of his self.

In the whole Bible, the person who spoke the most was
Job. God afflicted him with circumstances and also arranged
that he be surrounded by his four friends. In this way all the
words within him were drawn out. He had his own opinions,
his own ideas, and he did not yield to others' viewpoints. He
felt that he had done no wrong and that there was no need for
him to deal with sin, the world, or the conscience. Therefore,
he beat his chest, desiring to reason with the righteous One.
Indeed, the difficulty with Job was not sin, the world, or the
conscience. His difficulty was his self. His unbroken self was
a problem that prevented him from knowing God.

Many in the church are like Job; they have much to say.
Actually, a sinning one, or one who loves the world, does not
speak much, because he is aware of his mistakes and shortcomings. The conscience of all those who do wrong is defiled,
and they cannot lift up their head. Therefore, they do not
speak much and are easier to be helped and led. But those
who are of Job's type seemingly have no touch of sin, nor do
they love the world; yet they are extremely self-righteous and
always think they are right. Concerning the church and the
things of God they have many opinions and ideas. Thus, all
day long they talk about this and that and even speak of
things they do not know. This kind of people is the most difficult to be helped and led; they cause others to feel incapable
of helping them.

A person who is full of the self always brings many difficulties into the church. The reason for so many divisions in
Christianity today is not only the sinfulness and worldliness
of man but more so the self of man. Many people serve the
Lord by helping brothers and sisters, yet in reality they want
others to follow their ideas and opinions, their viewpoints

and methods. The result is many divisions in the church today. Martin Luther said that within him there was a greater pope than the one in Rome—himself. In the church, if the self is not broken, every person is a pope, and everyone will become a division.

Besides Job in the Bible, Peter is also a model example of one who was full of the self. Peter's self was expressed to the uttermost because he was the most talkative one and had the most opinions. On many occasions in the Gospels Peter spoke and expressed his opinions. There was not one subject concerning which he did not have an opinion or idea. Therefore, each time the Lord dealt with him, He dealt with his opinion and idea. The teaching of denying the self in Matthew 16 was spoken because of Peter. On the night of His betrayal, the Lord Jesus said to His disciples, "You will all be stumbled because of Me this night, for it is written, 'I will smite the Shepherd, and the sheep of the flock will be scattered'" (26:31). When Peter heard this, his self was immediately drawn out, and he said, "If all will be stumbled because of You, I will never be stumbled" (v. 33). The result was that he denied the Lord three times and failed greatly (vv. 69-75). This was a real breaking and dealing for Peter. But even after such a dealing, while the disciples were gathered together after the Lord's resurrection, it was again he who made a suggestion; he said, "I am going fishing" (John 21:3). He was really one who girded himself and walked where he wished (21:18).

In the New Testament there is still another who represents the self. It is Martha. Each time she is mentioned in the Gospels, she is always talking and giving her opinion. John 11 most clearly depicts her characteristics—many words and many opinions. We read there that her brother Lazarus died, and after four days the Lord Jesus came. When she saw the Lord, she blamed Him, saying, "If You had been here, my brother would not have died" (v. 21). This was her opinion. Then the Lord said, "Your brother will rise again" (v. 23). Martha said to Him immediately, "I know that he will rise again in the resurrection in the last day" (v. 24) This again was her explanation according to her own opinion of the words of the Lord. The Lord replied, "I am the resurrection and the life; he who believes into Me, even if he should die, shall live; and everyone who lives and believes into Me shall by no means die forever. Do you believe this?" (vv. 25-26). She answered and said, "I have believed that You are the Christ, the Son of God" (v. 27). What she answered was not what the Lord had asked; her comprehension of what the Lord had said was really remote. After saying this, she did not care whether the Lord had finished speaking with her; she returned home and called her sister Mary secretly, saying, "The Teacher is here and is calling you" (v. 28). This she fabricated on her own and made the decision for the Lord. Now when they had come to the tomb, and Jesus requested that the stone be removed, Martha again offered her opinion, saying, "Lord, by now he smells, for it is the fourth day that he is there" (v. 39). This story reveals Martha's opinion and viewpoint. She had so many opinions, which indicates that her self was very strong.

From these narratives relating to the people mentioned, we can clearly see that the expression of the self is in the human thoughts and opinions. Therefore, a person who is full of ideas and opinions is one who is full of the self.

I. THE DIFFERENTIATION OF SEVEN ITEMS

Now that we have clearly seen the definition of the self, we need to see the differences in seven related items: the old man, "I," the soul-life, the flesh, the temper, the self, and the natural constitution. If we wish to pursue the experience of the cross, we should know the definition and differentiation of these seven items very clearly, because these are the objects of the dealing of the cross.

Let us first give a simple definition to each of these seven items:

The *old man* refers to our very being, the created and fallen man.

"*I*" is the title by which the old man calls himself. The old man is the "I," and the "I" is the old man.

The *soul-life* is the life of the old man. The life that the old man possesses is the soul-life.

These three—the old man, "I," and the soul-life—are one

and the same. The old man is the man of the old creation that is in Adam, the soul-life is the life of this old man, and "I" is the title by which the old man calls himself.

The *flesh* is the living out of the old man, or the living of the old man. Before our soul-life is lived out, it is simply the old man, but once it is lived out, it is the flesh.

The *temper* is man's natural disposition, especially referring to the bad temperament.

The *self,* as we have seen, is the soul-life as expressed in the human idea and opinion.

The *natural constitution* is our natural ability, capability, and wit.

If we join these seven items together, we may state the following: There is a created, fallen man whose name is the *old man.* He calls himself "*I*." The life within him is the *soul-life,* which when being lived out is the *flesh.* In this flesh there is a part which is bad, the irritability and anger of which is called the *temper.* In the flesh there is also a good part, the opinion and idea of which is called the *self,* and the ability and capability of which is called the *natural constitution.*

These seven items are the objects of the dealing of the cross. Yet these dealings differ. In the whole Bible we find no reference saying that the Lord has put our soul-life, flesh, temper, the self, or the natural constitution on the cross.* We can only find that our old man has been crucified with the Lord on the cross (Rom. 6:6). What the Lord has crucified and put to an end on the cross is our old man. This is a fact which the Lord has accomplished. When we see this fact and acknowledge that the Lord has done away with the old man on the cross, then we can say, "I am crucified with Christ" (Gal. 2:20; 6:14). These two references acknowledge what the Lord has done for us. After this acknowledgement, we need to experience the cross in dealing with these last five items: our soul-life, our flesh, our temper, our self, and our natural constitution.

*Note: In Galatians 5:24, *they...have crucified the flesh* refers to our applying the cross through the Holy Spirit, not the Lord doing it for us. We have thoroughly discussed this matter in the previous chapter, "Dealing with the Flesh."

Therefore, the whole experience of the cross lies in the following three steps: first, the crucifying of our old man, which is an objective fact accomplished by Christ; second, when we acknowledge and receive this fact, it becomes "I am crucified with Christ"; third, when we go on to experience this fact subjectively, there are five different points, which are due to the five different aspects of the old man. First, the old man has a soul-life, which when being lived out is expressed in the flesh, temper, the self, and the natural constitution. As we apply in our experience the crucifixion with Christ through the Holy Spirit to our soul-life, that is dealing with the soul-life. Second, when we apply the death of the cross to whatever is lived out from our soul-life, whether it be good or bad, that is dealing with the flesh. Third, dealing with the flesh includes also dealing with the temper. Fourth, when we apply the death of the cross to our opinions and ideas, that is dealing with the self, or bearing the cross. Fifth, when we apply the death of the cross to our maneuvering, capability, ability, methods, wisdom, and knowledge, that is dealing with the natural constitution, or the breaking of the cross.

II. DEALING WITH THE SELF

How is the self dealt with? In other words, how should we deal with the self? We have already mentioned that the Bible only says that our old man has been crucified with Christ. The Bible never says specifically that our self has been crucified with the Lord. In spite of this, the way to deal with the self is still the cross, just as the way to deal with the flesh is the cross. In considering this matter, we will divide it into the objective fact and the subjective experience.

A. The Objective Fact

The objective fact in dealing with the self, just as in dealing with the flesh, rests in Christ; that is, our old man has been crucified with Him. This is because the self is part of the expression of the old man. With God, the problem of the old man has already been solved; thus, the self, which is of the old man, has also been solved. Therefore, on the objective side, the only fact is that our old man has been crucified; but on the subjective side, there is more to it. It is like having a chicken dinner: what we have killed is a chicken, but when it is being served on the table, there are many different parts, such as the breast, the legs, and the wings. Similarly, when the Lord was crucified, He solved the problem of our old man, but since the old man has various facets, there are likewise various aspects of dealings in our experience. One aspect is the dealing with the soul-life; other aspects are the dealings with the flesh, temper, and the self and the breaking of the natural constitution. These are our experience of the cross.

B. The Subjective Experience

The subjective experience in dealing with the self, just as in dealing with the flesh, is through the Holy Spirit. If we have seen the fact that our old man has been crucified, then in our daily living, whenever we discover the expressing of our own ideas or opinions, we must let the Holy Spirit work the death of the cross upon these ideas and opinions to put them to death. This is our subjective experience in dealing with the self.

III. THE PROCESS OF DEALING WITH THE SELF

A. Seeing That the Old Man Has Been Crucified

The process in dealing with the self is quite similar to that of dealing with the flesh. The first requirement is to see the fact that our old man has been crucified. This means that we must receive revelation from God so that we may see that our old man has been crucified with Christ.

B. Seeing That Our Opinions Are One of the Expressions of the Old Man

The second requirement is to see that one aspect of the expression of the old man is our opinions. The old man expresses itself not only in the flesh but also in the opinions, which are the self. If one only sees that the old man has been crucified and yet does not recognize the manners or ways in which the old man is being expressed, he cannot have the

subjective experience. Therefore, the first step in our dealing
with the self subjectively is to see that our opinions are one of
the expressions of the old man.

C. Applying the Crucifixion of Christ to Our Opinions

Once we know that our old man has been crucified and
done away with in Christ, and once we realize that opinions
and ideas are the expression of the old man, we naturally will
not allow the old man to express itself again in opinions.
Therefore, we will apply the crucifixion of Christ through the
Holy Spirit to our opinions. This is our subjective experience
in dealing with the self. This is also what the Lord refers to in
Matthew 16 as the denying of the self and the bearing of the
cross.

Today, in fallen Christianity, many truths have been mis-
understood. The truth of bearing the cross is a case in point.
Many people misinterpret the bearing of the cross as suffering. This is a wrong concept, a concept which we have
inherited from Roman Catholicism. We should realize that
the emphasis of the cross is not suffering but death. When a
person goes to the cross, the main thing is to go there not to
suffer but to die. When we mention execution by shooting
today, we understand that that means death. Likewise, in the
time of the Lord Jesus, whenever the cross was mentioned,
man's understanding of it was death. Therefore, the cross is
not only a painful punishment but also a deathly punishment. The cross does not cause man merely to suffer; the
cross puts man to death. Likewise, the bearing of the cross
is not a matter of suffering but of being put to death, not of
standing on the ground of suffering but of standing in the
place of death. To bear the cross is not to bear suffering but to
bear death, not to put ourselves under suffering but to put
ourselves under death. There is quite a difference between
the two meanings.

Thus, the bearing of the cross is nothing else but a declaration that in this universe the death of the cross is accomplished
by Christ. When the Word of God through the Holy Spirit
reveals the cross to us, we receive it by faith, thereby applying

the death of the cross to us and not departing from it. This is called the bearing of the cross. In other words, to bear the cross means to bear the death of Christ on us and allow the death of Christ to work on us continually in order to put our self to death.

The bearing of the cross differs from the crucifixion. The accomplished fact of Christ on the cross is called the crucifixion, whereas our daily experience of the cross is called the bearing of the cross. Hence, the crucifixion was accomplished by the Lord, and the bearing of the cross is our responsibility in experiencing it. The crucifixion on Calvary has been accomplished by the Lord once for all, and when we receive what the Lord has accomplished on the cross, we receive it once for all. But when we go on to experience this cross, we bear it continuously. Not only do we bear it daily and at all times, but we also bear it everywhere and in all places.

The Lord Jesus first bore the cross, and then He was crucified. But we are first crucified, and then we bear the cross. The Lord bore the cross all His life. There was an invisible cross that was laid upon Him. The cross was upon Him in His living and in His work. Then He bore the visible cross on the way to Golgotha (John 19:17), until finally He was nailed to this cross. The Lord not only bore the cross and endured the suffering, but He also endured death. Although He took only the form of a sinful body, without the reality of the flesh, and although He Himself is holy, yet He received the death of the cross unto Himself and allowed it to put Him to death. Finally, in His death at Golgotha, He put His whole being to death. Therefore, for the Lord it was first the bearing and then the crucifying.

After the bearing of the cross and the crucifixion, He was resurrected. From that time forth, with respect to Himself, He was delivered from the cross; but within His life, which passed through the cross, there is the very element of the death of the cross. Therefore, when after the resurrection He came into us as the Spirit, He automatically brought with Him the fact of the crucifixion and the element of the death of the cross that we may share His crucifixion.

All this has been done by the Lord for us, but on our part

we need the Holy Spirit to open our eyes so that we may see not only that the cross of Christ has put the Lord to death, but that at the same time our old man has been crucified and finished there. We actually have died with Christ. Once we receive this fact, the Holy Spirit will further reveal to us that our opinions and ideas are the expression of the old man. Since the Lord has crucified our old man, why then do I let the old man express himself in such a way? Hence, we will apply the death of the cross to us. Whenever we discover that we are about to voice our opinion and idea, we will immediately deny it and put it under the death of the cross. This is the bearing of the cross. Therefore, with us the crucifying is first, and then the bearing.

Though we present this matter of bearing the cross and dealing with the self in a simple way, I believe it is very clear to us. More than ten years ago, when we sought the Lord, we were not clear concerning the meaning of the cross, the bearing of the cross, and dealing with the self. At that time we were really groping. We worship the Lord that in these years the Lord has had mercy upon His church and has continuously shown us His light so that we may point out in detail these spiritual matters. Therefore, the Lord's children today, provided they have a seeking heart, will find it much easier to know and experience all these lessons.

IV. APPLYING THE EXPERIENCE
OF DEALING WITH THE SELF

A. In the Fellowship of the Holy Spirit

The applying of the experience of dealing with the self is first in the fellowship in the Holy Spirit. We may understand the crucifying of the old man and know that our opinions are the expression of the self, but if we do not live in the fellowship of the Holy Spirit, it is but an empty doctrine and does not afford any practical experience. If we do not live in the fellowship of the Holy Spirit and yet try to deal with the self, such exercise is exactly like the strenuous efforts practiced by the Buddhists, Hindus, and Chinese moralists; it is not a spiritual experience. Only the Holy Spirit is the Spirit of truth, the Spirit of reality; therefore, only as we live in the fellowship of the Holy Spirit is our seeing the real seeing and our experience the real experience. Therefore, if we desire to live continuously in the experience of dealing with the self, the basic requirement is to live in the fellowship of the Holy Spirit.

B. Letting the Holy Spirit Execute the Crucifixion of Christ upon Us

If we live in the fellowship of the Holy Spirit and touch the Holy Spirit, then we must allow the Holy Spirit to execute the crucifixion of Christ upon all our living and actions. This allowing is our cooperation with the Holy Spirit. When we allow the Holy Spirit to perform His work in us, it means that we are cooperating with Him. In this way it is on one hand that we apply the crucifixion of Christ through the Holy Spirit, and on the other hand that we let the Holy Spirit execute Christ's crucifixion in us. On one hand, it is our doing, and on the other hand, it is the working of the Holy Spirit—it is impossible to separate one from the other in the fellowship of the Holy Spirit. At this time we are living in Romans 8, in the law of the Spirit of life; we are putting to death all the expressions of the old man through the Holy Spirit.

If one who loves God has a pliable will, and he is willing to cooperate with the Holy Spirit, the Holy Spirit will bring him deeper and deeper into the cross and put his self thoroughly to death.

V. THE RELATIONSHIP BETWEEN SATAN AND SELF-OPINION

We have previously said that our opinions are one of the expressions of our old man. However, in the experience of our dealing with the self we must pay attention to a further matter—the relationship between the self and Satan. Very few people pay any attention to this relationship, and scarcely does anyone realize that Satan has a definite position in our self and in our opinions. Therefore, we must lay some stress upon this matter.

Hidden in the self of man is Satan. Not only is Satan the

sin in our body, but he is also the good opinions in our self. When speaking of sin, many people are aware of its corruption; therefore, they hate sin and condemn it. But when mention is made of opinions, many people think of them as good. Not only do they feel that their opinion is better than that of others, but they even feel that opinions themselves are essentially good. None of us hate our own opinions; we all love them and deem them to be good and admirable. In spite of this, the Bible reveals that not only is sin of Satan, but even the opinions that man deems to be good are also of Satan. The opinion in our soul is just as much the embodiment of Satan as is the sin in our body. We may say that Satan's "incarnation" in us causes him on one hand to become the sin in our body and on the other hand the opinion in our soul.

Because Satan has such a definite position in our body and soul, when he comes to possess, gain, and corrupt man, he works in these two parts of our being. On one hand, he stirs up the lust of the members of the body, and on the other hand, he arouses the opinions in the mind. Furthermore, when Satan works, he works on both parts at the same time. Whenever Satan comes to tempt man, he first causes man to have an opinion in his soul; then he causes the body to sin.

This applies to the fall of the human race when Satan tempted Eve in the beginning. He came first to stir up her mind by giving her a suggestion. In other words, by his crafty questions he caused the mind of Eve to entertain doubt, which in turn caused her to formulate opinions. Dr. Haldeman has said that in the beginning, when the serpent in the garden inquired in Genesis 3:1, "Did God really say?" its posture was in the form of a question mark, with the head raised and the body bent. This is indeed meaningful. Therefore, if we wish to know the spiritual principle of man's fall, we must realize that the first step of the fall was that man had an opinion and that his opinion was from Satan.

This opinion from Satan injected into man was the first opinion of the human race. When man was first created, before he was seduced by Satan, he lived in a very simple way before God, without doubt or opinion. The first opinion man had was derived from the suggestion Satan injected into the human mind. Hence, we see that the first step of Satan in entering into man was not by way of the fruit of the tree of the knowledge of good and evil, which man partook of by eating, but by way of an opinion transmitted into the soul of man. When the soul of man was stirred and received the suggestion of Satan, his body followed, and he ate of the tree of the knowledge of good and evil.

Because of this, we have said that opinion and sin are always related. When our opinion is expressed, nine out of ten times it is related to sin, for opinion does not issue from our self but stems from the originator of sin, who is Satan. Satan hides within the opinion, and we may say that opinion is the embodiment of Satan.

From Matthew 16:21-25 we see clearly the relationship between self-opinion and Satan. When the Lord Jesus showed His disciples that He must go to Jerusalem and die, Peter at that time had his own opinion, and taking hold of the Lord he said, "God be merciful to You, Lord! This shall by no means happen to You!" But the Lord turned and rebuked Peter, saying, "Get behind Me, Satan! You are a stumbling block to Me, for you are not setting your mind on the things of God, but on the things of men." The Lord here directly rebuked Peter as Satan because the Lord knew that Satan was hiding behind this opinion of Peter. Although Peter's opinion issued from his love for the Lord, although it was an excellent opinion and was for the interest of the Lord, this opinion was the very embodiment of Satan. We usually think of a bad opinion as being from Satan, but in the sight of the Lord, whether it be bad or good, as long as it is an opinion, it is of Satan. The best opinion of man is still in the sight of God the embodiment of Satan. We must be warned concerning this.

There is another place in the Bible that speaks clearly of the relationship between Satan and self-opinion. Ephesians 2:2-3 says, "You once walked according to the age of this world, according to the ruler of the authority of the air, of the spirit which is now operating in the sons of disobedience; among whom we also all conducted ourselves once in the lusts of our flesh, doing the desires of the flesh and of the thoughts..." This passage first shows us that all human beings today walk according to the working of the spirit of Satan within them. It then shows us that the result of Satan's work is to cause men to live in the lusts of their flesh, doing the desires of their flesh and of their thoughts. On the one hand, they fulfill the desires of the lusts of the flesh, and on the other hand, they fulfill the desires of their thoughts. Therefore, the working of Satan within men is of two aspects: in men's flesh and in men's mind. When Satan works in our flesh, it results in the lust of our flesh, which is sin; when he works in our mind, the result is opinion, or the self.

A brother once testified that whenever he encountered a situation and within him there was an opinion that he desired to express, if he did not express it, he would feel very "itchy" inside. This is really true. This itchy feeling is his desire within him. Whenever an opium addict is confronted with opium, he feels itchy; whenever a gambler sees the gambling devices, he feels itchy. In the same manner, when Satan works in man's mind and gives man an opinion, man becomes itchy within and cannot help but express it. Therefore, just as sin is the result of the desires of man's flesh, so also is our opinion the result of the desires of man's mind. Both are the result of the working of Satan within man.

We regret to say that in the past we have had too little knowledge with regard to our own opinion. Very few condemn their opinion, and even fewer realize that their own opinion is Satan. Everybody esteems his own opinions highly, treasures his own opinions, and feels very sweet when meditating upon them. We love our own children, but to my realization we love our own opinions far more than we love our children. To our feelings, opinions are always a most lovable thing.

We deeply need to ask the Lord to give us a full turn in our concept in the light of these words. We must see that if sin is horrible, much more so is our opinion. If to resist the enemy we need to resist sin, much more do we need to deny our opinions. We need to put to death all our opinions through the cross. Thus, we deny ourselves in a practical way, we deny thoroughly the place of Satan in us, and we overthrow Satan's stronghold in us.

VI. THE DIFFERENCE BETWEEN DEALING WITH THE SELF AND BEING MAGNANIMOUS

The dealing with the self that we are speaking of is entirely different from the magnanimity commonly spoken of among worldly people. Our dealing with the self is based upon our realization that opinion is not only an expression of the old man but also the embodiment of Satan. Therefore, we apply the cross to our opinion and thereby put it to death. Once the opinion is put to death, our self is dealt with as well. Nevertheless, this is not the case with those who are magnanimous. The magnanimous persons, when associating with others, never cause trouble by expressing their opinions. They endeavor to maintain peace with others; thus, in everything they seem to be very courteous and never quarrelsome. In all matters, however, they have their own opinion and idea. To their feeling, the opinion of others is never as good as theirs. But if others do not accept their opinion, they can restrain themselves from expressing it; they would never force others to accept it. They would even go to the extent, outwardly, of going along with the opinion of others and following others' way of doing things. In this way there is no disharmony with others. Therefore, they act outwardly in one way and inwardly in another. Outwardly, they do not insist on anything, yet inwardly, they never lay aside their own opinion; rather, they would keep it forever. This is called magnanimity.

Being magnanimous in such a way is absolutely not dealing with opinion or dealing with the self; on the contrary, it nurtures opinions. Once the opinion is nurtured, the self is developed, for the self grows in the soil of opinion. Opinion is the best fertilizer and hotbed for the self. The more human opinion there is and the more it is given existence and preserved, the better the self grows. Conversely, dealing with man's opinion is equal to slaying the self. Man is not willing to lay aside his opinion, because he is not willing to deny his self. Throughout the generations we see people whose self is strong to such a degree that you could cut off their head, but you could never make them relinquish their opinion. Hence, dealing with opinion and denying of the self are very difficult matters.

Being magnanimous, we repeat, is not dealing with the self. The magnanimous person never condemns his own opinion or idea. He always feels that his own opinion is the most correct and the best. The only reason he does not insist on his own opinion is that he is able to make allowances for others and bear with others. He practices broad-mindedness; he has a measure as broad as the sea. Yet this kind of person considers himself the wisest and his opinion the best. When others do not accept his opinion, he bears with them and manifests his broad-mindedness.

These persons are seemingly meek but actually are always self-righteous, seemingly humble but in fact most arrogant. They are in total darkness and are the most blind. They resemble the Pharisees, self-righteous and self-right, whom the Lord rebuked as in darkness and blindness. The more successful a person is in being magnanimous, the more he becomes a stranger in spiritual things. He never has the light of God, nor does he know the mind of God. He is void of any spiritual understanding; his whole being is like a brass and iron wall. He who is most magnanimous, he who is most able to bear with others, and he who is most able to adapt himself to others, is the most retarded in spiritual growth. This kind of person develops his magnanimity by human effort; therefore, the more magnanimous he is, the stronger and grosser is his self. A magnanimous person does not abandon his self; rather, he accumulates his self, until one day he will open his mouth and pour forth all the pent up opinions within; then he will be exactly like Job. He feels that he is the father of the orphans, the eyes of the blind, the feet of the lame, always helping others and bearing with others. This proves that his self is wholly sealed, and he has never decreased a bit.

Dealing with the self is an absolutely different matter. To be magnanimous is to hide your opinion, but to deal with the self is to reject your opinion. To be magnanimous is to temporarily swallow your opinion, but to deal with the self is to hand over your opinion to the thorough killing of the cross. Therefore, one who has really learned the lesson of dealing with the self has on one hand a firm decision in his spirit, and on the other hand, because he has been broken, he does not seem to have any opinion. If God does it his way, he says Amen; if God does it otherwise, he counts his opinion as nothing. Because the self has already been broken by the cross, he cannot lose his temper, nor can he be magnanimous, even if he wants to. Something within him has been broken. In this way he can have light. Therefore, we have seen that people who are frank, opinionated, and outspoken are more easily delivered than those so-called good people, those magnanimous persons who always bear with others. Since their self is exposed, after they are broken by the cross, it is truly dealt with; the result then is that they really have no opinion of their own.

Therefore, we should never have the concept that to deal with the self means to be magnanimous and thus become a magnanimous person. We must differentiate clearly the matter of dealing with the self from being magnanimous. For example, in the church or at home, once we have discovered that we have our own opinions, we should not let them pass lightly, but deal with them. Neither should we simply withdraw our opinion peacefully and let the matter go. The attitude of being tolerant will afford more growth to our opinion. We must see that we have already been crucified with the Lord on the cross; then whenever opinion and the self are being expressed, we should apply the killing of the cross through the power of the Holy Spirit to put to death this opinion and the self. It is only when we repeatedly apply this death that our self gradually decreases and the life of Christ gradually grows within us.

VII. A FINAL WORD

Among Christians there are very few who deal with the self and opinion. In regard to dealing with flesh and dealing with temper, all who have pursuit in spiritual things have had some experience. However, very few brothers and sisters are aware that the self needs to be dealt with. This is because we do not know the meaning of the self, nor do we know that opinion is the expression of the self, the embodiment of the self. But the biggest reason is that we think our opinions are good and lovable, not knowing that the self is hidden within them. We have mentioned several times that in Matthew 16 the opinion of Peter was commendable in showing his love for the Lord, but he did not know that the self and Satan as well were hidden within it. Only those who have been enlightened by the Lord know that man's opinion is the enemy of God's will as well as the opponent of the cross. Whenever we care for man's opinion, we will surely neglect the will of God. Whenever we set our mind on the things of men, we cannot set our mind on the things of God. Whenever our opinion comes to fruition, our self grows. Opinion is the fertile soil, and the self is planted therein. He who has the most opinions has the grossest self. Therefore, when we are together with young brothers or sisters, we need to grasp this principle and not permit their opinion to have any place. To give place to their opinion means to give their self the fertile soil to grow.

When we see the awfulness of the self and are willing to learn the lesson of dealing with the self in our daily living, we must beware of one thing—of ever taking the way of magnanimity, which is exactly contrary to the goal of dealing with the self. Unfortunately, most of us are not clear with regard to this aspect of the truth, and we unconsciously fall into the error of being magnanimous. While we are with others, we sometimes have our opinion; yet for the sake of not striving with others, we refrain from expressing our opinion. Similarly, in our homes we often are confronted with many situations that are incompatible with our opinion. We feel that it is useless for us to say anything, so we simply swallow our opinion and remain silent. In many churches and homes today, there are many such situations. According to man, this condition is much better than that of quarrelling. However, according to life, this state is much more difficult to deal with than that of quarrelling. Quarrelling exposes the corruption of man; thus, when man is enlightened by the Holy Spirit, he will fall before God. It is difficult for those magnanimous people who never quarrel to be enlightened. It is hard for the Holy Spirit to touch them or shine upon them. Those who always swallow their opinion are those who always seek the Lord's light for others. Actually, they themselves need light the most. Though a magnanimous person withdraws his opinion when it is rejected by others, he considers himself most right and praises his own opinion most highly. He continually lives in the self, not knowing that the self is the greatest enemy of God. Therefore, magnanimity does not cause us to be broken; on the contrary, it causes our self to grow and become tough.

This is not so with the matter of dealing with the self. In dealing with the self we must see that as long as we live and grow in ourselves, Christ will have no way to live or grow. Since we live in our opinion, we must condemn it by putting it to death, that is, putting our self to death. This is the work of the cross, which issues in Christ being increased in us. We are not taking the way of magnanimity; rather, we are taking the way of putting to death the self, thereby letting Christ have a place to grow and be formed in us.

Concerning the application of the experience of the cross, we must realize that all dealing with the flesh and the self is continuous and not once for all. All the objective facts in Christ are accomplished once for all, but all the subjective experiences in the Holy Spirit are continuous. Our opinions cannot be crucified all at once; neither can we deal with the flesh all at once. The farmer weeds the field; today the weeds are removed, but tomorrow they will grow again, and he must remove them again. He can never exert one supreme effort to gain eternal ease. Likewise, today we are still in the old creation, and the old man cannot refrain from expressing himself in various aspects. Therefore, when we apply the dealing of the cross through fellowship in the Holy Spirit, one application is not enough; we must apply it morning, noon, and night. When these subjective experiences become mature and deep, we may be able to apply a last thorough crucifixion and severe dealing to a certain expression of the old man, bringing it to an end. However, in the initial stage of our experience, we must apply the dealing time after time. Therefore, when speaking of the subjective dealing, the Lord said that we need to bear the cross, meaning that we cannot depart from the cross. While in the meeting, a certain brother may have an opinion: he condemns it and withholds himself from speaking, but after the meeting, in privacy, he speaks forth. This is not the bearing of the cross. It is not that you bear the cross when you

have an opinion during the meeting, and then after the meeting you throw off the cross. We should always be crucified on
the cross and always bear the cross. The meaning of bearing the
cross is not to depart from the cross.

Throughout the generations all those who have experienced the cross, such as Brother Lawrence and Madame Guyon,
have agreed that one who bears the cross cannot be separated
from the cross. A person who bears the cross is one with the
cross; he is inseparable from the cross. When he sees the fact of
the putting to death through the cross, he receives the mark
of death as a seal upon him, and thereafter he continually
applies the fact of death to his practical daily living. This is
called the bearing of the cross. Therefore, the acceptance of the
death of the cross is not once for all but a daily bearing of
the cross.

When the Lord touched upon the matter of dealing with
the self, He spoke about the bearing of the cross and not the
crucifixion. There are two meanings of crucifixion: one is to be
nailed to the cross; the other is to be put to an end. Many think
that once we accept the cross, our self is terminated, and there
is no further need to bear the cross. However, the Lord spoke
of our need of bearing the cross, thus showing us that our self
is not brought to an end simply by the acceptance of the truth
of the cross. We must still bear the cross and not be separated
from it. When we receive the fact of our being crucified, that
is crucifixion. But when we go on to experience the crucifixion, that is bearing the cross.

When the Lord Jesus was a man on this earth, He first
bore the cross; He bore it until one day He went to Golgotha
and was nailed upon the cross. This is called the crucifixion.
When the Lord was crucified on the cross, He died and was
brought to an end. When He died, He was separated from the
cross. So also are we. Factually, the Lord has crucified us
with Him on the cross, but experientially, we have not died.
Therefore, we need to bear the cross continually until we are
raptured and transfigured, at which time we can be separated from the cross. In reality, however spiritual a Christian
may be, he cannot for one moment depart from the cross.
Whenever he departs from the cross, he is living in his flesh

and by his self. When through the Holy Spirit we apply the cross so that we have the mark of the cross upon us continually, this is called bearing the cross. Therefore, dealing with the self is a lifelong lesson. During our entire life, we should apply the death of the cross to our self and be one who denies the self and bears the cross.

CHAPTER ELEVEN

DEALING WITH THE NATURAL CONSTITUTION

We now come to the eleventh experience of life—dealing with the natural constitution.

I. THE DEFINITION OF THE NATURAL CONSTITUTION

Constitution as used here means "the aggregate of man's physical and mental powers." In the Bible there is no such term as *the natural constitution,* and it is seldom mentioned among Christians; yet in our experience there is such a thing. It is an outstanding characteristic of the soulish man and a prominent expression of the living out of the old man. If we pursue the experience of the cross, we cannot neglect this aspect of dealing. Hence, we need the lesson of dealing with the natural constitution.

We have said that when the old man is being lived out, it has its various kinds of expressions, such as temper, flesh, the self, and the natural constitution. Some people lose their temper and get angry easily, which means that they are quick-tempered. Some people are very talkative and always express their own opinion; that means that their self is very strong. There are still others who may never have lost their temper and are not talkative, but they are very capable in whatever they undertake; that indicates that they are very strong in their natural constitution. Therefore, the natural constitution is the expression of the living out of the old man that has to do with human ability, capability, wisdom, cleverness, schemes, and skills.

When speaking of the self, we can use self-righteous and

talkative Job as a model. But when speaking of the natural constitution, Jacob, in the book of Genesis, is the best representative. We generally think that the record of Jacob points out his craftiness. But, actually, the most outstanding characteristic in the entire life of Jacob is his natural endeavoring and scheming. All those who scheme are inevitably crafty. So also was Jacob. His craftiness was but the superficial expression; his natural constitution was his hidden characteristic. Before Jacob became matured, all his history revealed his natural constitution. He was able, resourceful, full of schemes, and very capable and skillful; he was truly one who was exceedingly strong in the natural constitution.

Jacob's natural constitution was expressed even before his birth. In his mother's womb he took hold of Esau's heel, striving to come out first. When he grew up, he cleverly schemed to gain a position of advantage. He used intrigue and cheated Esau out of the birthright. Then by a clever device he obtained the blessing of the firstborn from his father. When he left home, in his wanderings, God appeared to him at Bethel and promised to bless him; then also he applied his skill and bargained with God. He said, "If God will be with me and will keep me in this way that I go and will give me bread to eat and garments to put on, so that I return to my father's house in peace, then Jehovah will be my God, and this stone, which I have set up as a pillar, will be God's house; and of all that You give me I will surely give one tenth to You" (28:20-22). God had promised to bless Jacob without any terms; nevertheless, he bargained with God on certain conditions. This only proves how smart and clever he was.

While he was with Laban, his uncle, he still employed schemes and devices according to his natural ability. Before long, he became very prosperous, acquiring many herds, servants, camels, and donkeys. At the ford of the Jabbok, God dealt with him by touching the socket of his hip, thereby causing him to limp. Yet soon after passing through the river to meet his brother Esau, he was still fulfilling his own scheming and plotting. According to his previously self-made plan, he divided the women and children, flock, cattle, and camels into two groups, putting his beloved wife and his beloved son

Joseph in the rear, so that in case of attack they would be able to escape.

The reason Jacob was so scheming is that he was strong in the natural constitution. Therefore, throughout his whole life, God especially dealt with his natural constitution. The afflictions, sufferings, and troubles that beset him were for the breaking of his natural constitution. The crisis in his life occurred when God touched the socket of his hip at Penuel. Finally, in Genesis 35, God asked him to go to Bethel and there make an altar to God who had appeared to him when he fled from the face of his brother. From thence Jacob ceased all his scheming, and his natural man fell before God. Later, when his son Reuben defiled his bed, though Jacob knew it, he took no action. When his sons cheated him by selling Joseph whom he loved into Egypt, he suffered it. Finally, when he was struck by famine, he had to beg his sons to buy food for him. All his ability, schemes, cleverness, and capability evidently disappeared and ceased. His whole being had changed completely.

When Jacob's natural constitution was thoroughly broken, his life in God attained to a mature and full stage. He was no more Jacob but Israel. He was no more a supplanter (the meaning of *Jacob*) but a prince of God (the meaning of *Israel*). As a result, he could bless Pharaoh and command abundant blessings upon his sons before he died.

We gather, therefore, from the record of Jacob's life that Genesis 35 was a great turning point. Before chapter 35 all that Jacob expressed was his natural ability, resource, cleverness, and capability, which issued from the living out of his old man. After chapter 35 he no longer used natural ability, resource, cleverness, and capability, because his natural constitution had been completely dealt with, and he became one who lived in the presence of God. Spiritually speaking, he was at this time completely delivered from being natural, and he entered into resurrection. In his whole life he was afflicted and dealt with by God in such a way that his natural constitution might be broken and that he might become a resurrected man. The natural man is useless before God; only the resurrected one can be of use before God. For this reason the natural constitution needs to be broken and dealt with.

II. THE DIFFERENCE BETWEEN THE NATURAL CONSTITUTION AND RESURRECTION LIFE

We have defined the natural constitution as that which pertains to human ability, capability, wisdom, and cleverness, because all these are derived from our natural life and not from the resurrection life of God. They are acquired naturally; they do not spring from resurrection by passing through the breaking in Christ. The difference between the natural constitution and resurrection life is indeed great. Our dealing with the natural constitution is so that our inherent ability, capability, wisdom, and cleverness may pass through the death of the cross, become resurrected, and thereby become acceptable and useful to God.

When some people hear about dealing with the natural constitution, they think that God does not want our ability and capability. This concept is wrong. In order to be useful to God, we definitely need our ability and capability.

From the revelation of the Bible, we clearly see that the work of God on this earth requires man's cooperation. It is impossible for man to cooperate with God without possessing any ability and capability. Just as wood and stone cannot cooperate with God, so also foolish and incapable persons cannot cooperate with God. We always say that a clever man is useless before God, but a stupid one is even worse. We also say that a capable man is useless before God, but that the incapable ones are worse. Actually, all those who are useless in this world are also useless in the hand of God. Throughout the generations, all those who have been used of God have been the capable ones gained from this world. We have to admit that Moses was a capable man with ability, foresight, wisdom, and cleverness; therefore, God could use him to deliver the Israelites from Egypt. Moreover, through him the most important books of the Old Testament, the Pentateuch, were written. We must also admit that Paul was a capable man who had great learning and was rich in thinking; therefore, he was able to receive revelation from God, which enabled him to write the deep and lofty truths in the New Testament. Though Peter and John were but fishers of Galilee, we can presume that they were among the best of the fishers and by no means ordinary men.

The greatest principle in spiritual service is that of man cooperating with God. Although God does all things, yet in all things God needs man to cooperate with Him. It can never be that those who do not know how to do anything and are incapable and unwilling to do anything can be used by God. We often hear brothers and sisters say, "I believe that God can do it," yet they themselves make no effort to cooperate. This kind of faith is vain. No doubt, God can do it, but it is also necessary that man be able to do it. If man cannot do it, though God can, He will not do it. God must seek those who are able and willing to cooperate with Him. God works as far as man is capable. God works according to the degree of man's cooperation. Therefore, we must be able and capable and learn to be a useful man in every aspect; then we are fit for His use.

However, God still cannot use one who is merely naturally capable. Natural capability, unless broken, is a hindrance to God. It must be broken; it must pass through death and be resurrected so that it may be used by God. Natural ability is similar to raw iron, which, because it is too hard and brittle, is not suitable for use and is easily broken. Resurrected ability is like wrought steel, firm but malleable, suitable for use and not easily cracked. Therefore, God cannot use one who is incapable; neither can He use one who is capable yet has not been broken. Those who are usable in the hand of God are those who are capable yet whose capability has been broken. If we examine all those who have been used by God throughout the generations, almost all were very capable, rich in soul-power, having foresight and cleverness, while at the same time they were broken by God.

The most outstanding example in the Bible is Jacob, of whom we have already spoken. Naturally speaking, he was capable and crafty. But one day he was broken by God and became Israel; then he lost his capability and craftiness. Yet when we observe him at the time he blessed the two sons of Joseph, he was by no means confused. He was exceedingly clear and had foresight. Moreover, the blessings that he commanded upon his children (Gen. 49) are great prophecies in the Bible. Those words are truly great and wonderful. If Jacob had been one who was insensible and stupid, how could he have uttered such words? On the other hand, if Jacob merely depended upon his natural mind, natural thought, or natural capability, he could not have uttered those words either. His natural mind, natural thought, and natural ability, having been broken by God, became resurrected and spiritual; thus, he could be used by God to speak forth those great prophecies.

The same principle applies to our understanding of God's will. God is an extremely wise and intelligent God. Therefore, in order to understand His will, human wisdom and intelligence are required. A stupid person can never understand the will of God. However, neither can a person who depends only upon his own wisdom and intelligence understand the will of God. What is necessary is that man have intelligence, wisdom, and clear thinking, and that he put all these beneath the cross, allowing the cross to put the stamp of death upon them. This kind of person has his own mind, wisdom, and thoughts, yet he does not do things according to himself, for himself, or depending upon himself; he is used only according to God, for God, and depending upon God. He does not have his own aim or elements of his own self, much less his own scheming hand. He relies only upon the mercy of God; he waits for His visitation and seeks His revelation. Only this kind of people can understand the will of God and be clear concerning His guidance.

From this we learn that natural ability and capability do not come to naught after having been dealt with. The brokenness and putting to death by the cross is not the final step. The real death of the cross always brings in resurrection. Jesus of Nazareth was put to death on the cross, yet Christ was resurrected. After Genesis 35, Jacob was completely dealt with and finished, yet a matured Israel came forth. Therefore, the dealing of the cross always brings in resurrection. The more one's capabilities are dealt with by the cross, the more capable one becomes. The more one's wisdom is dealt with by the cross, the wiser one becomes. Furthermore, this capability and wisdom are in resurrection.

For this reason, on one hand, we encourage people to read and study the Bible, to exercise their mind and foresight, and to learn how to behave as human beings, how to handle things, and how to work, to the end that they may be capable. On the other hand, we always tell people that education as well as capability are useless. When we say this, we mean that these must be broken and become resurrected. These two aspects apparently contradict each other, but for us they are practical and absolutely necessary.

How can we differentiate natural ability from resurrected ability? How can we tell which is an inherent ability and which is the ability that has been broken? There are seven points of comparison. We shall look first at natural ability:

First, all natural ability is selfish, and all its schemes and devices are for the sake of self. Second, all natural ability is mingled with the elements of flesh and temper; therefore, when it is disapproved, it becomes provoked. Third, all natural ability involves craftiness and maneuvering. Fourth, all natural ability contains pride and makes oneself feel capable, thereby resulting in boasting and self-glorification. Fifth, all natural ability is not under the control of the Holy Spirit and is extremely daring in doing anything. Sixth, all natural ability has no regard for the will of God; it acts entirely according to self-will. Seventh, natural ability does not rely on God and does not have to rely on God but relies wholly upon self.

Resurrected ability is exactly the opposite. First, all ability that has been broken and resurrected is not for self, neither does it contain any element of self. Second, all resurrected ability is devoid of the flesh. Third, resurrected ability does not scheme. Fourth, resurrected ability is not proud, nor does it boast in itself. Fifth, resurrected ability is controlled by the Holy Spirit and does not dare to act according to its wishes. Sixth, resurrected ability is for the will of God. Seventh, resurrected ability relies upon God and does not dare to act according to self, though truly able and capable.

Since we are clear now concerning the difference between natural and resurrected ability, we should examine ourselves in our experience. When we exercise our ability, is it for self or for God? Am I making decisions on my own and acting individually and egocentrically, or am I able to stand the criticism of others and suffer their opposition? Do I employ schemes, or do I look to the grace of God? Do I give glory to God, or do I boast and glory in myself? Am I controlled by the Holy Spirit, or am I acting as I wish? Do I fulfill my own desires, or do I care for the will of God? Do I attempt to achieve the goal by any means, or do I commit all things into the hand of God, trusting Him for the outcome? Am I depending solely on my own resources, or am I relying upon God with fear and trembling? If we examine ourselves strictly, we will discover that in our living and service, many areas are still in the natural constitution and of the old creation; therefore, we cannot bring forth fruit of resurrection. Hence, dealing with the natural constitution is the deliverance that we need most.

III. DEALING WITH THE NATURAL CONSTITUTION

A. The Objective Fact

Dealing with the natural constitution is the same as dealing with the flesh and the self—it is based on objective fact. Since our old man has been crucified with Christ, our natural constitution also has been dealt with in the old man. In the sight of God it is an accomplished fact. We too must see this by the Holy Spirit. Only those who see this objective fact will have the experience of the subjective dealing.

B. The Subjective Experience

Flesh, self, and the natural constitution—all three—are the expressions of the old man. Therefore, the principle in dealing with them is the same: on one hand, we have the objective fact, and on the other hand, we need the subjective experience. The objective fact is that Christ has already crucified our old man, whereas the subjective experience is the applying of the death of Christ through the Holy Spirit to ourselves. If we apply it to the flesh, it is the dealing with the flesh; if we apply it to our opinion, it is the dealing with self;

and if we apply it to our ability and capability, it is the dealing with the natural constitution.

IV. THE PROCESS OF THE EXPERIENCE
OF DEALING WITH THE NATURAL CONSTITUTION

The process of the experience of dealing with the natural constitution closely resembles that of dealing with self.

A. Seeing That Our Old Man
Has Been Crucified with Christ

This spiritual seeing is the first step toward our experience in dealing with the natural constitution. We must see that our old man has been crucified with Christ; then we shall experience the dealing that follows.

B. Realizing That the Natural Constitution Is
a Very Strong Expression of the Old Man

This also is a spiritual seeing. Of course, this also includes seeing what the natural constitution refers to and what its expressions are.

C. Receiving the Crucifixion of Christ
upon Our Natural Constitution

After we have seen the first two points, we will automatically receive the crucifixion of Christ upon our natural constitution. This also means that we apply the crucifixion of Christ through the power of the Holy Spirit to our natural expression. Once we receive and apply this, all our natural ability will be stamped with the mark of death and will gradually become withered. This receiving is a great spiritual crisis in our life; it may perhaps become our Penuel in experience. It is here that our natural ability and capability are touched by God, and the socket of our hip, wherein lies the strength of our body, becomes limp. Hereafter, we can no longer as before use our ability and capability as we wish. Thus, we pass a crisis in our dealing with the natural constitution; we gain an experience in a subjective way.

V. APPLYING THE EXPERIENCE OF DEALING WITH THE NATURAL CONSTITUTION

A. In the Fellowship of the Holy Spirit

In order to experience dealing with the natural constitution, we must first be in the fellowship of the Holy Spirit. Whether we are dealing with self or with the natural constitution, if we desire to have a continual experience, we must live in the fellowship of the Holy Spirit. In order to apply this experience, we need to apply the death of the cross through the Holy Spirit. If we do not live in the fellowship of the Holy Spirit, we cannot live in dependence upon the Holy Spirit, nor can we apply the death of the cross.

B. Letting the Holy Spirit Execute the Crucifixion of Christ upon Every Area of Our Natural Constitution as It Is Discovered

If we live in the fellowship of the Holy Spirit, we need to let the Holy Spirit execute the crucifixion of Christ upon every area of our natural constitution that we discover. In other words, every time we discover our cleverness, wiles, and capability, we must immediately apply the death of the cross to them. In this way the stamp of the death of the cross is applied to all the practical expressions of the natural constitution. This is not merely a once-for-all acceptance; it must also be a daily application. We must apply the cross to our natural constitution daily and moment by moment. From the very beginning, when we accept the working of the cross, we must allow God to touch every expression of our natural constitution in the fellowship of the Holy Spirit. We may be rich in thinking and very capable, yet we must be one who receives the cross and bears the cross. The cross must continually do the work of breaking us; then after a certain period of time, all that is of our natural constitution will gradually be in the state of having passed through death to resurrection.

A FINAL WORD

Dealing with self and dealing with the natural constitution are the deeper experiences in the stage of the cross.

Therefore, after studying these two experiences, we will summarize them together.

Dealing with self and dealing with the natural constitution are of extreme importance in spiritual experience. They are related not only to life but also to service. Dealing with self and dealing with the natural constitution are preparations for our service to God. If we wish to have the kind of service that is according to God's heart desire, dealing with self and the natural constitution is a must. Strictly speaking, those who have never been dealt with in the self and in the natural constitution cannot serve God.

This matter is clearly demonstrated in the life of Moses. Before God used him, the work that God did upon him was to deal with his self and his natural constitution. When he was forty years old, he was very strong in his natural constitution. He "was educated in all the wisdom of the Egyptians, and he was powerful in his words and works" (Acts 7:22). Therefore, he was about to use his own strength to deliver the Israelites. One day, when he saw an Egyptian beating a Hebrew, one of his brothers, he smote the Egyptian and hid him in the sand. That was his natural strength or device. However, this natural constitution of his, God could not use. God cannot use one who works for Him by using his own natural ability. Therefore, God raised up an environment that forced him to flee into the wilderness, and for forty years God afflicted him and dealt with him in order to terminate his natural constitution. When Moses wrote Psalm 90 he said, "The days of our years are seventy years, / Or, if because of strength, eighty years" (v. 10). It was not until he was eighty years old, which, according to his own calculation, was the time of his feeble and dying days, that God called and used him. Furthermore, at the time God called him, God caused him to see the vision of the bush burning, yet not being consumed—an indication to Moses that the power of God's work was to be manifested through him, yet not using what he had by birth, which was his natural constitution, as fuel.

When we study the life of Moses, we see that from the time he was called by God, he never again used his own power and ability to work for Him. From the time that he first saw

Pharaoh in Egypt till the time of his death on Mount Nebo (forty years), although he still had ability, it was no more natural but had passed through breaking and resurrection.

Furthermore, dealing with the natural constitution and dealing with self are closely related. Those who are able and capable always have many opinions. If anyone has no opinions or ideas, surely he must have no capability. Because Moses did not have his own opinions or ideas, his natural ability had been dealt with during his forty years of serving the Lord. Although he prayed to God, he was but seeking His counsel; he did not, except on one occasion, voice any of his opinions or ideas. The only exception was at the time that he was irritated by the Israelites, when he spoke rashly and smote the rock twice; other than this he made no mistake in forty years. He served God not according to his own strength or his own opinions. He was one who had indeed been wholly freed from self and the natural constitution. Therefore, he became the one who was most used by God in Old Testament times.

It was upon this same principle that God led the Israelites to serve Him in the wilderness. When the Israelites were led to the wilderness, where God desired them to serve Him, the first lesson for them to learn was to see that their strength and their opinions as well were to be laid aside. They could not serve God with their strength, nor could they serve according to their own opinion. The means by which they served God were the tabernacle and the offerings. The tabernacle signified that all their ways and activities pertaining to the service of God must be according to the pattern shown on the mount, according to God's revelation and not according to their own opinion. The offerings signified that their service could only be acceptable and satisfying to God if it were rendered through the sacrifices instead of by their own ability and capability. Therefore, when God at Mount Sinai prepared the Israelites to serve Him, He gave them on one hand the tabernacle, showing them the need for laying aside their own opinion, and on the other hand, He gave them the offerings, which implied the need for their laying aside the natural constitution. The service rendered through the tabernacle contained no self-opinion, and the service through the offerings contained no natural

constitution. Since both the tabernacle and the offerings typified Christ, we must take Christ as our wisdom and way as
well as our strength and ability, allowing Him to replace our
self-opinion and our natural constitution; thus, we can serve
God.

A person whose self has been denied and whose natural
constitution has been broken before God is weakened and
decreased; hence, Christ increases in him. Not only is this a
great crisis in his spiritual life and service, but it is in itself
a very serious matter in the eyes of God. Throughout the generations, God's purpose has been to lead His saints to pass
through the stage of the breaking of the natural constitution in order to attain to the fullness of Christ. We can see
this from the Bible in the life of many of the ones who were
led of God. Not only is this true of Moses but also of Abraham and Jacob. The period preceding and following the birth
of Ishmael in the life of Abraham and the twenty years of
Jacob's sojourn in Paddan-aram are equal to Moses' forty
years in the wilderness, all of which portray the condition of
man living in the natural constitution. Not until Abraham
was circumcised, the socket of Jacob's hip was touched and
became limp, and Moses reached the age of eighty, did their
condition portray the brokenness of their natural constitution. Having passed through this breaking, there was a great
change in their condition before God.

God not only led the Old Testament saints in such a way
but also used many objects and situations in the Bible to typify
this matter. For example, the establishing of the tabernacle
and the journey of the Israelites in the wilderness all typify
the spiritual experience of a Christian, in which the breaking
of the natural constitution occupies an important place.

Let us first consider the typology of the layout of the
tabernacle, divided as it was into the outer court, the Holy
Place, and the Holy of Holies. These three sections depict the
three stages of our spiritual experience. In the outer court
were the altar and the laver. The altar typifies the redemption
of the cross, with the emphasis upon solving the problem of
sin so that we may experience salvation. The laver represents
the cleansing of the Holy Spirit, with the emphasis upon

washing away our earthly defilements so that we may be renewed. Therefore, the outer court typifies the primary stage of our salvation, which is closely equivalent to the first two stages of our spiritual experiences of life.

The table of the bread of the Presence, the golden lampstand, and the golden altar of incense were in the Holy Place. The bread of the Presence typifies Christ as our life supply for our satisfaction and enjoyment. The golden lampstand typifies Christ as our light for our enlightenment. The golden altar of incense typifies Christ as our acceptance before God so that we may have peace and joy. These are the conditions of experiencing Christ as our life. These items approximate in typology the third stage of our spiritual life, a stage that involves deeper experiences. However, in these experiences there is still the element of the feeling of the soul. Therefore, the spiritual condition of those who are in this stage is full of ups and downs and is not very stable.

After the Holy Place was the Holy of Holies. In the Holy of Holies there was only an Ark, which contained the tablets of the covenant, the golden pot of manna, and the budded rod of Aaron (Heb. 9:4). The tablets of covenant typify Christ as the light, corresponding to the golden lampstand in the Holy Place. The hidden manna typifies Christ as the life supply, equivalent to the bread of the Presence in the Holy Place. The budded rod of Aaron typifies Christ as our acceptance before God, corresponding to the golden altar of incense in the Holy Place. Therefore, these three items in the Ark were the same in nature in typology as the three items in the Holy Place; however, the conditions were changed. In the Holy Place, the bread of the Presence was on display, the light from the lampstand was shining forth, and the golden altar of incense was giving forth fragrance, all of which were manifested outwardly. However, in the Holy of Holies, these three items became hidden. The bread of the Presence on display became the hidden manna, the shining lampstand became the hidden law, and the fragrant altar of incense became the hidden budded rod.

The condition in the Holy of Holies typifies the condition in our spirit. When a man turns to his spirit, he enters into the Holy of Holies. He no longer lives according to the feeling of his soul, nor does he display anything before men. Everything is hidden; it is no longer on the surface but deep within. At this time, his spiritual life attains the degree of maturity. Therefore, this condition in the Holy of Holies typifies the fourth stage of our experience in spiritual life.

How can we from the shallow experience of the outer court enter into the deep experience of the Holy of Holies? We need to pass two crises. First, we need to pass through the curtain that separates the outer court from the Holy Place. This curtain, according to the Bible, is not a very great separation and is not too difficult to pass. Second, in order to enter the Holy of Holies from the Holy Place, we need to pass through the veil. This veil is a tremendous crisis. For one to enter into the Holy of Holies, the veil must be rent. This rending of the veil typifies our being broken. Therefore, this type shows us that our being must be rent, and our self and natural constitution broken; then shall we be able to leave our shallow condition and enter into the depth of the spirit; then shall we have fellowship with God face to face and live in God's presence, that is, live in God. Therefore, the breaking of the natural constitution is truly a great turning point in our spiritual pathway.

Similarly, the journey of the Israelites entering Canaan also typifies the spiritual pathway of a Christian. Canaan refers to the heavenly realm and is comparable to the Holy of Holies. Those in Canaan were those living in the Holy of Holies. They wandered in the wilderness for forty years, until the old creation gradually passed away. The passing through the Jordan is comparable to the rending of the veil. From that time forth, their flesh was rolled away.

Therefore, we must start from the altar and go forward, until one day we experience the rending of the veil and enter into the Holy of Holies. We must also start our journey from Mount Sinai and go forward until we reach the Jordan, where our old creation is dealt with; then we can enter into the land of Canaan. The older generation of Israelites depicts all that pertains to the old creation within us, namely our flesh, the self, and the natural constitution. Therefore, the spiritual meaning of God rejecting the older generation of Israelites is that God rejects everything in us that pertains to the old creation. From the time we begin to learn to serve God, He causes us to daily experience death in order to put to death and nullify all that is of the old creation in us. God employs a long period of time and a lengthy journey to lead us, "the Jacobs" who have found favor before God and "the Israelites" who have been redeemed, to the end so that all the items of our flesh, self-opinion, and natural constitution might be revealed one by one in our practical experience; then one by one He puts them to death for us. Therefore, when at times we see our flesh and opinions exposed in the church, we need not fear or be troubled, for without being exposed, they will exist hiddenly, but once they are exposed, there is deliverance.

Of course, dealing with the flesh, the self, and the natural constitution requires many years. The Israelites in the wilderness did nothing for forty years but serve God; some carried the tent, some killed the sheep and oxen, and some arranged the bread of the Presence in the Holy Place. Whenever the pillar of cloud was lifted and the trumpet sounded, they all marched on. They lived in this manner for forty years before the oldness was completely purged away. Likewise, we as Christians today must pay the price, forsake the world, pursue the Lord, bear the testimony of God, serve God daily, and go on with Him. Then the incident at Taberah (Num. 11:1-3), the rebellion of Korah and Dathan, and Miriam's not submitting to authority, plus numerous other mixed conditions in us, of which we are not aware, will gradually be exposed. The more we are exposed, the more we are being purged. If we go on in such a way, and if it takes us eight to ten years to pass through the Jordan and purge away the old creation, it is a tremendous grace of the Lord. Contrariwise, if we still set our heart on the world, what we think and do are things outside of God; though we go to meetings or read the Scriptures occasionally, even after fifty years we still will not be able to pass through the Jordan; neither can we do it until the day we depart from the world. May the Lord have mercy upon us in order that we may see the way and walk therein.

CHAPTER TWELVE

ACCEPTING THE DISCIPLINE
OF THE HOLY SPIRIT

Now we will consider the twelfth experience in our spiritual life—accepting the discipline of the Holy Spirit.

I. THE MEANING
OF THE DISCIPLINE OF THE HOLY SPIRIT

The discipline of the Holy Spirit that we are now considering does not refer to the inward discipline of the Holy Spirit, for that is the function of the Holy Spirit within us as the anointing. The discipline of the Holy Spirit refers to what the Holy Spirit is doing in our outward environment; it refers to His arranging of all people, things, and happenings, through which we are being disciplined.

The major work of God toward us through the Holy Spirit, aside from the Holy Spirit as the anointing, is in His outward discipline. These two aspects comprise almost the complete work of the Holy Spirit. For example, Romans 8, which speaks of the work of the Holy Spirit, tells us in the first part that the Holy Spirit, which contains the law of life, is able to set us free from sin, and that by Him we can put to death the practices of the body. This chapter also tells us that the Holy Spirit guides us so that we may live according to Him, and finally, that He helps us in our weaknesses and prays for us. All these activities are the work of the Holy Spirit within us as the anointing. In the latter part of this chapter we read that "all things work together for good to those who love God" (v. 28). This speaks of the discipline of the Holy Spirit in our outward environment. The work of this outward discipline coordinates with His inward moving and leading. The Holy

Spirit arranges and determines all that comes upon us according to the will of God. Although in many instances this causes temporal pain and trouble, in the end it is for the good of those who love God, that they may be conformed to the image of His Son. This arrangement is what we mean by the discipline of the Holy Spirit.

The work of the Holy Spirit within us requires the coordination of outward discipline because usually the inward working of the Holy Spirit alone is not sufficient. We can say that the inward working of the Holy Spirit is largely for the obedient ones, and the outward discipline of the Holy Spirit is largely for the stiff-necked ones. When the Holy Spirit moves and anoints within us and we obey the feeling that He imparts, God's will is accomplished, and His attributes are increased within us. Therefore, the inward anointing of the Holy Spirit is to some extent sufficient for the obedient ones. However, if we are stubborn, if we do not obey the inner anointing and rebel time after time, the Holy Spirit is compelled to raise up an environment to chasten and discipline us, thereby causing us to submit. Therefore, the anointing of the Holy Spirit within us is a sweet act of God's love toward us and is His original desire, while the outward discipline of the Holy Spirit is an act of God's hand, an act that He is compelled to perform. It is something additional.

Hence, both in the original desire of God and in the New Testament teaching, the place of the discipline of the Holy Spirit is not as important as that of the anointing of the Holy Spirit. In God's Word much is said about the Holy Spirit as the anointing, such as the leading of the Holy Spirit, the enlightening of the Holy Spirit, the strengthening of the Holy Spirit, and our need to live in the Holy Spirit, walk according to the Holy Spirit, and bear fruit through the Holy Spirit. However, the Bible says very little in a literal way about the discipline of the Holy Spirit; indeed, it contains no such phrase. This is because the discipline of the Holy Spirit is not a matter that is pleasant to God's feeling. Such a condition may be likened to the fact that most fathers prepare good things for their children, not whips and rods. In many families the father is forced to resort to rebuking and whipping because of the children's stubbornness and rebellion. In fact, to the feeling of the father, such chastenings are never pleasant. Likewise, that which God has prepared for us in the New Testament is always positive, but due to our obstinacy, stubbornness, lawlessness, and disobedience, God is forced to discipline us. In a normal situation among the saints in the church, the anointing of the Holy Spirit should always exceed the discipline of the Holy Spirit; there should not be the constant encountering of discipline. It is always abnormal if the children in a family are spanked every day.

Therefore, when we accept the discipline of the Holy Spirit, we should not deem it to be a pleasant thing. Some brothers and sisters seem to glory in testifying of their experience while being disciplined by the Holy Spirit. This should not be. No child is proud after being punished by his father. In the same manner, we should feel ashamed when we receive the discipline of the Holy Spirit. We should be aware of our own obstinacy, stubbornness, lawlessness, and disobedience, which cause punishment from God our Father. No doubt, He chastises me because He loves me, but when I speak of His chastisement, it is not my glory. It is because I am so rebellious and stubborn, even as a mule without understanding, that God is compelled to discipline me. This is my shame. Therefore, we should not boast in regard to the discipline we receive. All those who boast concerning the discipline of the Holy Spirit are those who do not know the nature of the discipline of the Holy Spirit.

Because the discipline of the Holy Spirit is such an unpleasant thing, God in His original thought put greater emphasis on the inner anointing, which is of a positive nature, than on the outward discipline, which is of a negative nature. But judging from our condition, the discipline of the Holy Spirit is most needful, because we are by nature rebellious, lawless, and disobedient. We often disregard and disobey the moving and enlightening of the Holy Spirit. It seems that His anointing alone, which is His sweet act, is not enough to accomplish His purpose, but that we need in addition the outward discipline as the coordinating factor to chastise us and deal with us in order that we may be subdued. Therefore, the discipline of the Holy Spirit must not be neglected in our experience.

II. THE PURPOSE
OF THE DISCIPLINE OF THE HOLY SPIRIT

The purpose of the discipline of the Holy Spirit toward us can be divided into three aspects: chastisement, education, and breaking.

A. Chastisement

Hebrews 12:10 tells us that the Father of spirits chastens us "for our profit, that we may be partakers of his holiness." The chastisement mentioned here is the first intention or the first category of the discipline of the Holy Spirit.

Chastisement means punishment which is necessary because of our rebellion, stubbornness, and disobedience. Many times in our experience the Holy Spirit has already spoken within us and has anointed us to make known the will of God, but due to our stubbornness, rebellion, or some other reason we have disregarded the voice of God and paid no attention to the feeling of the Holy Spirit. Therefore God has arranged environmental situations through the Holy Spirit to cause us to feel afflicted, painful, suppressed, and miserable, that we may be punished and chastised.

For example, consider a brother who has gained his income in a dishonest manner and has been enlightened by the Holy Spirit to deal with the situation; yet, due to his pride and his concern for financial loss, he refuses to obey the will of God in this matter. Though the Holy Spirit repeatedly moves and urges him, he will not obey. At this time God has no other alternative but to use an outward environment to chastise him. It may be that he will be hit by an automobile. Though he does not die, nor is he critically injured, yet he suffers great pain. While he lies in the hospital, groaning in anguish, the Holy Spirit speaks to him again, reminding him of the former demand. He becomes humble and subdued and is willing now to deal with his behavior according to the will of God. Shortly after obeying and accepting the dealing, his wound is gradually healed. This is the environmental discipline arranged by the Holy Spirit according to the will of God and our need for chastisement. This is His dealing especially with our stubbornness and disobedience so that we may be disciplined.

The purpose of chastisement can be subdivided into two kinds. One kind deals with rebellion and consists purely of punishment for our rebellion. The other kind corrects our mistakes. This means that when we have gone astray and refuse to turn back at the teaching of the Holy Spirit, or when we are about to err, though the Holy Spirit has given us a certain sense, we proceed headlong into the error, then the Holy Spirit is forced to raise up an environment as a blow to us so that we might be warned and corrected from the mistake or kept from falling into the mistake. All these activities are counted as discipline.

B. Education

The second purpose or category of the discipline of the Holy Spirit is education. Strictly speaking, the chastisement we have previously mentioned is also a form of education. However, the chastening education is a punishment due to our fault, while pure educational discipline has nothing to do with punishment or our fault, for though we may be faultless, we still must be educated. Therefore, in this aspect, the discipline of the Holy Spirit is necessary for every one of us.

The education given through the discipline of the Holy Spirit coordinates with the anointing work of the Holy Spirit within us in order to fulfill the goal of God's mingling with man. We have often said that the purpose of the anointing of the Holy Spirit within us is to anoint God's element into us. Nevertheless, there are many elements of self within us that replace the elements of God and are contrary to them; thus, this presents a great difficulty to God. Hence, the discipline of the Holy Spirit for education is given to purge us of the contrary elements through raising up the environment, in order that God's element may be anointed into us. The chastening discipline deals only with our *fault* and is concerned with the problem of our outward behavior, whereas the educational discipline deals with our human *element* and is concerned with the problem of our inward nature. Regardless of whether our outward behavior is good or bad, our inward nature is always in opposition to God.

For example, we would find it rather difficult to apply an additional coat of paint to a small table that already has been painted with a thick layer of glossy paint. Such a surface simply cannot absorb the new paint. In other words, the original element becomes an opponent to the element that is to be added. Therefore, we must sand off the original paint so that the surface becomes rough and better able to absorb the new paint. Likewise, if we are filled with the element of self, the Holy Spirit finds it difficult to anoint us through His moving and anointing within. Hence, there is also the need for the Holy Spirit to raise up environments that act like sandpaper upon us. This kind of scraping is not to punish us for rebellion, neither is it to correct our mistakes, but to make us rougher, who otherwise would be shiny and glossy, untreated and hard, thereby enabling the Holy Spirit to anoint God's element into us.

There are many brothers and sisters who are like glass, slippery and hard. Although the Holy Spirit often speaks to them, they will not listen. They have listened to many messages; indeed they have become an "old pro" at them. Regardless of what the message is, they know every point in the proper sequence; yet in fact they have not touched the reality of the message at all. This kind can only be dealt with by the Holy Spirit through various difficulties of the environment cutting and scraping them here and there; then they will listen to the message in a serious manner. At this time the word of the Holy Spirit as well as the anointing and moving of the Holy Spirit will be effective. Therefore, the second purpose of the discipline of the Holy Spirit is to coordinate with the inner anointing of the Holy Spirit, thereby educating us so that we may be receptive to the working of the Holy Spirit.

To prepare a spiced egg, the shell must be cracked so that the spices can penetrate into the egg. When God desires to penetrate us by the Holy Spirit, we who are whole according to nature, like the shiny egg shell, need to be cracked as a coordinating process for the penetrating work of God. This is the educational purpose of the discipline of the Holy Spirit.

For the educational purpose, the discipline of the Holy Spirit is given not only to break us so that the element of God may mingle more with us but also to cook us, because we are so raw and wild by nature. When we cook rice, it is not because the rice is faulty and needs to be corrected. We put the rice in the pot and cook it with water over fire so that the rice, which is raw and hard, may become cooked and softened, savory and good for eating. Similarly, all of us, before being dealt with by God, are raw, wild, and hard. We need God's discipline through the Holy Spirit and by the environment to burn and cook us. Such cooking will cause us to suffer and be afflicted, as though we had passed through fire and water, but it is done so that our raw and tough condition may become matured and softened, and that we may obtain the fragrance of maturity and be able to supply and satisfy man's need.

A raw person not only is wild and hard but also has a foul smell, like any uncooked fish or meat, regardless of how good the quality may be. A raw brother may have many natural virtues: he may be very gentle and meek; he may love the Lord, pursue the Lord, and even fervently serve the Lord. This is all good; yet, because he is still raw, uncooked, and of the natural, unresurrected life, all his virtues carry a foul, human smell rather than the fragrance of Christ. If you meet such a brother after he has been placed in difficulties for a certain length of time or has passed through serious illness, you will find that he is still gentle and meek, he still loves the Lord, pursues the Lord, and serves the Lord; yet you will sense that all these qualities are different: the raw and smelly odor has been greatly eliminated, and a sweet savor flows forth from him. If so, we must bow in worship to the Lord and say that this brother has really been educated by the discipline of the Holy Spirit.

C. Breaking

The third purpose of the discipline of the Holy Spirit is the tearing down or breaking. We have repeatedly said that the work of God in us is for the central purpose of mingling and building His element into us. To achieve this goal we must first be torn down. The educational purpose of which we have spoken is trivial and minor when compared to this. The educational discipline causes us to have merely an opening or a crack, while the breaking smashes and demolishes us completely, to the end that all that is of the natural and old creation in us will completely disintegrate. Therefore, breaking is the most severe step as well as the final goal in the discipline of the Holy Spirit.

We regret to say that in our midst we have not seen many being disciplined by the Holy Spirit in such a severe manner; neither do many of us know the discipline of the Holy Spirit to such a degree. Contrariwise, we see some who, the more they are disciplined by the Holy Spirit, the tougher and more built up in their own beings they become. This is a wrong condition. Normally, the more a person is disciplined by the Holy Spirit, the more he is terminated. The end result of the discipline of the Holy Spirit is always that we may be torn down, broken, and reduced to nothing. It is through the discipline of the Holy Spirit that God completely tears down our old creation so that the element of His new creation may be built up in us.

If one considers the discipline of the Holy Spirit merely as a chastisement or spiritual education, then this kind of discipline will cause him to be built up and perfected. It will seem then that one who originally was incomplete has become complete through being disciplined by the Holy Spirit, or that one who originally was in a poor condition, after having been disciplined by the Holy Spirit, has shaped up. Notwithstanding, the discipline of the Holy Spirit was never intended for this. On the contrary, the discipline of the Holy Spirit is given to break and smash the one who is whole and to mess up the one who is in such perfect shape. The original intention of the discipline of the Holy Spirit is not to build us up but to tear us down. Therefore, if a person is always gentle, the Holy Spirit will trouble him to such an extent that he can no longer be gentle. If there is one who never contends with others, the Holy Spirit will trouble him to an extent that he is forced to contend. Never think that because a person is not gentle he is therefore being disciplined by the Holy Spirit. Some people are always gentle, yet the Holy Spirit raises up an environment to disturb them and compel them to stop being gentle, even causing them to lose their temper terribly. This terrible losing of their temper is a kind of breaking to them.

The reason God breaks us is that all our natural element has no place before God. The gentleness, obedience, and other good points of some people are of the natural constitution and are by virtue of birth. Some people are born with a good temper; therefore, they receive praises from man and esteem themselves praiseworthy, not knowing that such a natural, good trait is the greatest hindrance to the work of the Holy Spirit within them. Thus, their spiritual life is retarded. Therefore, the Holy Spirit will raise up environments again and again to irritate such a person and cause him to lose his temper. The day will come when he can no longer bear all the irritation; he will lose his temper in a terrible way. Then he will be discouraged, feeling that having lost his temper so badly, he can no longer serve the Lord, and his future will be terminated. He does not know that while he is afraid of being terminated, the Holy Spirit fears lest he will not be terminated. The reason the Holy Spirit continually irritates and pressures him is that he may be terminated. Such is the severe nature of the discipline of the Holy Spirit.

If we have experienced the Lord more, we must confess that the discipline given us by the Holy Spirit, whether it be chastisement or education, is for our breaking. Actually, there is neither chastisement nor education; all the discipline of the Holy Spirit is for the tearing down and breaking. Only when we define them can we categorize them into the three aspects of chastisement, education, and breaking. In fact, after all is said and done, the discipline of the Holy Spirit has only one purpose—to tear us down and break us.

Since the primary purpose of the discipline of the Holy Spirit is for breaking, it does not necessarily have to do with any mistake on our part. He disciplines us regardless of our mistakes. Of course, if we are disobedient, we will be dealt with; however, though we are obedient, we will still be dealt with. His purpose is not only to correct us or to cause us to be more obedient but to break us. The basic purpose of His discipline is breaking. The more whole a person is, the more he needs to be torn down. It seems that those whose behavior is disorderly do not need His disciplinary breaking; since they are already full of wounds, they need only a deep repentance on the day that they are enlightened. Rather, he who has never done anything wrong or has never fallen, he who is so whole and well-behaved, such a one needs the striking, beating, dealing, and breaking of the Holy Spirit through the environment until he becomes totally smashed and terminated.

God's salvation is very special. On one hand, He needs the goodness of man, while on the other hand, He breaks it. According to the human point of view, this is really contradictory. When a person disobeys, God wants him to obey, but when he is obedient, God smashes his obedience. If a person is not gentle, God wants him to be gentle, but when he becomes gentle, God smashes his gentleness. When we do not love Him fervently, He wants us to be fervent, and He will draw us to love Him; yet when we love Him fervently, He breaks us to pieces. In God's leadings, the work of God always seems so contradictory. Yet this contradiction is exactly the breaking work of the discipline of the Holy Spirit in us.

Therefore, in experiencing this lesson we must pay special attention to the aspect of breaking. We need to see that although the discipline of the Holy Spirit has the twofold purpose of chastisement and education, nevertheless the ultimate purpose is the breaking. To put it simply, all the discipline of the Holy Spirit is for our breaking. He breaks us whether we are right or wrong. He breaks us whether we are obedient or disobedient. He breaks us whether we are rebellious or not. Before God, our evil is worth nothing, and so also is our good; our being wrong is worth nothing, and so is our being right; both our disobedience and obedience are worth nothing; both our rebelliousness and our submissiveness are worth nothing. These all need to be broken. The discipline of the Holy Spirit is entirely for the breaking of man.

III. THE POSITION OF THE DISCIPLINE
OF THE HOLY SPIRIT

The position of the discipline of the Holy Spirit in the entire work of God is first outward, not inward. Although the discipline of the Holy Spirit deals with things within us, the discipline itself is in our outward environment. The Holy Spirit uses all kinds of environments outside of us to discipline us and break us.

Second, the discipline of the Holy Spirit is negative, not positive. We have said that the positive work of God through the Holy Spirit includes the inner anointing, guidance, enlightening, and strengthening. The Bible speaks much about these aspects, which are all glorious, sweet, and of chief importance in the eyes of God. However, within us there are many natural elements that must be removed; therefore, in the work of God there is an accessory part, which is the environmental dealing or discipline. According to our experience, these dealings and disciplines are extremely vital; however, they are painful and shameful and, in God's eyes, are not of chief importance; thus, they are negative.

Furthermore, the positive work of the Holy Spirit within us is always accomplished through the Spirit of God, whereas the negative discipline of the Holy Spirit in our environment is brought about by the deeds of Satan. All the people, things, and happenings used in the discipline of the Holy Spirit are of Satan's manipulation. For example, if someone is opposing us and causing us trouble, this opposition or trouble is definitely not directly of God but directly from Satan. Again, a thief who steals our clothing, or a fire that burns our house, is definitely not sent directly by God but by Satan. If someone is obstinate, rebellious, and sins against God, and as a result becomes seriously ill, this sickness is not sent directly from God but from Satan. Therefore, all the people, things, and happenings involved in the discipline of the Holy Spirit are measured to us by God according to our need. But the one who is acting behind the people, things, and happenings in order to harm us is Satan. Therefore, this is another major reason why we say that the discipline of the Holy Spirit is not sweet.

Since the position of the discipline of the Holy Spirit is outward and negative, we should not consider it more important than the positive anointing of the Holy Spirit within. The purpose of our experiencing the discipline of the Holy Spirit is that we may experience the anointing of the Holy Spirit. If there were only the discipline of the Holy Spirit but not the anointing of the Holy Spirit, it would be meaningless.

IV. THE CHARACTERISTICS
OF THE DISCIPLINE OF THE HOLY SPIRIT

There are two characteristics of the discipline of the Holy Spirit: one is temporal; the other is of long duration. The temporal discipline is only for a short period of time and usually comes suddenly and passes quickly. Take for example someone who is hit by an automobile and is seriously injured but who does not die. After two weeks in the hospital he recovers, and the discipline is ended. This is temporal discipline.

The discipline of long duration is of a longer period of time, the least lasting several years, and the longest following us throughout our entire life. Thus, the pain is great and the breaking severe. Suppose, for example, that God gives a brother a quarrelsome wife or that He gives a sister a most unreasonable husband, causing them to suffer daily, perhaps unbearably. Since, as Christians, they cannot be divorced, the wife becomes the lifelong discipline to the husband, and, likewise, the husband to the wife.

The disciplines of long duration are mostly in an environment that we contact regularly, such as our family, job, church, or relatives. Among these, the family discipline is of the longest duration and is the most severe. Many in China say that a family is a cangue.* This is very meaningful. The people of this world take marriage as an enjoyment, but practically speaking, when we marry, we receive a painful dealing, and we must prepare to carry the cangue and wear a lock. There is nothing that binds people so much as the family. He who has a family is one who receives a bondage and discipline from God. The husband is a lifelong discipline to the wife, and the wife to the husband.

The children in the family are also a means of discipline. Those who are childless always wish to have children, but in spite of their wish, some remain childless. Others, who have many children, do not want any more, yet the more they do

---

*A wooden collar three or four feet square used in Oriental countries for confining the neck and sometimes also the hands for punishment.

not desire them, the more they have. A certain sister may wish to have a child as gentle as Jacob, but unfortunately the child is as wild as Esau and creates much trouble in the home every day. She is made to feel that her home is like a kiln. Servants can be dismissed, but children must be kept whether she likes them or not. They follow her all through her life and serve as discipline of long duration to her.

The church is also a place where man is severely disciplined. God ordains that we cannot be isolated Christians; we must be in the church and in the Body, serving the Lord and being coordinated with the brothers and sisters. However, God also arranges some very peculiar brothers and sisters to be with us. They love the Lord and are consecrated, but they have such peculiar dispositions. They always conflict with us and make us suffer. This also is the Holy Spirit's discipline of long duration.

Throughout our lifetime there are many instances of this kind of discipline. Some, like Paul, live continually with a thorn in the body—it may be weakness of the physical body or a certain disablement. This is a discipline of long duration. Temporal discipline lasts only for a short period of time, so we may hope for deliverance; but the discipline of long duration is of a long period of time and does not leave or change its flavor; it always remains the same. Therefore, when the discipline of long duration comes upon us, we should not hope for its passing; rather, we must give up all hope and be willing to accept it all through our life. Actually, the discipline of long duration is the most precious; it alone can give us lengthy and severe breaking. Good lessons are learned by going through the discipline of long duration. Therefore, we should pay attention not only to temporal discipline but even more to the discipline of long duration.

V. THE SCOPE
OF THE DISCIPLINE OF THE HOLY SPIRIT

The scope of the discipline of the Holy Spirit is universal. Its dimensions are equal to those of the universe. All that is in the universe is included in this scope. Therefore, everything that comes to us, including people, things, and happenings, either great or small, is the discipline of the Holy Spirit. We must believe that nothing a Christian encounters is what the people of the world call coincidence or luck, but the arrangement and discipline of the Holy Spirit. It is not that certain aspects, certain kinds of things, or certain matters are the discipline and arrangement of the Holy Spirit, and all others are not. We must admit that in all our living, every matter is the discipline of the Holy Spirit. The reason you have such a job opportunity is due to the discipline of the Holy Spirit. The reason you meet such brothers and sisters is also due to the discipline of the Holy Spirit. You wish you were healthy, but unfortunately you are weak; this is the discipline of the Holy Spirit. You expect your work to expand so that you can render good service to the Lord, but unfortunately you encounter so many problems that you are unable to move at all; this also is the discipline of the Holy Spirit. Whether you can have a virtuous and prudent wife or marry the husband of your desire depends on the discipline of the Holy Spirit. Whether or not you have a perfect home life depends also on the discipline of the Holy Spirit. You may not care to have many children, yet your children are especially numerous; this is the discipline of the Holy Spirit. Or, you wish you had children, but unfortunately you have none; this is the discipline of the Holy Spirit. Even the loss of property, mismanagement of affairs, or failure in spiritual matters is the discipline of the Holy Spirit. We must apply the discipline of the Holy Spirit to all our living, to all our environment. We must especially admit that all those circumstances that are neither pleasant nor agreeable are within the scope of the discipline of the Holy Spirit. Thus, we will learn this lesson in a thorough way.

VI. THE ACCEPTANCE
OF THE DISCIPLINE OF THE HOLY SPIRIT

To accept the discipline of the Holy Spirit we must take note of the following points:

A. Acknowledging That It Is Discipline

Acknowledgment precedes acceptance. When we receive the Lord as our Savior, we must first acknowledge that He is the

Savior. Likewise, in accepting the discipline of the Holy Spirit, we must first acknowledge that all we encounter is of the discipline of the Holy Spirit. In other words, whenever we encounter something, we must realize that it is of the Holy Spirit and acknowledge it as the discipline of the Holy Spirit.

We have previously referred to Romans 8:28, which says that *all things* work together for our good. Matthew 10:29-30 says also, "Are not two sparrows sold for an assarion? And not one of them will fall to the earth apart from your Father. But even the hairs of your head are all numbered." These passages show that all things that come to us, even such a trivial matter as the falling of hair, have been permitted and measured by God to work together for our spiritual benefit. Therefore, with regard to all things, we must admit that they are the discipline of the Holy Spirit.

B. Finding the Purpose

Since we acknowledge that whatever comes to us is the discipline of the Holy Spirit, we must discover what the purpose of the discipline is. For example, someone hit by an automobile cannot ignorantly think that since this is the discipline of the Holy Spirit, it is good enough to just praise the Lord; if so, he cannot reap the benefit. He must ask, Why was I hit by the automobile? What is the purpose of the Holy Spirit in giving me such discipline? Is it for chastisement, education, or breaking? He must have a longing heart and a prayerful spirit; he must be quiet before the Lord, seeking Him until he is clear that it is a particular problem or need that caused him to be disciplined by the Holy Spirit. In this way he can learn the spiritual lesson and obtain practical benefit.

C. Confessing Regarding the Point of the Purpose of Being Dealt With

Once we ascertain that the purpose of the discipline of the Holy Spirit in dealing with us is a certain problem, we should confess it seriously before the Lord with regard to that particular problem. Were it not for that problem and difficulty we would have no need for the discipline of the Holy Spirit.

Since the Holy Spirit arranges the environment to discipline us concerning a specific point, we must realize that it is in that specific point that we have a problem before God, either because we are stubborn or proud, stiff-necked or disobedient, not willing to pay the price, or not willing to deny self; it is either one thing or the other that must be removed or broken, dealt with or torn down. At any rate, there exists a problem. We must remember that the discipline of the Holy Spirit never causes us to suffer without a reason; rather, it is always because there are areas within us that require dealing. The Holy Spirit had already anointed us many times, perhaps, yet we disobeyed; therefore, He has arranged such a discipline to assist His inward anointing. Hence, once we discover the purpose of the discipline of the Holy Spirit, we should have a thorough confession regarding the point in view.

D. Submitting

After we confess our sin, we must submit through the Holy Spirit. This submission implies acceptance. After we see that the purpose of this discipline is to deal with a specific point, we must submit ourselves in that particular point. It is only then that we accept the discipline of the Holy Spirit.

E. Worshipping

After we accept the discipline of the Holy Spirit, we need to worship God. Worship is the highest form of gratitude. We have to worship God for His work in us and His way regarding us. For His dealing with us, for His way in our life, and for breaking us in such a way, we should not only give thanks before Him but also worship Him.

The clearest picture in the Bible of man worshipping God is seen in Jacob. When he was dying, he worshipped God, leaning upon the top of his staff. This staff, which he carried throughout his lifetime, depicts on one hand the whole experience of his life, and on the other hand his life as a sojourner. We place more emphasis upon the aspect of his entire life's experience, because it includes his life of sojourning. Therefore, when Jacob worshipped God by leaning on the top of his staff, it means that he worshipped God according to his experience. When a person has the experience of being led by God, he is then able to render worship before Him. However, if one has never had the experience of being dealt with by God, it is difficult for him to render worship before God. All the worship of man to God is based upon man's experience before God. Therefore, after being disciplined before God, we need to have a very clear, sure, and solemn worship. At this time, we are really accepting the discipline from God in a solid way.

Sometimes it seems that we have accepted a discipline before God, yet we have neither confessed to Him thoroughly nor accepted the discipline and worshipped Him solemnly. It seems that we have accepted the discipline, but we have not accepted it fully; therefore, that acceptance is not solid. Henceforth, when we accept the discipline of the Holy Spirit, may we first discover the purpose thereof, acknowledge our shortcomings and weaknesses, submit from within, and, finally, worship God. In this way our acceptance is very solid.

VII. THE APPLICATION
OF THE DISCIPLINE OF THE HOLY SPIRIT

Application means a continuous acceptance. If the nature of the discipline is temporal, it passes away after we have accepted it. However, if the nature of the discipline is of an extended and long duration, we need not only to accept it but to know how to apply it.

Take for example the illustration we gave earlier concerning the automobile accident. That was a temporal discipline. While the brother who was hit was on the hospital bed, he realized the cause of being disciplined and submitted. Soon after, he was healed, and thus the discipline passed away. However, when God prepares a wife, a husband, or a co-worker for us, one who is daily at our side, this kind of discipline is not merely to be accepted once but to be applied continuously. To apply the discipline means that we cooperate with the Holy Spirit and help Him to discipline and deal with us. When little children take medicine, they sometimes need an adult to squeeze their nose and force the medicine down their throat. It is not so when adults take the medicine. Although

the medicine is bitter, they still take it by themselves. Therefore, in applying the discipline of the Holy Spirit, we must not
be as little children taking medicine, having to be forced by God
to accept it; we must rather voluntarily and willingly accept
and apply it.

We should believe that all the environment we are confronted with is not just a temporal, accidental arrangement of
the Holy Spirit, but that it has been prearranged by the Holy
Spirit in the eternal plan of God. Before we were saved, and
even before we were born, God has already prearranged our
parents, husband or wife, children, church, or co-worker. In
the whole universe God has exercised His wisdom greatly to
look for all these wonderful disciplinary measures in order
to deal with us. Hence, we should not always desire that God
would change the opposite party or the environment. We must
continue to accept and apply His discipline until we are torn
down and broken.

VIII. THE EXAMINATION OF THE RESULT

When we accept the discipline of the Holy Spirit, we need
to look back after a certain period of time and examine how
much result we have obtained from this discipline. Some
people have been disciplined continually, yet there is no result
whatsoever. A certain brother may have passed through ten
or twenty years of discipline and tasted all sorts of troubles,
such as being jobless, poverty stricken, sick, in distress, and
other bitternesses of life; yet with him there is no indication
of any crack, wound, or breaking. He is just like an unbreak-
able iron shell. No matter how many dealings he has passed
through, he remains sealed and untouched, without any result
from the discipline. This is indeed regrettable!

Do not think that we have no wound because there has not
been any discipline. Actually, all of us have been disciplined.
Our God never errs; His hand can be seen in all that we
encounter. As a rule, each of us should be broken and show
the result of having been disciplined. The longer a brother has
been in the church, the more brokenness he should have. To be
broken is to be torn down. By breaking after breaking, our natural constitution is terminated. However, if we pass through

discipline, yet have not been broken, neither do we show any scar of having been struck or torn down, it proves our lack of accepting and especially our lack of applying the discipline of the Holy Spirit. We have simply submitted everything to fate and allowed the environment to pass meaninglessly by us as time goes on.

Therefore, each one of us should always look back and examine the result obtained from the discipline. The result will show whether our spiritual condition is rich or poor. The more we accept the discipline of the Holy Spirit, the greater will be the result and the richer the spiritual condition. However, if we accept little discipline, the result will accordingly be small and our spiritual condition poor.

IX. THE TESTING
OF THE DISCIPLINE OF THE HOLY SPIRIT

The discipline of the Holy Spirit is not only given to deal with us or to break us but also to test us.

Some people have been in painful trials, but after a certain period their sufferings have passed away, and their life has become easy. There is no criticism given them, but praise; no suppression, but exaltation; everything goes well. Such a prosperous environment tests where we are.

Therefore, the discipline of the Holy Spirit consists not only of trials of sufferings but also of tests of prosperity. Some brothers and sisters can endure the trials of poverty but cannot pass the tests of being rich. Some can endure criticism and attack but cannot pass the test of being praised or exalted. Some who have never been exposed to riches claim that they do not love money. That is not dependable. Not until gold and silver are within their grasp will it be proved whether they really love money or not. Some say that they would love their wife, but that is because they do not have a wife; once they have a wife for them to love, it will be proved whether they love or not. In order to expose our inner condition we need the Holy Spirit not only to use a trial through a painful environment, but we often need the Holy Spirit to put us in a favorable environment to test us. Therefore, the discipline of the Holy Spirit works through both trials and tests simultaneously.

But normally, the discipline of the Holy Spirit through trials by suffering is always more frequent than through tests of prosperity.

X. A FINAL WORD

The discipline of the Holy Spirit is an important lesson to the saints. There are many positive lessons for the saints, but this is the only negative one. Although there are other lessons of dealings that have to do with the negative aspects, all these require the coordination of the discipline of the Holy Spirit. The forefathers in the Bible and all the overcomers in the way of life as recorded in church history have had rich and definite experiences along this line. Although they did not necessarily use this term, *the discipline of the Holy Spirit,* it is abundantly evident that they experienced various environments confronting them as trials and tests. The apostle Paul in Philippians 4 tells us that he knew how to be abased and how to abound; this is because he learned the lessons of the discipline of the Holy Spirit amidst all circumstances. Much more should we who seek the growth of life pay full attention to this lesson, not only to know the points fully but to accept the dealings thoroughly. Then we will allow the hand of the Potter to mold and shape us, the pieces of clay, that we may become a fit vessel, filled with the glorious image of His Son.

CHAPTER THIRTEEN

DEALING WITH THE SPIRIT

Now that we have seen the discipline of the Holy Spirit, we will study dealing with the spirit. We join these two lessons together because they are closely related in our spiritual experience. Many times our spirit is not upright or correct because we have not received the discipline of the Holy Spirit. Therefore, the discipline of the Holy Spirit usually reveals the condition of our spirit. Moreover, it is only when we have dealt adequately with our spirit that we can accept from deep within the dealing of the Holy Spirit.

I. SCRIPTURAL BASIS

Psalm 51:10 says, "Renew a *steadfast* spirit within me." A steadfast spirit is not what we originally have but is usually the result of God's visiting and dealing with us.

Second Timothy 1:7 says, "God has not given us a spirit of cowardice, but of *power* and of *love* and of *sobermindedness*." This kind of spirit, which is powerful, loving, and having a sober mind, is given by God.

Galatians 6:1 says, "In a spirit of *meekness*." The spirit of meekness, which can restore those overtaken in some offense and which is possessed by the spiritual man, must be the result of man having been dealt with by God.

First Peter 3:4 says, "The incorruptible adornment of a *meek* and *quiet spirit*." This kind of spirit is not only meek but also quiet and is therefore a most valuable adornment in the sight of God. This must also be the result of man having been dealt with by God.

Proverbs 16:19 says, "To be of a *lowly* spirit." A lowly spirit, a spirit that is not proud, is obtained through having been afflicted and dealt with.

Matthew 5:3 says, "*Poor* in spirit." This means that there is neither self-satisfaction nor self-righteousness in the spirit. This kind of spirit is obtained by having passed through severe smiting and discipline.

Second Corinthians 7:1 says, "Let us *cleanse* ourselves from all defilement of...spirit." This verse speaks of dealing with the spirit and removing all defilement therein so that we may have a clean spirit.

II. THE DEFINITION OF THE SPIRIT

If we desire to deal with the spirit, we must first be clear what the spirit is. Man is of three parts: body, soul, and spirit. The innermost and deepest as well as the loftiest part is the spirit. Furthermore, we must especially point out that the spirit is the most genuine part of man. We may say that the spirit is the genuineness of man, the genuine man.

The spirit is deeper than the heart. Hence, the spirit is more genuine than the heart. Our living and acting must be according to our spirit in order that we may be genuine. Only when we speak from our spirit are we speaking in genuineness. Only when we deal with others in our spirit are we dealing with them in genuineness. Even our spiritual activities, such as praying, fellowshipping, and preaching, must all be done in our spirit in order to be genuine. Any activity without the exercise of our spirit is outward, shallow, and also false. Any activity not originating from the deepest part is not genuine. It is not an intentional pretension but the use of a wrong organ. Therefore, we must learn to exercise our spirit and be a genuine person in the spirit.

Generally, a man is most genuine when he loses his temper, for at that time his spirit is released. When a man is not angry, he always follows a certain set of rules or etiquette outwardly, and his real situation being hidden within. But when he becomes extremely mad, to the point that he can neither bear nor hide his anger anymore, he explodes regardless of everything. What he feels inwardly, he speaks forth outwardly; how angry he feels within, he expresses without; his outward manner depicts his real condition within. At this time his spirit, that is his genuineness, comes forth. Therefore, one who is refined in appearance and who seldom loses his temper is usually a false man, whereas one who often loses his temper is genuine. His genuineness lies in the fact that his spirit is being released. In conclusion, the deepest and most genuine part of man is the spirit, and the spirit is the genuineness of man.

III. THE MEANING OF DEALING WITH THE SPIRIT

We must learn the lesson concerning the spirit in two aspects: one is to let the spirit come forth, and the other is to let the spirit come forth cleanly.

The purpose of the previous lessons on dealing with the flesh, the self, and the natural constitution is to let the spirit come forth. The result of the dealings is that the spirit may be released.

In God's original arrangement for man, He placed the spirit of man above his soul and body in order that man might live by the spirit, on one hand exercising the spirit to contact God and be ruled by Him, and on the other hand exercising the spirit to control his whole being. But after the fall, the body and the soul usurped the position of the spirit so that man no longer lived by the spirit but by the flesh and the soul. Thereafter, man's spirit gradually withered and approached deadness. Therefore, all those today who have not experienced salvation are living in the flesh and the soul. The spirit within them seems to exist, yet it is almost without any function. Furthermore, man's body has become flesh because of sin, while the soul has become self because of self-opinion and has become natural because of natural ability. The flesh, self-opinion, and the natural constitution tightly and securely surround the spirit. When God comes to save man, His Spirit enters into man's spirit so that it might be revived and strengthened, enabling man to live again by the spirit. Nevertheless, the spirit of man is surrounded by the flesh, self-opinion, and the natural constitution, plus the fact that man is so accustomed to live by these; therefore, God requires that man, through the killing effect of the Lord's cross, put all these to death, dealing with them and breaking them, so that there will be some crack or opening for the spirit to come forth. When man's spirit comes forth, it brings forth also the Spirit of God. Thus, man can live by the spirit, directing his soul, controlling his body, being a genuine man, living and acting, worshipping, and serving God by the spirit. Therefore, dealing with the flesh, the self, and the natural constitution, which were discussed before, are for the breaking of both the flesh and the soul of man to enable the spirit to come forth. This is the first aspect of the lesson we should learn with regard to dealing with the spirit.

It is not enough, however, if we simply experience the breaking of the outward surroundings of the spirit so that the spirit can be released, for when it is released, whether its condition is correct, upright, pure, and unmixed is still another aspect of the problem. Our experience proves that some brothers or sisters are truly very faithful in denying self and dealing with the natural constitution so that their spirit can come forth. However, when their spirit comes forth, it bears with it some improper conditions, such as being rude, haughty, crooked, or unfair. This proves that in their spirit there is much mixture unpleasing to God.

For example, we have said that when a man loses his temper, his spirit comes forth easily. But the spirit that comes forth at such a time is undoubtedly cruel, full of hatred, and rude. This is an improper condition of the spirit. As another example, consider a brother who is going to a certain place to preach. He knows from experience that he cannot rely on his outer man but that he must allow his spirit to be released; hence, he denies self and rejects the natural constitution. As a result, his spirit as well as the Holy Spirit within his spirit are really released so that many people are touched. However, while he is speaking, there is a desire to exhibit himself and gain the praises of man, as well as a desire to compete with others and surpass them. This improper condition of boasting is manifested along with the release of his spirit. Without doubt his spirit is released at this time, but the condition of its being released is neither right nor pure.

Strictly speaking, within our spirit there are many impure

elements, such as haughtiness, boastfulness, crookedness, unfairness, cunning, subtlety, rebellion, and stiff-neckedness. The condition is complicated and delicate beyond our imagination. Therefore it is a problem whether or not our spirit is released, but even more a problem whether it is clean when it is released. With regard to our spirit, not only should we allow it to be released without any hindrance, but we should also cause it to be clean, pure, and proper when released. This is the second aspect of the lesson we need to learn with regard to the spirit, the lesson that we call dealing with the spirit. In conclusion, with regard to the spirit, we need on one hand to be broken in order to release the spirit, and we need on the other hand to be dealt with so that the spirit may be clean, the latter being what we call dealing with the spirit.

IV. THE SPIRIT ITSELF IS NOT DEFILED

Though we have said that the spirit must be clean, the spirit itself is not actually filthy. Indeed, 2 Corinthians 7:1 says to "cleanse ourselves from all defilement of...spirit," but this defilement is not of the spirit itself but a defilement effected by the soul and body.

Our judgment regarding this is based upon the process of the human fall recorded in the Bible. In Genesis 3 we see that at the fall, man received the suggestion of Satan first in his soul; therefore, man's soul has been corrupted and made filthy. In addition, with his body man ate of the tree of the knowledge of good and evil; therefore, man's body has been contaminated by the mingling of the element of Satan. Yet at this time man's spirit was not involved. During man's first committing of sin, the spirit did not participate. Therefore, after the human fall, although man's spirit was deadened through the defiling influence of soul and body, yet there was no mingling of the element of Satan in the spirit. Hence, the spirit itself is not defiled.

For example, our conscience at times is contaminated and produces the feeling of offense; yet the conscience itself has no problem. This fact still remains until today, and it is proven by the unsaved, who, whenever their spirit is revived or their conscience is touched, always stand on the side of God. They

are able to differentiate between good and evil, and, through
the fellowship part of their spirit, have the concept of worshipping God. Even the strongest atheist, who denies the
existence of God, still has a sense deep within him of God.
These remaining functions of the spirit prove that the spirit
itself is clean.

V. THE PASSAGE OF THE SPIRIT IS FILTHY

If the spirit itself is not filthy, why does it sometimes manifest itself in an unclean and improper manner? It is because
the spirit must pass through many of our inward parts when
it comes forth. Within the inward parts is filthiness so that
when the spirit passes through them, it is defiled, and thus
the filthiness is brought forth also. Therefore, when the spirit
is released and manifested, it exhibits certain defiled and
improper conditions.

For example, the water from a hot spring often bears the
odor of sulphur. Actually, the water itself is clean and odor-
less, but as it flows out, it passes through a sulphur deposit
and brings with it the sulphuric element. Since there is the
element of sulphur in the water, it becomes sulphur water,
and when it flows out, it carries with it the sulphuric odor.

Likewise, the spirit in our innermost part is pure and
undefiled. However, surrounding the spirit are the soul and
body, both of which have been mixed with the wicked elements of Satan and are thus filthy and corrupt. Therefore,
when the spirit comes forth and passes through the soul and
body, it becomes contaminated by this filthiness and corruption. Hence, when being manifested, the spirit bears certain
filthiness, corruption, impurity, impropriety, and various
other undesirable conditions. If a person is proud in his soul,
the spirit also manifests itself in pride; if a person is angry
in the flesh, his spirit also reveals the anger. We often encounter the spirit of anxiety, the spirit of jealousy, a crooked spirit,
or a rude spirit, all of which are not the problem of the spirit
itself but the defiling influence of the undesirable elements of
the soul and body upon the spirit as it passes through them.
We can tell the kind of defilement from the kind of spirit, and
the kind of spirit reveals the kind of man.

That man's spirit carries this filthiness of the soul and body is indeed a dreadful thing. It seems that when the spirit is inert, the filthiness of the soul and body are not so critical, but when the spirit is activated and released, then all the filthiness of the soul and body are brought forth. This is very serious. We may liken this situation to dynamite, which, when kept in the storeroom, is not harmful. But when a fire breaks out in the storeroom, causing an explosion, the condition is serious. Fire itself is not explosive, but when it passes through the dynamite, the two will explode together. Likewise, if a person hates others in the soul, it is not too serious; but if his spirit is being released while he is hating others, it carries with it the hatred of the soul, and thus it becomes a spirit of hatred. This is rather serious.

Therefore, it is not enough for us to simply learn to release the spirit; we must completely deal with all the mixture in our spirit so that when the spirit is released, it will neither be dangerous nor cause trouble to others.

VI. THE SCOPE OF THE PASSAGE OF THE SPIRIT

The passage of the spirit can be summed up as the soul and the body, but when studied minutely it can be divided into the purpose of the heart, the motive, the aim, the intention, the heart, the mood of the heart, the will, and the flesh. The purpose of the heart has something to do with the heart, whereas the motive and intention can be either in the heart or in the soul. The flesh has to do with the physical body.

Since all these passages of the spirit surround our spirit, they naturally affect the spirit, which must pass through them in order to be released, and which also brings forth their elements and conditions. Hence, the condition of the spirit reflects the condition of all these passages. If our motive is not pure, the spirit also is not pure when released; if our intention is not clean, the spirit coming forth is also not clean.

We can see this more fully from the illustration we have used concerning preaching when it is used for showing off and for competition. When the brother is preaching, his spirit is released, but with the air of display and competition. This is because there are the elements of display and competition in the purpose of his heart and in his motive. With the purpose of heart for self-glory, the result is a showy and boastful spirit. His competitive motive, moreover, causes others to touch a competing and striving spirit.

Therefore, man's spirit is indeed the most genuine part of man. No matter what a man's condition is, it is manifested when his spirit comes forth. When we contact others or help others in spiritual matters, we should touch their spirit and know their intention and motive. Thus, we shall know the real condition of man deep within him.

Take for example a brother who comes to see the elders and says, "Brother So-and-so and I engaged in business together, and he has wronged me. I come not to accuse him but simply to have some fellowship with you, the responsible brothers." Although he declares that he does not come to accuse his brother, his spirit proves otherwise. His motive and intention in fellowshipping are to accuse his brother. Once we touch his spirit, his motive and intention can never escape our discernment.

The purpose of the heart and the motive in man's spirit are just like a person's accent—they are very difficult to disguise. For example, suppose a southerner insists on saying that he is a northerner. If he is silent, he might pass, but the more he argues, the more his accent reveals that he is a southerner. The day that Peter was in the court of the high priest, the more he defended himself by saying that he was not one of the Nazarenes, the more his Galilean accent betrayed him (Matt. 26:69-73). Likewise, someone may claim that he is humble, yet his spirit reveals his pride. Someone may declare that he is absolutely honest, yet his spirit causes us to sense his crookedness. Another may say that he would be happy to help if there were only an opportunity, yet you touch in him an unwilling spirit. Still another may say that he really wants to obey but that because of a certain difficulty he cannot obey, yet from his spirit we can tell that from the very beginning he has never wanted to obey. The situation in a man's spirit is much more complicated than the outward expression. Therefore, we must judge according to man's spirit, not according to his words.

All brothers and sisters desiring to serve the Lord in the church must especially learn this lesson. If we merely observe a man's outward attitude and listen to his words, we can easily be deceived. However, if we learn to touch his spirit, the purpose of his heart, his motive, his aim, and his intention cannot escape our observation. Since these are the passages of the spirit, and the spirit bears these conditions as it is being released, its condition reflects these exact conditions. There is no exception to this.

VII. DEALING WITH THE SPIRIT BY DEALING WITH ITS PASSAGE

Since the defilement of the spirit is due to the passage of the spirit (which includes the purpose of the heart, motive, aim, and intention), then dealing with the spirit is not dealing with the spirit itself but with the passage of the spirit, that is, with the purpose of the heart, motive, aim, and intention. Whenever we are about to act or speak, not only do we need to inquire whether what we are about to do is right or wrong, good or bad, but we must also discern whether or not our inner intention is clean, our motive pure, and our aim wholly for God. Is there any selfish purpose behind our action? Is there any self-inclination? This kind of dealing is dealing with the spirit.

For example, suppose a certain brother has a controversy with you, which causes you to be very angry and disgusted. When you mention him to others, although outwardly you speak lightly as if nothing really matters, nevertheless your words cause others to sense a spirit of condemnation and anger. One day, perhaps during a meeting or while in prayer, you receive mercy from the Lord and realize that since the Lord has forgiven you, you must certainly forgive your brother. At this time, from your deepest being, you deal thoroughly with your unforgiving purpose of heart and intention. Later, when you mention this brother to others, although you touch the controversial matter of the past, your spirit is undisturbed and upright. At this time, not only does your spirit come forth, but it comes forth cleanly without any other intention.

In the church, those who can really supply others and edify the brothers and sisters are those who have a clean spirit through this kind of dealing. If our spirit has never been dealt with, then even while praising others we cause an uncomfortable feeling in others. This is because our spirit is not clean. It may be that in our praising there is the purpose of flattering or the intention of gaining rewards from others. Contrariwise, one who has had his spirit dealt with may even rebuke others in a firm and straightforward manner, causing those who are rebuked to feel upset in the soul; yet their spirit will receive supply and enlightenment, and will thus feel refreshed and satisfied. This is because his spirit is clean and pure, having no other motive.

For this reason we need not only to have our flesh, self, and natural constitution broken so that the spirit can come forth, but we must go one step further and deal with all the negative purposes of the heart, undesirable intentions, impure inclinations, improper will, and mixed emotion to the end not only that the spirit can come forth but that it may come forth in an upright, clean, and pure manner. Therefore, we need these two steps of dealing. The first step is the dealing of breaking in order to release the spirit; the second step is dealing with all the elements in the passage of the spirit so that the spirit can come forth in a clean way. This dealing with all the elements is dealing with the passage of the spirit and also dealing with the spirit.

Since the passage of the spirit includes every part of our being, we need to deal with every part of our being when dealing with the spirit. This kind of dealing is deeper and more delicate than the various dealings mentioned before. If we compare dealing with sin and dealing with the world to our washing clothes, dealing with the conscience to taking a bath, dealing with the flesh to shaving, dealing with self to the flaying, and dealing with the natural constitution to cutting, then dealing with the spirit is comparable to taking out all the blood cells in order to examine and clean each one. Beginning with dealing with sin, every step of the dealings becomes deeper and finer as we go on. When we come to dealing with the natural constitution, we are being dealt with completely within and without. The only part remaining is the mixture coming forth with the spirit. When we have the spirit dealt with and cleansed from all mixtures so that not only does the spirit come forth but it comes forth as a clean, pure, and upright spirit, then our whole being is completely and thoroughly dealt with. Therefore, following this, we obtain the filling of the Spirit. When all the elements of our old creation have been completely dealt with, then the Holy Spirit can possess and fill our whole being.

VIII. THE DIFFERENCE BETWEEN DEALING WITH THE SPIRIT AND DEALING WITH THE CONSCIENCE

Dealing with the conscience and dealing with the spirit are very delicate dealings within us and are seemingly difficult to distinguish. However, when we compare them carefully, we realize that the objects of their dealings differ. Dealing with the spirit emphasizes dealing with the impure intentions, motives, and other mixtures within us, whereas dealing with the conscience emphasizes dealing with the feeling of the conscience toward all the mixtures.

For example, consider a sister who relates a certain matter to others. While she is speaking, there is a bad motive hidden within her. Afterwards, her conscience condemns her, causing her to feel that it was not right to speak with a bad motive. She confesses the matter before God and deals with it before others. At this point, she has dealt with the matter of speaking thus to others with a bad motive, and she has peace in her conscience. Yet she has not dealt with the bad motive itself. Hence, that element, that mixture, still remains within her, though it will not be manifested as long as she keeps quiet and does not release her spirit. However, as soon as she mentions the same subject, her spirit being released, that particular motive, that mixture, will automatically be brought forth. Later, when she is enlightened and sees what a base motive she has had and that it should no longer remain within her, she deals with that bad motive through the power of the Holy Spirit. At this time, she has not only dealt with her improper, outward behavior but also with the mixture itself within her. In dealing with the outward behavior, as far as the behavior is concerned, it is dealing with sin; as far as the feeling of the conscience toward the behavior is concerned, it is dealing with the conscience; and dealing with the inward mixture is dealing with the spirit.

Consider another example. A brother is very dissatisfied with another brother and has many feelings of criticism and complaint. Although these feelings have not been expressed, yet within his conscience he realizes that this is not right; therefore, he confesses this as sin before God. This is his dealing with his own conscience. Nevertheless, he is not willing to abandon these dissatisfied feelings and deal with these mixtures. Therefore, whenever he is reminded of this brother or mentions the brother, his spirit still contains these mixtures and is still a dissatisfied spirit, full of criticism. Up to this point he has only dealt with the feeling of the conscience but not the mixtures in his spirit. He has only the experience of dealing with the conscience but not the experience of dealing with the spirit. Therefore, he may have peace in his conscience but the mixtures in his spirit have still not been eliminated. Not until he receives mercy again and abandons the dissatisfaction hidden deep within him, so that there is no more such mixture in his spirit, will he have once learned the lesson of dealing with the spirit.

In conclusion, dealing with the conscience is only a matter of dealing with the feeling. We need to deal with the spirit in order to deal with the nature within. It is only when the nature is dealt with that the root of the matter is treated. Therefore, dealing with the spirit is deeper and more severe than dealing with the conscience. Dealing with the conscience is but a lesson in the second stage of the spiritual experience of life, whereas dealing with the spirit can only be experienced at the end of the third stage.

IX. THE WAY OF DEALING WITH THE SPIRIT

A. Our Initiative

The practical way to deal with the spirit is similar to that of the various dealings mentioned before. First, we need to condemn the mixtures, and second, to remove them by the power of the Holy Spirit. For example, if we have a crooked spirit, we must first condemn this crookedness as sin. Second, we must purge out this crookedness from within us by the power of the Holy Spirit. Although the condemning and the removal are through the power of the Holy Spirit, yet they are of our own initiative. We must be willing to have such dealings and desire them; then we can draw from the power of the Holy Spirit. The Holy Spirit requires the cooperation of our will; when He has this, He will supply us with the power for dealing. This is the most basic principle of our dealing in life.

The putting to death mentioned in Romans 8:13 means that we take the initiative to put to death; it does not mean that the Holy Spirit does it for us. The Holy Spirit is the means, but we must take the initiative. The Holy Spirit supplies the strength, but we must take the initiative to put to death the practices of the body by the Holy Spirit. We have spoken before of Galatians 5:24, which says that we who are of Christ Jesus have crucified the flesh with its passions and its lusts. This crucifying is also of our initiating, not of the Lord's. No doubt the crucifixion was accomplished by the Lord, but that is only an objective basis; our taking the initiative to crucify the flesh is our subjective application. We need to take the initiative to apply the cross and crucify the passages of the spirit, including our flesh, our self, our natural constitution, our purpose of heart, aim, intention, inclination, and motive.

B. The Cross as the Basis

This type of dealing initiated by us differs from human cultivation. Human cultivation is purely the work of man, whereas the dealing that we initiate is based upon the fact of the cross. It is because the Lord has already condemned sin on the cross that we can deal with sin. It is because the Lord has already judged the world on the cross that we can deal with the world. Likewise, it is because the Lord has done away with our old man on the cross, and our flesh, temper, self, natural constitution, and all other mixtures as well, that we can employ this fact as a basis upon which to deal with our flesh, temper, self-will, natural ability, and all the mixtures in the passages of our spirit.

C. The Function of Life

In dealing with the spirit, we have not only the accomplished fact of the Lord on the cross as the basis, but we have moreover the life of the Lord's death and resurrection as the power. Because this life issues from the death of the cross, it has within it the element of the death of the cross. Therefore, when His life flows into us, it brings us back to the death of the cross in order to unite us with the death of the cross, thereby joining us to the cross. This may be likened to the electric current following through the light bulb: it connects the bulb with the power plant, while at the same time the electricity of the power plant can manifest its function by causing the bulb to give forth light. Likewise, when the resurrection life of the Lord enters into us and moves within us, it produces the effect of death, which enables us to have the various dealings of putting to death. This life within us spontaneously gives us feelings that require us to deal with sin, the world, the feeling of the conscience, the boasting and desires of the flesh, the self-opinion, the ability of the natural life, and all the mixtures in the different parts of our whole being. All these dealings are in the accomplished fact of Christ on the cross and are now being experienced by us in the Holy Spirit.

Once we have the feeling derived from the life of the Lord within us, we need to exercise our will to cooperate with His life and immediately initiate the dealing. If we cooperate in this manner, this feeling of life becomes a killing power, enabling us to have the experience of the killing of the cross. At this time, the putting to death of the cross becomes manifest in our living in a very practical way by removing our unrighteousness, unholiness, offense in our conscience, flesh, temper, self-opinion, natural constitution, and all mixtures in the various parts of our being. At this stage, our whole being is not only broken so that the spirit can be released but also purified so that the spirit that is released is pure and upright, meek, and normal.

D. The Standard of Peace

The standard of our dealing with the spirit is still "life and peace." We only need to deal to the degree of having peace within; this is sufficient. However, concerning the degree of dealing whereby we can obtain peace, the Holy Spirit will be responsible to speak to us and give us a clear feeling. Many times the speaking of the Holy Spirit within us has a higher standard than the outward demand. If our growth in life reaches the degree of dealing with our spirit, then the demand of the Holy Spirit within us will not only be higher than the law of this world but higher and more severe than the regulations in letter in the Bible. Therefore, as long as we feel that there is no problem deep within, that is sufficient. If, however, there is some problem deep within that gives us no peace, we should not listen to outward reasonings. We must take heed to the inner demand of the Holy Spirit and thereby attain the standard required by the Holy Spirit deep within.

CHAPTER FOURTEEN

BEING FILLED WITH THE HOLY SPIRIT

We now come to the fourteenth experience of life, which is being filled with the Holy Spirit. This is a very complicated matter because it is a vast subject in the Bible. In the past two thousand years all Bible expositors as well as those with spiritual pursuit have had different views and various explanations regarding this subject. Therefore, to this very day many people, unable to find a common definition, are rather confused regarding this subject. However, if we accept the word of the Lord with a pure heart and compare our experience with it, we will feel that it is rather simple. As we presently discuss this subject, we will try to simplify it as much as possible, departing wholly from the nature of research and simply speaking about our experience in accordance with the Scripture.

When considering this matter of being filled with the Holy Spirit or the work of the Holy Spirit on us, we must be very clear that, as far as the Bible is concerned, it is divided into two periods—the Old Testament and the New Testament; and as far as our experience is concerned, it is divided into two great aspects—the outward and the inward.

I. THE CHARACTERISTICS OF THE WORK OF THE HOLY SPIRIT IN THE TWO GREAT PERIODS, THE OLD TESTAMENT AND THE NEW TESTAMENT

A. In the Old Testament the Spirit of God Coming upon Man Outwardly, Whereas in the New Testament the Holy Spirit Dwelling in Man Inwardly

The first characteristic of the work of the Holy Spirit on man in the two periods, the Old Testament and the New

Testament, is that in the Old Testament the Spirit of God came upon man outwardly, and in the New Testament the Holy Spirit dwells within man. The Old Testament often contains such sayings as, "The Spirit of God (or the Spirit of the Lord) came upon..." a certain person. This implies that the Spirit of God came upon man and moved man to do a certain work. Although in the Old Testament this action of the Spirit of God coming upon man to move him to work for God occurred quite frequently, in principle at that time the Spirit of God had not entered into man or dwelt in man and mingled with man. Since the Spirit of God merely came upon man, He would "not strive with man forever" (Gen. 6:3), and He could be taken away (Psa. 51:11). It was not until the New Testament period that the Holy Spirit began to enter into man and mingle with man; moreover, He will live in man forever, no more to be separated from man; thus, man can enjoy the blessing of the Holy Spirit eternally. Therefore, the indwelling is the most outstanding feature of the work of the Holy Spirit in the New Testament period.

B. In the Old Testament the Spirit of God Being Mainly for Empowering, Whereas in the New Testament the Holy Spirit Having Come Mainly to Be the Life (Nature)

Second, we must see clearly from the light of the Bible that in the Old Testament period the Spirit of God descended upon man to move man to perform God's work. The emphasis was upon the Spirit of God being the power to man. In the Old Testament, through generation after generation, the Spirit of God continually descended upon man as a divine power that moved man to work, fight, and speak for God, or as the excelling wisdom that enabled man to manage affairs for God. For example, after the Spirit of God descended upon Moses, he was empowered to fight with Pharaoh and speak for God. The Spirit of God upon him also became Moses' wisdom, enabling him to manage the affairs for God, take charge of the house of God, lead the Israelites, rule God's people, and build the tabernacle for God. All this work performed by Moses did not stem from his own power or wisdom but was the result of the descending of the Spirit of God upon him.

Although people in the Old Testament received the Spirit of God upon them as power and wisdom, in principle they did not receive the Spirit of God into them to mingle with them and be their life. In the Old Testament times, the Spirit of God merely descended upon man as power but did not enter into man as life; He only bestowed a divine power upon man but did not impart to man a divine nature. Therefore, in the Old Testament we see a number who possessed the power of God yet had nothing whatever of God's nature. Samson is the best example (Judg. 14—16). He had the supernatural power of God upon him, but at the same time he did not have the nature of God in him at all. Here we have a strong man whose power was beyond measure, yet whose nature was totally incompatible with God. It is rather difficult to find anyone in the Old Testament who was stronger than Samson; as far as power is concerned, Samson was undoubtedly a superman. But with regard to his nature and life, Samson was the poorest among all those used by God in the Old Testament. In nature and life Moses and David had something that was somewhat close to the presence of the Spirit of God, but with Samson such a condition did not exist at all. Therefore, with respect to power, Samson was full of the Spirit of God, but with respect to life, he did not have the Holy Spirit. This is because in Old Testament times the Spirit of God descended upon man as power, not as life. He descended upon man so that man might have God's power but not His nature. It is not until the New Testament times that the Holy Spirit formally entered into man and became man's life so that man might have God's nature.

C. In the Old Testament the Spirit of God Being Employed by Man, Whereas in the New Testament the Holy Spirit Being the Lord in Man

Based upon the above two points we can conclude that the Spirit of God who descended upon man in the Old Testament did not come in His person to be the Lord for man to obey but as a power to be employed by man. We know that the Holy

Spirit is a person, but in Old Testament times the Spirit of God did not descend upon man in His person. If He had descended upon man in His person, He would have come as Lord, and man would have had to obey Him. Nevertheless, in Old Testament times He descended as a power without His person; therefore, it seemed instead that He obeyed man and was employed by man.

Take for example the gasoline in a car: it is without a person; it is not the master of the car for the car to obey. It is because the car does not have the power to move that the car is filled with gasoline. The gasoline is the moving power of the car and is used by the car. Likewise, God desired that Moses deliver the Israelites out of Egypt and lead them into Canaan, but Moses found himself lacking in power. He lacked the power to speak to Pharaoh on behalf of God. He also lacked the power to lead the millions of Israelites through the wilderness. Neither did he have the power to rule the house of Israel nor the power to build a tabernacle for God according to the heavenly pattern. Undoubtedly, Moses was learned in all the knowledge of Egypt and was very capable; however, his limited learning and capability were not sufficient to meet the need of this great commission. Therefore, the Spirit of God came not to be his master for him to obey but to supplement his lack of power and be under his command. Moses was like a bicycle that could run only ten miles per hour, and the Spirit of God was like a motor added to the bicycle that increased its speed to seventy miles per hour. Actually, the Spirit of God coming upon man in the Old Testament was just like the motor added to the bicycle, the purpose of which was not to become the master of the bicycle nor to control it but to become its moving power and increase its effectiveness. This was exactly the meaning of the vision of the burning bush, which Moses saw when he was called (Exo. 3:2-3). The bush was Moses, and the fire was the Spirit of God that descended upon him. The bush was of little use, but the fire burning upon it became its strength.

Therefore, we must keep in mind the principle that in Old Testament times, although the Spirit of God descended and became a great moving power to man, nevertheless He did not descend in His person to become the Lord of man for man to obey; rather He descended upon man as a power to be employed by man.

However, the principle of the work of the Holy Spirit is entirely different in the New Testament. At this time, when He descends to work on man, He not only descends upon man to be the power to man, but He dwells within man and is mingled with man to be his life, thereby imparting God's nature into man. This means that now He comes in His person to dwell in man. Since He comes in His person to dwell in man, He comes to be the Lord of man, requiring man's obedience to Him. It is interesting that there is not a single sentence in the entire Old Testament saying that man ought to obey the Spirit of God. But in the New Testament we are told that the Holy Spirit takes the control over us (Acts 16:6-7) and that we ought to walk by the Spirit (Gal. 5:25). Second Corinthians 3:18 especially calls the Holy Spirit "the Lord Spirit." The Holy Spirit today is the Lord, a person. He dwells within us to be our Lord; therefore, we must commit ourselves to Him and submit ourselves to His rule. He is not only our power but also our Lord. He is not only the gasoline in the car but the Driver. He is not only the motor of the bicycle but the Owner who rides it. Not only does the moving power of the car depend on Him, but whether the car stops, proceeds, goes forward, or goes backward is all under His driving and operating. Our nature and our life is of Him. He is our life, our nature, and our Lord.

D. In the Old Testament the Spirit of God Being of a Single Aspect, Whereas in the New Testament the Holy Spirit Being of a Double Aspect

We who are under the New Testament dispensation enjoy the double blessings of the Holy Spirit, namely, the aspect of His being power to us and the aspect of His being our life and nature. Those living under the dispensation of the Old Testament enjoyed the Spirit of God only as the outward power, whereas those of the New Testament enjoy the Holy Spirit as the inward life as well. This does not mean that in New Testament times God terminates the aspect of the work that was done in the Old Testament, but rather He continues even more the former aspect and adds another aspect. In the Old Testament there was only one aspect, but in the New Testament there are two aspects. In the Old Testament there was only the outward, but in the New Testament there are both the outward and the inward. Therefore, under the dispensation of the New Testament, we can not only rely upon the Holy Spirit as the outward power to perform the work committed to us by God, but through the Holy Spirit as life within, we can mingle with God as one. What a glorious grace of God this is!

II. THE DIFFERENCE IN EXPERIENCING THE HOLY SPIRIT OUTWARDLY AND INWARDLY

We have seen the characteristics of the working of the Holy Spirit in the two great periods of the Old Testament and New Testament. We come now to see our experience of the Holy Spirit inwardly and outwardly.

A. The Inward Experience Being First; the Outward Following

People in Old Testament times did not experience the indwelling of the Holy Spirit but only the outward descending of the Spirit of God. However, in New Testament times man can have both aspects; moreover, man must first experience the indwelling of the Holy Spirit and later experience the outward descending of the Holy Spirit. Therefore, in New Testament times the indwelling of the Holy Spirit becomes the basis for His outward descending upon man.

1. The Lord Jesus as the Model

The first person in the New Testament who experienced the indwelling of the Holy Spirit was Jesus of Nazareth. When the Holy Spirit dwelt in Jesus of Nazareth, this great act of God marked the change of age. Since the history of the human race began, although many had experienced the descending of the Spirit of God upon them, moving them to do the work of God, there was not one among them who had the Holy Spirit indwelling him, mingling with him, and becoming his life and nature. Neither Moses nor David was such a person; neither

Elijah nor Daniel was such a person. For four thousand years there had not been such a person. It was not until four thousand years had passed that Jesus of Nazareth appeared, in whom the Holy Spirit dwelt and mingled and became His life and nature. This was because the very life within Him was from the Holy Spirit.

Since the Lord Jesus was the first to experience the indwelling of the Holy Spirit, and since He is the Head of the New Testament believers as well as of the church, then the manner of the Holy Spirit's work on the New Testament believers and the church is the same as that which was upon Him; the Holy Spirit works on the Body in the same manner as He worked on the Head. The experience of our Head, the Lord Jesus, with regard to the Holy Spirit, becomes the very pattern or example for us, the New Testament believers, in experiencing the Holy Spirit.

The experience of the Lord Jesus with regard to the Holy Spirit was clearly divided into two aspects: first the inward experience of the Holy Spirit as life, and then the outward experience of the Holy Spirit as power. He began to experience the Holy Spirit as life within when He was being conceived. The Lord Jesus was conceived by the Holy Spirit (Matt. 1:20). It was the Holy Spirit who entered into Mary, one of the old creation, and out from her was born Jesus the Nazarene. Therefore, from the time that the Lord Jesus was conceived, His inward life and nature was of the Holy Spirit. In other words, we may say that from the day He was born He was filled with the Holy Spirit.

From the day the Lord was born until He came forth to work for God—during these thirty years—He lived in the presence of God by the Holy Spirit as the life within Him. Isaiah 53:2 says, "He grew up like a tender plant before Him, / And like a root out of dry ground." This refers to His life before He was thirty years of age. It was entirely by the Holy Spirit infilling Him as His life that on one hand He was able to live humbly in the house of a poor carpenter as a son of man, while on the other hand He was able to walk according to the laws of God.

When He was thirty years old and was about to work for

God, the first outward event occurred: while He was being baptized in the river Jordan, the Holy Spirit descended upon Him as a dove, and He was filled with the Holy Spirit. After forty days of trials in the wilderness, He was even more filled with the power of the Holy Spirit and worked for God in the various regions round about Galilee (Matt. 3:16; Luke 3:21-23; 4:1-15). We see that this condition of His was exactly the same as that of the Old Testament people experiencing the Holy Spirit. When Ezekiel was by the river Chebar, the Spirit of Jehovah descended upon him, and he opened his mouth and spoke for God (Ezek. 1:1-3). In the same manner, when the Lord Jesus was in the river Jordan, the Holy Spirit descended upon Him, and He opened His mouth to preach the glad tidings of the kingdom of the heavens. This proves that the Lord Jesus experienced at this time another aspect of the work of the Holy Spirit: the descending of the Holy Spirit upon Him as a divine power, enabling Him to work for God.

From this we see that the Lord Jesus experienced the Holy Spirit in two aspects: the experience of the Holy Spirit within as life in order that He might have God's nature, and the experience of the Holy Spirit without as power, enabling Him to do the work of God. He first experienced the Holy Spirit within as life while He was being conceived; later, when He was being baptized, He experienced the Holy Spirit without as power. At this time He was filled with the Holy Spirit both inwardly and outwardly.

Some think that John the Baptist was the first one filled with the Holy Spirit in the New Testament. It was really not so. Concerning John the Baptist, Luke 1:15 says, "He will be filled with the Holy Spirit, even from his mother's womb." However, in the original text the filling here refers to the aspect of outward power, in the same principle as that of the Spirit of God descending upon the prophets outwardly in the Old Testament. Although with respect to time he received the Holy Spirit while he was in his mother's womb, this, however, was still of but one aspect—the outward aspect of power. It was unlike what the New Testament people have received, which is of two aspects—first the inward and then the outward, the aspect of life and then the aspect of power. Although John was the greatest among the prophets, the Lord said that the least in the kingdom of the heavens is greater than he (Matt. 11:11). Therefore, according to the principle of experiencing the work of the Holy Spirit, he was somewhat like those who were in the Old Testament period; his experience cannot be fully listed in the New Testament period.

2. The Experience of the Apostles

Immediately after the Lord Jesus, the apostles were the first group to experience the Holy Spirit. They also experienced first the indwelling of the Holy Spirit and then the outward descending of the Holy Spirit. As early as John 14, the Lord promised His disciples that He would ask the Father to send them another Comforter, even the Spirit of reality, to dwell within them so that they might live as the Lord lives (vv. 16-20). This word of the Lord indicated that they would experience the Holy Spirit inwardly as life.

On the night of the resurrection, while the disciples were together, the Lord came into their midst and "breathed into them and said to them, Receive the Holy Spirit" (20:22). Thus, the Lord fulfilled His earlier promise by causing them to have the Holy Spirit enter into them and become their life. On the day God created Adam out of the dust, He breathed into him so that he might have life and become a living man with a spirit. Now, in the same manner, the Lord breathed into the disciples so that they might have life and become regenerated men. However, that which God breathed into man at creation was not the Spirit of God; therefore, what man obtained was only his own spirit, plus a created life. On the night of the resurrection, what the Lord breathed into His disciples was His own Spirit; therefore, the disciples obtained the Holy Spirit plus His uncreated, eternal life, that they might live forever as the Lord Himself lives. Therefore, strictly, accurately, and practically speaking, Peter, James, John, and the rest of the apostles became regenerated by obtaining God's life on the night of the resurrection. The breath that the Lord breathed into them was the breath of life. It was wholly for life, not for power.

At Pentecost, the apostles experienced the other aspect of

the work of the Holy Spirit, namely, the Holy Spirit as power. Acts 2:1-4 says, "As the day of Pentecost was being fulfilled, they were all together in the same place. And suddenly there was a sound out of heaven, as of a rushing violent wind, and it filled the whole house where they were sitting. And there appeared to them tongues of fire, which were distributed; and it sat on each one of them; and they were all filled with the Holy Spirit and began to speak in different tongues, even as the Spirit gave to them to speak forth." From this time forth, the apostles preached the gospel with great power, bringing thousands and tens of thousands to salvation.

If we compare both instances of the experiences of the apostles in receiving the Holy Spirit, we can see the difference. The Holy Spirit of life, which they experienced on the night of the resurrection, was symbolized by the "breath"; whereas the Holy Spirit of power, which they experienced at Pentecost, was symbolized by three things—"wind," "fire," and "tongues." Both wind and fire typify power, whereas the tongue is for speaking and is also related to power. Furthermore, at Pentecost, the Holy Spirit "sat on each one of them"; He did not enter into them. Therefore, what they experienced then was the Holy Spirit upon them outwardly as their power. It was through this outward power of the Holy Spirit that they were able to speak the tongues of the nations, preach the gospel, and later work for the Lord in different regions.

Therefore, in the experience of the apostles, we can also see both aspects of the work of the Holy Spirit and that they experienced the inward aspect first and then the outward.

B. Both the Inward and the Outward
Experienced at the Same Time

After Pentecost, the experience of the Holy Spirit inwardly as well as outwardly was fully accomplished in the Head (the Lord Jesus) as well as in the Body (represented by the apostles). From this time onward, all those who desire to experience the work of the Holy Spirit can experience both the indwelling and the outward descending of the Holy Spirit at the same time. The proof of this was seen in the house of Cornelius.

In Acts 10 we see that Peter was sent to preach the gospel in the house of Cornelius, and while he was preaching, the Holy Spirit fell upon all those who heard, causing them to receive not only the indwelling Holy Spirit as life, but also the Holy Spirit as power descending upon them outwardly. Therefore, beginning with the household of Cornelius and continuing to this day, it is possible to experience the Holy Spirit's work within and without at the same time. The Holy Spirit within is the basis for the Holy Spirit without, while the Holy Spirit without is the proof of the Holy Spirit within. This is the most normal condition.

Of course, throughout the generations there have been many who experienced the Holy Spirit only as life within when they were saved; then after a certain period of time they experienced the Holy Spirit as power without. There have been also some who never experienced the Holy Spirit outwardly as power. In any case, in the dispensation of the New Testament, none can experience the Holy Spirit outwardly as power before experiencing Him inwardly as life. Neither can anyone only experience the Holy Spirit outwardly as power without experiencing Him as life within. Such cases can never occur in the New Testament dispensation.

III. THE WAY TO BE FILLED WITH THE HOLY SPIRIT

A. The Accomplishment of the Objective Fact

In order to be filled with the Holy Spirit, we need first to know that, as far as the objective fact is concerned, both aspects—the inward and the outward—have been accomplished by God. The Holy Spirit as life within was given on the night of the resurrection, while the Holy Spirit as power without descended on the day of Pentecost. The chorus of a hymn by A. B. Simpson says, "Doubt not the Spirit, / Given long ago" (*Hymns,* #248). The descending of the Holy Spirit is like the crucifying of the Lord Jesus—both are accomplished facts. Today the Lord Jesus does not need to be crucified again; neither does the Holy Spirit need to descend again. God does not have to give the Lord Jesus to man again to be crucified for man; neither does God have to send down the

Holy Spirit again to fill man within and without. God has already accomplished it all. The problem now is in our receiving it by faith. In order to gain Christ and experience Christ today, we need only to receive Him; likewise, in order to obtain the Holy Spirit, either inwardly or outwardly, we also need only to receive Him. To what extent we receive the Holy Spirit, to the same extent the Holy Spirit will fill us. We shall now study separately the two aspects of receiving the filling of the Holy Spirit.

B. The Way to Be Filled with the Holy Spirit Inwardly

The way to be filled with the Holy Spirit inwardly is as follows:

1. Emptying Ourselves

In order to receive the regeneration of the Holy Spirit, we must first confess, repent, and accept the fact that Christ has died for us. Likewise, in order to receive the infilling of the Holy Spirit, we must first accept the fact that we have died with Christ. Then we must deal with sin, the world, the flesh, our self-opinion, and our natural ability, to the end that we may completely empty ourselves of these, allowing none of them to have any more place in us, but rather allowing the Holy Spirit to gain all the ground in us. If we will respond to the demand of the Holy Spirit, removing that which must be removed and forsaking that which must be forsaken, thus emptying ourselves and letting the Holy Spirit have all the ground and authority in us, then automatically the Holy Spirit will fill us, and we will subjectively experience and enjoy the infilling of the Holy Spirit. For this reason we have placed this lesson of being filled with the Holy Spirit after all the experiences of the dealings.

2. Believing

After we have dealt with everything and emptied ourselves, we must believe that the Holy Spirit is filling us from within. We only need to believe in the filling of the Holy Spirit, without trying to feel whether or not we have been filled. Real faith does not depend on feeling. If we will only believe in this manner, the Lord will cause the filling of the Holy Spirit to become our practical experience.

C. The Way to Be Filled
with the Holy Spirit Outwardly

The way to be filled with the Holy Spirit outwardly is as follows:

1. Being Willing to Be Used by God

We have previously said that the Spirit of God descending upon man as power is for empowering, that man may be made competent for the work committed to him by God and that he may be used by God. Beginning in the Old Testament, whoever was really willing to be used by God obtained the descending of the Spirit of God upon him as power. Moses was such a person; so also were Samson, David, Elijah, Elisha, Ezekiel, and other prophets.

In the New Testament the principle is still the same. The first example in the New Testament of one upon whom the Holy Spirit descended was the Lord Jesus. The reason the Holy Spirit descended upon the Lord on the day He was baptized was that the Lord was testifying to heaven and earth through baptism that from that day He was going to be officially used by God. At the time when people in the world cared neither for God's will nor God's work, but lived only for themselves, Jesus of Nazareth stood forth before the whole universe, declaring that He desired to live for God, to be used by God, and to work for God. It was at this time that the Holy Spirit descended upon Him.

This was true also with the first group of apostles. Originally they were fishermen, but they gave up both the fish and the boat, and with their whole heart were willing to be used by God. They desired to continue the work of the Lord to fulfill God's work on earth. Their heart's desire and attitude prepared the way for God to pour out the Holy Spirit upon them at Pentecost.

Examples of this kind are innumerable in church history. About two hundred years ago, among the Moravian Brethren there was a great outpouring of the Holy Spirit. Before that, they also were prepared to be used by God; therefore, at a meeting of the Lord's table, the Holy Spirit greatly filled them. After this they were used by God in a surpassing manner.

Actually, if from the beginning all those who are saved would be willing to abandon everything for the Lord to be used by Him, then upon being saved each one would be in a position to receive both aspects of the filling of the Holy Spirit simultaneously, as occurred in the house of Cornelius. We regret to say that today there are too few who are willing to be used by God upon being saved. Most people are satisfied with just possessing eternal life and not having to perish. They completely disregard God's work and God's plan; neither do they desire to have power to work for God and fulfill His plan. Although each one when saved has to some extent the move of the Holy Spirit and a desire to work for God, nevertheless, because they are not willing to give themselves up to be used by God, they suppress the Holy Spirit's move and their desire. Even though the Holy Spirit within repeatedly moves them and puts demands upon them, they persist in refusing. When Rebekah was engaged to Isaac, she made no delay, but leaving her father's house, she followed the old servant to give herself to Isaac (Gen. 24). Many people today have believed in Christ and are saved, yet they refuse to give themselves to Christ. They linger in their original position, unwilling to let the Lord use them. Hence, our Lord always seems to be cheated by men. He gave salvation to men, yet men turn their backs on Him, refusing to give themselves to Him. Such a condition renders men unable to receive the outward filling of the Holy Spirit after they are saved.

Since man is so unwilling to be used by God, few obtain the outward filling of the Holy Spirit, causing this experience to become mysterious and rare. In fact, the outward aspect of the Holy Spirit is by no means more precious or more difficult to obtain than the Holy Spirit within, the only requirement being that we be willing to be used by God.

2. Believing

Once we have offered ourselves and are willing to be used

wholly by God, we must believe in the outward filling, the outpouring, of the Holy Spirit. This too must be taken by faith rather than by feeling. If we are so willing to be used by God and we believe in the outpouring of the Holy Spirit, then the outward power of the Holy Spirit will be manifested upon us.

Therefore, there is no need to beg for the outward filling of the Holy Spirit. All we need to do is to rise in answer to God's call, commit ourselves to the Lord to be at His disposal, and tell Him, "Lord, I know that You have saved me so that You can use me. Now I put my all in Your hands to be at Your disposal. I also know that according to my own strength I can do nothing; therefore, I need Your Spirit. Since I know that Your Spirit has already been given, I am here to receive it by faith." In this way, the experience of the outpouring of the Holy Spirit is not a difficult matter. As to the manner of the manifestation of the outward filling, we need to allow the Holy Spirit to bear full responsibility. Some admire others' outward manifestations and insist that they also speak in tongues, cry, or laugh as others do; if so, what they really desire is the speaking in tongues, the crying, or the laughing, not the outpouring of the Holy Spirit. Others insist not to cry or laugh, for they are afraid of being possessed by a demon. This also is a wrong concept. Our insistence often limits the free working of the Holy Spirit. Therefore, while we experience the outpouring of the Holy Spirit, we need to afford complete freedom to the Holy Spirit, neither insisting upon anything nor refusing anything.

In summary, the filling of the Holy Spirit within and without is a glorious blessing under the New Testament. It is also a fulfillment of the blessing promised to Abraham by God (Gal. 3:14). May we on one hand empty ourselves more so that the Holy Spirit together with the fullness of the Godhead may fill us from within, thereby enabling us to live out the glorious image of God. On the other hand, we need to give ourselves more to the Lord to be used by Him so that the Holy Spirit may descend upon us richly, giving us power and gifts. Then we can serve God, deal with God's enemy, and bring in the kingdom of God.

THE FOURTH STAGE—CHRIST'S FULL GROWTH IN US

Now we will consider the fourth stage of our spiritual experience. This is the last and highest stage of our spiritual life—Christ's full growth in us.

After we have passed through the previous stages, all difficulties in us relating to sin, the world, the offense in the conscience, the flesh, the self, and the natural constitution having been dealt with and purged, there remains in us nothing but God. God now has gained absolute ground in us, and our whole being within and without is entirely filled with the Holy Spirit. Now we enter the highest stage of the spiritual life, where Christ is fully grown and matured in us. We have, therefore, called this highest stage "Christ's full growth in us."

Let us look at the type in the Old Testament as shown in the account of the Israelites' departure from Egypt and their entrance into Canaan. At the outset of their journey, by passing through the Red Sea, they left Egypt, the land of bondage, while Pharaoh and his army were buried under the sea. Henceforth, the world with its usurping power was stripped off. Later, they fought with the Amalekites, which is a type of their dealing with the flesh. Then the Israelites wandered in the wilderness for forty years. The number forty in the Bible denotes testing and affliction. God led them to walk through the wilderness for forty years because He desired, by means of testing and affliction, to expose the wickedness of their flesh. His intention was that the flesh should be dealt with exhaustively. Our experience is the same. After baptism, it is not enough to deal with the flesh just once; we must be dealt with in the hand of God for months and years. Sometimes God leads us through the wilderness so that not only is our living difficult but even our spirit is dry, depressed, and miserable.

The only reason for this is that through testing and affliction our flesh might be dealt with.

When the Israelites fulfilled their days of wandering, God led them through the Jordan, and they were circumcised in Gilgal. On one hand, they entered the promised land of Canaan in a practical way; on the other hand, they were facing the seven nations of the Canaanites, and warfare was required in order to annihilate them and establish the kingdom of God. This prefigures the fact that when our days of testing in the spiritual wilderness are fulfilled and we have learned to let our flesh be dealt with to a certain degree, God will lead us through the spiritual Jordan, where the flesh will be completely rolled away (*Gilgal* means "a rolling") and cut off (Col. 2:11). Henceforth, we shall attain to the heavenly realm in a practical way, thereby inheriting all the fullness of Christ. Furthermore, it is at this very time that we contact the hosts of evil spirits in the heavenlies and begin the experience of spiritual warfare.

During their entire journey, the Israelites passed through two bodies of water: the Red Sea, and the river Jordan. The Red Sea was for the burial of Pharaoh and his armies, whereas the Jordan was for the burial of the Israelites themselves. When they passed through the Jordan, they brought twelve stones over with them and set up another twelve stones in the riverbed. These two groups of twelve stones represent the twelve tribes. They signify that the "old" twelve tribes were terminated in the Jordan, and the "new" twelve tribes passed over to the other side of the river to enter into the promised land. Both of these two bodies of water through which they passed typify the death of Christ. The water of the Red Sea is a type of the aspect of Christ's death that ends the power of the world. The water of the Jordan represents the aspect of Christ's death that brings our old man to an end. When the Israelites passed through the Red Sea, they could fight only with the Amalekites; not until they passed through the Jordan could they fight with the seven nations of the Canaanites. This means that in the beginning of our spiritual life, after our baptism, we can only have warfare with the flesh (Gal. 5:17). Not until our spiritual life has reached the climax, when our flesh has been completely buried and rolled away and all our difficulties within have been resolved, will we be able to deal with the enemy without and engage in spiritual warfare.

We understand by all these types that the first three stages of our spiritual life have transpired before we pass through the Jordan. The fourth stage occurs after we cross the Jordan and enter into the land of Canaan. All our difficulties have been dealt with on the other side of the river Jordan and in the river Jordan. Now we come to this side of the river to deal with God's difficulty, to fight against and totally destroy the seven nations of the Canaanites—the powers of spiritual darkness and wickedness in the heavenlies (Eph. 6:12)—who are usurping this promised land of God. Thus, spiritual warfare must be placed in the last and highest stage of our spiritual life. Only by passing through the various dealings and having our own problems solved can we engage in spiritual warfare.

From another point of view, God has a twofold purpose for all His redeemed ones: first, and most important, that we be filled with God Himself and manifest His glory; second, that we rule for God and deal with His enemy. When we reach the end of the third stage of our spiritual life, we are filled with the Holy Spirit, or God Himself; this, the first and most important purpose of God, has been fulfilled. It is at this time that God desires that we learn to fight for Him and deal with His enemy so that His secondary purpose can be fulfilled in us. This is what we will experience in this fourth stage of our spiritual life.

In this fourth stage, we shall cover five experiences: (1) knowing the Body, (2) knowing the ascension, (3) reigning, (4) spiritual warfare, or bringing in the kingdom of God, and (5) full of the stature of Christ. Now let us come to the first experience of this stage, that is, knowing the Body.

CHAPTER FIFTEEN

KNOWING THE BODY

Everyone who wants to engage in spiritual warfare must first know the Body. Nothing requires us to know the Body so urgently as spiritual warfare, because spiritual warfare is not an individual matter but a Body matter. No individual believer can fight with the enemy; it takes the whole Body. If we wish to learn spiritual warfare, we must first know the Body.

We must wait until the fourth stage to speak of knowing the Body, because the Body referred to here is the mystical Body of Christ, the church. This Body is formed by Christ as life in each of us, mingled with us. During the second and third stages of our experience of life, we are still living in our own life; therefore, we cannot know this life that mingles with us to form the Body. Only when our self life has been utterly dealt with and we have the experience of passing through the Jordan and entering into the fourth stage shall we be able to touch the reality of this life of the Body and come to know the Body.

Everyone who is saved is a member of the Body of Christ. Is the life in each one of us, then, a life pertaining to the *members* or to the *Body*? The Bible and our experience prove that though each one of us is a member of Christ, the life in each one of us is not a *member* life but a *Body* life. All the members of our body are sharing one life. Each member shares in common the same life together with all the other members, that is, the life of the entire body. For example, an ear, unless it has been cut off, shares the same blood that flows through the eye, the nose, and the whole body. Similarly, in the Body of Christ, when one member is joined to the Body or having fellowship with the Body, his life is the life of the Body, and the life of the Body is his life. It would not do for him to be separated from the other members, or vice versa, because the life both in him and in the other members is of the same Body; it can neither be distinguished nor separated. It is this life that joins us together to become the Body of Christ; or, to say it more precisely and emphatically, it is this life that mingles with us to become the Body of Christ.

We cannot, however, experience this before the difficulties of the self have been entirely dealt with. If we are still living according to the flesh, in ourselves, and serving the Lord in our natural ability, the life of the Body, which is Christ Himself in us, has no way of being manifested, and there is no way for us to know the Body. The more we live by the flesh, the less we feel the need for the support of the Body. If we live by our self-opinion, we find no need for the sustaining of the church. If we serve with our natural ability, we sense no need for the coordination of the members. Only when our flesh has been dealt with, the self-opinion has been broken, and the natural life has been smashed, shall the life within cause us to realize that we are simply members of the Body and that the life in us cannot be independent. Hence, this life requires us to have fellowship with all other members and be joined to them, and it also brings us into that fellowship and the experience of being joined together. It is at this time that we begin to know a little concerning the Body and become qualified to engage in spiritual warfare.

On one hand, we say that if we want to fight the spiritual warfare and deal with God's difficulty, we must first deal with our flesh, self, and soul-life, thus solving our own difficulties; on the other hand, we say that in order to fight the battle, we must first know the Body, and in order to know the Body and live in the Body, we must first deal with our flesh, self, and soul-life. Whether, therefore, we speak from the standpoint of fighting the warfare or knowing the Body, we all must first pass through the preceding three stages—coming out of the flesh, the self, and the soul-life—in order to attain to the fourth stage of the experience of life.

We shall now consider the matter of knowing the Body from several aspects, beginning with God's plan.

I. GOD'S PLAN

God's plan from eternity is to obtain a group of people to share His life, bear His image, and be united with Him as one. In the purpose of this plan there are two points that we should observe in knowing the Body.

A. God Wanting to Work Himself into Man and Make Man like Himself

This matter is absolutely related to His Son. The Bible reveals to us that God is in His Son; all that God is and all that God has, all the fullness of the Godhead, dwells in the Son (Col. 2:9). We can say that if there were no Son of God, there would be no God.

The usual concept of a son places the emphasis on the son being born of the father, and the son and the father existing as separate beings. But in the Bible the emphasis in relation to the Son of God is that He is the expression of God and cannot be separated from God. In John 1:18 we read, "No one has ever seen God; the only begotten Son, who is in the bosom of the Father, He has declared Him." This verse reveals that the Son of God is the expression of God, or the expressed God. No one has ever seen God, but now the Son of God has declared Him. When man sees the Son of God, he sees God. The Son of God is the expression of God and the manifestation of God. Outside of His Son, God has no expression or manifestation. Therefore, God and His Son are inseparable.

Since God and His Son cannot be separated, neither can the object of God's plan be separated from His Son. God wants to work Himself into man, which means that God wants to work His Son into man. God desires to make men like Himself, which means that God desires to have men like His Son. God wants men to be one with His Son. Genesis 1:26 shows us in figure that in creation God wanted men to have His image and share His likeness. In the New Testament it is pointed out clearly and practically that God wants men to have His image, which means that He wants them to "be conformed to the image of His Son" (Rom. 8:29). When men are conformed to the image of His Son, they bear God's image, because the Son is the image of God (Col. 1:15).

B. In God's Sight This Group of People, Which He Purposed to Be United with His Son and Bear The Image of His Son, Being Not a Number of Individuals but a United, Corporate Body.

We can trace this thought from the three different ways that the Bible speaks concerning our relationship with His Son:

(1) We are the brothers of God's Son (Heb. 2:11; Rom. 8:29). This aspect may seem to indicate that we as individuals are brothers of God's Son, but the Bible emphasizes the fact that we and Christ together express God. Before Christ came in the flesh, God had only one Son and one expression in the universe. After Christ came to this earth and became flesh, He imparted His life into us so that we may become sons of God and His brothers. Henceforth, God has many sons in the universe. As this one Son is God's expression, so all the sons are similarly God's expression. Therefore, in saying that we are Christ's brothers, the emphasis is that we and Christ together are God's sons and together are God's expression. Even so, the Bible does not infer that as brothers we are a number of separate individuals. For though we become brothers of Christ one by one, the Bible further states that we are the "house of God" (1 Tim. 3:15). Though we are many sons of God, the individual son is not the unit. The unit is the corporate unity of all the sons, who have come together as one house, one family.

(2) We are the bride of Christ (Eph. 5:31-32; 2 Cor. 11:2). Some may think that because there are thousands of saved ones, Christ has thousands of brides, as in a polygamous system; but the Bible shows that Christ has only one bride— the church, which is composed of all the thousands of saved ones. When the Bible says that we are the bride of Christ, the point of emphasis is that we have come out from Christ and are a part of Christ, just as Eve came out from Adam and was

a part of Adam. In the beginning Adam did not have many ribs removed but only one, that is, the rib that became Eve. Similarly, Christ did not have many segments removed (such as one segment for one brother to be saved, and another segment for a sister to be saved), but only one segment was taken from Him, and that was for the saving of the church. The church is the only part that came out from Christ. When we say that we are the bride of Christ, the idea of corporateness is expressed more specifically than when we refer to ourselves as the brothers of Christ.

(3) We are the Body of Christ. In Ephesians 1:23 we read that the church is the Body of Christ. In 1 Corinthians 12:27 we read, "You are the Body of Christ, and members individually"; in 1 Corinthians 10:17, "We who are many are one Body." These verses state that we are the Body of Christ, not that each one of us individually forms the Body of Christ. We are joined together to become the mystical Body of Christ, and we as individuals are members of this Body. The Body, therefore, can best express our corporate oneness.

The point to be stressed in what we have said regarding ourselves as the bride of Christ is that the church came out from Christ. When we refer to ourselves as the Body of Christ, the point to be emphasized is that the church and Christ are one. Just as Eve came out from Adam and was presented to Adam to become one flesh with Adam, so also the church came out from Christ and is presented to Christ to become one with Him. Christ is the Head; the church is the Body. The two cannot be separated. The church itself is one; the church and Christ are also one. This demonstrates even more clearly that what God desired for His Son was a corporate Body, not a number of separate individuals.

In summary, we see five points in God's plan: (a) God desired to work Himself into man and unite Himself with man so that man would resemble Him. (b) God is in His Son. Therefore, when He wanted to work Himself into man, He wanted to work His Son into man; when He wanted man to be united with Himself, He wanted man to be united with His Son. (c) The people whom God wanted to be united with His Son are the brothers of His Son, those who share the sonship with His Son and together with His Son express Him. (d) This group of people is the bride of His Son, a part of His Son, taken out from His Son. (e) This bride not only comes out from His Son but is presented to His Son to become the Body of His Son. When this Body appears, the plan of God has been fulfilled. To put it quite simply, the plan of God is to have a Body for His Son, and this Body is the church. The church is the Body of Christ; it is the sole object of God's plan. God's creation is for this; His redemption is for this; His work throughout all generations is for this. When this purpose has been accomplished, the Body of Christ will appear, the bride will appear, and the many brothers will appear. It is then that God's desire will be satisfied, His goal reached, and His plan fulfilled. Thus, if we want to know the Body, we must know the plan of God.

II. GOD'S CREATION

Second, we shall consider the creation of God. We have already said that God's heart desire is to get a group of people who will have His life and express Him. For this purpose He brought His creation into being. But when God created man, He did not create many men but only one—Adam. If God could create one man, He could have also created thousands of men. Why then did He not at the same time create thousands of men, instead of creating only Adam and letting thousands of men come out from him? The reason is that the thought of God is only one.

From the beginning of history, the number of human beings is countless, but since they have all come out from Adam, in God's sight there is only one man. To God there is but one man in the universe, not millions or billions of men. We can prove this by 1 Corinthians 15:45 and 47. In this passage the apostle speaks of Adam and Christ as "the first man" and "the second man." This second man is also "the last" one. Therefore, from the creation till now, in God's eyes there is only one other man besides Christ. In order to complete His purpose and fulfill His plan, God created only one man. It was not in God's thought to impart Himself to many individuals. His desire was to impart Himself to one corporate man and to express Himself through this one corporate man.

This same principle also holds true in the creation of woman. In the creation, God made only one woman; that is Eve. We know that Eve represents the church. He made only one man, which means that He desires only one corporate man to become His image. He created only one woman, which means that God desires only one corporate man, which is the church, to become the bride of Christ. In conclusion, in God's creation His thought is one, and this oneness is the Body that we speak about.

III. GOD'S REDEMPTION

Third, let us consider the redemption of God. In His redemption, His thought is still only one. Speaking from the standpoint of our experience, some have been saved recently, some scores of years ago, and some hundreds of years ago; some were baptized in the United States, and some in other countries. But though these events have taken place at different times and in different places, from God's standpoint, He never saves individually. When He saves, He redeems the whole church.

A good example of this is the account of the Israelites coming out from Egypt. When the entire house of Israel came out from Egypt, the lamb was eaten and the blood applied at the same place and at the same time. Then at the same time and at the same place they passed through the Red Sea. From our limited viewpoint, some ate the meat and applied the blood at one place, while others ate the meat and applied the blood several hundred houses away. When passing through the Red Sea, some were in the front of the procession, and others were in the rear of the procession; they may have been thousands of feet and many minutes apart. But in God's viewpoint, they ate the meat and applied the blood simultaneously in Rameses (Exo. 12:37), and their passage through the Red Sea (14:29) was also a simultaneous act.

For example, when an ant transports its food from one corner of the room to another, he considers that he is traveling quite a distance, but from our viewpoint he is simply moving about in one room. Similarly, in our understanding, salvation takes place earlier or later, here or there; but with God a thousand years is as one day (2 Pet. 3:8). Therefore, in the eternal view of God, we are all saved at one time. He did not save us one by one, individually; He saved us corporately, as one man. Therefore, in His redemption, as in His plan and in His creation, His thought is still one. He did not plan for His Son to have two bodies but only one; nor did He create two persons for His Son but only one. Whether in God's plan, in His creation, or in His redemption, the thought is one and one alone, and this oneness is the Body.

IV. IN CHRIST

After we were redeemed into Christ, our position in Christ is still one. In ourselves we are many, but in Christ we are only one. In Christ there is only one church. In Christ there is one mystical Body. This mystical Body of Christ is one. The spiritual meaning of the Body is one. Whenever we as Christians are not one, we are not in the Body, and we demonstrate that we have not seen what the Body is.

The Epistle to the Ephesians speaks especially about the church. It states that the church is the mystical Body of Christ. The Epistle to the Ephesians is also a book that mentions the matter of "one" the most. It mentions seven "ones": one Body, one Spirit, one hope, one Lord, one faith, one baptism, and one God (4:4-6). Seven is the perfect number. So this perfect "one" is in the Body, and this perfect "one" is the mystical Body of Christ.

V. IN THE HOLY SPIRIT

In Christ we are one; moreover, in the Holy Spirit we are one. This oneness in the Holy Spirit is what we commonly call fellowship. If we live in the Holy Spirit, we have this fellowship, and we have this oneness, which is the reality of the Body. When we lose this fellowship in the Holy Spirit, we do not have this oneness, and we do not have the Body.

VI. IN LIFE

In life we are still one. We have mentioned elsewhere that

the life within us is not a divided life but a complete life. Because of the fellowship in the Holy Spirit, the life in each one of us is complete and undivided. The life in me is the life in you and also the life in God. Therefore, His life in all of us is one. We are all one in this life. Not only the good Christians are one with us in life but also the failures, the weak ones, and the poor ones. This oneness in life is the mystical Body of Christ.

VII. IN FELLOWSHIP

The fellowship we refer to here is fellowship in life. Since we are all one in life, the fellowship issuing from this life is one. Whenever there is oneness, there is fellowship. When there is no oneness, there is no fellowship. Therefore, when we are in fellowship, we are one. Today, in Christendom, people often advocate unification. This proves already that they are not one and not in fellowship; that is why unification is necessary for them. If we live in fellowship, there is no need for unification, for we are already united; we are one. This oneness is the Body of Christ.

VIII. IN EXPERIENCE

Since all the seven points already mentioned indicate oneness, in our experience we should also be one. If in our experience we are one, we are conscious of the oneness, and we touch the oneness; then we know the Body and live in the Body. But in fact it is not so simple. In God's plan, in God's creation, in God's redemption, in Christ, in the Holy Spirit, in life, and in fellowship, all is one. We have no problem with these matters, because these are accomplished facts on God's side. But on our side, whether we are one in experience differs with individuals. Some already have a little experience, whereas others have none. What we shall stress now is this oneness in our experience.

First of all, we must know that our knowledge and experience of this oneness are definitely related to our spiritual age. With the young and immature, their knowledge and consciousness of this oneness is superficial and light; with the experienced and mature, it is deep and weighty. For example, a newly saved brother feels that he is far behind the other brothers who have been saved for five or ten years. But when this brother grows in his love to the Lord, he tends to feel that the other brothers and sisters who do not love the Lord cannot be compared with him. When he learns some spiritual lessons, he feels that he is much superior to those brothers and sisters who have not learned. Sometimes, when in a meeting with young brothers and sisters, he feels that their prayers, being poor both in content and in utterance, are not good; therefore, he will not open his mouth. This continuous feeling of being different from others proves that he does not have the consciousness of oneness and that he is still in an immature stage, not knowing the Body.

This is not the case, however, with the experienced brothers and sisters. There are two seemingly contradictory aspects to their feelings. On one hand, they feel that these younger brothers and sisters are really far behind them, but on the other hand, they feel that they are the same as all the brothers and sisters. Whatever the brothers and sisters feel, they feel likewise. The immature ones always feel different from others, but those who are deep in the Lord and developed in their spiritual experience feel no such difference. Therefore, the reason we cannot be one in our experience is because we are immature and shallow. When we arrive at this fourth stage in our spiritual experience, there is no feeling of difference but a spontaneous feeling of oneness with all. This is knowing the Body.

If we speak with regard to dealings, knowing the Body is also a kind of dealing, that is, a dealing with individualism. All those who do not know the Body are individualists. Their views, actions, living, and work are individual. All this individualism is because they still live in the flesh, the self, and the natural constitution. This resembles the parasitic vine, which winds itself about the tree and dies only when the tree of flesh, the self, and the natural constitution are cut down. Only when the flesh, the self, and the natural constitution have been severely dealt with will individualism be removed. When men no longer live as individualists, they come to know the Body.

Knowing the Body is not a doctrine that by speaking and hearing you may understand. Knowing the Body is the result of many past experiences. Having passed through all these experiences, we come at length to know the Body. When we go to visit a place of fame, we travel a certain distance; at length we arrive at our destination and see the object of our journey. So it is with knowing the Body. If we wish to know the Body and touch the reality of the Body in experience, we must walk a certain distance and climb certain slopes in the spiritual life. We must start from the experience of the clearance of the past and pass through the experiences of dealing with sin, the world, and the conscience, climbing diligently from one stage to the next. We must be severe with ourselves in learning the lessons one by one, especially in dealing with the flesh, the self, and the natural constitution. Only when we have experienced the first three stages of our spiritual life and attained to the fourth stage do we naturally arrive at the place where we can know the mystery of the Body of Christ.

Any spiritual knowledge in reality cannot be gained without experience. All is based on experience. True spiritual knowledge does not go beyond the lessons we have experienced. For example, there may be a Bible truth of which we cannot fully grasp the meaning because of our limited experience; all we have is a small feeling about it. If we would follow that feeling and try to experience it, the truth would one day become enlightened to us. On one hand, the truth brings in the experience; and, on the other hand, because of the experience, we know the truth. In this way we come to true spiritual knowledge.

Consider some other examples. If one has not experienced fellowship in life, he does not know the meaning of abiding in Christ. If one does not have the experience of walking according to the Spirit, he does not know the teaching of the anointing. Likewise, if the flesh has not been dealt with, self has not been abandoned, and the natural constitution has not been broken, he cannot know what the Body is. He may know a little regarding the doctrine of the Body, but he cannot touch either the actuality or the reality of the Body. The Body of Christ is not a doctrine; it is a reality. One must climb over the hills of experience before he is able to see and touch the Body. Knowing the Body does not depend on our supplication. Praying and fasting for three days and three nights will not enable us to see the Body. This is useless. The knowledge of the Body is the result of our experience and spiritual growth. After sufficient experience we arrive at a place where we naturally know the Body.

I will never forget the message given by Brother Watchman Nee in a special meeting. He repeatedly stressed the fact that before Romans 12 there must first be Romans 8. One must pass through the putting to death of the flesh of Romans 8 before he can attain to the knowledge of the Body of Romans 12. Therefore, from the beginning we must be very severe in dealing with ourselves, especially in regard to our flesh, our self, and our natural constitution. We must mean business and be thoroughgoing until we have the experience of Romans 8. Not until we have experienced the putting to death of the flesh in Romans 8 can we realize the Body in Romans 12. When our body (flesh) has been put to death, the Body of Christ will then be manifested. This is a spiritual reality wherein is no counterfeit and which cannot be counterfeited. There may be counterfeiting in other spiritual areas, such as humility, gentleness, faith, and love. We may even pretend to be spiritual. But no pretension is possible where knowing the Body is concerned. When our experience has attained to the degree of knowing the Body, then we know it. If in our experience we have not attained to this degree, we do not know it, and listening to much preaching on the subject avails nothing.

IX. PROOFS THAT WE KNOW THE BODY

Since knowing the Body is such a practical thing, how may we ascertain whether or not one knows the Body as yet? We can prove it in at least three ways.

A. Being Unable to Be Individualistic

The first proof of knowing the Body is that we cannot be individualistic. In all the seven points we have mentioned—in God's plan, in God's creation, in God's redemption, in Christ, in the Holy Spirit, in life, and in fellowship—all is oneness, inseparable, and non-individualistic. If we really know the Body and realize the oneness contained in these seven matters, there can be no individualism. Before one knows the Body, he is an individualist and can be individualistic. His life, his actions, his work, and his service are all individualistic. Outwardly, he appears to be one with the brothers, but there is no real coordination or knitting together. Not until he grows deeper in life and knows the Body to a certain extent does he see that being a Christian is a corporate matter and that he cannot go on without fellowship in the Body, nor can he depart from the coordination of the members. The Body of Christ becomes a practical matter to him. In the church life he can no longer serve alone. In the innermost part of his being, he feels that he needs to be a Christian together with others. Not only in great and important actions and work does he need the brothers and sisters, but even in Bible reading and prayer as well, he cannot do without other members. He cannot work without the coordination of the brothers and sisters, and he cannot live without the support of the church. It is at this stage that he is being knit together spontaneously with all the saints to become one Body, no more to be separated. All those, therefore, who can still be individualistic do not know the Body, and all those with a true knowledge of the Body definitely cannot be individualistic.

B. Discerning Those Not in the Body

The second proof of our knowing the Body is the ability to discern whether others are in the Body or not. One who has come to know the Body not only lives in the Body in a very practical way but also can clearly discern whether or not others are living in the Body.

This discerning ability after one knows the Body is absolutely due to the extent of the deep degree of fellowship he has in the Lord. Our fellowship with the Lord grows in depth in proportion to our experience of life, beginning with the initial stage of our spiritual life and continuing through the fourth stage. The degree of depth of fellowship differs greatly as we progress in the experience of life. When two people in different degrees of fellowship in the Lord come together, the

one having the deeper experience can go on with the one who
has the shallower experience and have fellowship with him,
but that fellowship is limited in proportion to the experience
of the latter. Should this fellowship go beyond the limit, it
will become rather incongruous and incomprehensible to the
latter. The one having deeper experience, therefore, can go on
with the one who has the shallower experience, but the shallower one cannot go along with the deeper one. This is a great
principle in spiritual fellowship.

It is because of this principle that those who are deep in
the Lord recognize those who are shallow, but those who are
shallow in the Lord do not discern those who are deep. If we
have been brought by the Lord to the fourth stage and are
having a deep fellowship in this stage, we can by fellowship
know whether others also have been brought to this stage
and as yet know the Body. But if we have not reached the
fourth stage and do not know the Body, we then have no way
of discerning others.

Let us use a most shallow illustration. When others spoke
regarding regeneration before we were born again, it sounded
incongruous to us. In addition, we were unable to know whether
others were born again. If we are already born again, we not
only can talk with others about regeneration, but we can easily
discern whether others have been born again. This proves
that we have indeed been born again.

Another illustration: If we have already consecrated ourselves and have had the experience of dealing with sin, we
can very readily recognize those who have not had this experience. Since their fellowship with the Lord has not reached
this stage, they will have no idea what we are saying, nor will
they be able to respond. Conversely, if we have not had this
experience, we will also not be able to recognize whether they
have been consecrated or have dealt with sin.

Not only can we through fellowship ascertain whether
others know the Body, but the experience of knowing the
Body is also in itself a matter of fellowship. If one is in
the Body, he is in fellowship; if one is not in the Body, he is
not in fellowship. Most Christians have lost the position
of fellowship, the reality of fellowship. This implies that they

do not see the Body and do not live in the Body. Living in fellowship, therefore, proves that we know the Body. If we really know the Body, we can ascertain whether others are in it or not. When others have not come to live in the reality of the Body, they are not in the fellowship of the Body. There is no possibility of fellowship between them and us regarding this point. We need only a contact, and we know it. Conversely, if we never sense that others are not in the Body, we demonstrate that we are not in the Body. We have not come to know the Body. Our inner feelings when contacting others, therefore, reveal to us whether we know the Body or not.

C. Recognizing Authority

The third proof of our knowing the Body is the recognition of authority. Whether or not one knows the Body depends upon whether or not he recognizes authority. Those who do not recognize authority do not know the Body. Knowing the Body and recognizing authority are inseparable. Recognition of authority is related to what we have mentioned regarding individualism in the first proof. If one recognizes authority, he cannot be an individualist. If one wants to determine whether or not he recognizes authority, he simply needs to determine whether or not he is still able to be an individualist. If he is still able to live as an individualist and feels that he can serve God alone without being coordinated with others, he demonstrates that he does not recognize authority, nor has he come to know the Body. Authority can only be manifested in the Body and in the coordination. If one member is individualistic and isolated, he has no relationship with others as far as authority is concerned. But if we have seen that God wants a Body, and that we, being members of this Body, can never go on alone (for once we are alone we are disjointed), we will learn to recognize authority, keep our position in the Body, and coordinate with all the brothers and sisters.

What is authority? Authority is simply the authority of Christ the Head, which is revealed in the order of the Body. Take our physical body as an example. The head is uppermost and is the authority of the whole body; from it, order is expressed throughout the whole body. Below the head are the arms, the trunk, and the legs. All the members follow a definite order; therefore, any member, unless it is detached, falls into such an order. Any member that is attached to the Body surely comes under this order. On one hand, it is under the authority of some of the members, and on the other hand, some other members are under its authority. For example: above the palm of the hand is the elbow, and below are the fingers; the elbow has authority over the palm, and the palm has authority over the fingers. This authority is in accord with their respective order in the body and is also the authority of the head as shown forth in the order of the members. When we speak of authority, we mean the authority of Christ manifested through the order of His Body. Since we are all members of the Body of Christ, we naturally have our right position and order. If we have been taught in our spirit and have been indeed led by God to recognize the flesh, if we have had self dealt with and the natural constitution broken, we will immediately recognize our own order when placed among brothers and sisters. We will know who is in front of us and who is behind us, who is in authority over us and over whom we are in authority. The authority of the Head in me and the authority of the Head in others makes it clear who is over me and who is under me. This is just like a family, where brothers and sisters know their own order—who should submit to whom and who is the authority of whom. This kind of authority is not assumed, nor is it by election, but it is the natural order in life, which Christ the Head has manifested in all the members of His Body. Only those living in the flesh, walking according to self-opinion and the natural constitution, are able to engage in ugly conflicts with one another in rivalry for authority. All those who have learned their lessons can recognize the authority of the Head over the Body and can rest in their own order in a very natural and satisfactory manner. This has nothing to do with either humility or pride. Coming under authority is a natural procedure, far removed from forcing oneself to submit. This kind of people recognize authority and know the Body because recognizing authority is equal to knowing the Body. Therefore, this matter of knowing the Body can also be called knowing authority.

If we do not know our order in the Body, we demonstrate that in our experience of life we have not reached the fourth stage. If in the first three stages we have passed through various kinds of dealings, being earnest and thorough, especially in dealing with the flesh, the self-opinion, and the natural constitution, then the Holy Spirit within will lead us in a very natural manner to know our respective order in the Body of Christ, causing our life and service to be full of the flavor of the coordination of the Body. Thus, the Body of Christ will gradually become manifest among us.

In conclusion, when we have come to know the Body, we can be aware of it, even though we may not know when we attained to this knowing; but if we have it, we will know it. This is similar to recovery from an illness. The exact time of recovery is difficult to discern, but we know that we have recovered, for in appearance as well as in feeling we are different. Likewise, in all true spiritual knowing, it is not easy to tell precisely at what day, hour, or minute we gained entrance, but the aftereffect is clearly discernible. Therefore, if one has a real knowing of the Body, sooner or later he will demonstrate the three proofs that we have mentioned. First, he can no longer be an individualist. Second, he can tell when others are not in the Body. Third, among brothers and sisters he knows clearly, without any special effort, his own order in the Body—who has authority over him, and over whom he has authority, that is, in whom rests the authority of the Head. These three points are proofs of our knowing the Body.

CHAPTER SIXTEEN

KNOWING THE ASCENSION

We now come to see the sixteenth experience of life, which is knowing the ascension. Although this lesson is rather profound, it is not difficult to understand. We will speak of this in several main points.

I. THE NEED OF KNOWING THE REDEMPTION OF CHRIST

In order to know ascension, we need first to know the redemption of Christ, because ascension is included in it. Concerning Christ's redemption, many comprehend only Christ's crucifixion, His dying for us. Some see something deeper; they realize that Christ's redemption includes also the resurrection. But if we read the Scriptures again carefully and examine our experiences, we will discover that His redemption includes ascension also. Christ's redemption consists of three main parts: death, resurrection, and ascension. If any part is missing, the redemption of Christ cannot be regarded as complete.

In these three main parts of Christ's redemption, Christ's death emphasizes deliverance from the negative aspects. That is, it saves us from sins, the world, the flesh, that which is natural, and all those things that are incompatible with God. Christ's resurrection emphasizes the entrance into the positive aspects. That is, it brings us into all the riches of the new creation, which God has in Christ. And Christ's ascension is the glorious conclusion of His death and resurrection. Christ's death and resurrection are not the conclusion of His redemption; His ascension is. We cannot say that Christ rested when He was raised from the dead. Christ did not rest in death or in resurrection; He rested in His ascension. The Scripture does not say that the Lord sits in resurrection but that He sits in the heavens (Eph. 2:6). Sitting signifies that the work has already been accomplished. Therefore, the redemptive work of the Lord was not considered accomplished until He ascended to the heavens. We can say that death and resurrection are only progressive stages of the Lord's redemption. Ascension is the final stage of the Lord's redemption. The Lord's death and resurrection are the path that leads to His ascension. Thus, ascension is the conclusion of His death and resurrection.

Since the Lord's ascension is the conclusion of His death and resurrection, all three steps are closely connected. When the Lord came forth from death and entered into resurrection, He had already reached the heavenly realm. Immediately following death and resurrection is ascension. In Christianity there is an inaccurate understanding that Christ ascended forty days after His resurrection. Actually, in the resurrection morning the Lord ascended to the heavens. In that morning the Lord appeared to Mary Magdalene and said to her, "Do not touch Me, for I have not yet ascended to the Father." And He continued, saying, "I ascend to My Father" (John 20:17). In the evening of the same day, the Lord again appeared to the disciples and said, "Touch Me and see" (Luke 24:39). By this time the Lord could let men touch Him. This reveals that before this time He had already ascended to the heavens and offered to God the freshness of His resurrection. Therefore, before His ascension in the sight of His disciples forty days later, He could say, "All authority has been given to Me in heaven and on earth" (Matt. 28:18). This authority was obtained from God when He ascended to the heavens on the resurrection morning. Thus, we see that Christ's death and resurrection are connected with His ascension. They cannot be separated. Finishing of school cannot be separated from graduation; when one finishes his study, he graduates. Likewise, when the Lord was risen from the dead, He ascended.

In Christ's ascension, He brought all that He had accomplished through His death and resurrection to the heavens. He brought the fruit of all His redeeming work into the heavenly realm. Thus, the Lord today, in the position of His ascension, applies the efficacy of His redemption to man. Certainly, the Lord's forgiveness of our sins is based on His blood shed on the cross. But if He had not ascended to the heavens, He would not have been able to apply His death or His blood. He has achieved redemption on the cross, but it is in His ascension that He applies His redemption. In the position of ascension, He gives man salvation. To speak accurately, all the redemptive grace experienced by the church, from forgiveness of sins to experiencing the ascension and obtaining various gifts, is being applied in a practical way by the Lord in His ascension. Therefore, the ascension in Christ's redemption occupies a very important place. All that Christ has accomplished through His death and resurrection is brought into the ascension for application. Without ascension, nothing in Christ's salvation can be applied to us in a practical way.

II. THE NEED OF KNOWING
THE POSITION OF OUR SALVATION

In order to know the ascension, we also need to know the position of our salvation. We were saved from being under judgment into the forgiveness of sins and were made alive from the condition of death and obtained God's life; however, the forgiveness of sins and the obtaining of life cannot be considered as the position of our salvation. Ephesians 2:5-6 tells us that "when we were dead in offenses, [God] made us alive together with Christ...and raised us up together with Him and seated us together with Him in the heavenlies." This shows that every man who is saved is not only one whose sins are forgiven, not only one who is made alive from death and has God's life, but also one who is seated in the heavenlies, a man of ascension. When Christ saves us, He causes us to ascend with Him and sit with Him in the heavenlies. Therefore, ascension truly is the final position of our salvation.

The position of ascension that we have obtained rests not only on the fact of ascension that God has accomplished in Christ but also on the life of ascension that we have obtained within us. In Colossians 3:1-4 the apostle asks us to set our mind "on the things which are above." This is based on the fact that Christ is our life. Christ is sitting in the heavenlies at the right hand of God. Because we have Him as our life, we also are hidden with Him in God. This reveals that neither in His death nor in His resurrection but in His ascension Christ caused us to obtain life and became our life. This life has passed through death and resurrection, yet it is in the position of ascension that Christ gives this life to us. This life is ascended and heavenly and is given from heaven. It is a life that reaches heaven. Therefore, once we obtain this life, we have fellowship with heaven and are joined to heaven. According to outward conditions we still live on earth, yet according to the inner life we are already in heaven. The situation is just like the Lord's during His time on earth. He said then that though He "descended out of heaven," He was still "in heaven" (John 3:13). This was due to the fact that His life is heavenly and connected with heaven.

For example, an electric light bulb gives light because of the electric current within it. This electric current originates from the power plant and is connected with the power plant. Therefore, externally speaking, its light shines forth in this room. But, in respect to the electric current within the bulb, its position is at the power plant. Likewise, we as saved ones can be manifested in this age as shining light (Phil. 2:15; Matt. 5:14-16) because of the ascended life that saves us and is now within us. This life flows into us from heaven, and it is also connected with heaven. It flows into us from heaven, and it also brings us to heaven. With this life that is connected with heaven, we are also a people who are connected with heaven. Therefore, just as from Christ's standpoint ascension is the conclusion of His redemption, even so from our standpoint ascension is the position of our salvation.

III. THE NEED OF KNOWING THE SPIRITUAL FUNCTIONS

In order to know the ascension, we also need to know the spiritual functions. All the spiritual gifts of Christians are given by the Lord in ascension (Eph. 4:8) and are for us to apply in the position of ascension. Therefore, if we do not know the ground of ascension or stand fast upon it, we will be unable to apply the spiritual gifts. The functions of the spiritual gifts can only be made manifest on the ground of ascension.

Genesis 1:17 tells us that God set light-bearers in the sky to shine upon the earth. This word is full of meaning figuratively. The sun, moon, and stars can shine upon the earth because they are set in the sky. Once a star is fallen from the sky, its function is lost. Its illuminating function depends entirely on its position in the sky. Likewise, whether we preach the gospel, visit people, edify the saints, or administer the church, the real function rests entirely on our position of ascension. Once we lose the position of ascension, we will surely lose the spiritual functions.

For example, the reason many brothers and sisters have visited people to no avail is that they have already fallen from the position of ascension and live in some situation on earth. If we want to visit people with much effectiveness, it is not necessary for us to speak much or preach many truths. We need only to maintain the position of ascension in our daily living; we need only to be continually touching heaven in our inner being and live in the heavenly condition, the heavenly atmosphere, which, when touched by others, will enable them to obtain the heavenly supply. This also applies to the prayers offered in meetings. The prayers of some brothers and sisters impart a feeling of emptiness and oldness to others because they have already lost the position of ascension. The phraseology of their prayers may be very attractive, but before God and before Satan there is no weight. There is also no effect in the spiritual realm. Other brothers and sisters, however, are not so. They stand fast in the position of ascension and live in the life of heaven. Their daily living is of heaven; therefore, their prayers also are of heaven. When they open their mouth, they give a heavenly taste. Only this kind of prayer can touch the throne in the heavens and shake the gates of hell, thereby producing much spiritual consequence. Therefore, regardless of what our spiritual functions are, we must apply them in the heavenly position and manifest them in the heavenly realm.

IV. THE NEED OF KNOWING THE POSITION OF WARFARE

In order to know the ascension, we also need to know the position of warfare. The position of spiritual warfare is absolutely in the heavenlies. Whenever we lose the position of ascension, we are unable to carry on any spiritual warfare. On the battlefield, all military strategists pay attention to the problem of position. Whoever takes the high ground against the low ground can win the battle. On the spiritual battleground, this principle is even more important. We can say that spiritual warfare depends solely on the problem of position. If we wish to win in the fight, the position of ascension must be absolutely known and kept.

We must see the fact that the spiritual warfare mentioned in the sixth chapter of Ephesians is based on the position of ascension in the second chapter. The second chapter of Ephesians declares that we are seated together with Christ in the heavenlies. Then the sixth chapter goes on to speak of our wrestling against the spiritual forces of evil in the heavenlies (v. 12). This means that we must first be men of ascension with the position of ascension before we can attack the enemy in the air from above. If we are men of earth and lose the position of ascension, we will fall into the hand of the enemy and cannot fight against him. Therefore, the position of spiritual warfare is absolutely in the heavenlies.

Genesis 3:14 tells us that after the serpent enticed Eve, God judged him by causing him to move about on his stomach and to eat dust all the days of his life. Moving on his stomach limits the sphere of his activity. He can only creep on the ground. Eating dust limits the object of his devouring. He can only eat things pertaining to the dust of the earth as food. The serpent in Genesis 3 is the embodiment of Satan. Therefore, the judgment against the serpent is also the judgment against Satan. Today the sphere of Satan's activity is earth, and the object of his devouring is the man of earth. First Corinthians 15:47-48 tells us that Adam and all those belonging to him are earthy. Therefore, whenever we live in the earthly life of Adam, we are earthly and also on earth. We not only cannot fight against Satan, but we also fall into the sphere of his activity and become the object of his devouring. Contrariwise, whenever we live in the heavenly life of Christ, we are heavenly and are in heaven. Thus, we transcend Satan's sphere of activity and are no longer the object of his devouring. Hence, we can attack him and overcome him.

This principle of warfare is also very evident in our practical daily living. Whether in the church, at home, or at the place of our employment, whenever we have a touch of sin, a love for the world, a display of temper, a dealing in craftiness, or a living in the earthly life, we simply cannot be strong before the enemy and fight against him. At this time we are already earthly and have fallen into the hand of the enemy. On the other hand, if we constantly have fellowship with the Lord, walk in spirit, and live in the heavenly life, we are heavenly and abide in the position of ascension. Then we can stay on higher ground over against lower ground and deal with Satan. At this time, should the church encounter difficulties, we can engage in prevailing prayer before God, demanding God to come forth to judge His enemy. We can rise to express our attitude to God, saying, "We will not allow these things to happen in the church." We can also say seriously to Satan, "We are disgusted with this. We are against this." When we make such a severe declaration and strong expression, the entire host of Satan will retreat. His work will also be completely destroyed. But if we live in the earthly life, using natural methods and means, we will never be able to solve these problems. We have already fallen from heaven and have lost the position of warfare. We have no way to deal with God's enemy and nullify his works.

Why does the position of ascension cause us to be victorious in battle? It is because only in the position of ascension may we have heavenly authority. In order to wage spiritual warfare, we need to depend upon heavenly authority. There is only one place where we can obtain heavenly authority: this place is heaven. If we pass through death and resurrection to reach the heavenly realm, we will surely obtain heavenly authority. Therefore, we will surely be victorious in battle.

Many Christians today are greatly concerned with the problem of power. But the Lord has saved us not only to the state of possessing power but also to the place of having authority. Those in the heavenly realm not only have power but also authority. Those with power can only cause others to be moved. But those with authority cause others not only to be moved but also to be reverent and fearful. For example, consider some brothers and sisters who love the world and live according to the flesh. When they see brothers or sisters loving the Lord, seeking Him, and living in the spirit, they admire them very much and are moved. This is a matter of power. But if they meet other brothers or sisters who are living in the realm of ascension, they feel not only a certain power that causes them to be moved but also a certain phenomenon that causes them to be reverent and fearful. With such brothers or sisters there is the heavenly reality; therefore, they are also full of heavenly authority. Thus, while they are walking among men, they bring with them a certain fearsomeness, which causes others to be reverent.

When we read the Song of Songs in the Old Testament, we see that the one who is seeking the Lord grows in life to such an extent that her expression is exceedingly noble and awesome. Song of Songs 6:10 says, "Who is this woman who looks forth like the dawn, / As beautiful as the moon, / As clear as the sun, / As terrible as an army with banners?" Here the morning light, the moon, and the sun are all things in the heavens. Therefore, by this time the condition of this one is altogether heavenly. In other words, her experience of life has reached the realm of ascension. Thus, her condition gives others the feeling of fearfulness. This is because she is in the position of ascension and has the heavenly authority. It is this authority that causes others to be fearful and filled with reverence.

The authority we obtain in the position of ascension is the basis upon which we deal with Satan and overcome him. In Luke 10:19, the Lord said, "Behold, I have given you the *authority* to tread upon serpents and scorpions and over all the *power* of the enemy, and nothing shall by any means hurt you." The serpents mentioned by the Lord refer to Satan, and the scorpions are the evil spirits, the messengers of Satan. These are our enemies. All they have is *power*, but what the Lord gives us is *authority*. The Lord gives us authority in order to deal with all the power of the enemy. We may illustrate this by an automobile moving along the road. It is full of power, yet a traffic policeman has authority over it. When he blows his whistle, the car must stop. Again, it is like an army. It has great power, yet the general has the authority. When he gives an order, the army must obey. This proves that authority is over power and can control power; therefore, authority is greater than power.

But authority depends entirely upon position. With the position, there is the authority; without the position, there is no authority. A policeman without his uniform and not standing in the assigned post has no authority to direct the cars. A general taking leave from his duty has no authority to command an army. Likewise, our heavenly authority depends solely on our position of ascension. Whenever we lose the position of ascension, we also lose the spiritual authority. Therefore, in order to engage in spiritual warfare, we must first know the position of ascension and, second, keep the position of ascension. Only then can we deal with the enemy.

In Paul's second journey, when he was preaching in Philippi, a certain slave girl with a spirit of Python followed, crying out after him. Paul, being greatly troubled, turned and said to the spirit, "I charge you in the name of Jesus Christ to come out of her." And the spirit came out that very hour (Acts 16:16-18). Paul here was standing in the position of ascension and exercising heavenly authority to halt the enemy's disturbing power. Likewise, today, if we stand in the position of ascension, we can directly command the environment, rebuke difficulties, and destroy all the works of the enemy.

Unfortunately, the prayers of the church today contain all too few authoritative commands. On the contrary, the prayers are mostly tearful pleadings. Therefore, they cannot deal with the enemy; they can only appeal to God's mercy. This only proves that our actual position is still on earth and has not yet ascended to the heavenlies. Since we are not in the position of ascension, we do not have the heavenly authority. We cannot pretend in this matter. On the other hand, if any man has the reality of ascension, he has no need to pompously display his power or assume airs; he is naturally clothed with a heavenly appearance; he is full of a heavenly atmosphere and adorned with beauty as the moon and purity as the sun. This causes him to appear awesome. Not only do men fear him; even the evil spirits are afraid of him. Only this kind of man can stand in the heavenly position, exercise heavenly authority, and engage in spiritual warfare. Therefore, in order to know the ascension, we must know also the position of warfare.

V. THE EXPERIENCE OF ASCENSION

We obtain the position of ascension the moment we are saved. But how can we *experience* ascension? Simply speaking, the experience of ascension is the outcome of our experiencing resurrection through death. Even as Christ ascended to the heavenlies through death and resurrection, so also we may experience ascension through death and resurrection.

Let us consider the history of the Israelites entering the land of Canaan. Once they left their wilderness wanderings and crossed the Jordan, they entered Canaan. The land of Canaan signifies the all-inclusive Christ in the heavenlies. At the same time, it also typifies the heavenly realm. Therefore, when the Israelites entered Canaan, typically speaking, they entered the heavenly realm. When they crossed the Jordan, they buried twelve stones at the bottom of the river, signifying their death and burial. Then they removed twelve stones from the bottom of the river, signifying their resurrection. They brought these twelve stones into the land of Canaan, signifying their passing through death and resurrection and entering into the heavenly realm. Therefore, their entering Canaan after crossing the Jordan typifies our experiencing the ascension through death and resurrection. Whenever we experience death and resurrection, we reach the realm of ascension.

Let us look again at the one who seeks the Lord in the Song of Songs. She also, through the experience of death and resurrection, gradually attains to the reality of ascension. In Song of Songs 1:9 the Lord praises her for the first time, saying that she is like "a mare among Pharaoh's chariots." A mare among Pharaoh's chariots is an Egyptian horse. Though fast and strong, it is still of Egypt, which typifies the world. This shows that, though at that time she was exceedingly swift and full of strength in her seeking the Lord and following after Him, she was still earthly. Then in 2:2 the Lord praises her by saying that she is "as a lily among thorns." This means that, though as a lily she lives a clean life and a life that receives God's tender care, she still grows on earth.

When we come to 3:6, the Lord speaks of her as one coming "up from the wilderness / Like pillars of smoke, / Perfumed with myrrh and frankincense, / With all the fragrant powders of the merchant." The wilderness signifies the state of a Christian's spiritual wandering. As a matter of fact she had been wandering in the wilderness. Now she comes up from the wilderness, leaving behind her life of spiritual wandering. At the same time, she is perfumed with myrrh and frankincense and all the powders of the merchant. Myrrh expresses Christ's death, frankincense expresses Christ's resurrection, and the powders of the merchant signify the spiritual riches obtained at a price. Now because she has paid a price in her seeking, she is perfumed with Christ's death and resurrection. Therefore, her condition is likened to pillars of smoke ascending from the earth. She has passed through death and resurrection and has begun to have a little experience of ascension. Further on, in 6:10, the Lord's praise for her is altogether heavenly. At this time, her spiritual condition is as the morning light, as the moon, and as the sun. She truly resembles the sun, the moon, and the stars of Genesis 1:16-17, arrayed in the sky and shining upon the whole earth, that the people on earth may receive her supply. At the same time she also has heavenly authority with her; she is dignified and awesome. Now she has fully experienced ascension.

In conclusion, ascension is the result of resurrection from death. Once we pass through the death of the cross and enter into resurrection, we reach the realm of ascension. Thus, if we want to experience ascension, we must first seek to experience death and resurrection. We must severely put to death by the Lord's cross everything of sins, the world, the temper, the flesh, the self, and the natural constitution, and enter into the Lord's resurrection by the Holy Spirit. Then we can experience ascension and be a heavenly people in the realm of ascension.

Chapter Seventeen

REIGNING

In the previous chapter we have seen the matter of knowing the ascension; now we will go on immediately to see the experience of reigning. Both lessons are closely related in experience.

I. THE DEFINITION OF REIGNING

Simply speaking, to reign is to exercise authority for God—to rule all things and in particular to deal with His enemy. We have repeatedly mentioned in the past that in the creation of man God had a twofold intent and desire. On one hand, God wanted man to possess His image so that he may express God Himself. On the other hand, God wanted man to represent Him with His authority in order to deal with His enemy. Therefore, when God created man, on one hand, He created him in His image and likeness so that man might be like Him. On the other hand, God caused man to "have dominion over the fish of the sea and over the birds of heaven and over the cattle and over all the earth and over every creeping thing that creeps upon the earth" (Gen. 1:26). This means that God gave man authority so that he might reign for Him.

The Old Testament records many instances of men reigning for God after Adam. Exodus 14 tells how God wanted Moses to lift the rod and stretch it forth to divide the Red Sea. Joshua 10 tells how Joshua prayed to God that the sun might stand still in the sky. First Kings 17 through 18 relates how Elijah prayed to control the rainfall. Daniel 6 tells how Daniel shut the lions' mouths in the den. All these instances show us that through the ages, as long as there are men willing to live for God, God desires to grant them authority in order that all things might come under their dominion.

This matter is even more evident in the New Testament. The first one in the New Testament who ruled for God was the Lord Jesus. He commanded illness to recede (Matt. 8:8-9), cast out unclean spirits (Mark 1:27), and rebuked and calmed the storm and the raging sea (Matt. 8:26-27). All these incidents speak of His reigning. Later, when the apostles continued the Lord's works, they also had many experiences of reigning for God by healing and casting out evil spirits (Acts 3:6-7; 14:8-10; 19:12; 16:18). To the present day, this kind of experience is often repeated in the church. Then in the future and in the kingdom, the overcomers will reign with Christ and rule the nations (Rev. 2:26-27). Finally, in eternity all those who are saved will reign as kings forever and ever (22:5). At that time we will truly and fully enjoy the blessing of reigning for God.

All these instances reveal that from the beginning until eternity, God's one intention is that He may gain man to reign for Him in the universe. This was one aspect of God's purpose in creating man. Even more, this was one aspect of God's intention in redeeming man.

Therefore, from the point of view of authority, reigning is the final goal of God's salvation. It is the summit of our spiritual experience. As for God, had He not saved us to the extent that we could reign for Him in the heavenly realm, the goal of His salvation would not have been considered fully accomplished. Furthermore, although this matter of reigning will not be completely realized until the coming of the kingdom and in eternity, today God wants us to have a beginning on earth. As for us, if any Christian has not yet reached the degree of reigning for God, he is not yet up to the standard. A Christian who is up to the standard has not only been delivered from sin, overcome the world, had his flesh dealt with and his natural constitution broken, been filled with the Holy Spirit, and is sitting in the heavenly realm, but even more he is reigning with Christ in all things. Whether in God's work, in the church, at home, or in any encounter in his environment, he can reign and rule over that which God wants him to rule. There must

be such people gained by God so that through them the authority of God can be executed, and the kingdom of God can come
upon the earth.

II. THE EXPERIENCE OF REIGNING

We must seek the experience of reigning. For this, two
things must not be lacking.

A. Knowing Our Position

First, we must know our position. We have mentioned in the
previous chapter, "Knowing the Ascension," that the basis of
spiritual authority is the position of ascension. To have *power*
depends on one's *condition,* but to have *authority* depends on
one's *position.* A car with sufficient gasoline and horsepower
will have *power.* This is a matter of *condition.* But a traffic
policeman standing at his assigned post has *authority* to direct
the cars, that they may proceed in order. This is a matter of
position. Therefore, authority depends entirely on position. If
we are in the position of ascension, we have authority and can
reign. If we are not in the position of ascension, we do not have
authority and cannot rule.

Even in the case of the Lord Jesus, the basis of reigning
depended on His position of ascension. Not till after His resurrection and ascension did He obtain all authority in heaven
and on earth (Matt. 28:18) and have dominion over all things
(Eph. 1:20-22). Therefore, if we would reign, we must be in
the position of ascension.

But if we want to be in the position of ascension and reign
for God, we need to accept all the dealings of the cross, that
we may pass through death into resurrection and thereby
experience ascension. In other words, the experience of reigning is the result of all the foregoing experiences. Only after
we have experienced death, resurrection, and ascension,
can we obtain the experience of reigning.

God's children today show forth very little of the reality of
reigning. The main reason is that we are not in the position
of ascension. Many still live in an earthly condition. They are
still involved with sins and the world. They have not put off
the flesh and their temper. They have not denied the self and

their natural constitution. There are some who have put these off and have a little experience of ascension, yet because they cannot maintain this experience, they become defiled again with those things pertaining to the old creation; thus, they lose the position of ascension. Both conditions can cause us to lose the basis of reigning, and as a consequence we cannot rule for God. Once, there was a brother who was constantly hindered by his wife from drawing near to God and serving Him. One day he could bear it no longer; so in his anger he rebuked his wife and beat her, saying, "Today the Lord wants me to really discipline you." Obviously, this is not reigning. Because he lost his temper, he lost the position of ascension and fell into the hand of the enemy. How then could he deal anymore with the enemy? Therefore, in order to reign we must know and keep the position of ascension.

Our reigning is based not only on the position of ascension but also on the position of order arranged by God. Therefore, if we want to reign for God, not only do we need to be in the position of ascension, but we must also keep the position of order given to us by God—that is, to submit to the authority to which we should submit. All the authority of the traffic policeman previously mentioned depends not only on his standing at the assigned post but also on his submitting to his superior. If he leaves his assigned post, he will not be able to direct the cars. If he rebels against his superior, he will lose even his official rights. Therefore, a policeman's executing of his authority depends on keeping the position of his duty on one hand, and on keeping the position of his rank on the other hand. The position of his duty is equivalent to our position of ascension, and the position of his rank is equivalent to our position of order.

Matthew 8:5-13 tells us of a centurion who came to ask the Lord to heal his servant's sickness. His faith was based on his knowledge of the position of order. He said, "Lord, I am not fit for You to enter under my roof; but only speak a word, and my servant will be healed. For I also am a man under authority, having soldiers under me. And I say to this one, Go, and he goes; and to another, Come, and he comes; and to my slave, Do this, and he does it." Since he himself was under authority, he could command those under him. Therefore, he believed that the Lord needed only to exercise His authority and give a word of command, and the matter would be done. He really knew the relationship between the position of order and authority. He knew that in order to reign, he first had to submit to the reigning. In order to be the authority, he first had to submit to authority.

When God created man in the beginning, God gave man authority to have dominion over all the creatures in the sea, in the air, and upon earth. At that time, man was submitting to God's authority; hence, God's authority was with him, and all creatures were made to submit to man. But once man fell and rebelled against God, unwilling as he was to submit to God's authority, he then lost the authority of God. As a result, all the creatures under man were no longer in subjection to man's authority. Therefore, not only can the poisonous snakes and wild beasts harm us today; even the tiny mosquitoes and fleas can bite us. This indicates that the entire fallen universe is full of the creatures' rebelliousness and insubordination.

But in this rebellious and confused universe, whenever there is one who is still willing to accept God's authority, God's authority will be manifested upon him so that he may be able to reign. Moses was an example. He was a man who submitted to authority and thereby reigned for God. Nearly every time he was confronted with the rebellion and quarrelling of the Israelites, he submitted himself to God's authority. Especially at the time that Korah, Dathan, Abiram, and those with them rebelled and assembled themselves together against him, he behaved even more in this way. They attacked Moses and Aaron, saying, "You take too much upon yourselves, for all the assembly are holy, every one of them, and Jehovah is among them. Why then do you exalt yourselves above the congregation of Jehovah?" (Num. 16:3). Their word touched the matter of Moses' authority; their intention was to overthrow his authority. At that time, Moses did not consider himself as the authority and seek to solve the problem himself. On the contrary, he fell on his face before God and let God vindicate him. His falling on his face before God was his keeping the position of order. He knew that authority rested not in him but in God. His submission to God's authority caused others also to submit to him. Therefore, the result of his behaving each time in this way manifested even more clearly that God's authority was upon him.

Let us consider David. In his entire life, David submitted not only to God's authority but also, in an absolute way, to the authority of order. He recognized that Saul was God's anointed one, that Saul was in the position of king, and that Saul was arranged by God to be his authority. He realized that he was only a subject of Saul. Therefore, no matter how Saul persecuted and hated him as an enemy, he never dared to rebel against him. In this way, he always kept the position of order and was a man who submitted to authority. Consequently, the day came when God also anointed him king, that he might reign for God in the nation of Israel.

Nevertheless, these men who submitted to God's authority had their own blemishes and weaknesses. It was not until the Lord Jesus came as the Word become flesh that there was in this rebellious universe a man who submitted absolutely to God's authority. In the life of the Lord Jesus, every word and action, every move and cessation, were in accordance with God's will and in subjection to God's authority. Philippians 2:8 says, "He humbled Himself, becoming obedient even unto death, and that the death of the cross." Therefore, God also highly exalted Him, that every knee in heaven, on earth, and under the earth should bow to Him, and every tongue should call Him Lord—all in submission to His authority (vv. 8-11). Because the Lord Jesus submitted to the authority of God the Father and kept the position of order, He obtained authority and was able to reign for God.

The Lord has also given this authority now to His church, that is, to us. Therefore, we also need to submit to God's authority as the Lord did. Furthermore, each one of us must submit to the order of authority established by God, that is, to the representative authority of God. Then we, the church, can exercise this authority of the Lord to rule over all things and reign for God. Today in this rebellious and confused universe, we are to succeed the Lord to be a testimony of submission to authority, with the younger ones submitting to the elderly ones, those who are being taught to those who teach, and all of us submitting one to another; thus, we are submitting to God's authority. When we stand in our respective position of order, God's authority will be made manifest in our midst; thus, we will be able to reign for God. Therefore, the authority in the church is neither self-obtained nor self-assumed, but it comes through submission. For example, the elders must not continually think of themselves as being more mature and older than others; if so, they will frequently make use of their position and title in dealing with the brothers and sisters or in their administration. They should be like Moses. Whenever anything occurs among the brothers and sisters, they must immediately fall on their faces before God, submitting to the position of order. By their submission to God's authority, God's authority will be with them, and they will be able to reign and rule for God over all things. If they themselves do not submit to God's authority, but assume the position of eldership, demanding that others submit to them, this is the breaking out of the flesh, not reigning. It will be difficult for others to submit to them.

In conclusion, in order to gain the experience of reigning, we must first solve the problem of position. We must know and keep the position of ascension, and we must also know and keep the position of order. Knowing the position of ascension is the experience of knowing the ascension, which has previously been mentioned. Knowing the position of order is the experience of knowing the Body, which has also been mentioned. We must know and experience these two aspects before we can reign for God. We must know the position of ascension, which He has caused us to obtain in His salvation, and the position of order, which He has arranged for us in His Body, before we can exercise His authority and reign for God. Simply speaking, we must be in the position of ascension and in the position of order in the Body before we can have the experience of reigning.

B. Desiring to Reign

Second, we must have the desire to reign. This means that

we must positively and actively reign for God, ruling over all things. Once we have the position of ascension and order, we may reign. If our experience has reached this stage, we ought to reign. Some brothers and sisters, however, have neither the thought nor the desire to reign. Their spirits are loose and lazy. They neither care for the difficulties arising in the church nor inquire about the problems springing up in the Lord's work. They simply allow Satan to work and destroy at will. Hence, according to their growth of life, they are able to reign, yet in reality, due to their laxity and unwillingness to reign, they still cannot obtain the experience of reigning. Therefore, if one desires to reign, his spirit must not be lax or timid but willing to exercise God's authority and positively and actively deal with all the works of the enemy. Thus, God's authority will immediately be manifested in the church, and many rebellious and unlawful matters in the church will be subdued.

In the church today we lack the kind of people who desire to reign. Therefore, many situations that should not exist often arise. For example, some of the fellowship and breaking of bread meetings are weak and confused. Some of the brothers and sisters should have prayed, but they did not; some should have spoken, but they withheld from speaking. On the contrary, many unnecessary prayers and meaningless testimonies were released. The meetings thus are disturbed, and the brothers and sisters are not edified and lose heart toward meetings. This condition is mainly caused by those who should have reigned but did not reign. They have just behaved like bystanders, allowing others to act in the meetings in whatever manner they chose. They even regard such a way as being very spiritual, not by man's doing but by the Spirit's move. As a result, they cause the church to suffer great loss.

We often say that certain meetings are very dead and depressed. This kind of depression comes from Satan, because Satan is the devil, who has the authority of death. Therefore, whenever a meeting is dead and depressed, it means that Satan is reigning there as king. At that time, someone should rise up to reign for God, either by a word, a hymn, or a prayer to control the meeting, change the atmosphere, and release the life of God, thereby swallowing up Satan's death.

Satan works not only in meetings but also in many lives. Sometimes he sends unnecessary poverty or sickness. If we live in the realm of ascension, we can tell which poverty and sickness is permitted by God and which is inflicted by Satan. Once we have discerned the matter, we must learn to reign by denying and opposing the poverty and sickness inflicted by Satan.

Furthermore, if we have had some experience in spiritual warfare, we can see that all things tending either to disrupt God's works or disturb the church are the deeds of demons. For example, sometimes in the meetings some are dozing, others have wandering thoughts, or children are running around. All these are the work of the demons. Even some prayers and messages are also the works of demons. Actually, anything in this world, except that which is moved by the Holy Spirit, can be said to come from evil spirits, that is, from demons. Hence, how we need men who are willing to rise and stand in the position of ascension and order, men who will positively and actively exercise authority for God to rule over all the confused and lawless situation and destroy the antagonistic works of the enemy! We must not be like old Eli. In 1 Samuel 3 we see how he was indifferent and in deep sleep. One who is indifferent and in deep sleep cannot reign for God. If we want to reign, our spirit must be strong and positive. A reigning spirit must be strong and living, active and not passive, positive and not negative, diligent and not loose. One who has such a spirit not only keeps the position of order and submits to God's authority but also has strong faith and exercises God's authority consistently in the position of ascension. Thus, he reigns and rules over his environment, over his work, and over all the meetings and affairs in the church.

In order to reign, we must express our attitude in three directions: first, toward God; second, toward Satan; and third, toward persons, events, and things. Take for example a brother in the church who does not behave properly. The reigning ones need to go before God and express their attitude, saying, "Lord, concerning this brother who misbehaves in such a way in the church, we neither agree nor approve." Then they need also to declare to Satan that this comes from his disturbance, and they are opposing and judging it. Finally, if necessary, they still need to solemnly express their attitude toward the persons, events, and things concerned, saying, "We do not agree and will not allow this matter to take place." When we express these attitudes, God will work and manifest His authority. Many times God's working depends on our attitude expressed toward Him. When a person lives in sins and the world, God will not respect his opinion. But when one has reached the position of ascension, his opinion will be greatly respected by God. When one reaches the realm of ascension, his opinion is almost the same as the mind of God. Therefore, he can be active and express his attitude, and God will respect him and trust him and reign through him.

Therefore, with regard to the goal of God's salvation, we need to reign for Him. With regard to our growth in life, we also need to reach the stage of reigning. With regard to Satan's unlawfulness, we need even more to rise and reign. In view of this we ought to take heed to learn this lesson well. This experience is considerably high and deep, yet we already have some beginning in the second and third stages. If we continue to seek diligently, the Lord will bring us into the realm of reigning. May the Lord be gracious to us!

Chapter Eighteen

SPIRITUAL WARFARE

Concerning the fourth stage of spiritual life we have seen the first three experiences: knowing the Body, knowing the ascension, and reigning. Now we shall continue by considering the fourth experience of this stage, spiritual warfare. This is an important experience in the fourth stage. The reason we must know the Body, know the ascension, and reign is that we may have spiritual warfare. Hence, the fourth stage is called the stage of spiritual warfare.

I. SCRIPTURAL BASIS

The purpose of spiritual warfare is to bring in the kingdom of God. This is a subject of great significance in the Bible. We will select two most important passages as the basis.

Let us first read Matthew 12:26, 28-29: "If Satan casts out Satan, he is divided against himself. How then will his kingdom stand?...But if I, by the Spirit of God, cast out the demons, then the kingdom of God has come upon you. Or how can anyone enter into the house of the strong man and plunder his goods unless he first binds the strong man? And then he will thoroughly plunder his house." In this passage of the Lord's words, there are several important points related to spiritual warfare. First, the Lord said here that Satan has his kingdom. Not only is there the kingdom of God in this universe but also the kingdom of Satan. Second, the Lord said that if He cast out demons by the Spirit of God, then the kingdom of God had come upon men. Hence, we see that to cast out demons by the Spirit of God is to bring in the kingdom of God, which is to engage in spiritual warfare. Third, since to cast out demons is to bring in the kingdom of God, then before the demons are cast out, it is the kingdom of Satan that reigns. It is through the demons that Satan usurps men and reigns. Fourth, the strong man that the Lord mentioned here is Satan. Satan is a strong man; he has that which he usurps and has seized by force. Fifth, both the kingdom of Satan and the house of the strong man are mentioned here. The kingdom of Satan is the house of the strong man. Therefore, the people in the world are on one hand the subjects in the kingdom of Satan and on the other hand the possessions in the house of Satan. It says here that a certain man enters into the strong man's house and plunders his goods. This refers to the Lord coming to the kingdom of Satan to rescue men out of Satan's usurpation and possession. Sixth, it says here also that in order for one to plunder the goods of the strong man, he must first bind the strong man. This means that when the Lord comes to rescue us, He must first overcome Satan and bind him.

Now let us read Matthew 6:9-10: "Our Father who art in the heavens, let thy name be sanctified, let thy kingdom come, let thy will be done as in heaven so upon the earth" (J. N. Darby's New Translation). Also, verse 13b says, "For Yours is the kingdom and the power and the glory forever. Amen." This passage of the Lord's word concerning prayer is of great significance in the Bible. The meaning contained therein is very much related to spiritual warfare.

As the Lord taught us how to pray, He began with three *lets*. "*Let* thy name be sanctified, *let* thy kingdom come, *let* thy will be done as in heaven so upon the earth." These three *lets* set forth the central meaning of what the Lord wants us to pray. Then, at the conclusion, He said, "For Yours is the kingdom and the power and the glory." Again three factors are revealed here. The three *lets* at the beginning and the three factors at the conclusion show us the goal of spiritual warfare.

Let thy name be sanctified means also "let thy name be separated unto holiness." The Bible shows us that the name of God is a great matter. After the fall of mankind, at the time of Enosh (grandson of Adam), men began to call upon the name of the Lord (Gen. 4:26). God desires that only His name be upon earth and that men call only upon His name. But when men built the tower of Babel, rebelling together against God, they put the name of God aside and propagated their own name (11:4). God's will is that His name be sanctified on earth and become the only name worthy of all honor. However, Satan united rebellious mankind to put aside the name of God and replace it with many other names. Thus, the name of God was made common and ordinary. Hence, the name of God is not being sanctified or hallowed by men on earth today—an evil consequence of Satan's reigning.

We know that name and authority are related. A name in great measure represents authority. A man's name follows wherever his authority goes. The fact that a man's name is in a certain place proves that his authority is there also. Generally speaking, the name appearing on a certain object identifies the object as belonging to the person of that name. If the name of God is on the earth, that means the earth recognizes God's ownership over it. If the name of God is rejected on earth, that means the earth denies God the ownership over it. Since the earth was created by God, it must have the name of God upon it and recognize God's ownership. But Satan took possession of man by causing man to rebel against God. Hence, God's name was forsaken and no longer hallowed.

For this reason, when God works on this earth, He pays attention continually to the matter of His name being sanctified. When God brought the Israelites into the land of Canaan, He told them to gather together in one place to worship Him; that was the place where He chose to set His name (Deut. 12:5-6). God did this so that His name alone would be sanctified among His people. Today, in the dispensation of the New Testament, God has not given any other name under heaven among men, in which we must be saved, but the name of the Lord (Acts 4:12). When we are baptized, it is into the name of the Father, the Son, and the Holy Spirit (Matt. 28:19). When we pray, it is in the name of the Lord (John 14:13-14; 16:23-24). When we meet, it is also in the name of the Lord (Matt. 18:20). Therefore, we are those who belong to the name of the Lord, and His name is being sanctified in us. The Lord Jesus came to this earth for the purpose of gaining the people on this earth.

Through them He intends to recover the earth to God's ownership so that the name of God will again become the only name that is sanctified. In that day, men truly will praise God, saying, "O Jehovah our Lord, / How excellent is Your name / In all the earth!" (Psa. 8:1).

Following the name is the kingdom. The second point that the Lord wants us to heed when praying is to let God's kingdom come. This proves that the kingdom of God is not yet on this earth. What is the kingdom of God? God's kingdom is the sphere of God's reign. Any nation, however great or small, is a sphere for reigning. If the earth does not recognize the name of God, God's reign is not on this earth. If the name of God is being sanctified on the earth, God's kingdom or God's reign comes upon this earth. Therefore, after the Lord said, "Let thy name be sanctified," He said, "Let thy kingdom come."

The Bible reveals that there are three important parts of the universe: the heavens, the earth, and the air. Since Satan rebelled against God, he took possession of the air and the earth, leaving only the heavens as the place where God has complete dominion. Hence, Satan became the ruler of the authority of the air (Eph. 2:2), and through the messengers under his hand he rules in the air and over the earth (6:12). Consequently, the people on earth abandon the name of God and reject His reign.

Although God does not have His kingdom on earth as yet, He has not abandoned the earth. Beginning with Genesis, we see the continuous line of God's work on the earth throughout the generations to set up His kingdom and reign on earth. The purpose of God in calling Abraham was to obtain a family and from it to produce a nation (Gen. 12:1-2). Later, God delivered the Israelites, the heirs of Abraham, out of Egypt so that they might become a kingdom (Exo. 19:4-6). Then, through the tabernacle. He reigned among them.

After the Israelites entered Canaan, the day came when they again rejected God and refused His reign. They followed the nations of the earth by desiring a man to rule over them instead (1 Sam. 8:4-7). Because of this, God was very displeased; it was a setback for His kingdom on earth, and it gave Him no place to reign on earth. After Saul passed away,

David was raised up. David was a man after God's heart; thus God was able to reign among the Israelites through David. However, after Solomon, the Israelites failed again. Since then, God has not been able to gain a kingdom on this earth wherein He may reign freely.

It was under such circumstances that God sent the man called John the Baptist. When he began to preach, his first word was, "Repent, for the kingdom of the heavens has drawn near" (Matt. 3:2). Later, when the Lord Jesus came forth to preach, His first statement was also, "Repent, for the kingdom of the heavens has drawn near" (4:17). Again, later, when the Lord sent the disciples to preach the gospel, He commanded them that as they went, they should preach, saying, "The kingdom of the heavens has drawn near" (10:7). Finally, what the Lord desires His church to preach throughout the whole earth is still "the gospel of the kingdom" (24:14; Acts 8:12; 28:31). For two thousand years God has been sending men to preach the gospel, the purpose of which is to gain a sphere for Him to reign on earth and thus set up His kingdom. This is the meaning of the second *let* in the prayer that the Lord taught us.

Finally, the Lord desires us to have the third *let;* that is, "let thy will be done as in heaven so upon the earth." God's will and His reign are inseparable. God's will can only be done in the place where He reigns. God's will can only be accomplished in heaven, not on earth, because the kingdom of God is still not on earth for Him to reign. And God's kingdom is not found on earth because His name is not sanctified on earth. Where God's name is sanctified, there His reign is, and where His reign is, there His will is being done. Therefore, in teaching us to pray, the Lord's interest is that God's name, God's reign (His kingdom), and God's will might reach to the earth.

In the prayer that the Lord taught us, the conclusion says, "For Yours is the kingdom and the power and the glory." The kingdom is a sphere for reigning. God exercises His authority or power in His kingdom, and glory is made manifest through His reigning. These three items—the kingdom, the power, and the glory—are God's forever. It is based on these three factors that the Lord prayed for God's name to be sanctified,

His kingdom to come, and His will to be done, as in heaven, so
also on earth.

Today, although the kingdom of God has not yet completely come upon this earth, although God has not yet
gained a sphere wherein He can exercise His authority in
a full way, and although His glory has not yet been made
fully manifest, nevertheless there is a small place, a small
sphere, thank the Lord, where there still exists the condition
of God's partial reign, which thereby manifests a portion of
God's glory. This is the church. Today the church is a model
of God's reign. What God desires today is to expand His reigning sphere according to this model and through this model. It
is through the church that God will bind Satan and destroy
his power. Thus, His name will be honored in the whole earth,
His kingdom set up, and His will done. This is the commission of the church. This also is the purpose of the church's
spiritual warfare.

II. THE KINGDOM OF GOD VERSUS
THE KINGDOM OF SATAN

We have said that in the universe there is the kingdom of
God, and there is also the kingdom of Satan. The spiritual
warfare we are speaking of is the warfare between these two
kingdoms. Therefore, in order to engage in spiritual warfare,
we must first know the opposition between the kingdom of
God and the kingdom of Satan.

God's kingdom is eternal, both in time and in space. Since
God Himself is from eternity to eternity, so also is His kingdom
from eternity to eternity. Furthermore, since God Himself is
in light, so also is God's kingdom in light.

Satan's kingdom is not eternal. As to time, it is limited in
time; as to space, it is limited to the air and the earth. Furthermore, Satan's kingdom is in darkness, the exact opposite
of the kingdom of God.

In addition, there is still another great difference: God's
kingdom is legal, whereas the kingdom of Satan is illegal.
The whole universe was created by God and belongs to Him;
hence, God has the legal right to reign. On the contrary, Satan's

kingdom was established by rebellion against God; hence, it is entirely illegal.

In Isaiah 14:12-15 and Ezekiel 28:11-17, through the king of Babylon and the king of Tyre (both of whom had been instruments utilized by Satan), God relates the process of Satan's rebellion. Satan was originally an anointed cherub, the archangel, who occupied a special place before God. Because he was proud in heart and desired to exalt himself to equality with God, he rebelled against God and tried to overthrow God's authority, thereby establishing his own authority. Since then, there has existed in the universe the illegal kingdom of Satan.

Satan's kingdom is the sphere of Satan's reign. The Lord Jesus once called Satan "the ruler of the world" (John 14:30). This reveals that Satan not only has his kingdom but also reigns in his kingdom. Moreover, within his kingdom are his messengers of various ranks, all of which were angels who followed Satan in rebelling against God. Today these are the rulers, authorities, world-rulers, dominions, and spiritual forces of evil in the heavenlies, Satan being their head (Eph. 6:12; 2:2; 1:21).

Furthermore, in Satan's kingdom there are many demons, evil spirits, who serve as his servants. Based on the various records in the Bible, we can ascertain that before the six days' recovery work of the heavens and the earth (Gen. 1), there existed a world wherein lived a group of living beings with spirits. When Satan rebelled against God, they all followed him and rebelled together. Therefore, God judged that world, on one hand, by shutting off the sun and moon in the sky so that they gave forth no light and, on the other hand, by destroying the earth and the living beings with water. These living beings, judged as they were by water, became separated in spirit and body. These disembodied spirits who dwell in the waters of judgment are the demons, the evil spirits, mentioned in the Bible.

Therefore, originally, there were three groups of characters in the kingdom of Satan: first, Satan, the head, the ruler; second, the angels who followed Satan in rebelling against God and who served as ministers and officials to rule for him in the air; and third, the disembodied spirits, or the demons, the evil spirits, who acted as Satan's servants to run his errands on earth.

Later, after men were created, Satan came to entice men and succeeded in seducing them. Men became his kingdom's subjects, the ones who were handled and abused by him. Therefore, there are four classes of personalities in Satan's kingdom today. In the air are Satan and his messengers, and on earth are his servants and subjects, the innumerable demons and the myriads of people. At the time when the Lord Jesus was preaching the gospel on earth, He met people everywhere who were possessed by the demons. Today there are still flocks of demons who are maneuvering among people in this world. Although their dwelling place is in the sea, they like to seek a body where they can live. When we say that a person is possessed by a demon, we usually refer to the human body being possessed by a demon.

In summary, the kingdom of Satan consists of these four classes of personalities. They are organized altogether into a system through which Satan usurps the air and the earth to the end that he may overthrow God's authority and set up his own kingdom. Therefore, this kingdom, organized by Satan's rebellious force, is absolutely illegal.

It was not till four thousand years after the fall of the human race, at the beginning of the dispensation of the New Testament, that the Lord Jesus came forth to His ministry and declared, "Repent, for the kingdom of the heavens has drawn near." What the Lord meant was that before this it was the kingdom of earth, the kingdom of Satan, wherein Satan ruled, that held sway; but now it is the kingdom of the heavens, the kingdom of God, coming upon this earth to reign. Later, He taught the disciples to pray, "Let thy kingdom come." The full accomplishment of this matter will be seen at the sound of the seventh trumpet in the future (Rev. 11:15). Then the kingdom of this world will become the kingdom of God and Christ. Thus, God's kingdom will practically and completely come upon the earth.

Before that day arrives, the period in which we are living is the time for the people of God to fight for Him on earth. From the time the Lord Jesus came forth to minister, until the time of His second coming, all the works that the people of God are doing for Him are instances of spiritual warfare. God's desire is to rescue, through those who belong to Him, the people who were captured by Satan, and to recover the earth, which was usurped by Satan. This rescuing and recovering is, according to what the Lord has shown us in Matthew 12, the warfare between the kingdom of God and the kingdom of Satan.

III. ALL SPIRITUAL WORK IS A WARFARE

Since warfare exists between the kingdoms of God and Satan, all the spiritual work that we are doing for God, whatever form it may take, as long as it touches the things of the spiritual realm, is in nature a warfare. For example, preaching the gospel, according to Acts 26:18, is "to open their eyes, to turn them from darkness to light and from the authority of Satan to God." This shows us that preaching the gospel is not only to open men's eyes and turn them from darkness to light but also to deliver them from the authority of Satan. Again, Colossians 1:13 says, "Who delivered us out of the authority of darkness and transferred us into the kingdom of the Son of His love." To be delivered from the authority of darkness is to be delivered from the power of Satan or the kingdom of Satan. And to be transferred into the kingdom of the Son of God's love is to be transferred into the kingdom of God. Therefore, preaching the gospel is wholly a spiritual warfare to drive out the power of Satan in men and bring in the kingdom of God. A person who does not believe in the Lord obviously rejects the name of God, does not have God's reign in him, and has nothing to do with the will of God. Instead, he is fully under the power of Satan, and his whole being is in the dark kingdom of Satan. When a person is saved, he first believes in the name of the Lord; second, he calls on the Lord's name; and third, he is in the name of the Lord; he belongs to the Lord's name. Hence, he is delivered from the power of Satan and belongs to the name of the Lord. Once the name of the Lord is upon him, the authority of the Lord follows. Once the authority of the Lord comes upon him, Satan's authority is removed. Therefore, strictly speaking, preaching the gospel, bringing salvation to men, and leading them to the Lord is a kind of spiritual warfare.

Edifying the saints is also a matter of spiritual warfare. To edify the saints is to deliver them from the rule of Satan, that is, from sins, the world, the flesh, and everything relating to the old creation, all of which are used by Satan to rule over man. Thus, they will be further delivered from the satanic power of darkness, they will know the name of the Lord more deeply, and they will allow the Lord to increase His reign in them and thereby let the kingdom of God come more fully upon them.

Second Corinthians 10:3-5 says, "Though we walk in flesh, we do not war according to flesh; for the weapons of our warfare are not fleshly but powerful before God for the overthrowing of strongholds, as we overthrow reasonings and every high thing rising up against the konwledge of God, and take captive every thought unto the obedience of Christ." This word shows us that even after a Christian is saved, it is possible that a large portion of his mind and thoughts remains the stronghold of Satan, and many of his ideas and concepts still serve as the base usurped by Satan. Therefore, when the apostles edify the saints, their purpose is to cast down through warfare all the strongholds and bases of Satan in the saints and eventually bring their thoughts into captivity unto the obedience of Christ. Hence, edifying the saints is also a kind of spiritual warfare.

Moreover, even administering the church is a warfare. The purpose of administering the church is to deliver the church out of the power of darkness, to let God gain the place of rule in the church, to let the name of God be exalted in the church, to let His will be done in the church, and to let the glory of God be increasingly manifested in the church. Hence, administering the church is also a kind of warfare.

Even all our prayers, whether they be for ourselves, for our family, for the revival of the church, or for anything else, are for the purpose of delivering us out of the satanic power of darkness; hence, they are also a kind of warfare.

If our eyes have been opened by the Lord, we will see that the nature of our work in serving the Lord is that of warfare.

All our spiritual work, whether it be delivering men from sin, from the world, from illness, or from problems, has an ultimate goal: to rescue men out of the power of Satan and drive out the satanic power of darkness from within men so that men might be gained by God and gained even more by God. Thus, God's name will be sanctified in men, God's kingdom will reach unto men, His will shall be done in men, and thereby His glory will be manifested upon men. Therefore, the nature of all this work is that of spiritual warfare.

IV. THE PRINCIPLES OF SPIRITUAL WARFARE

To experience spiritual warfare in a practical way, there are several basic principles that we must keep:

A. Not Using Fleshly Weapons

The first principle of spiritual warfare is that we cannot use fleshly weapons. The apostle Paul tells us this clearly in 2 Corinthians 10:3-5, which we have quoted already. He says, "Though we walk in flesh, we do not war according to flesh; for the weapons of our warfare are not fleshly." These fleshly weapons not only refer to the losing of temper but include all human schemes and natural methods. For example, we may feel that a certain brother is in error and that this error has already become a problem in the church. We want to correct him, yet we feel that to do so is inappropriate. Later, we remember that there is another brother who is rather intimate with him, so we ask that brother to go and talk with him. Even this kind of maneuvering is a fleshly weapon; it will eventually prove futile in solving the spiritual problem. In society and the business world, many such schemes are employed, but on the spiritual battlefield we cannot use schemes. Whenever we use the schemes of our flesh, we have already fallen into the hands of the enemy. How then shall we be able to deliver others from the hands of the enemy?

We see that Paul was a man who never used fleshly weapons. In his dealings with the churches and his contacts with the saints, he was perfectly straight—as straight as an arrow. He would rather be treated as a fool than employ ingenious scheming for a moment. For this reason he could be "powerful before God for the overthrowing of strongholds" and thereby gain the victory in the spiritual warfare.

In the same manner, if we wish to win the victory in all our spiritual works and be effective, we must forsake all fleshly weapons. For example, in preaching the gospel it is all right to use illustrated tracts as helps for presentation, but if we continually rely on various methods or use material benefits to attract people, that is using fleshly weapons. The most it can do is to help people become church members; it cannot deliver them out of the hands of Satan. Therefore, the first principle of spiritual warfare is to forsake all fleshly, carnal weapons.

B. Keeping the Position of Ascension

The second principle of spiritual warfare is to keep the position of ascension. We have spoken much concerning spiritual warfare; in fact, however, there is only one kind of people who can engage in spiritual warfare—those who have received salvation, have been raised from death, and are now sitting with Christ in the heavens. Only this kind of men can attack the enemy in the air from a transcendent position in the heavens. Therefore, in order to engage in spiritual warfare we must keep the heavenly position. Whenever we are not heavenly enough, whenever we lose our heavenly condition, everything is finished. If our gospel is powerless, it is because we are not heavenly enough; we ourselves are earthly, and we are using earthly methods or fleshly weapons to preach the gospel. As a result, we may get some saved, but their condition will be muddled, and they will be unable to be completely delivered out of the power of Satan. If we really desire to deliver men out of Satan's power so that they are not only saved but completely delivered from the hands of Satan, we who are preaching the gospel must be men who are sitting in the heavens and keeping the ascended position.

The same principle applies in edifying the saints. If we lose the position of ascension, we can neither supply nor help the saints. If the messages we preach are mere doctrines and the fellowship we give mere knowledge, containing no element of warfare, the most we can impart is teachings for the mentality and stirring in the emotions; we cannot deliver people out of the power of Satan and turn them to God in a practical way. Therefore, if we want our work to have the effect of war, work which is able to deliver men from Satan's hands, we must keep the position of ascension and live continually in the condition of the heavens. This is an extremely important secret.

Since many of us have not yet reached the realm of ascension in our experience, why then is it possible that we can lead people to be saved and love the Lord? This is due to the fact that, after all, there is still a part in us that is heavenly or bears the heavenly condition; therefore, through that portion we are able to help others and edify them. Although we are defiled with sin, love the world, and mind the flesh, yet part of our condition is still heavenly; thus, we are able to chase away part of the power of darkness in men and cause them to turn to the Lord and love Him. Hence, the principle remains the same. Only those who live in the realm of the heavens can deal with the power of darkness in the air and chase the devil out. The help, the deliverance, that we afford others is based solely on that part which is of the heavenly nature in us. The extent to which we chase out the power of darkness is directly dependent on our heavenly condition. If we have more element of the heavens, we can engage more in spiritual warfare. If we have only a little element of the heavens, we can by no means have much element of spiritual warfare. The two are in direct proportion to one another. When a man has utterly reached the heavenly realm, his whole being, living, works, and actions are spiritual warfare. He is able to chase out the power of darkness from every place to which he comes and from all the people whom he meets. Therefore, when we in our experience have reached the position of ascension and are able to reign, that will be the time we can fight for the kingdom of God, recover the lost earth for God, and bring in the kingdom of God.

C. Using Spiritual Weapons

The third principle of spiritual warfare is that we must use spiritual weapons. When engaging in spiritual warfare, it is not enough to merely keep the heavenly position; we must be able to actively employ the spiritual weapons. Spiritual weapons refer to the "whole armor" mentioned in Ephesians 6:10-17, which includes the girdle of truth, the breastplate of righteousness, the shoes of the gospel of peace, the shield of faith, the helmet of salvation, and the sword of the Spirit. All these weapons are spiritual, and when we use them, we must be in spirit. We can say that the basic principle of employing the spiritual weapons is that all our activities must be of the spirit. Preaching the gospel, edifying the saints, and administering the church are of the spirit. Whatever kind of activity we are engaged in, everyone must be of the spirit, and everyone must release the spirit. Anything that is not of the spirit, anything that is according to our own view, our own idea, our own wisdom, or our own intelligence, is unavoidably a kind of human scheme and thus a fleshly weapon, not a spiritual weapon. Therefore, when we are fighting, all our activities must be of the spirit, touching the feeling from within our spirit. This also is an extremely basic principle.

D. Praying Fighting Prayers

The fourth principle of spiritual warfare is to have fighting prayers. After the apostle mentions the various kinds of spiritual weapons in Ephesians 6, he says, "Praying at every time in spirit" (v. 18). Spiritual warfare cannot neglect prayer, for spiritual warfare largely depends on prayer. What Satan fears most is the saints' bended knees before the Lord, or the prayer of the church before God. Even in the Old Testament we can see a few examples of warring prayers. For example, when Daniel prayed, there was action on the throne. But when the answer came down from the throne, it met resistance in the air. Daniel prayed continually. His prayer was a kind of warfare. A person who keeps the position of ascension reigns in heaven. He can also employ spiritual weapons, and the prayer that comes forth from him avails much; it can touch the throne of God and affect the power of Satan. God desires that His saints have this kind of prayer to work together with Him and fight for Him.

E. Through the Blood, the Word of Testimony, and Not Loving the Soul-life

In spiritual warfare, besides forsaking the fleshly weapons, keeping the position of ascension, employing the spiritual weapons, and offering fighting prayers, we must also apply the blood, testify the word, and love not our own soul-life (Rev. 12:11). This is also a very important principle in spiritual warfare.

To engage in spiritual warfare through the blood means to apply the blood of the Lord as our covering and to take the Lord's blood to counter Satan's accusations and attacks. Since we are still to this very day on the earth and in the body of flesh, we cannot help but have some defilement, corruption, weakness, shortcoming, and other undesirable conditions. When we fight with Satan, the first thing he does is to point out all the weaknesses and shortcomings in our conscience and then to accuse and attack us. Satan's accusation is not only within; sometimes it is spoken without. Once, when someone was casting out a demon, the demon pointed out his hidden weaknesses and revealed them publicly through the one possessed by him. This kind of incident is even recorded in the Old Testament. Zechariah 3:1-5 speaks of Joshua wearing the filthy garment and Satan coming to oppose and attack him. These are things that the devil will certainly do in spiritual warfare. At such a time we need to know the power and effectiveness of the blood. Thus, we can apply the blood to answer all Satan's accusations. We can tell him, "Although we have these weaknesses, the Lord's blood has been shed, and God is satisfied." Thus, we can be strong and of good courage before the enemy and fight with him.

Second, we must testify. That is, we must declare what the Lord Jesus has accomplished—the victory of the cross, the attainment of resurrection, and the position of ascension. This is not a matter of preaching but of testifying and declaring with words.

Satan is indeed a very subtle accuser. Sometimes when we just start to talk about overcoming the world, he immediately accuses us within, saying, "Are you not still loving the world?"

The moment he interrupts and asks such a question, we faint inwardly. This is the time that we ought to immediately declare the Lord's victory. We must say, "Although I have not been delivered from the world, the Lord Jesus has overcome the world." Thus, we can prevail against his attacks.

Third, we must not love our own lives; we must have no self-love or self-care. Loving and caring for ourselves will cause us to lose the position of warfare and to be unable to fight the battle. Hence, in order to fight the battle, we must not love our soul-life, even unto death.

In conclusion, all spiritual work is a form of spiritual warfare. There is not one time when we rise to work that we do not encounter the attacks of the enemy. In the day when Nehemiah restored the city of Jerusalem, because of the disturbance caused by the enemy, everyone with one of his hands wrought in the work and with the other hand held a weapon (Neh. 4:17). Likewise, we who serve the Lord today ought to work with one hand and fight with the other. We ought not to care for our gain or loss, but through the blood, in the position of ascension, declare the Lord's victory. Then, exercising the various spiritual weapons to deal with Satan, we can overthrow his power and bring in the kingdom of God. We must not neglect any of these principles while we are engaging in spiritual warfare in a practical way.

V. THE RESULTS OF SPIRITUAL WARFARE

The first result of spiritual warfare is the bringing in of God's authority. How much we fight determines how much God's authority will be brought in. God's authority can only be executed in the place of our fighting. If this warfare transpires in an individual, then God's authority reaches that individual; if it occurs in the home, then God's authority reaches the home; if it takes place in the church, then His authority reaches the church. Therefore, the first result of spiritual warfare is the bringing in of God's authority.

The second result of spiritual warfare is that Satan is driven out and chased away. This is true in the individual, in the home, and in the church as well. So also it is even in the air and on the earth. The place where the saints maintain the spiritual warfare is also the place where God's authority is brought in; consequently, Satan is driven out from that place.

Among the children of God there are not enough who are fighting the warfare, and the element of spiritual warfare is too little; hence, Satan still rules in the air and on the earth. When our spiritual experience is rather shallow, our sense of spiritual warfare is very weak. We still feel that our problem is with sin, the world, the flesh, the self, and the natural constitution. When we deal with these and enter into the fourth stage of spiritual life, our experience is deepened, and we see that the Body that God uses in the universe is the church. Then we have a strong sense toward spiritual warfare, knowing that whatever we do—our every action, word, and attitude—is an influence upon Satan and an attack against him. Only then will we feel strongly that our only problem is Satan and that we are here as warriors to deal with this enemy of God. We will see that our preaching the gospel is not merely to save souls but even more to cast out the devil; our edifying the saints and administering the church are not merely for the building up of the church but even more to fight for God and chase away the power of darkness that usurps men. Thus, God's authority can come upon a group of people or on certain matters and reign over them. Upon arriving at this stage, whether we are preaching the gospel, edifying the saints, or administering the church, our attitude is always to aim at Satan as the object of our dealing. We know that what hinders the gospel is not the outward environment but Satan. We know that what usurps men and causes them not to love the Lord is neither human ties, nor the world, nor the flesh, but the satanic power of darkness. We know also that the reason for all the confusion, striving, indifference, and corruption in the church is naught else but Satan. Therefore, we do not deal with things that appear on the surface, but, through the position and authority of ascension, we deal with the power of darkness that schemes behind these things and reigns on the earth.

Revelation 12 reveals that once the man-child, who typifies the overcomers, is caught up to heaven, warfare immediately takes place. The moment they are caught up into heaven, they enter into conflict with Satan and cast him down from the air to the earth. Later, the Lord Jesus brings them with Him in His descent to the earth and casts Satan, who is on the earth, into the bottomless pit. At that time the power of darkness in the air and on the earth will be completely expelled, and no trace of Satan will be found again in heaven or on earth; thus, the kingdom of God will come in a practical way. At that time, all the overcoming saints will reign together with Christ and for God a thousand years.

Finally, at the end of the millennial kingdom, the enemy will be released for a short time and will rebel for the last time. But again he will be dealt with by the Lord and the overcomers and will be cast into the lake of fire burning with brimstone. All those who belong to him will perish with him forever. At that time, the former heaven and earth will pass away, and a new heaven and new earth will begin. There, in the new heaven and new earth, God's name will be uniquely honored, all creatures will be subject to God's authority, God's will shall be done in the whole universe, and His glory will be fully manifest. Thus, through spiritual warfare, God's eternal purpose is completely accomplished.

CHAPTER NINETEEN

FULL OF THE STATURE OF CHRIST

We shall now study the nineteenth lesson concerning life, which is also the last experience of life—being full of the stature of Christ. We shall deal with this subject in a rather simple manner because many of the related aspects have already been discussed in the previous chapters, leaving very little to be said at this point. Furthermore, we have only experienced this lesson very little; therefore, we do not have much to say.

When we speak about being full of the stature of Christ, we mean that our life in Christ has attained to the realm of full maturity. If we have really experienced all the lessons of life mentioned previously, then the life of Christ can be fully wrought into us. At this time, we will be full of the stature of the fullness of Christ.

The growth of the stature of Christ within us can be divided into five steps. First, Christ enters into us to become our life. Second, Christ living within us through the Holy Spirit gradually grows in us. Third, Christ is formed in us. Fourth, Christ is manifested through us. As Christ grows and is formed in us and manifested more and more, one day every part of our being will be filled with His elements; then we will attain to the fifth step—Christ becoming matured in us, or we being full of the stature of the fullness of Christ. At this time our experience of life in Christ has reached its climax.

Every saved Christian has the experience of the first step—Christ entering into them to become their life. If anyone has not experienced this first step, he is not saved; neither can he speak of the experiences of life that follow. Concerning the second step—Christ living and growing within us—every seeking Christian is in the process of this experience. As to the third step—Christ being formed in us—many have not attained to this stage. When we come to the fourth step of Christ being manifested through us, even fewer have experienced it. Finally, as to the fifth step—Christ being matured in us and we being matured in His life and full of His stature—people with this experience can rarely be found in all the churches on earth today. Therefore, in this lesson of being full of the stature of Christ, there is not much that we can say. We simply list a few main points and discuss them briefly.

I. IN THE BODY

Concerning being full of the stature of Christ, we must first realize that none can attain to this stage individually. This experience is attainable only in the Body. It is entirely an experience that is gained in the Body.

A Christian who has experienced the brokenness of the flesh and the natural constitution will automatically see the Body of Christ. From this time forth, he deeply realizes from his experience that apart from the Body of Christ he cannot live—he can neither live in the Lord nor touch His presence. If he is detached from the Body of Christ, he cannot even be a Christian. Therefore, from the time he sees the Body of Christ until he becomes mature in the life of the Lord, his spiritual life is in the Body and so also is his whole spiritual experience. Hence, his being full of the stature of the fullness of Christ is also an experience in the Body.

Not only is it impossible for anyone to experience being full of the stature of the fullness of Christ outside of the Body, but, practically speaking, even in the Body, none can be full of the stature of Christ individually. To be full of the stature of Christ is a Body matter. Therefore, only the Body can be full of the stature of Christ.

Being full of the stature of the fullness of Christ is mentioned only once in the Bible—in Ephesians 4:13. In this passage the writer is not referring to individual saints, but rather pointing out the fact that one day the Body of Christ, which is the church, shall attain to such a stage. In Ephesians 3:18, we read that to apprehend the breadth, the length, the height, and the depth of Christ, we need a togetherness with all saints. From these two Scripture references we see that the stature of the fullness of Christ and the unsearchable dimensions of Christ cannot be experienced by ourselves individually but by being in the Body and joined together with all the saints.

Therefore, simply speaking, the maturity of the Christian life takes place in the Body. We should never expect that we can attain to the maturity of life individually. In fact, when one sees the Body, he can no more be individual.

II. BEING FULL OF THE LIFE AND NATURE OF CHRIST

Concerning the content, being full of the stature of Christ means that we are full of the life and nature of Christ. When a person's experience of life reaches its climax, the life and nature of Christ have permeated all the various parts of his being. The different parts of his spirit as well as the mind, will, and emotion of his soul are filled with the life and nature of Christ. Even his physical body at times is supported by this strength from the spirit. (Christians today cannot as yet be full of the element of Christ in their body; this can only be attained when we are raptured and transfigured.) At this time his life comes to maturity.

There are many among us who have believed in the Lord for years, but to this day there is but little of the element of Christ in them. Their thoughts are filled largely with themselves. Though there is little filthiness or corruption in their thoughts, there is also little of Christ. This also means that in their thoughts there is very little of the stature of Christ. With regard to their will, though it may not rebel against God, oppose Him, or seem to be wrong in any way, the element within it is largely of themselves and very little of Christ. With regard to their emotion, their mood, desire, and inclination may be blameless, but they are still not filled with the element of Christ. This proves that the stature of Christ within them has not reached full measure and that they have made very little progress in spiritual growth.

How can we gradually be filled with the life and nature of Christ? We know that man has three parts: spirit, soul, and body. The spirit is the center, the body is the outer circumference, and between these two is the soul. When we are regenerated, Christ as the Spirit enters into our spirit. From this time, He lives and grows within us. First He fills us in our spirit; then He spreads outward from our spirit to the mind, emotion, and will in our soul. He uses the cross to deal with our self and our natural constitution, that is, to deal especially with our soul-life which is in our mind, emotion, and will. The more our mind, emotion, and will are dealt with and broken by the cross, the more Christ as the life-giving Spirit can enter into these parts. At a certain point, all the elements of our mind, emotion, and will are Christ; then the stature of Christ is fully grown in us.

At this time, all the considerations, concepts, ideas, and viewpoint of our mind; all the pleasure, anger, sorrow, joy, delight, and inclination of our emotion; and all the judgment, decision, intention, and choice of our will are filled with the element of Christ. Our mind is like the mind of Christ, our delight is His delight, and our intention is His intention. In other words, when we think, it is Christ who thinks; when we delight, it is He who delights; and when we intend, it is He who intends. At this time, every part of our inward being has been dealt with by the cross, and there is no place for self or the natural constitution; all the ground has been given over to Christ. We can say that our whole being is filled with Christ's life and nature.

This is like pouring grape juice into a glass of water, with the water representing us, and the grape juice typifying the life and nature of Christ. One who is newly saved can be compared to a glass of water with a little grape juice added, the greater part being water. There are Christians who seem at times to have, and at other times not to have, a little grape juice in the bottom, causing others to doubt their salvation. With others, one can be certain that they contain the grape juice, though very little. Formerly, it was purely water; now there is the element of grape juice within it. When there is more growth in life, it is as if the grape juice increases, and the color thus becomes deepened. Before, when loving others, the love of such a person was solely of himself; now in his love for others there is undoubtedly an element of Christ added. Before, he looked at things in a certain way with a certain concept; now it is different; there is the element of Christ added. Likewise, his emotion and will have the element of Christ added into them. Whatever he loves or delights in, whatever he considers and decides upon, may still be mixed with impure elements, but to some extent the element of Christ has been increased, and the color of Christ deepened. This means that Christ has grown within him.

With regard to Christ being formed in us, we may use as an illustration grape juice whose color is deep enough to be easily recognized. Before Christ is formed in us, we may be likened to grape juice that is very lightly colored, making it difficult to be identified. However, when Christ is formed in us, men can definitely see the grape juice inside. Proceeding a little further, the water in the glass will no longer be seen; it will be swallowed up and overshadowed by the grape juice. This means figuratively that the life and nature of Christ have increased in us to such a degree that Christ has become all in us, overshadowing and swallowing up all our own elements. What is manifested is completely the element and color of Christ. This we call the maturity of life, or being full of the stature of Christ.

III. SHARING THE SAME POSITION WITH CHRIST

When a person arrives at the full stature of Christ, he is in the same position as Christ, not only in objective fact but also in experience. Christ is seated in the heavens, and so also is he; Christ is on the throne, and so is he. At this time he is not easily shaken; neither can he fall easily.

Before a man's spiritual life attains to maturity, he is not stable. A month ago he may have been greatly uplifted and zealous for the Lord; the next month he may be exceedingly depressed and weak to the point of even being unwilling to come to the meetings. Some brothers and sisters, when they are well received and lifted up, become overjoyed and beside themselves; but when they are opposed and troubled, they become depressed and downcast. These ups and downs prove that their life is still immature. However, when man's life has

attained maturity and is seated with Christ on the throne in
the heavens, he does not rise and fall or waver easily. When you
welcome him, he is a certain kind of person; when you oppose
him, he remains the same. If you lift him up, he is on the
throne; if you trouble him, he is still on the throne. When the
prophet Elijah heard that Jezebel desired to kill him, he became
exceedingly fearful; he fled and sat under a broom shrub,
requesting that he might die (1 Kings 19). This is because
he had descended from Mount Carmel. Likewise, when one
descends from the heavenly position, he is easily confused and
frightened. Nevertheless, one who has attained to maturity of
life lives in the spirit, in the life of Christ; he shares His position and is not easily disturbed or excited. Just as Christ is
stable and sure in the heavens, so also is he. One whose life
has attained unto maturity is one who is stable and steady.

As Christ Himself is unshakable in the heavens, so are
those who are full of the stature of Christ and who share the
same position as Christ. He changes not because of place or
time; no matter what kind of environment he encounters, he
remains seated in the heavens, unchanged. He shares the same
position as Christ. This is the condition of one who is full of
the stature of Christ.

IV. REIGNING WITH CHRIST

Another condition of one who is full of the stature of
Christ is that he reigns with Christ. One must attain to the
position of reigning with Christ in order that his life might
become mature. If we desire to learn whether or not we are
mature in life, we should ascertain whether or not we can
reign in the spiritual life. We cannot ask a six-year-old child
to rule; even if we crown him king and give him reign, with
everything subject to his control, he will run off to play ball. If
the life is insufficient, there is no possibility of reigning.
When one's life attains to maturity, he reigns automatically.
Consider the woman in the Song of Songs. It was not until
her inner life became bright as the morning, beautiful as the
moon, and clear as the sun, that she manifested her majesty
and was terrible as an army with banners (6:10). If one has
not attained to this transcendent and heavenly state and yet

claims himself to be experienced and standing in a high position, he is only displaying his own glory and power; it is an ugly display and certainly not reigning. Therefore, reigning is not only a matter of position but also of life. In order to reign, one needs the position and much more, the life.

This is true not only of the spiritual life but also of the physical life. A statement made by a child is of very little significance. The same statement, in the same situation, at the same time, when spoken by an adult, has some measure of weight, and when spoken by an elderly person of seventy or eighty years of age, is more weighty. The weight of the word is measured according to age. When a certain age is attained, the word has depth. In like manner, authority is based on life. When life matures, it can reign. Therefore, the experience of reigning depends on the maturity in life.

In Numbers 17, in order to prove that Aaron was invested with His authority, God caused his rod to bud, blossom, and bear almonds. This budding, blossoming, and fruit-bearing is the story of life. The rod represents authority. Among the twelve rods, only one budded and bore fruit. This proves that only those whose life matures can reign.

When our life attains unto maturity and fullness, we will be raptured and transfigured. At that time, we will be seated with Christ on the throne and reign with Him. All that we are will be full of the stature of the fullness of Christ, and all that we do will be to reign with Christ. The same principle applies today to the maturity of life. When our life attains to the full stature of Christ, then we are able to reign with Christ.

V. TOGETHER WITH CHRIST, DEALING WITH THE ENEMY

Another issue of one who is full of the stature of Christ is that of dealing, together with Christ, with the enemy. To deal with the enemy is to fight the warfare. However, we should not use the term *warfare* here, because it does not convey the meaning of full maturity in life. When we are really full of the stature of Christ and our life has attained unto full maturity, our spiritual warfare is over. Then we are seated far above all in a victorious position and need only to deal with the enemy.

It was in the same process that the Lord Jesus fought the battle. From the time of His temptation at the beginning of His ministry, He continually fought with Satan. But when He ascended to the throne, He ceased fighting. Nevertheless, He continues to deal with the enemy, until eventually he will be subdued beneath His feet and become His footstool (Heb. 1:13). When we attain to the stage of dealing, together with Christ, with the enemy, it is proof that our life has attained to its highest peak.

For a victorious one, there is no need to fight. All he needs to do is to be situated in a certain place; then all the robbers and prowlers will disappear completely, daring no more to act foolishly or do evil. His awe-inspiring reputation has been gained through much warfare in the past. This example explains the principle of Christ in dealing with the enemy. If neither Christ nor His name were in this universe today, imagine how much more violent Satan would be! It is simply because Christ is dealing with the enemy today that wherever the name of Christ is lifted up, the enemy flees, and the power of darkness vanishes.

Sometimes we see the same condition in the church or in the work. As long as there are one or more who have a deeper life, trouble can hardly arise in the church or in the work. Once those persons leave, however, many problems arise. This is because they are in authority dealing, together with Christ, with the enemy. Their presence there subdues the enemy. It is as if there were no need for dealing, but in reality their presence is the dealing. Therefore, dealing with the enemy is superior to fighting the warfare.

When the life of a Christian reaches this stage, every part of his being comes to maturity. He is waiting to be raptured to enter into glory with Christ. The Bible uses the reaping of the harvest to illustrate the rapture of the saints. When the harvest is ripe, it is ready to be reaped. Therefore, we should not view the matter of rapture merely as prophecy. Rapture is a matter of life. As the life of the church or the life of the saints grows and matures continuously in Christ, at a certain stage it becomes fully ripened and, in the sight of the Lord, is ready to be reaped from the field of the world into the barn of heaven.

This occurs at the time of the Lord's return, the time of the rapture of the church (Rev. 14). When we are raptured, we will be brought by the Lord into His glory to enjoy the glory with Him. Thus, the purpose of God's salvation is fulfilled.

Therefore, when the life experience of a Christian attains to the full stature of Christ, it has reached the climax. He shares the same position with Christ, and he reigns and deals with the enemy together with Christ. His whole being is filled with the element of Christ. Aside from the fact that the body has not yet been transfigured into the body of glory, all else has reached its highest or final point. The life experience of a saint in Christ thus comes to a conclusion. Other than waiting to be raptured and entering into glory, there is nothing else left to be desired.

OTHER BOOKS PUBLISHED BY
Living Stream Ministry

Titles by Witness Lee:

Titles by Watchman Nee:

Available at

Christian bookstores, or contact Living Stream Ministry

2431 W. La Palma Ave. • Anaheim, CA 92801

1-800-549-5164 • www.livingstream.com